Noble Strategies

Habent sua fata libelli

Noble Strategies

Marriage and Sexuality in
the *Zimmern Chronicle*

Judith J. Hurwich

Sixteenth Century Essays & Studies 75
Truman State University Press

Cover illustration: Lucas Cranach the Elder, *The Adoring Husband,* 1537. Courtesy of
Akademie der Bildenen Künste, Gemäldegalerie, Vienna.

Cover and title page design: Teresa Wheeler
Type: Minion Pro © Adobe Systems Inc.
Printed by Thomson-Shore, Dexter, Michigan USA

Library of Congress Cataloging-in-Publication Data

Hurwich, Judith J.
  Noble strategies : marriage and sexuality in the Zimmern Chronicle / Judith J. Hurwich.
    p. cm. — (Sixteenth century essays & studies ; v. 75)
  Includes bibliographical references and index.
  ISBN-13: 978-1-931112-59-8 (alk. paper)
  ISBN-10: 1-931112-59-2 (alk. paper)
    1. Zimmern family. 2. Family—Germany—Swabia—History—16th century.
3. Marriage—Germany—Swabia—History—16th century. 4. Sex customs—Germany—
Swabia—History—16th century. 5. Nobility—Germany—Swabia—History—16th
century. I. Title. II. Series.
HQ626.15.S93H87 2006
306.80943'46—dc22

                                                                    2006017257

CONTENTS

FIGURES AND TABLES

ACKNOWLEDGMENTS

I first became fascinated by the *Zimmern Chronicle* when I was assigned to write a paper on it in a graduate seminar on the Renaissance given by Felix Gilbert as a visiting professor at Princeton. My first reaction to the colorful chronicle of the spectacularly dysfunctional Zimmern family was "how typical are they?" At that time, this question was impossible to answer, since little research had as yet been done on the history of the family and virtually none on the German noble family. As a student of Lawrence Stone's at Princeton, I was introduced to the pioneer work in the history of the family and I resolved to return to the *Zimmern Chronicle* once the field was sufficiently developed to allow me to place the chronicle in a broader German and European context.

Since I have spent my career outside the university, I am particularly grateful to members of the Sixteenth Century Society and Conference who encouraged me to continue with my research, including Raymond Mentzer, Merry Wiesner-Hanks, and Gerald Strauss. Karl-Heinz Spiess helped me obtain recent articles from German publications and kindly allowed me to use his unpublished research on the German princes. Raymond Mentzer and the anonymous readers for the Truman State University Press gave me much-needed help in editing the manuscript. I would especially like to thank Kathryn Reichard for her invaluable assistance as listener and sounding board over the many years of this project, and for her editorial suggestions. Lastly, I would like to thank my husband, Bob, for his patience and practical advice.

CHAPTER 1

The *Zimmern Chronicle* and the Zimmern Family

In the mid-1560s, the Swabian Count Froben Christoph von Zimmern sat down to write a chronicle of the history of his family, which had made a remarkable comeback from political and economic disaster. Looking back over generations of happy and unhappy marriages and extramarital affairs, births (both legitimate and otherwise), family honors and family scandals, he left a remarkably frank and detailed account of the Zimmern family. Largely unknown for two centuries, the *Zimmern Chronicle,* or *Chronicle of the Counts of Zimmern,* came to light in the late 1700s. Since that time, it has been regarded as a unique and valuable source of cultural history in Germany in the sixteenth century. It has a well-established "reputation for being one of the most colorful representations of Swabian noble culture" and for giving an unparalleled "glimpse into the minds, habits, and bedrooms of the premodern nobility."[1]

The *Zimmern Chronicle* is unique among the chronicles of German noble families not only for its great length (1581 pages of manuscript, of which three-quarters are devoted to the period from the 1480s to the 1560s) but also for its inclusion of a large amount of incidental material drawn from popular culture, including many *Schwänke,* or bawdy "merry tales." It is this incidental material, rather than the narrative of the Zimmern family itself, that has made the *Zimmern Chronicle* famous since the eighteenth century as a source for the study of German literature, popular culture, and law.[2]

Until recently, however, little attention has been paid to the chronicle as a source for the history of the noble family in early modern Europe. German nobles

---

Unless otherwise noted, all translations are by the author.

[1]Bastress-Dukehart, *The Zimmern Chronicle,* 11, 27.

[2]See, for example, Franklin, *Die freien Herren und Grafen von Zimmern;* and Nadler, "Die Herren von Zimmern."

of the fifteenth and early sixteenth century left few diaries, autobiographies, or personal letters giving glimpses into their motives and personal feelings. Although such sources are available for this period for the English gentry and nobility and for the German urban patriciate, they do not become common for the German nobility until the end of the sixteenth century.[3] The *Zimmern Chronicle* helps to fill this gap through its inclusion of much material that was either autobiographical or handed down orally within the family.

Froben Christoph von Zimmern's richly detailed account of his own marriage negotiations, for example, demonstrates that a young nobleman did not merely acquiesce in a candidate selected by his elders, but could manage the negotiation process himself and reject a candidate he disliked. The *Zimmern Chronicle* is remarkably candid about tensions within the family, portraying fratricidal quarrels over the inheritance, estrangements between fathers and sons, and separations between husbands and wives. The chronicler has more than one occasion to echo Ovid's lament that "love or unity between brothers is a rare bird" (*ZC* 2:329; similar sentiments are expressed at 2:134, 3:291–92). While warnings against the damage quarrels between brothers could inflict on the wealth and reputation of the lineage can also be found in other noble house chronicles of the period,[4] the *Zimmern Chronicle* stands alone in its emphasis on emotional relationships within the nuclear family and especially in its condemnation of the extramarital sexual relationships noblemen took for granted. "Their wives had to see it, live with it, and keep quiet, even if it stabbed them to the heart," exclaims the chronicler (*ZC* 3:389). Froben Christoph himself confronted and became permanently estranged from a father who neglected his wife and legitimate children in favor of a concubine.

The *Zimmern Chronicle* strongly emphasizes the lineage (male line of descent) and relegates women to secondary roles. It evaluates them according to the benefits they conferred on the Zimmern lineage by bringing large dowries, providing valuable alliances with other noble families, bearing sons to continue the male line, or defending the Zimmerns' claim to their estates. By the chronicler's criteria, for example, his aunt Apollonia von Henneberg was a distinct disappointment. The Zimmerns had initially expected that the status of their lineage would be enhanced

---

[3]For the English gentry, the most important such source is the fifteenth-century Paston letters: Gairdner, *The Paston Letters, 1422–1509*; and Bennett, *The Pastons and Their England*. For the peerage, the most important collection of correspondence is that of the Lisle family in the early sixteenth century: Byrne, *The Lisle Letters*. Studies of the fifteenth- and sixteenth-century German patriciate draw primarily on the letters, diaries, and family account books of families in Augsburg and Nuremberg. See Beer, *Eltern und Kinder*, and the works of Ozment, including *Magdalena and Balthasar*, *Three Behaim Boys*, and *Flesh and Spirit*. Studies of the German nobility based on similar sources include Hufschmidt, *Adelige Frauen im Weserraum zwischen 1550 und 1700* (on the lower nobility); and Bastl, *Tugend, Liebe, Ehre* (on the nobility of the imperial court from the late sixteenth through the eighteenth centuries).

[4]For example, the early sixteenth-century *Truchsessenchronik*, the house chronicle of the Waldburg family, "over and over again emphasizes the destructive effect of divisions of estates and family quarrels as the greatest deficiency in the family history." Wolf, *Von der Chronik zum Weltbuch*, 84.

by the marriage in 1511 of Gottfried Werner von Zimmern to this "countess of princely rank" (*gefürstete Gräfin*), who belonged to one of the wealthiest and most powerful noble families of Franconia. But Apollonia's dowry proved to be less than her husband had hoped for and she bore him only daughters. Worst of all, she failed to outlive her childless brothers, so the eagerly awaited Henneberg inheritance never came to the Zimmerns after all.

Despite its male bias, however, the chronicle provides valuable insights into the lives of noblewomen in an era when they left few records apart from formal appearances in legal documents. A careful examination of the women in the Zimmern family shows the variety of roles they played at different times in their lives. As daughters, they were assets or burdens in their parents' inheritance strategies, dutifully following their parents' wishes in marriage or resisting an unwelcome union. As wives, they may have been valued for the money, property, and prestige they brought, but they often ended up trapped in an unhappy marriage, tied to a man more loyal to his concubine than his wife. As for the nonnoble women who were concubines of nobles, their position and that of their children grew increasingly precarious as public attitudes became less tolerant, and ecclesiastical and secular authorities sought to enforce stricter sexual morality.

Until recently, the history of the family received much less attention in Germany than in France and England, where two new approaches to the field were established by the 1960s. The first approach was historical demography, which used the new methodology of family reconstitution, based on parish registers, to analyze household size, age at marriage, and the life cycle. This methodology was developed in the years after World War II by the Institut National d'Études Démographiques in France and the Cambridge Group for the History of Population and Social Structure in England.[5] The second new approach was the study of *mentalités,* or "mental habits," which drew not only on family documents, but also on literature and art to illuminate attitudes toward the family. Popularized by Philippe Ariès in *L'Enfant et la vie sociale sous l'Ancien Regime* (1960), this approach led to a spirited debate over the structure of the family and over the emotional relationships among its members. In his *Family, Sex and Marriage in England, 1500–1800* (1977), Lawrence Stone proposed a model of the stages of development of the European family that provided the framework for the next decade of studies of the European noble family. In Stone's view, the family before the eighteenth century (especially in the upper classes) was characterized by patriarchal structure, focus on the extended kin rather than on the nuclear family, and weak ties of affection between family members.[6]

[5]Early studies in historical demography that were especially influential in shaping views of the early modern European nobility include Hajnal, "European Marriage Patterns in Perspective," which set forth the hypothesis of a distinctive European marriage pattern; Peller, "Births and Deaths among Europe's Ruling Families"; and Hollingsworth, "The Demography of the British Peerage."

[6]Ariès, *Centuries of Childhood;* and Stone, *Family, Sex and Marriage.* Other important contributions

Neither family reconstitution nor the analysis of *mentalités* was applied to Germany until the 1970s, when German scholars published works on the peasant family using both of the new approaches.[7] In the 1980s, research on the early modern German family focused primarily on the cities and on the impact of the Reformation.[8] The noble family did not receive as much attention from scholars of early modern Germany as it had from scholars of France and England.[9]

By the 1990s, however, the German noble family began to attract greater attention from both American and European scholars. At a theoretical level, Paula Sutter Fichtner argued that the inheritance and marriage strategies of German Protestant princes were affected by their religious ideology.[10] At the same time, concrete evidence to test prevailing assumptions about family structure and marriage strategies became available in a series of regional studies of the nonprincely nobility spanning the period from the High Middle Ages to the nineteenth century.[11] Studies of women and gender roles since the early 1990s have also examined marriage patterns and attitudes toward marriage and sexuality in the nobility.[12]

The *Zimmern Chronicle* itself has attracted new attention as an example of the genre of the German noble house chronicle. Until 2002, only one monograph on the chronicle existed: Beat Jenny's biography, *Graf Froben Christoph von Zimmern* (1959). That year witnessed the publication of two more: Gerhard Wolf, *Von der Chronik zum Weltbuch,* and Erica Bastress-Dukehart, *The Zimmern Chronicle.* Both authors explore how sixteenth-century noble family chronicles "used literary tropes, strategies, and invented elements in the service of their vision of history," creating works that glorified the family and sought to legitimize its claims to prestige and power.[13] Wolf emphasizes the literary strategies used in the *Zimmern Chronicle,* which, in his words, "towers like a monolith over the house chronicles

---

to the debate include Laslett, *The World We Have Lost;* Flandrin, *Families in Former Times;* and Shorter, *Making of the Modern Family.*

[7]See Imhof, *Historische Demographie als Sozialgeschichte;* and Mitterauer and Sieder, *The European Family.*

[8]Some of the most important contributions on these topics have been made by American scholars, including the works of Ozment cited above. See also Wiesner, *Working Women in Renaissance Germany;* Roper, *The Holy Household;* and Harrington, *Reordering Marriage and Society.*

[9]A significant exception is Mitterauer, "Zur Frage des Heiratsverhaltens."

[10]Fichtner, *Protestantism and Primogeniture.*

[11]On the ministerials of Salzburg 1100–1343, see Freed, *Noble Bondsmen.* On the counts and barons of the Mainz region 1200–1550, see Spiess, *Familie und Verwandtschaft.* On the imperial knights of the Rhineland in the seventeenth and eighteenth centuries, see Duhamelle, "Parenté et orientation sociale." Useful earlier works include Reif, *Westfälischer Adel 1770–1860;* and Pedlow, *The Survival of the Hessian Nobility 1770–1870.* Despite the dates in their titles, both works include material on the noble family in the sixteenth and seventeenth centuries.

[12]On the nobility of the Hapsburg court from the late sixteenth through the eighteenth centuries, see Bastl, *Tugend, Liebe, Ehre.* On the lower nobility of the Weser region between 1550 and 1700, see Hufschmidt, *Adelige Frauen im Weserraum.* Hufschmidt includes an extensive bibliography of recent publications on early modern German noblewomen. Although Wunder (*He Is the Sun, She Is the Moon*) deals primarily with nonnoble women, it also contains useful material on noblewomen.

[13]Johnson, "It All Makes Sense Now." Review of Gerhard Wolf, *Von der Chronik zum Weltbuch."*

of southwest Germany."[14] Bastress-Dukehart, on the other hand, emphasizes the historical content of the chronicle and sets it in political context. She focuses on the feud between the Werdenberg and Zimmern families (1488–1504) as the key event that defined the Zimmern family's perception of itself and its history.

The present study will draw chiefly on the portions of the *Zimmern Chronicle* that recount the family's history after the end of the feud. These biographical and autobiographical chapters, interspersed with chapters of "merry tales," make up about two-thirds of the entire chronicle. They focus on the lives of the chronicler, Froben Christoph von Zimmern (1519–66), his father, Johann Werner II (1480–1548), and his uncles, Gottfried Werner (1484–1554) and Wilhelm Werner (1485–1575). It will utilize both the *mentalités* approach and the historical demographic approach; in addition to analyzing the chronicle's depiction of the values of mid-sixteenth-century Swabian nobles, it will undertake a demographic analysis of the family strategies of the Zimmerns and the families with whom they intermarried. Not surprisingly, actual behavior did not always reflect the ideals expressed in the chronicle.

Since modern scholarship in the history of the family began with scholarship on England and France, these countries have generally been taken as the norms by scholars dealing with other countries. Comparative studies of European nobilities in the late Middle Ages and early modern periods rarely discuss German nobles except as conspicuous exceptions to the norms of England and France. While other European aristocracies were moving toward primogeniture or other inheritance systems that consolidated wealth in the hands of a single male heir, German nobles remained stubbornly attached to a system of partible inheritance that divided lands among several sons. German historians of the noble family, for their part, tend to ascribe the inheritance and marriage patterns of German nobles to regional factors and to draw relatively few comparisons to other European nobilities. But did German nobles actually differ in their attitudes and behavior from other European nobles? Recent research on the noble family in other European countries in the fifteenth and sixteenth centuries has questioned the generalizations made by pioneering scholars like Stone, and has made it possible to set the behavior of German nobles in a broader European context.[15]

In drawing comparisons among European nobilities with respect to marriage and sexuality, three issues deserve particular consideration: the kinship system and its effects on inheritance and marriage strategies; the concept of equality of

---

[14]Wolf, *Von der Chronik zum Weltbuch,* 130.

[15]Particularly useful are: on France, Nassiet, *Parenté, noblesse et états dynastiques;* on Castile, Beceiro Pita and Córdoba de la Llave, *Parentesco, poder y mentalidad;* and on England, Rosenthal, *Patriarchy and Families of Privilege,* and Harris, *English Aristocratic Women, 1450–1550.* Although they deal with urban patriciates rather than landed nobilities, studies of Italian city-states are valuable for comparative analysis of elites: Molho, *Marriage Alliance in Late Medieval Florence;* Kuehn, *Law, Family, and Women;* and Kuehn, *Illegitimacy in Renaissance Florence.*

birth as related to the definition of nobility; and the conflict between ecclesiastical and lay views of marriage and sexuality.

KINSHIP SYSTEMS AND FAMILY STRATEGIES

All European nobilities from the High Middle Ages onward faced a conflict between competing elements in the kinship system, which affected their strategies of inheritance and marriage. The kinship system of early Germanic societies was bilateral, tracing descent in both the male and the female lines. However, in order to control access to office and to preserve landed property, the landed elite in the High Middle Ages superimposed upon it a patrilineal system (tracing descent only in the male line).[16]

The older Germanic bilateral system favored the *kin* (the living relatives) at the expense of future generations and emphasized the equality of all members of the sibling group. It placed the highest priority on obtaining alliances for the living kin by giving the maximum number of sons and daughters sufficient property to marry and support a family. It therefore practiced partible inheritance, dividing property among all siblings.[17]

In contrast, the patrilineal system adopted by the medieval nobility favored the *lineage* (those tracing descent in the male line from a common ancestor) over the living kin. It placed its highest priority on passing ancestral property intact down to future generations in the male line. Inheritance practices favored sons over daughters and one son (usually the eldest) over the others.[18] When carried to its logical conclusion, these trends resulted in impartible inheritance with the title and ancestral lands descending to the eldest son, and in the preference for collateral male kin such as brothers and nephews over daughters as heirs. Primogeniture and the exclusion of female succession have thus been viewed as the hallmarks of lineal consolidation. [19]

At the time the *Zimmern Chronicle* was written, no western European aristocracy had completely adopted both of these inheritance practices. However, England and northern France had proceeded furthest toward the goal of consolidating property in the hands of the male line of descent. In the sixteenth century, legal settlements entailing estates on the eldest son to prevent division of the patrimony were widely used in England, France, Castile, and Italy.[20] Although they did exclude females from the succession, German nobles were conspicuous in their

---

[16]Herlihy, "Making of the Medieval Family."

[17]On inheritance law in southwest Germany, see Röhm, *Die Vererbung des landwirtschaftlichen Grundeigentums in Baden-Württemberg;* and Hess, *Familien- und Erbrecht im württembergischen Landrecht von 1555.*

[18]Herlihy, "Making of the Medieval Family," 124.

[19]On the two hallmarks, see Spiess, *Familie und Verwandtschaft,* 501–2.

[20]Cooper, "Patterns of Inheritance and Settlement by Great Landowners," 192–98. On Castile, see also Beceiro Pita and Córdoba de la Llave, *Parentesco, poder y mentalidad,* 232–42.

reluctance to abandon partible inheritance and the ideology of equality among brothers. Even modern German scholars often express exasperation with the seemingly irrational behavior of medieval German nobles who persisted in dividing their estates.[21]

Unlike other European nobles, German nobles consistently divided the paternal estates to create collateral lines that were equal in status to the original line. In the fifteenth century, some families—including the Waldburgs and the Zollerns—established the office of head of the entire lineage (*Seniorat*), but this office was not necessarily held by a member of the original line. Rather, this office was held by the oldest living head of one of the individual lines, and passed on his death to the next oldest head of a line.[22]

This German insistence on the equality of all collateral lines contrasted with the system adopted by the French and Iberian aristocracies, where the eldest son received all or most of the paternal estates, while younger sons were endowed with lands acquired through maternal inheritance or purchase. These younger sons established cadet branches inferior in status to the senior line, and often held their lands in fief from the senior branch.[23] German practice stood in even more marked contrast to that of England, where only the eldest son (as sole heir to the paternal estates under the system of primogeniture) ranked as a nobleman, while younger sons and their descendants were considered only gentry.[24]

Giving younger sons a share of the patrimony would enable more sons to marry, or at least to marry within their own social order. The German nobility also preserved, to a greater degree than other western European aristocracies, several other features of the original Germanic kinship system: an inheritance system that granted equal shares to daughters as well as to sons, a system of marital payments favorable to the bride's side, and a strategy of maximizing marriage alliances by not only allowing several sons to marry but also marrying off as many daughters as possible.

Equality of Birth and the Definition of Nobility

The definition of nobility played an important role in marriage strategy and attitudes toward the illegitimate children of noblemen. While all European nobilities sought to narrow their definitions of membership in the fifteenth and sixteenth centuries in the face of increased competition from the bourgeoisie, the German

---

[21]Spiess, *Familie und Verwandtschaft*, 199.

[22]Dornheim, *Familie Waldburg-Zeil*, 78–79; and Ulshöfer, *Hausrecht der Grafen von Zollern*, 25.

[23]On the establishment of such cadet lines in France, see Duby, "Philip Augustus's France," 124; and Nassiet, *Parenté, noblesse et états dynastiques*, 44–52. On the inferior status of lines descended from younger sons in the Castilian aristocracy in the late Middle Ages, see Beceiro Pita and Córdoba de la Llave, *Parentesco, poder y mentalidad*, 90, 276.

[24]Stone, *Crisis of the Aristocracy*, 789.

aristocracy was especially notable for its stringent definition of nobility and strong barriers against marriages between noblemen and women of lower social status.

Both early modern French theorists of nobility and modern French scholars assert that the attitudes of German nobles toward misalliances and bastardy differed from those of French nobles, and that these differences were based on the differing German and French definitions of nobility. The German system of reckoning nobility *by quarters* required noble ancestry on the mother's as well as the father's side, whereas the French system, like that of most other European nobilities, reckoned noble descent through the father alone.[25]

The practices of the English landed elite stood in even sharper contrast to those of the German nobility. Genealogist Andreas Thiele expresses his astonishment at the frequent intermarriage of the English peers with their social inferiors and the absence of legal consequences for such misalliances:

> Every heir was considered legitimate and eligible to inherit as long as the parents had contracted a legally valid marriage. Thus it happens over and over again that, in the English peerage, the crassest misalliances took place—and still take place—that would have meant the disinheritance of the children in Germany or France, but not in England.[26]

In Germany, the marriage of a nobleman to a nonnoble woman—even to a wealthy member of the urban patriciate—carried the legal disability of inequality of birth (*Unebenbürtigkeit*). This meant that the children of the marriage could not inherit the title or estate of the higher-ranking parent. For example, the inheritance pacts signed by the counts of Werdenberg in 1451 and 1494 stated that a count's estates would pass to his brothers or to his brothers' heirs in the absence of male heirs of equal birth (*männliche ebenbürtige Erben*).[27]

From the fifteenth century onward, the German nobility further protected its exclusivity by requiring members of elite cathedral chapters and tournament societies to prove four generations of purely noble ancestry. The *Zimmern Chronicle* draws a direct analogy between the rules for membership in cathedral chapters and those for participation in tournaments. When Johann Christoph von Zimmern was sworn in as a canon of Strasbourg in 1531, he was required to prove that "fourteen ancestors of his father and fourteen ancestors of his mother were princes, counts, or barons" and that none of his ancestors were of lower rank. The chronicler comments, "It was just like a tournament,… where each had to prove his rank and descent" (*ZC* 3:206).[28]

---

[25]French writers on the nobility comment on the stringency of the German definition: Labatut, *Les noblesses européennes,* 79–81; and Contamines, *La noblesse au royaume de France,* 57.

[26]Thiele, foreword to *Erzählende genealogische Stammtafeln,* vol. 4, *Die Britische Peerage.*

[27]On inequality of birth and its legal consequences, see *Handwörterbuch zur deutschen Rechtesgeschichte* (hereafter cited as *HRG*), s.vv. "Ebenbürtigkeit," "Missheirat." On the Werdenberg pacts between brothers, see Vanotti, *Grafen von Montfort und von Werdenberg,* 401, 450.

[28]In the fourteenth century, cathedral chapters began to require proof of noble descent on both

A nobleman's marriage to a nonnoble wife could thus affect the prospects of his descendants for more than a century. This German view that the status of children depended on the rank of the mother as well as the father even influenced attitudes toward marriages that were not unequal in the eyes of the law, such as those between the different orders of the nobility. Moreover, it had important consequences for the legal and social position of noble bastards, who were generally regarded as nobles in France and other countries where nobility was defined solely by the status of the father.

ECCLESIASTICAL AND LAY MODELS OF MARRIAGE

Views on marriage and sexuality in all European elites were affected by the competition between the church and the kin group for control over these areas of life. From the eleventh century onward, what Georges Duby calls the "ecclesiastical" model of marriage triumphed over what he calls the "aristocratic" or "lay" model. In the lay model, derived from Germanic custom, marriage was controlled by the kin group. It was founded on a marriage pact between two houses, in which the woman was handed over from the authority of the head of her natal household to that of her husband.[29] The lay moral code permitted extramarital affairs for men but condemned adultery by the wife as an offense against the authority of her husband. Polygamy was practiced and husbands were allowed to repudiate their wives. Moreover, there was a strong tendency toward endogamy (marriage within the kin group), especially marriages between cousins.[30]

Competing with this lay model was an ecclesiastical model, which viewed marriage as a monogamous and indissoluble union, branded all sexual activity outside of marriage as illicit, and placed in ecclesiastical hands the power to deal with all issues related to the validity of a marriage or to marital breakdown. The ecclesiastical model regarded adultery as an offense against the institution of marriage that could be committed by husbands as well as by wives. It also set stricter limits on marriage to close kin than Germanic societies had done, finally fixing them in 1215 at the fourth degree of kinship (that is, a common ancestor within four generations).[31] As James Brundage remarks,

> exogamy and indissolubility clearly emerged as hallmarks of Catholic marriage during this period.... As a consequence the laity, even at the highest

---

the father's and the mother's side. In the course of the fifteenth century the chapter of Cologne (reserved for the high nobility) increased its requirements to eight, sixteen, and finally thirty-two noble ancestors, although those of Trier and Mainz (dominated by the lower nobility) still required only four noble ancestors in the sixteenth century. Veit, *Stiftsmässige deutschen Adel,* 11, 15–16.

[29]Duby, *Medieval Marriage,* 7–8.

[30]Duby, *Medieval Marriage,* 4–5.

[31]On the changes in Germanic marriage practices and family structure brought about by the Catholic Church, see Goody, *Development of the Family and Marriage in Europe,* 34–47. On the calculation of the prohibited degrees of marriage, see ibid., 134–46.

social levels, lost much of its former control over the marriages of family members. The old-style capacity of families to arrange the marriages, divorces, and remarriages of their kin was rapidly disappearing.[32]

The gap between the lay and the ecclesiastical views of marriage widened in the twelfth century as canon lawyers and theologians adopted a definition of marriage as based on consensus: that is, on the consent of the partners themselves, without the necessity of a public ceremony or of parental consent.[33] The Catholic Church now "held marriage to be a sacrament which the spouses administered to themselves by the exchange of consent," which was to be based on affection (*dilectio*) or "what we might call love" between the spouses rather than on the interests of the kin.[34]

> The [Catholic] Church thus...tended to take a stand against the power of the heads of households in matters of marriage, against the lay concept of misalliance, and, indeed, against male supremacy, for it asserted the equality of the sexes in concluding the marriage pact and in the accomplishment of the duties thereby implied.[35]

By the end of the Middle Ages, aspects of the ecclesiastical model of marriage and sexuality had been accepted in southern Germany by the middle classes and by secular authorities. In the late fifteenth century, merchants and patricians in Augsburg viewed the potential for affection between spouses as a significant criterion in marriage negotiations, and the towns of southern Germany were among the most active in Europe in legislating against nonmarital sexuality.[36] German nobles in this era continued to view the kin group as playing a dominant role in matters of marriage and sexuality, and to reject the church's view that sexual activity must be limited to marriage. However, imperial and territorial law codes of the sixteenth century imposed upon all social classes the ecclesiastical definition of adultery. Some scholars have suggested that the ecclesiastical model thus had greater impact on nobles in Germany than on those in countries like France, where secular law did not accept the view that infidelity by the husband constituted adultery.[37] The *Zimmern Chronicle* presents a richly detailed account of this conflict between the two models of marriage and sexuality. Froben Christoph von Zimmern, who had internalized the ecclesiastical model to an extent quite remarkable for a layman, repeatedly confronted a father, an uncle, and a social

---

[32]Brundage, *Law, Sex, and Christian Society,* 225.

[33]Pope Alexander III (1159–81) "consistently sought to free marriages from the control of parents, families, and feudal overlords and to place the choice of marriage partners under the exclusive control of the parties themselves." Brundage, *Law, Sex, and Christian Society,* 332–33.

[34]Duby, *Medieval Marriage,* 21, 36, 59.

[35]Duby, *Medieval Marriage,* 16–17.

[36]Beer, *Eltern und Kinder,* 86–96; and Brundage, *Law, Sex, and Christian Society,* 444, 514–15.

[37]*HRG,* s.vv. "Ehebruch," "Konkubinat"; Sprandel, "Diskriminierung der unehelichen Kinder im Mittelalter," 491; and Potter, "Marriage and Cruelty among the Protestant Nobility," 26–28.

milieu that continued to view a husband's extramarital affairs as a prerogative of his noble status and to expect a wife to turn a blind eye to them.

THE *ZIMMERN CHRONICLE* AND THE ZIMMERN FAMILY

House chronicles or chronicles of noble families first appeared in Swabia at the end of the fifteenth century and became fashionable among counts and barons in the sixteenth century. German nobles in this period began to compile systematic genealogies in order to buttress their position against recently ennobled parvenus. Under the influence of humanist historians, they also sought to enhance the reputation of their lineages by tracing their origins back to the Romans or Franks.[38] Among the southwest German counts and barons who commissioned house chronicles or genealogies in the sixteenth century, in addition to the Zimmern, were the families of Württemberg, Fürstenberg, Zollern, Montfort, Werdenberg, Waldburg, Limpurg, Geroldseck, Helfenstein, and Eberstein.[39]

The *Zimmern Chronicle* is unique among such chronicles because it was written by a member of the noble family itself rather than by a professional humanist. Scholars agree that the research on which the chronicle is based was undertaken by the family's most famous member, the jurist Wilhelm Werner von Zimmern (1485–1575), although they disagree on the extent to which he was responsible for the actual writing. The immediate inspiration for the chronicle may have been Charles V's grant of the title of count to Wilhelm Werner and his brothers in 1538,[40] for house chronicles were often commissioned as propaganda at a key point in a family's fortunes. They served to legitimate a noble family's claims to property and titles and to assert its status vis-à-vis other noble families.[41]

Although the chronicle traces the history of the Zimmern family back to legendary origins in Roman days, less than a quarter of the text is devoted to the period before the 1480s. The remainder of the chronicle presents what Wolf calls a tale of "catastrophe and salvation."[42] It traces the fall and rise of the Zimmern family from its nadir in 1488, when all of its estates were confiscated during the Werdenberg-Zimmern feud, to its recovery of wealth and status by the time the chronicle was written.

---

[38]On the development of genealogy, heraldry, and family chronicles in Germany, see Isenburg, "Die geschichtliche Entwicklung von Sippenkunde und Sippenforschung," 1–13; Seigel, "Zur Geschichtsschreibung," 93–118; Jenny, *Graf Froben Christoph von Zimmern*, 24–34; Wolf, *Von der Chronik zum Weltbuch*, 17–33; and Bastress-Dukehart, *Zimmern Chronicle*, 12–25. On similar interest among the French and Castilian aristocracies, see Nassiet, *Parenté, noblesse et états dynastiques*, 41–42; and Beceiro Pita and Córdoba de la Llave, *Parentesco, poder y mentalidad*, 90. In England, the interest in genealogy, heraldry, and family history did not reach a similar level of intensity until the late sixteenth and seventeenth centuries. Stone, *Crisis of the Aristocracy*, 23–27.

[39]Seigel, "Zur Geschichtsschreibung," 94–98.

[40]Wolf, *Von der Chronik zum Weltbuch*, 379.

[41]Wolf, *Von der Chronik zum Weltbuch*, 458; and Seigel, "Zur Geschichtsschreibung," 10.

[42]Wolf, *Von der Chronik zum Weltbuch*, 274.

The *Zimmern Chronicle* was completed about 1566 but remained in manuscript form until the nineteenth century. Two manuscript versions of the chronicle were first recorded in 1770 as part of the collection belonging to the Fürstenberg family, who had inherited the Zimmern lordship of Messkirch. The manuscript on parchment, containing many corrections, is known as MS A (Cod. Donauschingen 581); the manuscript on paper, an illustrated copy now bound in two volumes, is known as MS B (Cod. Donauschingen 580). Both copies remained in the Fürstenberg family archive at Donauschingen until 1993, when they were transferred to the Württembergische Landesbibliothek in Stuttgart.[43]

Although excerpts and abridged versions were published in the early nineteenth century, the first complete edition of the *Zimmern Chronicle* was published by Karl Barack in 1869; this is the edition used in this study. Barack also published a second edition in 1882, which was reprinted in 1932.[44] Both Barack editions insert the chronicler's numerous addenda into the body of the text, an arrangement that, in Wolf's opinion, "obscures the unity of the text from a literary point of view."[45] In the 1960s, Hansmartin Decker-Hauff and Rudolf Seigel undertook a new edition, which was intended to place the addenda at the end as they appear in MS B. However, only three of the projected six volumes were published.[46]

Scholars who have studied the chronicle agree that it was written by one or more members of the Zimmern family; however, its exact authorship has been a subject of controversy. Until the mid-nineteenth century, the chronicle was attributed to Wilhelm Werner von Zimmern (1485–1575), a judge of the Imperial Chamber Court (*Reichskammergericht*) and an antiquarian who owned a famous library and a collection of natural curiosities (*Wunderkammer*). In addition to his historical works—notably a five-volume chronicle of the archbishopric of Mainz and its suffragan bishoprics—Wilhelm Werner was known to have taken an active interest in family history and to have compiled genealogies for other Swabian families.[47] However, in the course of editing the *Zimmern Chronicle*, Barack came to the conclusion that Wilhelm Werner carried out the research on which the chronicle

---

[43]On the history of the manuscripts and the question of authorship, see Jenny, *Graf Froben Christoph von Zimmern*, 17, 34, 40–46; Bastress-Dukehart, *Zimmern Chronicle*, 30–36; and Wolf, *Von der Chronik zum Weltbuch*, 130–47.

[44]Barack, *Zimmerische Chronik* (1869); Barack, *Zimmerische Chronik* (1881–82); and Hermann, *Zimmerische Chronik* (1932).

[45]Wolf, *Von der Chronik zum Weltbuch*, 146.

[46]Decker-Hauff, *Die Chronik der Grafen von Zimmern*.

[47]Wilhelm Werner's major work, "Chronik von der Erzstifte Mainz und dessen Suffraganbistümer," was completed about 1550. The portions relating to the dioceses of Würzburg and Eichstatt have been edited by Wilhelm Kraft and published as *Die Würzburger Bischofschronik des Grafen Wilhelm Werner von Zimmern und die Würzburger Geschichtsschreibung des 16. Jahrhunderts* (1952), and *Die Eichstätter Bischofschronik des Grafen Wilhelm Werner von Zimmern* (1956). On works written by Wilhelm Werner, see *ADB*, s.v. "Zimmern, Wilhelm Werner"; and Bastress-Dukehart, *Zimmern Chronicle*, 31n79. On his library and *Wunderkammer*, see ibid., 36–38.

was based, but did not do the actual writing. Barack argued that the chronicle was written by Wilhelm Werner's nephew, Froben Christoph von Zimmern (1519–66), with the assistance of his secretary, Johannes Muller.

The theory of Froben Christoph's authorship of the chronicle has been accepted by most twentieth-century scholars, though they have rejected Barack's view that the secretary made a significant contribution.[48] However, Erica Bastress-Dukehart maintains that the chronicle should be seen as a collaboration between Wilhelm Werner and Froben Christoph. In her view, the older man was responsible not just for the research but for the actual writing of the sections of the chronicle dealing with events through the Werdenberg feud (chapters 1–84). She accepts Froben Christoph as the principal author—though not necessarily the sole one—of the biographical and autobiographical sections dealing with the period after 1504 (chapters 85–209). The question of authorship is not of central importance for this study, since almost all of the chronicle's discussions of family relationships and sexuality occur in the sections that even Bastress-Dukehart ascribes to Froben Christoph. It will be assumed in subsequent discussion that Froben Christoph von Zimmern is the author of the *Zimmern Chronicle,* and that the opinions expressed in the chronicle on family relationships and sexuality represent his point of view.

❧ ❧ ❧

The *Zimmern Chronicle* provides several different types of evidence for the study of the history of the noble family: summaries of legal documents and other materials from the Zimmern family archives, stories about family members or contemporaries that are autobiographical or based on oral transmission, and the frankly literary inventions, the *Schwänke.*

None of these sources can be taken at face value as presenting unvarnished historical fact. House chronicles were literary works that aimed "to give the mere assembling of facts about the family the quality of a unified epic," and to create a commemorative monument that would enhance the reputation of the family.[49] To achieve this goal, the Zimmerns, like the authors of other house chronicles, had no compunction about filling in gaps in the distant past with generations of wholly fictitious ancestors, or embellishing the achievements of genuine ancestors with family legends or heroic deeds modeled on those in courtly epics.

The autobiographical material and material based on oral transmission were also shaped to fit the agenda of the author. Above all, Froben Christoph wished to present himself as the savior who had rescued the Zimmern lineage from the

---

[48]Jenny, *Graf Froben Christoph von Zimmern,* 45; and Wolf, *Von der Chronik zum Weltbuch,* 141.
[49]Wolf, *Von der Chronik zum Weltbuch,* 458.

disasters caused by the banishment of his grandfather and the fratricidal quarrels between his father and his uncles.[50]

Lastly, the anecdotes and *Schwänke* had the twin goals of instruction and entertainment.[51] Not only do many of the anecdotes about the Zimmerns and other families teach a moral lesson about the need for unity between brothers, but even the bawdy tales about sexual pranks may be intended as commentaries on the serious themes treated in the narrative.[52] Even though the chronicle is a mixture of fact and fiction, it provides a unique insight into the values of Swabian nobles of the fifteenth and sixteenth centuries and indicates the assumptions the chronicler expected his audience to share.

Although the chronicle covers the history of the Zimmern family from its legendary origins down through the chronicler's own lifetime, over three-quarters of the text is devoted to the period from the 1480s to the 1560s. It describes in great detail three generations of the family: that of Johann Werner I (1455–95), the protagonist of the Werdenberg-Zimmern feud; that of his three sons, Johann Werner II (1480–1548), Gottfried Werner (1484–1554), and Wilhelm Werner (1485–1575); and that of his grandsons, the chronicler, Froben Christoph (1519–66), and his brothers, Johann Christoph (1516–56/57) and Gottfried Christoph (1524–70).

Despite the chronicle's fanciful effort to trace the descent of the Zimmern family from the Germanic tribe of Cimbri, the family first appears in historical records in the eleventh century. Its members are described as *freie Herren*, or "freeborn lords," a title equivalent to baron. The Zimmerns were typical of these small independent nobles, whose landed possessions were often made up of scattered holdings and whose political influence was confined to their local region Along with the counts (*Grafen*), the barons (*freie Herren*) belonged to the *Hochadel* or nonprincely high nobility. Membership in this order was based on free birth, landed possessions, and the exercise of the right of high justice over lordships (*Herrschaften*). The *Hochadel* made up the second of the three orders of nobles represented in the Reichstag. They ranked below the order of princes (*Fürsten*), which consisted of dukes (*Herzoge*), margraves (*Markgrafen*), and landgraves (*Landgrafen*). However, they ranked above the order of the lower nobility (*Niederadel* or *Ritteradel*), which consisted of knights (*Ritter*) and "mere" nobles (*Edelleute*). Unlike the freeborn princes and higher nobility, the lower nobility were descended from unfree *ministeriales* (serf-knights).[53]

---

[50]On Froben Christoph's view of himself as the renewer of the lineage in contrast to his feckless father, see Wolf, *Von der Chronik zum Weltbuch,* 320.

[51]Walter, *Unkeuschheit und Werk der Liebe,* 159.

[52]For example, Wolf, *Von der Chronik zum Weltbuch,* 246, 250, 273, 389. Wolf also argues (152) that the chapters of *Schwänke* serve the structural function of marking important points of chronological or thematic transition in the chronicle.

[53]For an overview of the development of the nobility in southwestern Germany from the thirteenth to the sixteenth century, see Spiess, *Familie und Verwandtschaft,* 1–4.

The original seat of the Zimmern family was at Herrenzimmern in the Black Forest near Rottweil.[54] In the mid-fourteenth century, the family greatly increased its wealth and prestige by acquiring the lordship of Messkirch through marriage to an heiress. Messkirch, located south of the Danube River in the Swabian Alb, became the family seat.[55] Their territorial acquisitions brought the Zimmerns into competition with other local noble families, notably the counts of Werdenberg. Friction increased after 1399, when the Werdenbergs acquired the fief of Sigmaringen, adjacent to Messkirch. An open feud between the two families developed after Johann Werner I von Zimmern succeeded to the Zimmern estates in 1483.[56]

As a councilor of Archduke Sigismund of Tyrol, Johann Werner I was drawn into the archduke's quarrels with Emperor Frederick III. In 1488, the emperor declared twelve of Sigismund's councilors guilty of treason, banished them from the Empire, and confiscated their lands. Although the emperor soon restored the lands of most of the archduke's other banished councilors, he refused to restore the Zimmern estates. The *Zimmern Chronicle* blames Johann Werner's misfortunes on his old enemy Hugo von Werdenberg, who was one of the emperor's chief advisers and—as the head of the Swabian League—his right-hand man in carrying out imperial policy in southwest Germany. Although J. N. von Vanotti's chronicle of the Werdenberg family denies that Hugo was responsible for the exile of Johann Werner, it acknowledges that Hugo did "capitalize upon the Zimmerns' disgrace with the emperor to enrich and improve the standing of his family, all at the Zimmerns' expense."[57]

The case dragged on long after the deaths of Emperor Frederick III in 1493 and Johann Werner I in 1495. The latter's sons were eventually able to reconquer their

[54]A note on geographical terms used in this study: Southwest Germany is used by modern geographers to describe the area east of the Rhine River encompassing the valleys of the Main, Neckar, and upper Danube Rivers. This region was included in two of the basic or "stem" duchies of medieval Germany, Swabia (Schwaben) and Franconia (Franken). In the sixteenth century, the names of the duchies were still used to designate these regions and their inhabitants, although the names no longer corresponded to actual political entities.

Swabia is the southern region centered on the upper reaches of the Neckar and Danube Rivers; the western portion includes the Black Forest. It corresponds roughly to the modern German state (*Land*) of Baden-Württemberg, although the eastern portion around Augsburg is part of the state of Bayern (Bavaria). The medieval duchy of Swabia also included Alsace and much of Switzerland.

Upper Swabia, where the Zimmern lived, is the highland region of Swabia. It includes the upper Danube valley and the mountainous region extending south to Lake Constance, known as the Swabian Alb.

Franconia lies to the north of Swabia and is centered on the Main River. It corresponds roughly to the modern German state (*Land*) of Franken (Franconia), although the southeastern districts around Nördlingen are part of the state of Bayern (Bavaria).

[55]For details of the territorial acquisitions of the Zimmern family, see Bastress-Dukehart, *Zimmern Chronicle*, 60–68. On their strategic significance, see Wolf, *Von der Chronik zum Weltbuch*, 247, 250.

[56]Wolf, *Von der Chronik zum Weltbuch*, 254.

[57]Vanotti, *Grafen von Montfort und von Werdenberg*, 438. Translation quoted from Bastress-Dukehart, *Zimmern Chronicle*, 97–98.

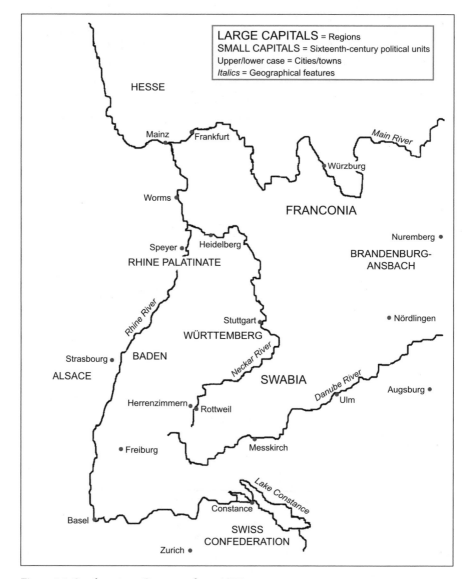

Figure 1.1: Southwestern Germany about 1525.

lands with military support from territorial princes who had their own quarrels with the emperor, and from Swabian nobles who resented the Hapsburgs' efforts to increase imperial control over the nobility of the region. In 1504, Emperor Maximilian I formally ordered the restoration of the property and privileges of the Zimmern family and issued a posthumous pardon to Johann Werner I (*ZC* 2:133–45).[58]

After their recovery, the Zimmern estates were heavily encumbered by debts. Nonetheless, the lands were divided in 1508 between Johann Werner II and Gottfried Werner, the two oldest surviving sons of Johann Werner I. The third surviving son, Wilhelm Werner, planned to enter the church but became a jurist after failing to obtain entry to a cathedral chapter (*ZC* 2:189–91).[59]

The two older brothers then left princely service and devoted themselves to managing (or in the view of the chronicler, mismanaging) their estates. They avoided holding office and took no part in the major political events of the Reformation era, for fear of placing their estates in jeopardy again if they backed the losing side. According to the chronicler, Gottfried Werner turned down offers both from the Hapsburgs and from their opponent, his old patron Duke Ulrich von Württemberg.[60]

> He was a clever, wise, and intelligent lord, capable of fulfilling his duties with dignity and courage, and was recognized as such by others. Nevertheless, because of the troubled and doubtful times, and especially the divisions in religion, he did not want to enter [princely] service or favor one party over another. (*ZC* 2:606)

Turning his back on the knightly life and on politics, Gottfried Werner devoted himself to patronizing the arts, and especially to building the Renaissance castle at Wildenstein. He ignored Froben Cristoph's criticism of his lavish expenditures on building projects, which his nephew (and heir) believed jeopardized the economic well-being of the Zimmern lineage. Jenny suggests that Gottfried Werner "did not want to save up for [the benefit of] future sons-in-law," since Froben Christoph's first three children were daughters and no male heir to ensure the continuation of the Zimmern lineage was born until 1549.[61]

---

[58]For details of the Werdenberg-Zimmern feud, see Bastress-Dukehart, *Zimmern Chronicle*, 80–155. On the significance of the feud in the politics of southwest Germany, see also Carl, *Der Schwäbische Bund*, 137–38, 268.

[59]On the careers of the three Zimmern brothers and their portrayal in the chronicle, see Jenny, *Graf Froben Christoph von Zimmern*, 52–53 (Johann Werner II), 55–65 (Wilhelm Werner), 332–38 (Gottfried Werner); Wolf, *Von der Chronik zum Weltbuch*, 318–21 (Johann Werner II), 328–38 (Gottfried Werner), 342–47 (Wilhelm Werner); Bastress-Dukehart, *Zimmern Chronicle*, 156–61, 165–68 (Johann Werner II), 161–65, 193 (Gottfried Werner), 36–42, 168–86 (Wilhelm Werner); and *ADB*, s.v. "Zimmern, Wilhelm Werner."

[60]Duke Ulrich von Württemberg, who had been deposed and driven out of his territorial state by the Hapsburgs in 1519, later became a Protestant. He regained the throne of Württemberg in 1534 with the help of the Protestant princes of the League of Schmalkalden.

[61]Jenny, *Graf Froben Christoph von Zimmern*, 57, 109, quote at 109. In addition to Wildenstein, where construction went on from 1520 to 1550, Gottfried Werner rebuilt the castle of Herrenzimmern

In contrast to the studied neutrality of his two older brothers, Wilhelm Werner spent his career in the service of Emperor Charles V as a judge in the imperial court at Rottweil and (after 1529) as an assessor at the Imperial Chamber Court at Speyer. As a reward for this service, Charles V granted Wilhelm Werner and his brothers the title of count in 1538. Wilhelm Werner also gained a reputation as a historian and an antiquarian.

The chronicler presents the history of these three brothers as a morality tale demonstrating the disastrous effects of placing individual self-interest above the good of the family as a whole. Gottfried Werner, who had received the smaller portion of the estate in the division of 1508, maneuvered his feckless elder brother Johann Werner II into an exchange of estates. Feeling that he had been swindled, Johann Werner II deliberately sold ancestral estates just to spite his brother. The chronicler criticizes both men for mismanagement and for indifference to the larger interests of the lineage as a whole: "There was no unity or loyalty in the Zimmern family; each one had his own state [*republicam*]" (ZC 2:134).

The elevation of the Zimmern family to the rank of count in 1538 completed the estrangement of the three brothers. Johann Werner II refused to adopt the new coat of arms that had been awarded along with the title; instead, he decorated his castle of Falkenstein with his personal device, a green bird. To the chronicler, the new official arms quartering the lions rampant of Zimmern with those of Wildenstein seemed all too apt a symbol of the dissension in the family:

> Perhaps it would have been better if the quartered lions had stood one behind the other rather than scratching and scowling at each other. A courtier once said, the old lords had deliberately chosen this quartering and could not have expressed their activities more clearly than painting their own discord on their coat of arms, for the lions were confronting one another. (ZC 3:292–93)

THE CHRONICLER FROBEN CHRISTOPH VON ZIMMERN

In the autobiographical sections that make up much of the remainder of the chronicle, Froben Christoph von Zimmern presents himself as rescuing his lineage through his single-minded devotion to its interests. Jenny regards these autobiographical passages as a historically accurate reflection of Froben Christoph's life and personality, whereas Wolf regards them as a "literary representation" of what he wanted his audience to believe about himself.[62] Even if one accepts the latter characterization, the persona that Froben Christoph presents in the chronicle is

---

and the parish church of St. Martin in Messkirch. The castle of Wildenstein was decorated with frescoes depicting scenes from courtly romance. Gottfried Werner also commissioned important paintings from the Master of Messkirch: *The Wildenstein Altarpiece* (1536), which includes donor portraits of Gottfried Werner and Apollonia von Henneberg, and the *Three Kings* triptych (1535–38) for the high altar of St. Martin's Church in Messkirch.

[62]Wolf, *Von der Chronik zum Weltbuch*, 143. Jenny entitles his closing section "The Chronicle as a Self-Portrait of the Chronicler." *Graf Froben Christoph von Zimmern*, 192–99.

full of contradictions: a champion of the Zimmern cause who was brought up by a Werdenberg, a defender of lineage solidarity who was estranged from his own father, and an exemplar of sexual rectitude who filled his family chronicle with bawdy stories.

Froben Christoph was actually born and brought up at the home of his grandmother, Countess Elisabeth von Werdenberg, and her second husband, Philipp Echter. His mother, Katharina von Erbach, had gone back to her mother's home to give birth because the plague was raging at Messkirch, and when Johann Werner II came to fetch his wife and child home six months later, "the grandparents were unwilling to let Froben go, since he had been born at their house. They brought him up until his twelfth year, as if he had been their own son" (*ZC* 2:379). Froben Christoph von Zimmern was the third child and second surviving son of Johann Werner II von Zimmern and Katharina von Erbach. His parents' marriage in 1510 had been arranged by his mother's uncle, Count Christoph von Werdenberg, to heal the rift between the Werdenberg and Zimmern families. Nevertheless, the chronicler states that "[Johann Werner's] mother, the Countess of Oettingen, and his brother, Gottfried Werner, were greatly displeased with it. Because of the injuries and insults they had received from the Werdenbergs in the past; they did not want to have a reminder before their eyes every day." Even though "the resentment diminished with time, and Katharina herself was not to blame" for the past actions of her relatives (*ZC* 2:194), tensions between the two families were still a vivid memory when the chronicler was born in 1519.

It is unclear whether Froben Christoph had any contact with his mother during his childhood, but he apparently had none with his father or other Zimmern relatives. His insistence that Philipp Echter "maintained an honorable port, even equal to that of a count," suggests that he felt defensive about his grandmother's marriage to a mere knight (*ZC* 2:384). Froben Christoph's obsession in the chronicle with the importance of lineage and the need to maintain the social barriers between the higher and the lower nobility may reflect a fear that he was not considered a real member of the Zimmern lineage or a real member of the high nobility.

At the age of twelve, Froben Christoph was summoned home by his father to accompany his older brother, Johann Christoph, on his university studies. From 1531 to 1542, Froben Christoph studied at a series of universities in Germany and France, at first in the company of Johann Christoph and then of his younger brother, Gottfried Christoph. His father begrudged the expenses of these studies, complaining that the boys should finish one book before buying another (*ZC* 3:215). However, his uncles Gottfried Werner and Wilhelm Werner interceded with the father to allow the boys to continue their education, and they eventually paid some of the costs themselves (*ZC* 3:218, 306, 324).[63]

---

[63]For a detailed account of Froben Christoph's studies at Tübingen, Strasbourg, Bourges, Cologne,

Although Johann Christoph was required to undertake university studies as a prerequisite for becoming a cathedral canon, Froben Christoph's university education was probably intended to prepare him for a career in the service of a prince. However, he rejected a political career as too risky in this period of strife between the emperor and the Protestant princes. He claimed to have had a dream telling him that "he should not enter the service of the emperor or of any prince, or become involved in their affairs, or he would fall into the greatest misfortune, and his life would even be in danger" (*ZC* 3:334). At the age of twenty-three he returned to Messkirch to act as secretary (*Schreiber*) to his uncle Gottfried Werner, the de facto head of the Zimmern family. Since his younger brother, Gottfried Christoph, also became a cathedral canon, Froben Christoph was the only lay male member of his generation and the only one to marry and beget children. He became the sole owner of the Zimmern estates after the deaths of his father in 1548 and his uncle in 1554.

Froben Christoph devoted his life to restoring the family's fortunes through the aggressive use of lawsuits. He sought to recover all the lands claimed by the Zimmerns, to prevent Johann Werner II and Gottfried Werner from alienating any more ancestral lands, and to cut out all claims to the estates by collateral relatives and females, especially Gottfried Werner's daughter Anna and her husband Jos Niklaus von Zollern.[64]

His achievement was short-lived, for the Zimmern family died out in the male line when his only son Wilhelm died without issue in 1594. However, Wilhelm's career as a privy councilor and steward at the Hapsburg court, as well as the marriage of eight of Froben Christoph's daughters into high-ranking families, demonstrated that the Zimmerns had indeed restored their reputation. Jenny views the splendid alliances gained through the marriage of the daughters as the summation of Froben Christoph's life work. The imperial general Lazarus von Schwendi, who married Froben Christoph's daughter Leonora, said of this marriage, "She has six sisters married to the leading counts and barons of Germany. Therefore I have achieved very extensive connections through marriage with the noblest families. (Habet sex sorores cum *praecipitus comitibus et baronibus Germaniae* nuptas. Itaque *amplissimam affinitatem* et necessitudinem cum *nobilissimis familiis* consecutus [sum])."[65]

In portraying himself as the savior of the Zimmern lineage, Froben Christoph consistently contrasts himself with an unworthy father who squandered ancestral estates. The tone of Froben Christoph's relationship to his father was set

---

Louvain, Paris, Angers, Tours, and Speyer, see Jenny, *Graf Froben Christoph von Zimmern,* 69–95.

[64]Jenny, *Graf Froben Christoph von Zimmern,* 97. For a summary of Froben Christoph's career, see ibid., 95–121; and Bastress-Dukehart, *Zimmern Chronicle,* 191–94.

[65]Jenny ends his book with this quote (emphasis in the original). *Graf Froben Christoph von Zimmern,* 199.

when they quarreled on the very first day the twelve-year-old boy set foot in his father's castle at Falkenstein. Of one visit home during his university career, Froben Christoph writes, "Since he and his father could not agree, he only stayed overnight and left early the next morning. But he wrote with chalk a saying from scripture, 'the stone that the builders rejected has become the cornerstone,' and wrote his name under it" (*ZC* 3:307).

In a passage with Freudian overtones, Froben Christoph describes how, after his father's death, he and his two brothers gleefully destroyed all the representations of the green bird Johann Werner II had adopted as his personal coat of arms. "They drove away all these birds, they flew out of the beautiful stained glass in the windows. The stained glass coats-of-arms were shattered in the wind, the paintings washed off, and the...correct arms painted in their place" (*ZC* 3:292).

Froben Christoph's quarrels with his father had a deeper cause than the latter's mismanagement of the Zimmern estates. He was deeply hurt by his father's neglect of his mother in favor of a concubine. Although such extramarital relationships were common in the aristocracy, Froben Christoph took the slight to his mother personally and viewed himself as her champion (*ZC* 3:307–8). Probably it was this personal experience that led him in the chronicle to express empathy with the suffering of wives and to denounce extramarital affairs by husbands.

Although his own sexual behavior was unusually restrained by the standards of his society, Froben Christoph seems to have had an obsession with sexuality and its consequences that grew stronger in the course of writing the chronicle. The *Zimmern Chronicle* is unique among German house chronicles in interpolating into the narrative large numbers of *Schwänke,* many of them sexual in content. In the portions of the chronicle that recount the activities of Froben Christoph's own generation, there is a regular alternation of serious chapters and farcical chapters.[66] Moreover, many of the addenda to the chronicle are sexual in nature, including several tales about bastards that probably reflect Froben Christoph's concerns about the threat posed to the lineage by the illegitimate children of his father and uncle.

Scholars disagree on Froben Christoph's motives for including these sexual anecdotes in the house chronicle. Jenny sees the text as autobiographical and believes that Froben Christoph sublimates his own sexual anxieties and neuroses through telling the tales.[67] Wolf, however, sees the discourse on sexuality in the chronicle as a literary device rather than as a direct reflection of the author's character. He argues that the *Schwänke* are often meant to be instructive, and that they advocate the use of cunning and cool rationality (*Kaltsinnigkeit*) to extricate oneself from difficulties.[68]

---

[66]On these *Schwankkapital,* see Wolf, *Von der Chronik zum Weltbuch,* 152, 364–65.

[67]Jenny, *Graf Froben Christoph von Zimmern,* 193.

[68]Wolf, *Von der Chronik zum Weltbuch,* 144–45; 389. For other examples of Wolf's interpretation

In reading the chronicle, one must keep in mind that it reflects the author's experience and idiosyncrasies, and that its views may not always be typical of the nobles of its region and era. Froben Christoph's concern with lineage solidarity reflects a sentiment that was widespread in the nobility, but it may be particularly acute because he feared not being accepted as a real Zimmern. His candid descriptions of marital breakdown, concubinage, and bastardy are unparalleled in the writings of contemporary German nobles and clearly based on his personal emotional experiences. The *Zimmern Chronicle* is exceptional not only in being written by a member of the family it describes but also in offering a commentary on marriage and sexuality by one nobleman who is writing not as a Christian moralist or a jurist but as an ordinary layman.

---

of the *Schwänke,* see ibid., 249–50, 342, 377.

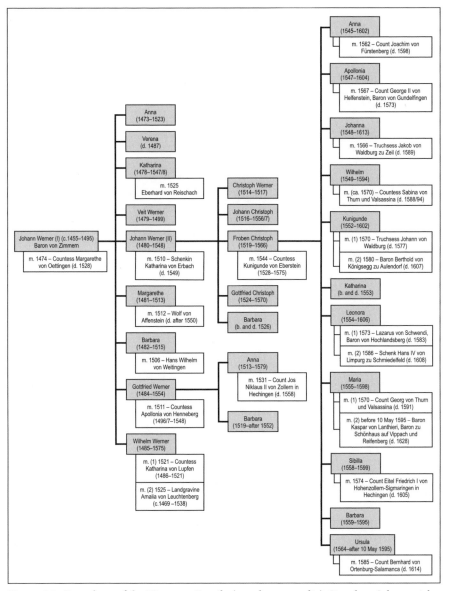

Figure 1.2: Genealogy of the Zimmern Family (see also appendix). Based on Schwennicke, *Europäische Stammtafeln NF,* 12, table 84, "Die Grafen von Zimmern."

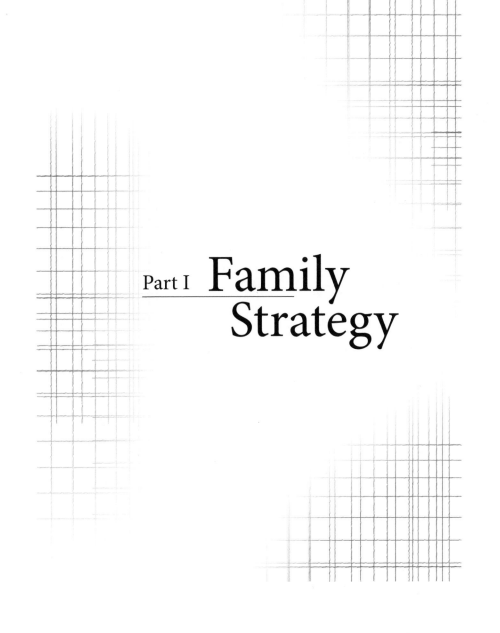

Part I Family
Strategy

CHAPTER 2

Inheritance and Dowry

Inheritance and marriage are interconnected elements of family strategy, for children could marry only if they received sufficient property as inheritance or as a "portion" or dowry. The kinship system of medieval and early modern European nobles combined two conflicting elements with different priorities for family strategy, with the older bilateral kin system favoring living kin through partible inheritance systems that maximized marriage alliances and the patrilineal system favoring future generations in the male line through impartible inheritance practices that favored sons over daughters and one son over the others.[1] The exclusion of females from succession to the parental inheritance was linked to changes in the system of marital payments from bride-price to dowry in the High Middle Ages. The burden of marital payments shifted from the groom's family to the bride's family; the marriage of a daughter to secure an alliance thus became a financial cost to her family rather than a financial advantage. As the size of the dowry increased, it became a premortem inheritance, replacing the daughter's claim to a share of the estate at her father's death.[2]

Decisions about the number of children who would marry thus involved decisions about whether to divide the patrimony to provide estates for more than one son, and about how much of the patrimony to use to provide dowries for daughters rather than to pass it on to future generations of male heirs. Although German nobles were affected by the trends towards consolidation of property in the hands of the lineage and substitution of the dowry for female inheritance, they

---

[1]Herlihy, "Making of the Medieval Family," 124.

[2]Diane Owen Hughes ("From Brideprice to Dowry," 276–78) dates this shift to the eleventh and twelfth centuries in northern Italy and southern France. In northern France in the eleventh century, "married women no longer received anything other than their dowry." See Duby, "Family Structures in the West," 108–9. In Castile, dowry did not become the dominant form of marital payment until the end of the thirteenth century. See Beceiro Pita and Córdoba de la Llave, *Parentesco, poder y mentalidad,* 184.

retained elements of the older Germanic systems of inheritance and marital payments that were becoming obsolete in other European nobilities. They continued to espouse an ideal of equality among brothers, although in practice they adjusted the number of heirs in response to economic circumstances. They also continued to give a substantial morning gift (a payment from the groom to the bride) long after this had become merely a token payment in other western European aristocracies, and allowed women who had already received dowries to make additional inheritance claims under certain circumstances. Moreover, they limited dowries to a narrow range based on rank even at a time when dowry levels in other nobilities were rising rapidly. This rigid dowry system lessened the financial burden of marrying off several daughters in a single generation and also made it difficult for women of lower social rank to marry into the high nobility by bringing exceptionally large dowries.

To compare the family strategies of southwest German counts and barons to those of other German nobles and other European elites, this section examines inheritance and marriage practices from 1400 to 1700 through the genealogies of the Zimmern family and of seven Swabian and three Franconian families with whom they intermarried in the fifteenth and sixteenth centuries. All these families lived within a hundred miles of the Zimmern seat at Messkirch.[3] Nine of these eleven families survived in the male line until at least the end of the sixteenth century and can be used for a comparison of religious confessions; of these, four families (and one branch of another) became Protestant.[4]

Information is available on 753 individuals (384 men and 369 women) in these eleven families who were born, married, or died between 1400 and 1699 and who survived to the age of fifteen. Individuals who died before that age are excluded because genealogies in the fifteenth and sixteenth centuries frequently

---

[3]These families are the counts of Eberstein, the *Schenken* (later counts) of Erbach, the counts (later princes) of Fürstenberg, the barons of Geroldseck, the barons of Gundelfingen, the counts of Kirchberg, the counts of Königsegg, the *Schenken* (later counts) of Limpurg, the counts (later princes) of Oettingen, the barons (later counts) of Zimmern, and the counts of Zollern (later princes of Hohenzollern). Their genealogies are found in Isenburg, *Europäische Stammtafeln*, 1:153–55 (Zollern), 3:93–96, (Limpurg); 4:27–31(Fürstenberg), 4:132–33 (Eberstein); 5:21–27 (Erbach), 5:72–73 (Geroldseck), 5:117–19 (Königsegg), 5:122 (Kirchberg), 5:123 (Zimmern), 5:125 (Gundelfingen), 5:150–55 (Oettingen). An update is currently in the process of publication (Schwennicke, *Europäische Stammtafeln, NF*), in which the Zimmern genealogy appears in 12:83–84. Where possible, data from the Isenburg edition have been corrected and amplified by data from the Schwennicke edition and from studies of individual families. In addition to the studies previously cited, these include Müller, "Das Geschlecht der Reichserbschenke zu Limpurg." The Erbach, Limpurg, and Oettingen families were Franconian; all the other families were Swabian.

[4]The families that became Protestant were Eberstein, Erbach, Geroldseck, and Limpurg; those that remained Catholic were Fürstenberg, Königsegg, Zimmern, and [Hohen]zollern. The Oettingen family divided into four lines; the main branch became Protestant while the three younger branches remained Catholic. The Kirchberg and Gundelfingen families died out in the male line before the end of the sixteenth century.

omit children who died young, making it difficult to draw accurate comparisons with later periods. As a practical matter, family heads only had to plan careers and/or marriages for those children who survived to their midteens.[5] The study extends beyond the date of the *Zimmern Chronicle* itself in order to compare the strategies of Protestant and Catholic families and to facilitate comparison with demographic studies of other European elites. It ends with the cohort born in the late seventeenth century, since all but one of the Protestant families died out in the male line in the early eighteenth century.

After 1650, the German princes had adopted primogeniture and demographic evidence is available for northern as well as southern European nobilities. It is thus possible by the late seventeenth century to investigate whether the non-princely German nobility followed inheritance strategies similar to those of princes, whether Protestant and Catholic German nobles followed different inheritance and marriage strategies, and whether German nobles followed marriage strategies different from those of Catholic and Protestant elites in other countries.

INHERITANCE IN THE *ZIMMERN CHRONICLE*

In the period when the *Zimmern Chronicle* was written, German nobles were conspicuous among western European landed elites for their reluctance to adopt primogeniture or other forms of impartible inheritance. In southwest Germany, the fourteenth-century compilation of laws known as the *Schwabenspiegel* had provided for equal division of the inheritance among all children, daughters as well as sons.[6] Although German nobles excluded daughters from the inheritance by the late fifteenth century, they continued to believe in the equality of all male members of the sibling group. Both princes and members of the nonprincely high nobility in the late Middle Ages and early modern periods frequently invoked the ideal of equality among brothers, which could be fulfilled either by dividing the estates among them or by leaving the undivided estate to be held in common by all the brothers.[7]

---

[5]For the same reasons, Peller's classic demographic study ("European Ruling Families," 88) includes only children who survived their fourteenth birthday. Survival to age fifteen is used in this study in order to facilitate comparisons with works of historical demography that calculate survival rates at five-year intervals. In the European demographic system, family reconstitution based on parish registers in England, France, and Switzerland shows that in the period between 1550 and 1750, 50 percent of the children born alive did not survive to age fifteen. See Flinn, *European Demographic System*, 94, 130–31. Survival rates were higher among the nobility. Hollingworth ("British Ducal Families," 363) states that in British ducal families, fathers born between 1480 and 1679 saw 31 percent of their children die under the age of sixteen. Peller ("European Ruling Families," 94) states that in European ruling families, children dying under the age of sixteen made up 29 percent of the children of parents married between 1500 and 1600 and 37 percent of the children of parents married between 1600 and 1699.

[6]Southwest Germany may have favored female inheritance more than other regions of medieval Germany. See Siegel, *Das Deutsche Erbrecht nach den Rechtsquellen de Mittelalters*, 48–50.

[7]Fichtner, *Protestantism and Primogeniture*, 28; and Spiess, *Familie und Verwandtschaft*, 240.

Among the families of counts and barons that played a leading role in the politics of Swabia, the Fürstenbergs, Montforts, Zollerns, and Waldburgs were especially notable for undertaking repeated divisions of their estates during the High and late Middle Ages. The Zimmerns, a less wealthy and powerful family, normally followed a strategy of individual succession before the mid-fifteenth century. Once they acquired a second lordship at Messkirch, however, they divided their estates as soon as demographic circumstances permitted. This suggests that their earlier strategy was based on economic necessity, not on ideological preference.[8]

During the period of agricultural depression that followed the Black Death, southwest German families of counts and barons attempted to limit the number of heirs to their impoverished estates. Formal agreements regulating the succession proliferated in the fourteenth and fifteenth centuries, culminating in house treaties like those of the Waldburg and Zollern families, which had the force of law for their members up to modern times. Whether or not they enacted such house laws, families by the mid-fifteenth century demonstrated their increasing lineage consciousness by passing regulations to ensure that property of the lineage would not pass into the hands of outsiders. They often created a *Stammgut* (imposing restrictions on the sale or mortgage of the ancestral castle and other core possessions of the lineage) and engaged in inheritance pacts between brothers (*Erbverbrüdering*), which provided that in the absence of male issue, male collateral relatives such as brothers, uncles, or nephews were to succeed in preference to daughters. Some families such as the Waldburgs and Zollerns also instituted formal mechanisms such as the *Seniorat* (overall headship of the lineage) to maintain close cooperation among collateral lines and prevent inheritance quarrels in the future.[9]

However, this trend toward lineal consolidation was not permanent. Both the nonprincely higher nobility and the imperial princes resumed divisions of their estates after the return of agricultural prosperity in the early sixteenth century.[10] The era in which Froben Christoph von Zimmern was writing the *Zimmern Chronicle* was thus one in which the counts and barons of southwest Germany were reasserting the ideal of equality among brothers. In his zeal to recover and consolidate the Zimmern lands, Froben Christoph von Zimmern frequently criticized both his ancestors and his contemporaries for dividing estates to create collateral lines. Nevertheless, the *Zimmern Chronicle* shows that even such an ardent

---

[8]The estates were first divided in 1444 between Werner VII and Gottfried III, the grandsons of Johann III. Although the Zimmerns had acquired Messkirch in 1354, and therefore could have supported two heirs almost a century before they actually did so, the division of the estate was delayed by demographic accident. The next three generations each contained only one son who survived to adulthood.

[9]Spiess, *Familie und Verwandtschaft,* 77–79; and Ulshöfer, *Hausrecht der Grafen von Zollern,* 25.

[10]Spiess, *Familie und Verwandtschaft,* 278; and Fichtner, *Protestantism and Primogeniture,* 24.

proponent of lineage loyalty as Froben Christoph von Zimmern was still wary of a strategy of primogeniture, since it conflicted with the ideal of equality among brothers.

For southwest German counts and barons, as well as for imperial princes, the ideal form of succession was a community of heirs, and the second best was an equal division of the estates. Sons should rule dynastic lands jointly, partitioning them only if collective government proved unworkable. The principle of exact equality was to be observed in territorial disputes and divisions.[11] If, out of economic necessity, the estate was left to one son, nobles preferred to avoid a fixed principle of primogeniture. Instead, they resorted to ad hoc arrangements such as placing all the other sons in the church, or requiring lay younger sons to promise celibacy. Even in cases of individual succession, the ideal of equality among brothers was maintained through the tradition of selecting the son who was considered the best qualified to become the head of the family.

Among the nonprincely higher nobility of southwest Germany, the strategy of placing a large number of unmarried sons in the church was most often practiced by relatively poor families of ministerial origin, such as the Schenken of Erbach and the Schenken of Limpurg. However, even the most prominent families of counts sometimes placed all but one son in the church. This strategy was not as risky as it might appear, for clergymen could return to the lay world and marry if their brothers failed to produce male heirs. Most noblemen who entered the church were cathedral canons, who could easily be recalled since they were only in minor orders and were capable of contracting a valid marriage. Count Hans III von Werdenberg stipulated in his testament of 1451 that if none of his three lay sons or their male heirs were alive at the time of his death, "one of my clerical sons who is not yet a priest and who wishes to become a layman should take over the lordship."[12] Papal dispensations were required for priests who had taken major orders and monks who had taken binding vows. Nevertheless, some parish priests such as Count Wilhelm V of Montfort-Tettnang left the church and succeeded to the family estate in order to continue the family line.[13]

The wealthiest and most powerful families of counts—including the Fürstenbergs, Oettingens, Werdenbergs, and Zollerns—chose military careers for their unmarried sons rather than the church, which they saw as the preserve of the lower nobility.[14] These families adopted a strategy of designating one son as the

[11]Fichtner, *Protestantism and Primogeniture*, 21–24.

[12]Vanotti, *Grafen von Montfort und von Werdenberg*, 403. The southwest German families examined in this study include three clergymen who were recalled to secular life to succeed a brother who died without sons: Conrad von Erbach (d. 1423, cleric until 1411), Ulrich von Oettingen (d. 1477, canon until 1423), and Johann IV von Limpurg (1543–1608, canon until 1585).

[13]Spiess, *Familie und Verwandtschaft*, 286–87; and Burmeister, *Grafen von Montfort*, 106.

[14]On the withdrawal of high-ranking nobles from ecclesiastical careers, see Sablonier, *Adel im Wandel*, 203–4; and Andermann, *Geschichte des pfälzischen Niederadels*, 204–5. Veit (*Stiftsmässige deutsche Adel*, 11) states that in the cathedral chapters of Franconia, Swabia, Westphalia, and the

successor while one or two other sons remained lay *Ersatzregenten* (substitute family heads).[15] The latter promised not to marry unless their brother failed to produce male heirs. For example, the 1464 marriage contract between Count Georg I von Werdenberg and a daughter of Margrave Karl von Baden stipulated that Georg's two younger brothers Ulrich and Hugo were not to marry without special permission unless Georg had produced no male heirs after ten years.[16] Like many unmarried lay younger sons in other noble families, Ulrich and Hugo von Werdenberg entered the service of a prince in order to supplement their small annuities while they awaited an opportunity to marry. The *Zimmern Chronicle* claims that the Zimmern family in the High Middle Ages followed this strategy of placing younger sons in princely service rather than sending them into the church. However, this may be an effort to associate the family with the practices of wealthier and more prestigious noble families rather than a description of historical reality.[17]

Lower Rhine, "from the end of the fourteenth century there is an unmistakable tendency to exclude the higher nobility."

[15]On *Ersatzregenten*, see Spiess, *Familie und Verwandtschaft,* 296–300. According to Ulshöfer (*Das Hausrecht der Grafen von Zollern,* 37) the sixty counts of Zollern "from the beginning up to 1575" included forty-six laymen (twenty-seven married and nineteen unmarried) and fourteen clerics. In percentage terms, this means that 45.0 percent of the sons of counts of Zollern married, 31.7 percent remained unmarried laymen, and 23.3 percent entered the church. Nevertheless, even fathers with several unmarried lay sons might also place several sons in ecclesiastical careers, for all the sons born after the second or third one would be placed in the church. The three laymen Georg, Hugo, and Ulrich von Werdenberg also had three brothers who entered the church. See Vanotti, *Grafen von Montfort und von Werdenberg,* 402.

[16]Vanotti, *Grafen von Montfort und von Werdenberg,* 424–25.

[17]The genealogical data contained in the *Zimmern Chronicle* include many fictitious elements, but indicate what family members believed about their own past. The chronicle implies that between the twelfth and the mid-fifteenth centuries, the Zimmerns' preferred strategy was to marry one son and one daughter per generation and that they made little use of the church. The chronicle describes twelve generations preceding that of the chronicler Froben Christoph. Eight of these generations are said to have contained more than one son who survived to adulthood. In each such generation, a second and sometimes a third son who was not the designated heir is said to have remained unmarried, following a military career in the service of a prince. Sons are said to have been placed in the church only when there were three or more sons in a single sibling group. Only four unmarried daughters are named in the chronicle, all of them nuns.

The most up-to-date genealogy of the Zimmern family (Schwennicke, *Europäische Stammtafeln NF,* 12:83–84) is fragmentary before the thirteenth century. It provides no confirmation for the careers—or even the existence—of many of the eleventh- and twelfth-century barons of Zimmern mentioned in the *Zimmern Chronicle*. It does confirm that no divisions of estates are documented before 1444 and that before this date, the Zimmerns normally allowed only one son per generation to marry. The modern genealogy implies that the Zimmerns relied more heavily on the church in its family strategy than the chronicle acknowledges. In the nine generations preceding that of the chronicler Froben Christoph, ten Zimmern men survived to the age of fifteen but did not participate in the succession to the Zimmern estates. Four of these were clergymen (the last of whom flourished around 1350) and six were laymen (including all three of the men born after 1430). However, the latter category includes two eldest sons who died at the ages of eighteen and twenty; both would have succeeded

The *Zimmern Chronicle* makes it clear that Catholic counts and barons in southwest Germany in the second half of the sixteenth century continued to value the ideal of equality among brothers and that they regarded primogeniture as ethically dubious. The chronicler Froben Christoph von Zimmern often expresses a negative view of partible inheritance, particularly the division of the Zimmern estates between the sons of Johann Werner I. However, he also voices the view—widespread among German nobles—that the ability to establish collateral lines is a manifestation of a family's wealth and power. He remarks of the Gundelfingen family, "the first barons were so successful that they divided into three lordships and lines" (*ZC* 2:367). He also sees collateral lines as a means of ensuring the survival of the family. He criticizes Gottfried III for rejecting advice to marry even though his brother Werner VIII had only one son (*ZC* 1:416). He also states that the Zimmern family elders were reluctant to allow Froben Christoph's younger brother Gottfried Christoph to enter the church since the survival of the lineage would now depend on only one married son who had yet to produce a male heir (*ZC* 3:519).

The chronicler hopes that divisions of estates can be avoided by the holding of lands in common by several brothers. As a model, he invokes the legendary ten sons of the eleventh-century Gottfried I von Zimmern. The chronicler praises their cooperation after the castle of Herrenzimmern was destroyed in the wars of Emperor Henry IV: "through the unity of the ten brothers and the good management of their father Gottfried, they improved their goods and reputation in a few years so much that they quickly made good the damage" (*ZC* 1:73–74). He also comments approvingly on the fifteenth-century Geroldseck brothers who "held all their estates in common and undivided until their death.... They were able through such brotherly love and unity to live in great state and to greatly restore their family, which a little while earlier had been condemned to destruction" (*ZC* 2:332–33).

Such a preference for a community of heirs was frequently stated by other southwest German counts and barons in the fifteenth and sixteenth centuries, and the counts of Werdenberg actually succeeded in holding much of their property in common for long periods between 1416 and 1508. However, most such arrangements were short-lived. Karl-Heinz Spiess points out that a family head had to realize that "although a common exercise of governance by his sons was certainly desirable, it had little prospect of lasting success because of the many sources of friction. A division was therefore unavoidable sooner or later."[18] Even

---

to estates if they had lived longer. It also includes Wilhelm Werner, who originally planned to enter the church. Only two unmarried daughters, both of them nuns, are identified in the modern genealogy in the nine generations preceding that of the chronicler himself.

[18]Spiess, *Familie und Verwandtschaft,* 275.

in the Werdenberg family, the community of heirs usually lasted only as long as a powerful family elder remained alive to enforce it.[19]

In the eyes of Froben Christoph von Zimmern, primogeniture and other forms of individual succession lacked the legitimacy of governance by a community of brothers. This ambivalence was shared by the Zollerns, one of the families that instituted primogeniture in the sixteenth century in an effort to end a long history of quarrels between brothers. The counts of Zollern had lost much of their property and power in the early fifteenth century due to "divisions, alienations, and family quarrels," including the deposition of one brother by another in 1429. After the Zollerns had rebuilt their possessions and increased their power, Eitelfriedrich II von Zollern provided in his will in 1512 that the entire inheritance should go to Franz Wolfgang, the eldest of his six sons.[20]

Since Froben Christoph von Zimmern deplored fratricidal quarrels that squandered family property, one might expect him to extol the Zollerns' adoption of primogeniture as an example of a successful solution to this problem. However, the chronicler merely reports without comment that Eitelfriedrich "had ordered in his lifetime that his oldest son, Franz Wolf, would be the ruling lord and pay each of his [two lay] brothers a pension of fifteen hundred gulden, with which they should be content" (*ZC* 2:460).[21] He does not endorse this arrangement as a model, as he does the communal ownership by the Geroldseck family.

The Zollerns themselves had ethical reservations about individual succession and were by no means convinced that this strategy was the best way to ensure harmony between family members. In 1575, Count Karl I undertook one last division of the Zollern lands, arguing that the inheritance agreement of 1512 which had given them all to a single heir "was contrary to God's justice and reason and had resulted only in quarrels among those who had not received estates."[22]

The ideal of equality among brothers continued to influence inheritance practices among southwest German counts and barons more than a century after the *Zimmern Chronicle* was written, for the genealogies of the eleven families

[19]The sons of Eberhard von Werdenberg (d. 1416) divided their estates after the death of their maternal grandfather Johann III von Zimmern (d. 1441), and the sons of Georg von Werdenberg (d. 1500) divided theirs after the death of their uncle Hugo von Werdenberg (d. 1508), who had acted as de facto head of the family. The only generation that never divided its estates was that of Hugo himself, who was fiercely devoted to enhancing the wealth and prestige of the Werdenberg family. He was willing to remain unmarried in order to ensure that the undivided Werdenberg estates would descend to the sons of his brother Georg. See Vanotti, *Grafen von Montfort und von Werdenberg*, 423, 452.

[20]Ulshöfer, *Hausrecht der Grafen von Zollern*, 21, 33.

[21]The pensions were actually only 500 gulden per year. See Ulshöfer, *Hausrecht der Grafen von Zollern*, 39n159.

[22]Ulshöfer, *Hausrecht der Grafen von Zollern*, 75. The house law of Karl I divided the Zollern lands into three portions, but instituted primogeniture in the future for each the three lines. The sentiments expressed by the Catholic Karl von Zollern are identical to those expressed by the Protestant princes cited by Fichtner (*Protestantism and Primogeniture*, 23), that primogeniture brought "trouble, unfairness, and inequality."

examined show that the traditional preference for establishing collateral lines persisted well into the eighteenth century. These families did not keep estates united even when the extinction of collateral lines resulted in the accidental consolidation of all the estates in the hands of a single heir; in four such cases in the sixteenth and seventeenth centuries, the estates were divided again as soon as demographic circumstances permitted. These practices are consistent with the ideal of equality among brothers and with the view that the establishment of collateral lines was a manifestation of the family's wealth and status, as well as an assurance for its continued existence.

Despite this evident continuity in values, actual inheritance strategies varied markedly between 1400 and 1700. To understand changes in inheritance strategy and to compare the strategies of Catholics and Protestants, it is not enough to know how often estates were divided. Thus number might fluctuate due to demographic accident, since divisions are possible only when a father is survived by two or more potential heirs. Of the 231 landowners dying in the period of this study, 99 (43 percent) were survived by two or more sons. Despite the ideal of equality among brothers, the majority of fathers with two or more surviving sons did not divide the estate (see table 2.1). Fathers adjusted the number of heirs to the economic resources of the estate through three main strategies: placing surplus sons in the church, establishing a community of heirs, or designating a single heir in a testament or house law.

Between 1400 and 1749, fathers divided their estates in about one-third of the cases in which divisions were possible, with little difference overall between Catholic and Protestant fathers. However, there were considerable changes over time in the frequency of divisions and in the strategies used to avoid division. In the early fifteenth century, fathers divided their estates in almost half the cases in which division was possible and rarely used the church to eliminate potential divisions. In the late fifteenth century, however, divisions took place in less than one-fourth of all the cases in which they were possible, and fathers avoided almost a third of all the potential divisions by placing all but one son in the church.

In the sixteenth century, territorial divisions became more frequent among southwest German nobles, occurring in 33 percent of all possible cases in the first half of the century and 44 percent of all possible cases in the second half. Catholic families made little use of the church to avoid divisions in the Reformation era. Between 1500 and 1650, there was only one case in which all but one son entered the church, and this was not a deliberate strategic decision: in 1544 Gottfried Christoph von Zimmern chose to become a cathedral canon against the wishes of the family elders.

Although the preference for a partible inheritance system persisted throughout the period, there were significant changes in actual behavior after 1550. The strategy of avoiding divisions through a community of heirs was permanently

Table 2.1: Divisions of Estates 1400–1749, Southwest Germany

Date of death	Possible divisions[a] (N)	Division (n)	Division (%)	Held in common (n)	Held in common (%)	Left to one heir (n)	Left to one heir (%)	Left to eldest son (n)	Left to eldest son (%)	Avoided by use of church (n)	Avoided by use of church (%)
1400–49	13	6	46	1	8	6	45	4	31	1	8
1450–99	13	3	23	2	15	8	62	4	31	4	31
1500–49	12	4	33	3	25	5	42	1	8	1	8
Subtotal 1400–1549	38	13	34	6	16	19	50	9	24	6	16
1550–99	16	7	44	1	6	7	50	7	44	0	0
(Catholic/Protestant)	(10/6)	(5/2)	(50/33)	(1/0)	(10/0)	(4/4)	(40/67)	(4/3)	(40/50)	(0/0)	(0/0)
1600–49	13	6	46	0	0	7	54	7	54	0	0
(Catholic/Protestant)	(10/3)	(5/1)	(50/33)	(0/0)	(0/0)	(5/2)	(50/67)	(5/2)	(50/67)	(0/0)	(0/0)
1650–99	17	2	12	0	0	15	88	14	82	2	12
(Catholic/Protestant)	(11/6)	(1/1)	(9/17)	(0/0)	(0/0)	(10/5)	(91/83)	(9/5)	(82/83)	(2/0)	(18/0)
1700–49	15	6	40	0	0	9	60	6	40	3	20
(Catholic/Protestant)	(12/3)	(4/2)	(33/67)	(0/0)	(0/0)	(8/1)	(67/33)	(5/1)	(42/33)	(3/0)	(25/0)
Subtotal 1550–1749	61	21	34	1	2	39	64	34	56	5	8
(Catholic/Protestant)	(43/18)	(15/6)	(35/33)	(1/0)	(2/0)	(27/12)	(63/67)	(23/11)	(53/61)	(5/0)	(12/0)
Total 1400–1749	99	34	34	7	7	58	59	43	43	11	11

Note: Southwest Germany = 11 families of counts and barons, including the Zimmerns and 10 families with whom they intermarried between the years of 1400 and 1600. The sample includes all members of these families who were born, married, or died between 1400 and 1699 and who survived to the age of 15 years.

[a]Number of cases in which the father was survived by two or more sons.

abandoned, and the strategy of placing all but one son in the church was never used between 1550 and 1650. There was also a shift away from the traditional strategy of choosing the best-qualified —not necessarily the eldest—son in cases of individual succession. Over the entire period of 1400 to1749, the eldest son was chosen in only a bare majority of cases of individual succession, and in the first half of the sixteenth century, only one of the five sole heirs was an eldest son. However, after 1550 there was a clear preference for the eldest son in cases of individual succession. The result was that between 1550 and 1750, the estate was left undivided to the eldest son in the majority of the cases in which the father was survived by more than one son. In this limited sense, one can say there was a trend toward primogeniture among southwest German counts and barons even though divisions of estates continued. This willingness to divide estates continued into the early seventeenth century but ended abruptly in the second half of the seventeenth century, a period of agricultural depression. Only one Catholic and one Protestant landowner divided their estates between 1650 and 1699, and Catholic fathers once again made use of the church to avoid some potential divisions. In the late seventeenth century the inheritance system of southwest German nobles was one of primogeniture in all but name: in fourteen out of the seventeen cases in which a landowner was survived by two or more sons, the entire estate went to the eldest son. However, both Catholics and Protestants resumed the practice of partible inheritance in the early eighteenth century, carrying out divisions almost as frequently as in the sixteenth century.

These chronological trends are consistent with those described by Spiess for counts and barons of the Mainz region through 1550 and by Fichtner for imperial princes in the sixteenth and seventeenth centuries. Spiess notes that divisions of estates decreased after 1350 and reached their lowest point in the late fifteenth century before rising again in the early sixteenth century.[23] Fichtner describes a similar upward trend in the sixteenth century among German princes: although princes evinced interest in primogeniture at the turn of the sixteenth century, they increased the number of territorial divisions between 1550 and 1650.[24] However, after 1650 the princes permanently adopted primogeniture, in contrast to the southwest German counts and barons, who resumed partitions of estates after 1700.

The persistence of the southwest German counts and barons in a strategy of partible inheritance after 1700 may not be typical of all German nobles. Some non-princely German nobles followed the princes in adopting primogeniture after 1650 and maintaining this policy into the eighteenth century. Entails (*Fideicommisse*) were first introduced in Austria in the second half of the seventeenth century and became the general practice among nobles in the eighteenth century.[25] After 1650,

[23]Spiess, *Familie und Verwandtschaft,* 278.
[24]Fichtner, *Protestantism and Primogeniture,* 24.
[25]Mitterauer, "Zur Frage des Heiratsverhaltens," 188–89.

the imperial knights of the Rhineland adopted a strategy of impartible inheritance that was to become permanent. Only one son, who inherited the lands and capital, married and perpetuated the lineage, while his brothers entered ecclesiastical careers.[26]

In her influential *Protestantism and Primogeniture* (1989), Fichtner argues that religious ideology was an important factor in the reluctance of Protestant princes to adopt primogeniture in the period between 1550 and 1650, when major Catholic states had already instituted the practice. Not only did Protestantism eliminate the church as a resource for the support of unmarried sons and daughters, she argues, but it also provided religious support for the traditional German ideal of equality among brothers.[27]

Fichtner's argument is based primarily on the religious motives cited in the preambles to princely testaments. She states that, although both Catholic and Protestant princes

> passed their dynastic holdings either collectively or already divided to their heirs with an eye both to the world beyond as well as to the one at hand…, Luther seems to have had an especially strong influence on his followers when it came to this question. "Since we are children we are all heirs" (Romans 8:17) was one influential passage. Duke Wolfgang of the Palatinate-Zweibrucken (1526–69) took his guidance from *Ecclesiasticus,* a book that the Wittenberg reformer especially recommended to heads of households. Thus, the biblical command, "When the end comes, and you must take your leave, then divide your inheritance" prompted Wolfgang and others to do just that…. John William of Saxony-Weimar regarded partible inheritance as the will of God.[28]

In the absence of quantitative data on the inheritance practices of imperial princes, it is not possible to compare the practices of princes in the period from 1550 to 1650 with those of princes before the Reformation, or to compare the practices of princes in the Reformation era to those of contemporary counts and barons. However, the data on counts and barons of southwest Germany do not, on the whole, support the hypothesis that religious ideology caused Protestant nobles to follow inheritance strategies that differed from those of their Catholic counterparts. There is no indication that Protestant fathers were more likely than Catholic fathers to reject primogeniture or favor younger sons.

Among southwest German counts and barons, Protestant fathers were actually more likely than Catholic fathers to favor eldest sons over their younger brothers and to practice de facto primogeniture. Of the landowners who died between 1550 and 1750 leaving more than one son, 61 percent of the Protestants, as compared to 53 percent of the Catholics, left the estate undivided to the eldest son. Moreover,

[26]Duhamelle, "Parenté et orientation sociale," 65–67.

[27]Fichtner, *Protestantism and Primogeniture,* 4, 12–14, 24–33.

[28]Fichtner, *Protestantism and Primogeniture,* 28.

Catholic fathers were more likely than Protestant fathers to exercise their traditional option of choosing the best-qualified son regardless of birth order.

Eight of the 43 Catholic fathers (19 percent of those with more than one surviving son) excluded their eldest son from the succession; four of these cases occurred during the economic depression of the late seventeenth century. By contrast, only one of the 18 Protestant fathers (6 percent of those with more than one surviving son) excluded his eldest son. Six of the Catholic fathers excluded the eldest son by placing him in the church, an option not open to Protestant fathers. All of the laymen among the eldest sons excluded from the succession (two Catholics and one Protestant) outlived their fathers but died in their twenties; one of the Catholic sons was killed in battle. Possibly these young men were considered unlikely to live long and beget heirs.

The practice of excluding eldest sons had been more common before 1550: in 38 cases between 1400 and 1550 in which fathers were survived by more than one son, 10 fathers (26 per cent), excluded the eldest son by placing him in the church. The resurgence of this practice among Catholic fathers in the late seventeenth century is noteworthy since it contradicts the general trend after 1550 toward favoring eldest sons in cases of individual succession.

In only one case is there evidence of the motive behind the decision to exclude an eldest son from the succession. It is not entirely clear why Johann Christoph von Zimmern, the eldest son of Johann Werner II, was passed over as heir and sent into the church although he had little inclination to the priesthood. The decision could hardly have been based on his father's personal affection for a younger son. Johann Christoph had been brought up at home, whereas his younger brother Froben Christoph had resided with his grandmother since birth and had had virtually no contact with his parents.

The chronicler implies that the decision was based on Johann Christoph's intellect or his health: "Since the boy in his youth was stupid [or timid: *blöd*] and [not] very strong, some of the relatives thought it would be good for him to be ordained in the church" (*ZC* 3:205).[29] Nevertheless, the family elders remained ambivalent about a clerical career for Johann Christoph. The chronicle mentions negotiations for a marriage for him in 1531, the very year in which he became a canon (*ZC* 2:368–69).

If the family elders were afraid that Johann Christoph might not beget heirs to continue the lineage, their fears were justified by subsequent events. Despite long-term relationships with concubines, he had no children; the chronicler attributes Johann Christoph's sterility to sexual encounters during his university

---

[29]The text in the manuscript reads "Und seitmals der jung herr in seiner jugendt ganz blöd und zum sterkesten, ward durch etliche der freundschaft für guet angesehen, das er zum gaistlichen stand sollte geordnet werden" (*ZC* 3:205). In the Decker-Hauff edition (*Die Chronik der Grafen von Zimmern,* 3:71) this is amended to "[nit] zum sterkesten."

career (*ZC* 3:231). However, the family elders could scarcely have foreseen this when they decided to send the eight-year-old Johann Christoph to learn Latin in preparation for a career in the church.

The option of placing sons in ecclesiastical careers clearly gave Catholic fathers more flexibility than Protestant fathers in their family strategy. However, economic factors, rather than changes in values or in religious ideology, were probably the most important cause of changes in inheritance strategies between 1400 and 1700. The limitation of the number of heirs in the fifteenth century and the increase in the number of heirs in the sixteenth and early seventeenth century correspond to a period of economic depression followed by one of economic expansion. Population decline after the Black Death led to an agricultural depression that lasted until the early sixteenth century, severely affecting the income of nobles who depended on rents and feudal dues. Moreover, nobles' opportunities for secular careers were limited as private warfare decreased and fewer great nobles retained local nobles as councilors or court officials to ensure their loyalty. Nobles faced increasing competition for such posts from burghers with university degrees in civil law.[30]

The sixteenth and the beginning of the seventeenth centuries, in contrast, were an era of agricultural prosperity: grain prices reached high levels by the end of the second half of the sixteenth century, and income from seigneurial rents and dues peaked in the years just before and just after 1600. It is hardly coincidental that this is the period when nobles were most willing to divide their estates and to allow large numbers of both sons and daughters to marry. In the era of political stability between the Peace of Augsburg and the Thirty Years' War, territorial princes expanded their courts. Nobles (including the Zimmerns) began to acquire university educations in order to compete more effectively for positions as judges and councilors, and the development of a distinct officer's career gave the nobility a dominant position in the new standing armies. With more secular careers available, nobles became less dependent on the church to support younger sons.[31]

Southwest Germany was devastated by the Swedish and French armies in the Thirty Years' War and by the subsequent invasions of Louis XIV. The sharp drop in population led to a decline in both grain prices and land values after the Thirty Years' War, and income from seigneurial rents and dues did not reach prewar levels again until the new agricultural boom of the eighteenth century was well under

[30]On the effects of the population decline on agriculture and noble revenues, see Holborn, *A History of Modern Germany* 1:56–57. Grain prices remained depressed until the middle of the sixteenth century, when population growth finally led to an increase in demand. See Abel, *Geschichte der deutschen Landwirtschaft*, 128. On noble careers, see Holborn, *History of Modern Germany*, 1:31; and Hofacker, "Die Schwäbische Herzogswürde," 77. On the economic condition of the Swabian nobility in the fifteenth and sixteenth centuries, see also Müller, "Zur wirtschaftlichen Lage."

[31]Robisheaux, *Rural Society*, 168–69; Abel, *Geschichte der deutschen Landwirtschaft*, 169–70; Holborn, *History of Modern Germany*, 1:54; and Zeeden, *Deutsche Kultur*, 56–57.

way. Under these circumstances, it is not surprising that nobles drastically restricted the number of heirs in the late seventeenth century and resumed divisions of estates only when economic conditions improved in the early eighteenth century.[32] Since only those sons who inherited estates were likely to marry, it is to be expected that trends in the number of sons who married per generation closely paralleled trends in inheritance.

MARITAL PAYMENTS

These economic trends also affected other aspects of family strategy, including dowry levels. Unfortunately, information about marital payments among German elites is less readily available than information about divisions of estates. However, it is possible to analyze trends in dowry levels for the counts and barons of southwest Germany in the fifteenth and early sixteenth centuries, the period discussed in detail in the *Zimmern Chronicle,* and to draw on studies of marital payments in the lower nobility in other regions of Germany in the late sixteenth and seventeenth centuries.[33]

In the Germanic customs of the Early Middle Ages, the burden of marital payments fell more heavily on the groom's family than on the bride's. The major marital payment was the morning gift (*Morgengabe*), which was given by the groom to the bride. In the High Middle Ages, the burden of marital payments shifted to the bride's family, and the dowry became a premortem inheritance. In southwest Germany by the fifteenth century, daughters of noblemen made a formal renunciation of inheritance rights as a condition for receiving their dowry. The link between inheritance and dowry is explicitly stated in pacts between brothers that excluded females from the succession but granted them dowry in compensation. For example, an inheritance agreement in the Waldburg family in 1429 provided that in the case of the death of a brother without a legitimate son, the estate should go to his brother. "In addition, it was reemphasized that daughters were completely excluded from inheriting from males (*männliche Erbe*) but were granted dowry as a replacement, as compensation for their renunciation of the same."[34] In a related development, provisions for widows changed from a dower system, which assigned the widow the income from all or part of her husband's property, to a system of widows' pensions based on the amount of her dowry.[35]

[32]Holborn, *History of Modern Germany,* 2:25; Abel, *Geschichte der deutschen Landwirtschaft,* 243–44, 251–54; and Robisheaux, *Rural Society,* 242.

[33]Hufschmidt, *Adelige Frauen im Weserraum,* 269–437; Bastl, *Tugend, Liebe, Ehre,* 25–148.

[34]Dornheim, *Familie Waldburg-Zeil,* 77–78.

[35]The matching payment or widow's dower first appeared in the thirteenth century and became general among the nobility of southwest Germany in the fourteenth century. On its development, see Freed, *Noble Bondsmen,* 168–70; Spiess, *Familie und Verwandtschaft,* 139; and Ulshöfer, *Hausrecht der Grafen von Zollern,* 55. On the similar English system of jointure, see Spring, *Law, Land and Family,* 47–52. It is unclear how widely jointure was actually practiced among the English landed elite before it

As in the case of male inheritance, the system of female inheritance and marital payments among German nobles retained several features of the older Germanic system that were becoming obsolete in other European elites. These
archaic features tended to favor women. The morning gift, a remnant of the
brideprice system, remained a more significant payment among German nobles
than it did among German townsmen or than its counterparts did among other
European nobilities. It provided the wife with an income of her own during the
marriage, whereas other provisions for her support took effect only when and if
she was widowed.[36]

Although the dowry functioned as a premortem inheritance, a daughter still
retained all her inheritance rights under customary law unless she specifically
renounced them. She could reserve some of these rights even when making a
renunciation. Daughters usually renounced the right to inherit from fathers and
mothers and often from brothers and sisters; sometimes they added a renunciation of the right to inherit from kinsmen in general. However, renunciations
almost always reserved the right of sole succession (*ledige anfal*), in which the last
surviving member of a sibling group became the sole heir to the parents' estate.
Thus even a daughter who had made a renunciation could lodge a claim against
the parental estate if she outlived her brothers.[37] In 1521 Apollonia von Henneberg reserved the right to inherit from her four childless brothers. Twenty-
seven years later, her daughter, Anna von Zimmern, in turn reserved the right to
inherit from her mother, in the hopes that the Henneberg inheritance would
come to Apollonia and then to her (*ZC* 2:450, 4:73–74).

These surviving rights of female inheritance, which made it necessary to
obtain a daughter's renunciation to eliminate possible female claims against the
estate, gave a daughter and her husband considerable leverage in negotiating a
more advantageous marriage settlement. Anna von Zimmern delayed her renunciation for seventeen years after her marriage in 1531. This strategy enabled her
and her husband Jos Niklaus von Zollern to obtain 2000 gulden from her father
Gottfried Werner von Zimmern in addition to her original dowry of 4000 gulden
and trousseau of 1000 gulden (*ZC* 4:71–74).

---

became the legal norm in the Statute of Uses of Henry VIII in 1536. Rosenthal (*Patriarchy and Families of Privilege*, 196–202) states that fifteenth-century English nobles continued to follow the common
law practice of dower, granting a lifetime interest in one-third of husband's real property. However,
Harris (*English Aristocratic Women*, 25) states that among the peerage, jointure had become the conventional method of providing for widows at least seventy-five years before the Statute of Uses.

[36]The morning gift had become merely a symbolic payment in many German towns during the
late Middle Ages. See Harrington, *Reordering Marriage and Society*, 193. Its equivalent in Roman law
(the *donatio contra nuptias* or *arras*), also became a token payment in parts of Mediterranean Europe,
even among the nobility. See Klapisch-Zuber, *Women, Family and Ritual*, 121–22, 223, 280; and
Beceiro Pita and Córdoba de la Llave, *Parentesco, poder y mentalidad*, 175–76, 184, 246–77.

[37]Spiess, *Familie und Verwandtschaft*, 332–33; and Ulshöfer, *Hausrecht der Grafen von Zollern*,
41. For examples of such renunciations with reservations in the Zimmern family, see *ZC* 1:84, 2:458.

In the system of marital payments practiced by counts and barons of southwest Germany in the fifteenth and early sixteenth centuries, the principal payment from the bride's family was the dowry (*Heimsteuer,* also known as *Aussteuer, Mitgift,* or *Zugeld*), which was paid in cash; the principal payment from the groom's family was the matching payment (*Widerlegung* or *Widerlage*), made up of lands pledged to provide a widow's pension (*Wittum*). The matching payment was the hallmark of marriages among the elite and was not given by lower social classes. Although the ratio of the matching payment to dowry varied in different regions and periods, a 1:1 ratio was the norm among nobles in southwest Germany from the beginning of the fourteenth to the middle of the sixteenth century.[38]

Despite the norm of equality between dowry and matching payment, the ratio varied in individual cases. Before the middle of the fifteenth century, the counts of Zollern often gave a matching payment smaller than the dowry. According to Spiess, a higher dowry than matching payment indicated that the bride's side was the more eager for the marriage. The ratio might also vary depending on the relative financial worth of the marriage partners.[39]

In addition to these major marital payments, the bride's family also provided a trousseau (*Abfertigung*) in clothing, jewelry, and silver plate, while the groom's family also provided the morning gift in land. The morning gift, which might amount to as much as one-third to one-half the value of the dowry, became the property of the bride and provided her with income during the marriage.[40]

The widow's pension, to which the bride was entitled only after the death of her husband, was based on the value of the dowry, matching payment, and morning gift. These three marital payments taken together comprised a fictive entity called the *Hauptgeld* (capital sum), on which the widow received interest at a rate specified in the marriage contract and based on the normal rate of return on land. The widow was also provided with a residence (called a widow's seat), to which she usually retired after her husband's death, or after her oldest son came of age. If she remarried, she had to leave her widow's seat but took all of the marital payments from her first marriage into her second marriage.[41]

---

[38]For a detailed analysis of the system of marital payments used by nobles in southwest Germany in the late Middle Ages, see Spiess, *Familie und Verwandtschaft,* 131–62. Ulshöfer (*Hausrecht der Grafen von Zollern,* 53–60) provides a case study of payments in the Zollern family in the fifteenth and sixteenth centuries. On the ratio of dowry to *Widerlegung* in different regions and time periods, see Schröder, *Geschichte des ehelichen Güterrechts in Deutschland,* 2:82–83, 237–38; Freed, *Noble Bondsmen,* 171–76; Spiess, *Familie und Verwandtschaft,* 139–45; and Hufschmidt, *Adelige Frauen im Weserraum,* 317–18.

[39]Ulshöfer, *Hausrecht der Grafen von Zollern,* 56; Spiess, *Familie und Verwandtschaft,* 139–40; Burmeister, *Grafen von Montfort,* 291; and Vanotti, *Grafen von Montfort und von Werdenberg,* 395.

[40]On the value of the morning gift, see Spiess, *Familie und Verwandtschaft,* 143.

[41]On the widow's pension, *Wittum,* see Spiess, *Familie und Verwandtschaft,* 146–50; and Ulshöfer, *Hausrecht der Grafen von Zollern,* 58–60.

AMOUNT OF DOWRY

The amount of the dowry was based primarily on social rank and reflected both the status of the bride's family and that of the groom. Fathers paid more to marry a daughter to a husband of higher social status and less to marry her to a husband of lower status. In the mid-fifteenth century, the counts of Württemberg gave 30,000 gulden to marry a daughter to Duke Albrecht of Bavaria but only 16,000 gulden to marry another daughter to Count Hans III von Werdenberg.[42]

The amount of dowry also depended on the number of daughters for whom a father had to make provision. The house regulations and house laws codified in individual families in the fifteenth and sixteenth centuries attempted to limit the amount of the family's wealth that could be expended on dowries. In the Waldburg family, an inheritance agreement of 1429 limited dowries to 2000 gulden to prevent fathers from injuring the patrimony by paying unusually high dowries to marry their daughters to higher-ranking husbands. The Waldburg house law of 1463, which remained binding on future generations, raised the ceiling on dowries to 4000 gulden but reiterated that with this settlement the daughters lost all claim to the *Stammgut* (core possessions of the lineage).[43]

In his testament of 1512, Count Eitelfriedrich II von Zollern stipulated that no father could spend more than a total of 6000 gulden on the dowries of his daughters. If two daughters married, they were to receive 3000 gulden apiece; three daughters were to receive 2000 gulden apiece. Any additional daughters were to enter convents. In this case, Eitelfriedrich II had not practiced what he now preached: in marriage contracts of 1495 he promised dowries of 4000 gulden apiece to two daughters, Wandelberte and Salome. Karl I reiterated the same restrictions on dowry levels in his binding house law of 1575, though he permitted a larger total sum to be expended on dowries. A count who could afford it could now marry off more than three daughters; he himself married off five. In this case, dowries were not to exceed 3000 gulden apiece and must be paid for out of annual income from the estates; under no circumstances was the father to go into debt.[44] Though the specific provisions had been adjusted to meet changing economic conditions, the underlying principle is clear: the patrimony was not to be burdened by payments to daughters at the expense of future generations of male heirs.

Dowries among German nobles remained fixed (at least in face value) for long periods of time, including some eras of rapid dowry inflation in other European

[42]Vanotti, *Grafen von Montfort und von Werdenberg,* 395. For other examples of different payments from the same family to husbands of different ranks, see Spiess, *Familie und Verwandtschaft,* 346, 361–62.

[43]Dornheim, *Familie Waldburg-Zeil,* 77–78. These limits were not always observed; in the Sonnenberg line of the Waldburg lineage, Countess Veronika von Sonnenberg brought a dowry of 6000 gulden to her marriage with Count Ludwig von Oettingen in 1477. On limits to dowries in other house regulations, see Spiess, *Familie und Verwandtschaft,* 364–66.

[44]Ulshöfer, *Hausrecht der Grafen von Zollern,* 54, 79–80.

elites.[45] A spectacular rise in dowries is documented in the late fifteenth and early sixteenth centuries in Florence, Venice, and Castile.[46] Spiess finds it "truly amazing" that among counts and barons in the Mainz region, there is no observable increase in dowry size from the thirteenth to the fifteenth centuries. However, he notes that marriage contracts in the fifteenth century often contained provisions for supplemental payments after the death of the father; this would increase the effective amount of the dowry even though its face value remained unchanged.[47]

In the fifteenth and the early sixteenth century, dowries for daughters of German knights ranged from a few hundred gulden to about 1200 gulden, comparable to the 1000 gulden given by members of the urban patriciate, while members of the elite of the lower nobility usually gave around 2000 gulden. In the Mainz region, counts and barons gave dowries that usually ranged between 3000 and 5000 gulden, with an average around 4000 gulden; dowries between 6000 and 10,000 gulden were given by a few families of wealthy counts who aspired to a status equal to princes. Daughters of princes were in a category all their own, with dowries of over 20,000 gulden.[48]

The limitation of dowries for each social class within a narrow range meant that there was little opportunity for wealthy members of the patriciate or the lower nobility to marry their daughters into the high nobility by providing extraordinarily high dowries.[49] There are occasional examples of fathers from the lower nobility paying dowries of 6000 to 13,000 gulden to marry their daughters to counts and of counts paying dowries of over 30,000 gulden to marry their daughters to princes.[50] However, such marriages (usually of heiresses) were less

---

[45]Freed, *Noble Bondsmen,* 172.

[46]On Florence in the fifteenth and early sixteenth centuries, see Herlihy and Klapisch-Zuber, *Tuscans and Their Families,* 223–26; and Molho, *Marriage Alliance,* 324–26. On Venice, see Chojnacki, "Dowries and Kinsmen." On Castile in the fifteenth century, see Beceiro Pita and Cordóba de la Llave, *Parentesco, poder y mentalidad,* 185–96. On Castile in the sixteenth century, see Casey, *The History of the Family,* 82–83. In France, the members of the Parlement of Paris experienced "an enormous inflation of dowries" in the last third of the sixteenth century. Nassiet, "Réseaux de parenté," 119. In the English aristocracy, Harris (*English Aristocratic Women,* 46, 264n21) characterizes dowry size as "remarkably stable throughout the period" from 1450 to 1550. However, Stone (*Crisis of the Aristocracy,* 641, 790) describes the average size of portions as rising from £500 in 1475–1524 to £700 in 1525–49, an increase of 40 percent, and as increasing tenfold between the second quarter of the sixteenth century and the third quarter of the seventeenth century.

[47]Spiess, *Familie und Verwandtschaft,* 364.

[48]On dowry levels in general, see Schröder, *Geschichte des ehelichen Güterrechts,* 2:82–83, 237–38. Patricians of Ulm and Augsburg gave 1000 gulden in the fifteenth and early sixteenth centuries. See Spiess, *Familie und Verwandtschaft,* 345; and Roper, *Holy Household,* 148–49. On dowries at different levels of the nobility, see Freed, *Noble Bondsmen,* 173–80; Spiess, *Familie und Verwandtschaft,* 344–45; Peter Müller, *Die Herren von Fleckenstein,* 319; Reif, *Westfälischer Adel,* 254–56; and Hufschmidt, *Adelige Frauen im Weserraum,* 291–300, 313–19.

[49]Freed, *Noble Bondsmen,* 179.

[50]For examples of exceptionally high dowries see Spiess, *Familie und Verwandtschaft,* 347, 352–54; and Euler, "Wandlung des Konnubiums," 67.

common than in England or France. The limitation of dowries also made it easier for German nobles to pursue a strategy of maximizing alliances by marrying off several daughters from a sibling group even when marriages of sons were limited to one or two per generation.

The income of the fifteen families of counts and barons Spiess examined in Mainz ranged from 2000 to 20,000 gulden a year, while the average value of dowries for the same families ranged from 1000 to 9400 gulden. This suggests that in the fifteenth century, dowries normally represented about half of the annual income from the father's estate.[51]

Dowries among southwest German counts and barons in this study were somewhat lower than those reported in the Mainz region. Even leading families of counts such as Zollerns and Werdenbergs gave and received dowries of about 2000 gulden in the first half of the fifteenth century, while the highest dowries at the end of the century (except in the case of heiresses) were about 4000 gulden. The largest dowry on record is that of the heiress Magdalena von Oettingen-Wallerstein, who brought a dowry of 7000 gulden plus a maternal inheritance of 5000 gulden when she married Count Ulrich VII von Montfort in 1485.[52]

The *Zimmern Chronicle* says that the Zimmerns gave and received dowries ranging between 2000 and 5000 gulden for marriages from the late fourteenth to the mid-sixteenth century. However, some of its figures for the distant past appear to be inflated in order to bolster the family's prestige. It is unlikely that the Zimmerns actually gave dowries of 5000 gulden to Anna, daughter of Werner VII, when she married Ulrich von Schwarzenberg in 1372, and Anna, daughter of Johann III, when she married Eberhard von Werdenberg in 1402 (*ZC* 1:184, 239). In this era, the most prominent Swabian counts offered less than half this amount. Moreover, documents in the Werdenberg archives show that in 1402 Eberhard von Werdenberg acknowledged receipt of his wife Anna's dowry of "2266 ll. in Italian Heller."[53]

Legal documents quoted in the chronicle show that in 1441, Verena and Anna, granddaughters of Johann III, were each bequeathed 3000 gulden dowry plus 1000 gulden trousseau (*ZC* 1:315). In 1531 Anna, daughter of Gottfried Werner, was promised 4000 gulden dowry plus 1000 gulden trousseau at her marriage to Jos Niklaus von Zollern (*ZC* 4:290).[54] In contrast, Margarethe and

[51]Spiess, *Familie und Verwandtschaft,* 362, 537.

[52]For dowries of Swabian counts, see Ulshöfer, *Hausrecht der Grafen von Zollern,* 54; Burmeister, *Grafen von Montfort,* 280; Vanotti, *Die Grafen von Montfort und von Werdenberg,* 402; and Weiss, *Grafen von Montfort.* On the dowry of Magdalena von Oettingen-Wallerstein, see Vanotti, *Grafen von Montfort und von Werdenberg,* 141.

[53]Vanotti, *Grafen von Montfort und von Werdenberg,* 386. *Ll* is either an abbreviation for pounds, or a mistranscription of *fl,* the abbreviation used for gulden. A *Heller* is a small German coin. The entry suggests that the payment was made in Italian coins but not in golden florins, the customary money of account.

[54]On the dowry brought by Anna von Zimmern to her husband Jos Niklaus von Zollern, see also

Barbara, daughters of Johann Werner I, received dowries of only 2000 gulden apiece when they married husbands from the lower nobility in 1507 and 1512 (ZC 2:161, 163). Dowries were proportional to the rank of the husband; moreover, Margarethe had married without her brother's consent.

The only two dowries received by the Zimmerns whose value is stated in the chronicle were both smaller than those normally given by the bride's family. The dowry of Countess Margarethe von Oettingen, who married Johann Werner I von Zimmern in 1474, may have been as little as 2000 gulden.[55] In this case, the Zimmerns probably accepted a relatively low dowry as the price they had to pay for a prestigious political alliance. Margarethe's brother, Wolfgang "the Rich" von Oettingen, served along with Johann Werner I on the council of Archduke Sigismund of Tyrol; he was also one of the leading members of the Swabian League.[56] In 1521, Countess Apollonia von Henneberg, the wife of Gottfried Werner von Zimmern, received a dowry of 4000 gulden (ZC 2:450). This was a disappointment to the Zimmerns, for they had hoped to receive more from the Hennebergs, the highest-ranking counts of Franconia.[57] However, half a loaf was better than none. Apollonia had married without the consent of her father, who at first refused to grant her a dowry; it took Gottfried Werner ten years of negotiations to secure any dowry at all (ZC 2:450).

Dowries of 3000 to 4000 gulden given and received for marriages to their social equals in the mid-sixteenth century placed the Zimmerns at the same level as other leading Swabian noble families such as those of Waldburg, Zollern, and Montfort.[58] The Zimmerns were also typical of counts and barons of southwest Germany in paying a morning gift of 1000 gulden, which corresponded to a quarter to a third of the value of the dowry. Morning gifts of 1000 gulden were received by Verena von Zimmern in the 1440s and by Katharina von Erbach in 1509 (ZC 1:315, 350; 2:399). While the sum of 1000 gulden was standard for counts and barons, members of the lower nobility paid less than 300 gulden and princes up to 10,000 gulden as a morning gift.[59]

Ulshöfer, *Hausrecht der Grafen von Zollern,* 56.

[55]In 1495, the widowed Margarethe von Oettingen received an annual income of 230 gulden a year from her combined dowry, matching payment and morning gift (ZC 2:31). At a return of 5 percent a year, her *Hauptgeld* would have been 4600 gulden, suggesting that her dowry was about 2000 gulden. This seems low in view of other dowries of 4000 gulden paid by the Oettingen family in this period. See Burmeister, *Grafen von Montfort,* 280.

[56]On the role of Count Wolfgang I von Oettingen-Oettingen in the Swabian League, see Carl, *Der Schwäbische Bund,* 274–77. He served as head of the League from 1497 to 1502.

[57]In the first half of the sixteenth century, the Hennebergs already enjoyed the rank of princes and usually married into princely families rather than into other families of Franconian counts. Schmidt, *Das fränkische Reichsgrafenkollegium,* 12n13, 13.

[58]Ulshöfer, *Hausrecht der Grafen von Zollern,* 54; Dornheim, *Familie Waldburg-Zeil,* 77–78; and Weiss, *Grafen von Montfort,* 11.

[59]Spiess, *Familie und Verwandtschaft,* 141–43.

There is some evidence for an increase in dowry levels among the southwest German nobility in the second half of the fifteenth century. Since this was a period when the income of noble landowners was affected by a severe agricultural depression, families must have found these higher dowries a significant financial burden. Wolfram Ulshöfer states that in the Zollern family, "dowry levels were influenced by the general inflation of prices from the end of the fifteenth century." The counts of Zollern regularly gave dowries of 2000 gulden in the fourteenth and early fifteenth centuries, but the amount doubled to 4000 gulden in marriage contracts of 1495.[60] An increase during the fifteenth century is also suggested by the fact that the Truchsessen of Waldburg fixed 2000 gulden as their maximum dowry in their house treaty of 1429 but raised it to 4000 gulden in that of 1463.[61] This doubling of the dowry in the course of the fifteenth century was probably related to the decline in the rate of return on land from 10 percent to 5 percent, which meant it now took twice as much dowry to produce the same widow's pension.[62]

In Italy, Spain, and England, dowry inflation in the sixteenth and early seventeenth centuries has been seen as the cause of increasingly restrictive marriage strategies for daughters. For the English aristocracy, Stone states, "Between the second quarter of the sixteenth and the third quarter of the seventeenth century, portions given with daughters of the aristocracy increased approximately ten times," keeping pace with the general rise of agricultural prices in the sixteenth century but rising much faster than prices after 1600.[63] Therefore, he says,

> we must conclude that in the seventeenth century parents were devoting a very much higher proportion of their incomes to marrying off their daughters than were their grandparents in the sixteenth. By the early seventeenth century few fathers, and then only those with numerous children, were offering less than the equivalent of one year's income as portions for their daughters.[64]

In Valencia, dowries given by lesser aristocrats in the late sixteenth and early seventeenth centuries often exceeded a year's rents, and those given by the dukes of Gandía were twice their annual income.[65] Florentine marriage portions in the sixteenth century reached even greater heights, as much as five years' income for a moderately wealthy family.[66]

However, dowry size evidently followed somewhat different chronological trends in southwest Germany than in many other European elites. The chronicler

---

[60]Ulshöfer, *Hausrecht der Grafen von Zollern,* 54.

[61]Dornheim, *Familie Waldburg-Zeil,* 77–78; and Burmeister, *Grafen von Montfort,* 291.

[62]On the declining rates of return on land and their effect on widows' pensions, see Spiess, *Familie und Verwandtschaft,* 149.

[63]Stone, *Crisis of the Aristocracy,* 641.

[64]Stone, *Crisis of the Aristocracy,* 642.

[65]Casey, *Early Modern Spain,* 147.

[66]Litchfield, "Florentine Patrician Families," 203.

Froben Christoph von Zimmern says, apropos of a marriage in the 1530s, that the wife "brought with her a considerable dowry, as was then customary among counts and barons" (ZC 3:163). As a father who was involved during the 1560s in marriage negotiations for at least two of his nine daughters, Froben Christoph should have been well aware of current dowry levels. Nevertheless, he did not perceive them as higher than dowries a generation earlier. In the Zollern house law of 1575, Karl I reiterated the same ceilings on dowries that had been fixed by Eitelfriedrich II in 1512, suggesting that there had been no substantial inflation in dowry levels in the meantime.[67]

Although no studies on dowries in the southwest German high aristocracy are available for the period between 1550 and 1700, studies of the lower nobility in other regions of Germany in this period show that nobles continued to fix dowries within a narrow range that varied little over time. Members of the lower nobility in the Weser region of Westphalia in the late sixteenth and seventeenth centuries saw a standard dowry of 2000 gulden as appropriate for marriages within their social group, and this ideal remained unchanged despite the great economic fluctuations in this period. Anke Hufschmidt notes that

> with regard to the level of dowries, it must be further noted that, disregarding all fluctuations in the value of money, the sum of 2000 gold florins [or gulden], later [called] Reichsthaler, played a central role from the middle of the sixteenth to the end of the seventeenth century when families determined the dowry. Between 1588 and 1691, not only did many house treaties specify this standard portion, but it is actually found in about a quarter of all the marriage contracts concluded.... It can...be assumed that this is a matter of a sum rooted in customary law, for 2000 Reichsthaler is an especially common sum provided for a dowry even after 1700.[68]

In ten cases between 1594 and 1685 in which the dowries specified in marriage contracts could be compared to annual income from estates, Hufschmidt finds that dowries ranged from one-half of one year's income (the most common sum) up to four years' income; the median was one year's income.[69]

The dowry of 2000 gulden or Reichsthaler that the lower nobility of the Weser region took as their standard is comparable to the dowries given by the higher-ranking families of the *Ritterstand* (lower nobility) in other German regions in the late sixteenth and early seventeenth centuries. In Pomerania and Mecklenburg, the mean value of dowries given by middling families of the lower nobility in the sixteenth century was 2000 gulden; 600 gulden was considered a small dowry. In Brandenburg at the end of the sixteenth century, dowries averaged between 1000 and 2000 gulden, with a few elite families giving dowries of

---

[67]Ulshöfer, *Hausrecht der Grafen von Zollern*, 80.
[68]Hufschmidt, *Adelige Frauen im Weserraum*, 299–300.
[69]Hufschmidt, *Adelige Frauen im Weserraum*, 281 and table 9.

4000 to 5000 gulden. A territorial ordinance issued in Lower Austria in 1654 specified dowries of 1000 gulden for members of the *Ritterstand* (knights) and 2000 for the *Herrenstand* (lords).[70]

The dowries given by the lower nobility in southwest Germany in the sixteenth and seventeenth centuries appear to fall at the lower end of the range found in other German regions. In Franconia around 1600, the lower nobility (who included many poor imperial knights) customarily gave dowries ranging between 600 and 1000 gulden. In the Kraichgau region of Swabia, dowries given between 1532 and 1661 ranged between 1000 and 3000 gulden, with very few over 3000 gulden. These figures suggest that dowry levels among the lower nobility of southwest Germany had changed very little since the fifteenth and early sixteenth centuries, when dowries given by knights ranged from a few hundred gulden to about 1200 gulden, and those given by elite families of the lower nobility were typically about 2000 gulden.[71]

Even though the ideal level of dowries might remain fixed at a standard sum, dowries actually paid varied considerably over time. Surprisingly, dowry levels recorded for the German lower nobility over the period 1550 to 1700 did not rise steadily throughout the period. Dowry levels in the Weser region as well as in the Münster region of Westphalia reached their peak between 1620 and 1640, that is, during the Thirty Years' War. Despite the damage caused by the war, agricultural prices—and therefore noble incomes—remained high in this period. After 1640, dowries fell to prewar levels, and the severe agricultural depression of the second half of the seventeenth century forced many families to offer dowries in 1700 that were substantially lower than they had given a century earlier.[72] No such development has been documented in other European nobilities, where dowry levels rose without interruption throughout the seventeenth century.

Evidence on dowry levels among the lower nobility and from other regions cannot be extrapolated directly to the counts and barons of southwest Germany. The severe agricultural depression of the late seventeenth century affected their inheritance strategies with regard to sons, as fathers practiced de facto primogeniture, but no studies are available on the value of dowries paid to daughters in this period. Nonetheless, the evidence from the lower nobility demonstrates that the ideal of a standardized dowry based on rank continued to appeal to German nobles in the late sixteenth and seventeenth centuries, and that trends in dowry levels among German nobles may have differed significantly from those in other European nobilities. In an era characterized in other European aristocracies by

---

[70]Hufschmidt, *Adelige Frauen im Weserraum,* 316.

[71]Hufschmidt, *Adelige Frauen im Weserraum,* 316; and Schröder, *Geschichte des ehelichen Güterrechts,* 2:82–83, 237–38.

[72]Hufschmidt, *Adelige Frauen im Weserraum,* 292.

primogeniture and rapidly escalating dowries, German nobles attempted to preserve fixed dowry levels for daughters as well as partible inheritance for sons.
These limitations on dowries facilitated a strategy of marrying several daughters
per generation and helped to maintain strong barriers against intermarriage
between different social orders.

CHAPTER 3

Age at Marriage and Proportions Marrying

The *Zimmern Chronicle*'s detailed description of four generations of the Zimmern family between the 1480s and the 1560s vividly illustrates the dilemmas families faced in arranging marriages and ecclesiastical careers for their children. It sheds light on the ages at which men and women were expected to marry, strategies the family elders preferred to adopt when they had to provide for more than one son and/or one daughter per generation, and also how the demographic, economic, and personal factors beyond the control of the family head could affect those strategies.

In 1474, the chronicler's great-grandfather Werner VIII von Zimmern arranged the marriage of his son Johann Werner I to Countess Margarethe von Oettingen, the sister of one of his colleagues on the council of Archduke Sigismund of Tyrol. Through this marriage of his only surviving son at an early age—Johann Werner I was probably only nineteen at the time—Werner hoped to ensure the birth of an heir before his own death (*ZC* 1:423).[1] However, the sons of Johann Werner I had to postpone their marriages until they were much older, since they had to wait for the recovery of their late father's estates. The oldest son, Veit Werner, died unmarried at the age of twenty in 1499, five years before the Werden-berg-Zimmern feud was ended (*ZC* 2:76–78). When Johann Werner II divided the newly recovered estates with his brother Gottfried Werner in 1508, he undertook to marry within a year in order to ensure the succession (*ZC* 2:191). Johann Werner II carried out this promise by marrying Schenkin Katharina von Erbach in 1510 when he was thirty years old. The match was promoted by Katharina's uncles, Count Christoph von Werdenberg and Schenk Christoph von Limpurg, as a means

---

[1]Schwennicke (*Europäische Stammtafeln NF,* 12:83) gives the date of birth of Johann Werner I as "about 1455," although Isenburg (*Europäische Stammtafeln,* 4:123) gives it as 1444, the year of his parents' marriage.

of restoring peace between the Werdenberg and Zimmern families (ZC 2:194–95). Meanwhile, Gottfried Werner had met Countess Apollonia von Henneberg at the court of Württemberg. With the help of his patron, Duke Ulrich von Württemberg, he succeeded in marrying this *gefürstete Gräfin* (countess of princely rank) despite the opposition of her father (ZC 2:443–47). Gottfried Werner was twenty-seven and Apollonia was about fifteen at the time of their marriage in 1511. Wilhelm Werner, the youngest son of Johann Werner I, did not participate in the division of the estates, and was not able to marry until he had saved up sufficient money from his salary as an imperial judge. When he married Countess Katharina von Lupfen in 1521, he was thirty-six and his bride was one year younger. Katharina died only six weeks after the wedding due to a fall from a horse (ZC 3:41–32). Four years later, at the age of forty, Wilhelm Werner married the fifty-six-year old widow Landgravine Amalia von Leuchtenberg. He had originally set out to court Amalia's teenaged daughter, Countess Margarethe von Haag, at the urging of his old friend Count Christoph von Tengen, who was a good friend of Margarethe's father. However, Wilhelm Werner found Amalia herself a more attractive match, because of the larger financial settlement she promised to bring to the marriage (ZC 3:41–42).

Johann Werner I also had four daughters who survived to adulthood. The two oldest girls were placed in the Frauenmünster in Zurich: Anna in 1488 at the age of fifteen and Katharina in 1492 at the age of fourteen (ZC 2:155–56). Since daughters destined to become nuns were usually sent to the convent between the ages of five and twelve,[2] it is probable that the Zimmern elders originally expected these daughters to marry and only placed them in the church after it became clear that their exiled father would not be able to provide dowries for them. They allowed the two younger daughters, Margarethe and Barbara, to remain laywomen in the hopes that the estates could be recovered by the time they reached marriageable age. However, even after the recovery of the Zimmern estates, Johann Werner II proved reluctant to provide dowries for his sisters and arrange suitable marriages for them. Each of the women then took matters into her own hands and married a husband from the lower nobility. Barbara married her brother's close friend Wilhelm von Weitingen in 1506, when she was twenty-four years old. Margarethe, a lady-in-waiting to the Margravine of Baden, met Wolf von Weitingen at the court of Baden and married him either in 1507 or in 1512. The marriage of Margarethe, who was now between twenty-five and thirty-one years old, was abetted by her mother, Margarethe von Oettingen (ZC 2:159–64).[3] Even the former abbess Katharina von Zimmern married after her convent was shut down by the

---

[2]Spiess, *Familie und Verwandschaft*, 377.

[3]The *Zimmern Chronicle* cites a renunciation given by Margarethe von Zimmern "in the year 1507 on the Friday after Oculi in Stockach" (ZC 2:163). However, Schwennicke (*Europäische Stammtafeln NF,* 12:84) gives the date of Margarethe's marriage as 29 July 1512.

town council of Zurich in 1525. At the age of forty-one, she married the Zwinglian Eberhard von Reischach, a citizen of Zurich (*ZC* 2:156–58).

Gottfried Werner von Zimmern and Apollonia von Henneberg had no sons but did have two daughters. The older daughter, Anna, was brought up in her parents' castle in Messkirch. However, the younger daughter, Barbara, was brought up from the age of two by her grandmother, Margarethe von Oettingen, at her widow's seat in the town of Messkirch.[4] After the young Barbara was blinded by measles, her father sought the advice of his kinsmen and reluctantly agreed that she should enter a convent where she could be cared for the rest of her life. But her redoubtable grandmother refused to give up the companionship of the child; not until after the death of Margarethe von Oettingen in 1528 did the ten-year-old Barbara enter the convent of Inzigkofen in 1529. Here she "found good playmates" among Werdenberg and Limpurg cousins who were already in the convent (*ZC* 2:262).[5] In 1531, her older sister Anna married (at the age of eighteen) Count Jos Niklaus von Zollern, the seventeen-year-old nephew of the wife of Count Christoph von Werdenberg. Christoph vigorously promoted this match to reinforce his old friendship with Gottfried Werner von Zimmern. He had originally hoped that Anna would marry his own son Joachim, who died at the age of fourteen before Anna was old enough to marry. Gottfried Werner had earlier rejected overtures from other suitors who were interested in Anna's hand only if she, rather than her cousin Froben Christoph, inherited her father's estate at Messkirch (*ZC* 2:452–54).

As for Froben Christoph himself, he states that "the old lord [Gottfried Werner] made up his mind to marry the young man into an honorable family" when he was twenty-five years old (*ZC* 3:506). After a search that lasted several months and involved at least four candidates (one of them probably still a child), Froben Christoph married sixteen-year-old Countess Kunigunde von Eberstein in 1544. This match was promoted by members of the Zollern family, who were eager to secure an alliance with the Zimmerns and prevent them from backing the Zollerns' political rival, Count Friedrich von Fürstenberg (*ZC* 3:506–21).

Although the Zimmern family elders had decided many years earlier to place Froben Christoph's older brother, Johann Christoph, in the church, they fully

---

[4]It was not unusual for relatives who were childless (or whose children were grown up) to ask to keep a young child with them for the sake of companionship. Froben Christoph von Zimmern was brought up until the age of twelve by his grandmother Elisabeth von Werdenberg. His second daughter, Apollonia, was "brought up only a few years by her father and mother" before being sent to the household of her childless cousin Anna von Zimmern, the daughter of Gottfried Werner, and Anna's husband Jos Niklaus von Zollern. Here she was brought up along with her cousin Jacobe von Zollern "for many years, until she was grown up" (*ZC* 4:17).

[5]Barbara's entry into the cloister at Inzigkofen was arranged by her father's good friend and kinsman by marriage, Count Christoph von Werdenberg. Like many convents, Inzigkofen was the repository of the unmarried females of its founding family, in this case the counts of Werdenberg.

expected his younger brother, Gottfried Christoph, to marry to provide additional assurance for a male heir. They were alarmed when the twenty-year-old Gottfried Christoph announced at his brother's wedding in 1544 that he intended to enter the church, for this left the survival of the Zimmern lineage dependent upon only one married son (*ZC* 3:519). Gottfried Christoph's decision to enter the church was indeed surprising, for the young man had spent his boyhood days dreaming of tournaments and was noted in his student days chiefly for his enormous capacity for liquor and his taste for crude practical jokes (*ZC* 3:253–54, 324). However, the Zimmern family elders eventually gave their consent, for a canon could easily be recalled to the lay world if his brother failed to produce male heirs.

The chronicler does not describe how Gottfried Christoph explained his decision to the family elders, but he makes the cryptic remark, "I later heard him say many times that he never regretted his decision and desire to enter the church, for reasons that were later evident in his character and his life" (*ZC* 3:519). Possibly Gottfried Christoph felt that the income from an ecclesiastical benefice would allow him to maintain a noble style of life more easily than the income from the small estate he could expect to inherit as a younger son. Canons were only in minor orders and did not have to reside permanently in their cathedral chapter; they were able to travel and to remain in close contact with their families. Many wore secular clothing, attended tournaments, and in general led a noble style of life.[6] When the three sons of Johann Werner II were negotiating an inheritance agreement after their father's death in 1548, Froben Christoph argued that the prebends held by the canons Johann Christoph and Gottfried Christoph allowed them to live according to their rank more easily than he, the only lay son, could do as the heir to an estate burdened with debts (*ZC* 4:123).

Froben Christoph had only one son, Wilhelm, whose marriage to Countess Sabina von Thurn und Valsassina allied him to an influential family at the Hapsburg court. Sabina's father was the governor of Moravia. The exact date of the marriage is unknown, as are the ages of Wilhelm and Sabina at the time. It is likely that the marriage took place around 1570, when Wilhelm would have been in his early twenties. Wilhelm died without issue in 1594 but was survived by nine sisters.

Eight of these nine daughters of Froben Christoph von Zimmern married in the years between 1562 and 1585, at ages ranging from fourteen to twenty-one. Froben Christoph undoubtedly arranged the marriages of the two daughters who married in his lifetime: Anna, the oldest daughter, who married Count Joachim von Fürstenberg in 1562, at the age of seventeen; and, Johanna, the third daughter, who married Truchsess Jakob von Waldburg zu Zeil in 1566, at the age of eighteen. He may also have arranged the marriage of Apollonia, the second daughter, who was twenty years old when she married Count Georg II von Helfenstein in 1567, a few months after her father's death. However, it is more likely that Apollonia's

---

[6]Spiess, *Familie und Verwandtschaft*, 302–3, 468.

marriage was arranged by her cousin Anna von Zimmern and the latter's husband Jos Niklaus von Zollern, who had brought her up since early childhood.

The marriages of five other daughters of Froben Christoph von Zimmern were undoubtedly arranged by their brother Wilhelm. Kunigunde, the fourth daughter, married Truchsess Johann von Waldburg in 1570, at the age of eighteen; Maria, the sixth daughter, married Count Georg von Thurn und Valsassina in 1570, at the age of fourteen; Leonora, the fifth daughter, married the imperial general Lazarus von Schwendi in 1573, at the age of eighteen; Sibilla, the seventh daughter, married Count Eitel Friedrich I von Hohenzollern-Sigmaringen in Hechingen in 1574, at the age of sixteen, and Ursula, the ninth daughter, married Count Bernhard von Ortenburg-Salamanca in 1585 at the age of twenty-one. Barbara, the eighth daughter, remained an unmarried laywoman. She died at the age of thirty-six in 1595, a year after the Zimmerns had become extinct in the male line with the death of her brother Wilhelm.

Five of the eight marriages of the daughters of Froben Christoph von Zimmern reinforced traditional marriage alliances with other families of Swabian counts. However, three of the marriages arranged by Wilhelm—those of Maria, Leonora, and Ursula—reflected the new political and social connections that Wilhelm had made at the imperial court.

In the years between 1474 and 1585, the age at first marriage for Zimmern sons ranged from nineteen to thirty-six, and the age at first marriage for Zimmern daughters ranged from fourteen to forty-one. Despite this wide range of ages at marriage, it is clear that men were normally expected to marry in their late twenties or even later. The two marriages at younger ages each involved an only son who was under pressure to produce an heir as quickly as possible. Women, on the other hand, usually married in their teens; they feared being left old maids if their father or brother had not arranged a marriage by the time they reached their early twenties. The ages of men and women in the Zimmern family were also typical of other southwest German counts and barons in this period.

Decisions about family strategy were made by consultation among the family elders, not by the father alone. It is not clear whether female members of the family were formally consulted; however, the formidable matriarch Margarethe von Oettingen was able to block arrangements by her sons Johann Werner II and Gottfried Werner von Zimmern when they displeased her. The Zimmerns preferred to marry off at least one son and one daughter per generation, and more than that whenever demographic circumstances permitted. An only son or an only daughter always married, even if he or she had siblings of the opposite sex. The Zimmerns divided their estates in 1508 to allow two sons to marry, even though the estates were heavily burdened with debt, and they married off an extraordinary total of eight daughters between 1562 and 1585, long before they could have known that the family was about to become extinct in the male line.

The Zimmerns' preference for allowing more than one son to marry was shared by other southwest German counts and barons, as evidenced by their continued practice of partible inheritance. Their preference for allowing more than one daughter to marry was also shared by counts and barons of the Mainz region in the Middle Ages and early sixteenth century.[7]

Factors beyond the control of the family head could drastically affect family strategy. The most significant was demographic accident. Of the seven heads of households in the last five generations of the Zimmern family, two married but had no issue (Wilhelm Werner and Wilhelm); one had daughters but no sons (Gottfried Werner), and two had only one son (Werner VIII and Froben Christoph). Some other fathers with several surviving children did not have to make any decisions as to how many out of several sons or several daughters should marry. Only two sibling groups contained more than one son who survived to adulthood (the children of Johann Werner I and the children of Johann Werner II), and only three contained more than one surviving daughter (the children of Johann Werner I, Gottfried Werner, and Froben Christoph). In addition, the poor health or physical handicaps of some children, such as blind Barbara, made it unlikely that they could find spouses.

Economic circumstances also influenced family strategy; the children of Johann Werner I married at unusually late ages because of the long struggle to regain the Zimmern estates. Family heads might also find that their best-laid plans went awry due to the decisions of the children themselves. The daughters of Johann Werner I arranged their own marriages despite the opposition of their brother, Johann Werner II, and Gottfried Christoph decided to enter the church instead of marrying to beget additional heirs. Lastly, the Protestant Reformation could alter available career options, as when Katharina von Zimmern's convent in Zurich was shut down. All of these factors obviously affected other families as well as the Zimmerns.

It is difficult to draw comparisons between the family strategy of southwestern German counts and barons and that of other German and European nobles over the entire period between 1400 and 1700, since few systematic demographic studies are available for the years before 1650. Religious divisions add further complications. Although both Catholics and Protestants are included in the southwest German families, most studies of other German regions and foreign nobilities include only one religious confession or the other. However, it is possible to draw some comparisons with studies of the counts and barons of the Mainz region in the period between 1200 and 1550, the nobility of Lower Austria between 1500

---

[7]Spiess (*Familie und Verwandtschaft*, 368–69 and table 4) finds that in the period between 1200 and 1550, the majority of families with two or more daughters actually married off at least two daughters.

and 1800 (largely Protestant in the late sixteenth and early seventeenth century, but Catholic thereafter), the Protestant knights of Hesse between 1650 and 1899, and the Catholic imperial knights of the Rhineland between 1600 and 1803.[8]

It is also possible to draw comparisons for parts of the period from 1400 to 1699 with studies of elites in Italy, Iberia, France, England, and the Netherlands (the English and the Dutch were Protestant after the mid-sixteenth century.)[9] It is thus possible to compare Catholic and Protestant German nobles with their co-religionists in other countries and to analyze the extent to which the Reformation affected family strategy.

Data on age of first marriage and marriage rate (nuptuality) are available for noble families of southwestern Germany and can be compared to similar data on nobles and nonnobles in Germany and to nobles in other countries. This comparison shows the extent to which the nobility continued to use a strategy closely associated with the medieval aristocracy: the marriage of children in their early teens or even in childhood. The data also allow an analysis of trends over time in the proportion of sons and daughters who married, examining differences between strategies for sons and those for daughters, and differences between the religious confessions.

AGE AT MARRIAGE

Southwest German nobles in the fifteenth century adhered to a medieval marriage pattern in which sons married in their late twenties (at an average age of 27.8 years) while daughters married under the age of 20 (at an average age of 18.8

---

[8]Spiess gives statistics on the marriage rates of counts and barons in *Familie und Verwandtschaft,* 279, 367, tables 19 and 33, and on those of imperial princes in "Social Rank in the German Higher Nobility." Statistics on other regions are given in Mitterauer, "Zur Frage des Heiratsverhaltens"; Pedlow, *Survival of the Hessian Nobility;* and Duhamelle, "Parenté et orientation sociale."

[9]Demographic data on other European elites are taken from the following sources:

General: Cooper, "Patterns of Inheritance and Settlement"; and Peller, "Births and Deaths among Europe's Ruling Families," 87–100.

Britain: Harris, *English Aristocratic Women;* Hollingsworth, "Demographic Study of the British Ducal Families"; Hollingsworth, "Demography of the British Peerage"; Stone, *Crisis of the Aristocracy;* and Stone, *Family, Sex and Marriage.*

France: Arnaud, "Le Mariage et ses enjeux"; Henry and Lévy, "Ducs et pairs sous l'ancien régime"; Labutat, *Les ducs et pairs de France;* Le Roy Ladurie and Fitou, "Hypergamie féminine et population saint-simonienne"; Lorcin, *Vivre et mourir en Lyonnais;* Nassiet, *Noblesse et pauvreté;* and Nassiet, *Parenté, noblesse et états dynastiques.*

Italy: Herlihy and Klapisch-Zuber, *Tuscans and Their Families;* Litchfield, "Demographic Characteristics of Florentine Patrician Families"; Molho, *Marriage Alliance;* Sperling, *Convents and the Body Politic;* and Zanetti, *Demografia del patriziato Milanese.*

Netherlands: Marshall, *The Dutch Gentry;* and Nierop, *The Nobility of Holland.*

Portugal: Boone III, "Parental Investment and Elite Family Structure"; and Gonçalo Monteiro, "Casa, reproduçao social e celibato."

Spain: Beceiro Pita and Córdoba de la Llave, *Parentesco, poder y mentalidad;* and Gerbet, *La noblesse dans le royaume de Castille.*

years).[10] There was thus a large age gap between the spouses. During the sixteenth and seventeenth centuries, the age for men fluctuated between approximately 26 and 28 years. The average age for daughters rose to over 20 after 1500, to about 21 between 1550 and 1650, and to 22.6 years between 1650 and 1699. By the late seventeenth century, therefore, the southwest German nobility was moving closer to the European marriage pattern practiced by the nonnoble population, in which men married in their late twenties and women married at the age of 23 or above, with a relatively small age difference between the spouses (see table 3.1).[11]

In the late seventeenth century, the first period for which demographic analysis is available for German commoners, the average age at first marriage for sons of counts and barons was similar to that of nonnoble men. Daughters of counts and barons were slightly older at first marriage than nonnoble women in Mainz, but younger than nonnoble women in the Hessian town of Giessen and the nearby village of Heuchelheim.[12]

Comparisons with other German elites are possible only for certain time periods. The average age of marriage for both sons and daughters of counts and barons in southwest Germany in the fifteenth century is slightly higher than for those of counts and barons of the Mainz region in the same time period and for offspring of the counts of Wetterau in the period between 1450 and 1510.[13] The average age at marriage for sons in the southwest German high nobility was similar to that of Austrian nobles throughout the period between 1500 and 1699, but daughters in the southwest German high nobility consistently married at a younger age than noble daughters in Austria.[14] In the second half of the seventeenth century, sons and daughters of Hessian knights married at a later age than did the children of the high nobility in the southwest German and Austrian studies.[15]

[10]The term "average" as used in the discussion refers to an arithmetical mean: that is, the numerical result obtained by dividing the sum of two or more quantities by the number of quantities. The term "mean" is used in the statistical tables themselves to avoid any possible confusion. The mean, especially in a small group of items, may be heavily affected by a few extremely high or extremely low quantities. In such cases, a more useful measure is the median (the middle number in a series containing an odd number of items or the number midway between the two middle numbers in a series containing an even number of items), since it is not affected by the actual value of the highest and lowest items. The median is used in the discussion of the proportion of children marrying at young ages.

[11]On the medieval and European marriage patterns, see Hajnal, "European Marriage Patterns in Perspective," 101–35.

[12]The mean age at first marriage for men ranged between 26 and 28 years both for the counts and barons and for men in Mainz, Giessen, and Heuchelheim. Women in Mainz married at a mean of 21.3 years of age between 1681 and 1700; women in Giessen married at an average age of 24.3 years between 1651 and 1700, and women in Heuchelheim married at a mean age of 24.1 years between 1691 and 1700. See Rödel, *Mainz und seine Bevölkerung*, 263; and Imhof, *Historische Demographie als Sozialgeschichte*, 315. For additional statistics on age at marriage from the seventeenth and eighteenth centuries, see Wunder, *He Is the Sun, She Is the Moon*, 29–30.

[13]Spiess, *Familie and Verwandtschaft*, 415; and Schmidt, *Das Wetterauer Grafenverein*, 492.

[14]Mitterauer, "Zur Frage des Heiratsverhaltens," 179–81.

[15]Pedlow, *Survival of the Hessian Nobility*, 38; and Mitterauer, "Zur Frage des Heiratsverhaltens," 180.

Table 3.1: Mean Age at First Marriage in German Nobilities

Date of birth	Sons				Daughters			
	SW Germany (yrs)	Austria[a] (yrs)	Mainz[b] (yrs)	Wetterau[c] (yrs)	SW Germany (yrs)	Austria[a] (yrs)	Mainz[b] (yrs)	Wetterau[c] (yrs)
1400–99	27.8	—	—	—	18.8	—	—	—
1400–1530	—	—	25.9	—	—	—	18.6	—
1450–1510	—	—	—	25.1	—	—	—	17.8
1500–49	25.8	27.6	—	—	20.2	21.3	—	—
(Catholic/Protestant)	(25.8/25.8)	—	—	—	(18.5/23.6)	—	—	—
1550–99	26.1	27.8	—	—	21.4	24.0	—	—
(Catholic/Protestant)	(25.0/27.7)	—	—	—	(18.9/23.9)	—	—	—
1600–49	28.2	27.6	—	—	21.1	21.9	—	—
(Catholic/Protestant)	(29.1/27.2)	—	—	—	(21.1/21.2)	—	—	—
1650–99	27.3	27.7	—	—	22.6	—	—	—
(Catholic/Protestant)	(27.2/27.6)	—	—	—	(24.0/20.8)	—	—	—

[a]Mitterauer, "Zur Frage des Heiratsverhaltens," 179.
[b]Spiess, Familie und Verwandtschaft, 415–16.
[c]Schmidt, Wetterauer Grafenverein, 492.

For sons of southwest German counts and barons, birth order affected age at first marriage. After the fifteenth century, eldest sons consistently married at an earlier age than younger sons (see table 3.2). Many of the younger sons succeeded to collateral relatives and could not marry until they inherited the estate; the number of nonheirs who married is too small to affect the averages. The age gap between eldest and younger sons was greater in southwest Germany in the sixteenth and seventeenth century than it was in Austria.[16] It is difficult to make comparisons with eldest and younger sons in other European elites, since younger sons outside Germany did not benefit from the division of the paternal estates.

Catholics and Protestants in the southwest German high nobility showed no consistent differences in age at marriage for sons, but striking differences for daughters. Protestant daughters born in the sixteenth century married at a mean age four years higher than that of Catholic daughters, who continued to marry at the same age as in the preceding century. The high marriage age for Protestant daughters presumably reflects the difficulty of marrying off all or almost all daughters, especially in large sibling groups; some of the daughters in the first generation of Protestantism were over thirty years old when they married.

Between 1550 and 1649, the average age at first marriage for Protestant daughters was similar to that of Austrian nobles (the majority of whom were also Protestant in this period). However, the average age at first marriage of Protestant daughters in southwest Germany declined in the seventeenth century, whereas that of Catholic daughters rose until it was actually higher than that of Protestants in the second half of the seventeenth century. The Protestant noblewomen in this group included an unusually large number of heiresses, which may account for their lower average age at marriage. Studies of nonnoble German populations have not found significant differences in age at marriage between Catholic and Protestant women in the late seventeenth century.[17]

Few systematic studies on ages at marriage in other European elites before 1550 are available. According to Sigismund Peller, the average age at first marriage in European ruling families in the sixteenth century was 25.9 years for men and 20.2 years for women; in the seventeenth century, the average age rose to 27.5 years for men and 22.7 years for women.[18] The average ages at first marriage for sons and daughters of southwest German counts and barons were thus close to the European averages, though Catholic daughters in southwest Germany in the sixteenth century married younger than the average age for all European elites (see table 3.3).

---

[16]However, Mitterauer ("Zur Frage des Heiratsverhaltens," 186–87) emphasizes the increasing gap between eldest and younger brothers in the eighteenth century.

[17]Zschunke, *Konfession und Alltag in Oppenheim,* 174.

[18]Peller, "Births and Deaths among Europe's Ruling Families," 88.

Table 3.2: Mean Age of Sons at First Marriage, Southwest Germany and Austria

	SW Germany				Austria[a]		
Date of birth	All sons (yrs)	Eldest heir (yrs)	Younger heir (yrs)	Nonheir (yrs)	All sons (yrs)	Eldest son (yrs)	Younger son (yrs)
1400–99	27.8	28.5	27.5	>30	—	—	—
1500–49	25.8	24.4	26.9	24.5	27.6	29.0	26.7
(Catholic/Protestant)	(25.8/25.8)	(23.7/26.3)	(27.3/25.5)	(27.0/22.0)	(—/—)	(—/—)	(—/—)
1550–99	26.1	23.5	28.0	26.7	27.8	27.4	28.3
(Catholic/Protestant)	(25.0/27.7)	(23.6/23.4)	(26.0/30.0)	(26.7/NA)	(—/—)	(—/—)	(—/—)
1600–49	28.2	24.5	30.5	38.0	27.7	27.6	27.6
(Catholic/Protestant)	(29.1/27.2)	(24.0/24.7)	(30.4/30.8)	(38.0/NA)	(—/—)	(—/—)	(—/—)
1650–99	27.3	25.0	28.5	32.5	27.7	26.6	29.7
(Catholic/Protestant)	(27.2/27.6)	(24.3/28.5)	(29.1/27.3)	(32.5/NA)	(—/—)	(—/—)	(—/—)

Note: NA = not applicable, no Protestants in this group.
[a] Mitterauer, "Zur Frage des Heiratsverhaltens," 179.

Table 3.3: Mean Age at First Marriage in Other European Elites

Area / social group	Date of birth	Sons (yrs)	Daughters (yrs)
Britain / dukes[a]	1330–1479	22.4	17.1
	1480–1679	24.3	19.5
Britain / peers[b]	1550–74	25.3	20.3
	1575–99	25.7	19.9
	1600–24	26.0	20.7
	1625–49	27.4	22.0
	1650–74	26.9	21.5
	1675–99	28.1	22.7
France / dukes and peers[c]	1650–99	25.5	20.0
Brittany / petty nobles[d]	1581–1640	23.6	24.4
	1641–1700	29.0	25.8
Savoy / nobles[d]	1641–1700	30.4	22.7
Geneva / patricians[d]	1581–1640	29.1	24.3
	1641–1700	32.6	26.2
Florence / patricians[e]	1450–99	29.3	18.5
	1500–49	29.4	18.2
	1550–99	33.6	19.0
	1600–49	34.5	20.2
	1650–99	36.4	19.3
Netherlands / gentry[f]	1500–29	31.3	24.2
	1530–49	30.8	28.2
	1550–69	27.8	21.0
	1570–89	29.0	24.6
	1590–1609	25.8	23.0
	1610–29	26.5	28.0
	Date of father's marriage		
Portugal / grandees[g]	1601–50	24.8	<18
	1651–1700	23.6	19.3

[a]Hollingsworth, "British Ducal Families," 365.
[b]Hollingsworth, "Demography of the British Peerage," 16–18.
[c]Henry and Lévy, "Ducs et pairs," 813.
[d]Nassiet, *Noblesse et pauvreté*, 267.
[e]Litchfield, "Florentine Patrician Families," 199.
[f]Marshall, *Dutch Gentry*, 36.
[g]Gonçalo Monteiro, "Casa, reproducao social e celibato," 915.

In the fifteenth century, the sons of southwest German counts and barons married at a younger age than the average for sons of Florentine patricians, but older than the average for sons of British dukes.[19] After 1550, the sons of counts and barons of southwest Germany married at an age similar to that of sons of British peers and Dutch gentry (late sixteenth and seventeenth centuries),[20] and higher than the average for sons of Portuguese grandees or French dukes and peers (late seventeenth century).[21]

The age of first marriage for daughters of counts and barons in southwest Germany was similar to or slightly lower than that of daughters of Florentine patricians in the fifteenth and early sixteenth centuries, though higher than that of daughters of British dukes.[22] It was much lower than that of daughters of Dutch gentry, who in this period were still Catholic. In the late sixteenth and seventeenth centuries, their average age at first marriage was higher than that of daughters of British peers, Portuguese grandees, French dukes, or Florentine patricians, but lower than that of daughters of Dutch gentry, who were now Protestant.[23]

Marriages at Young Ages

The rising mean age at marriage among sons and especially among daughters of southwest German counts and barons from the sixteenth to the late seventeenth century suggests that fewer marriages were taking place at very young ages. In order to ensure that marriages of sons and daughters achieved the goals of broader family strategy, aristocratic parents in the Middle Ages often arranged marriages even before the children had reached the canonical ages of twelve years for women and fourteen years for men. Such promises of future marriage (*verba de futuro*) had to be reconfirmed by the later consent of the children; when both parties had reached the canonical age of marriage, they could exchange marriage vows (*verba de praesenti*). These vows, followed by consummation, constituted a valid marriage in the canon law. The marriage contracts were thus often executed many years before the wedding ceremony took place; if the bride was young, the consummation might not take place until still later.[24]

---

[19]Herlihy and Klapisch-Zuber, *Tuscans and Their Families,* 86–87. Memoirs (*ricordi*) of Florentine patrician families indicate a mean age of about thirty in the fifteenth century. On British dukes, see Hollingsworth, "British Ducal Families," 365.

[20]Hollingsworth, "Demography of the British Peerage," 16–18; and Marshall, *Dutch Gentry,* 36.

[21]Nassiet, *Noblesse et pauvreté,* 267; and Gonçalo Monteiro, "Casa, reproduçao social e celibato," 915.

[22]Molho, *Marriage Alliance,* 307; and Hollingsworth, "British Ducal Families," 365.

[23]Hollingsworth, "Demography of the British Peerage," 16–18; Nassiet, *Noblesse et pauvreté,* 267; Gonçalo Monteiro, "Casa, reproduçao social e celibato," 915; and Marshall, *Dutch Gentry,* 36.

[24]Spiess, *Familie und Verwandtschaft,* 113–14, 118. Among the English aristocracy, many marriage contracts specified that the dowry was to be repaid if either party died before reaching the age of sixteen. This suggests that marriages were not consummated until that age even if they were solemnized earlier. See Harris, *English Aristocratic Women,* 45.

Among the high nobility of Castile, where such child marriages made up a high proportion of all marriages in the late Middle Ages, the final stage of the marriage ceremony took place when the boy was between sixteen and twenty and the girl between fourteen and eighteen years old, with an age difference of four to five years between the spouses.[25] Child marriages were also common in the nobility of Burgundy in the fifteenth century.[26] In the English aristocracy between 1450 and 1550, child marriages were rare except in the case of heiresses, but even daughters who did not inherit an estate usually married between the ages of thirteen and sixteen.[27]

Early marriages were also common in German princely families in the late Middle Ages (see table 3.4). Richard Koebner finds that in five princely families between 1300 and 1520, about a third of all sons married at the age of nineteen years or younger, and about a third of all daughters married between the ages of thirteen and fifteen.[28]

Demographic evidence from the sample of southwest German counts and barons suggests that the sixteenth century witnessed a decline in marriages arranged in childhood. Without documentary evidence, it is not possible to tell whether marriages at young ages were actually negotiated while the parties were under the canonical age of consent. However, marriage ceremonies at very young ages decreased sharply in the course of the sixteenth century.

Marriages in the fifteenth century show a very large age gap between spouses, with men marrying at a median age of 28 years and women at a median age of 13.5 years. Seventy-five percent of the girls married before the age of sixteen years, and (despite the high median age of marriage for men) 22 percent of the men married in their teens. These statistics suggest that marriages negotiated in childhood made up a significant proportion of all marriages of southwest German counts and barons. However, age at marriage is known in only a small number of cases in the fifteenth century and these chiefly come from families of counts who later achieved the rank of princes. Such families may have been more likely than other counts and barons to marry their children at young ages.

This practice of marrying a substantial proportion of all sons and daughters at a young age continued into the early sixteenth century, when 20 percent of all men married in their teens and 28 percent of all women married between the ages of thirteen and fifteen. The pattern changed abruptly after 1550, when marriages of men before the age of twenty years declined to about 5 percent of all marriages. Marriages of women before the age of sixteen years also declined, though more slowly among Catholics than among Protestants. In the second half

---

[25]Beceiro Pita and Córdoba de la Llave, *Parentesco, poder y mentalidad,* 167.
[26]Caron, *La noblesse dans le duché de Bourgogne,* 202.
[27]Harris, *English Aristocratic Women,* 56–57.
[28]Koebner, "Die Eheauffassung des ausgehenden deutschen Mittelalters."

Table 3.4: Age at First Marriage—Range, Median, and Percent Marrying Young

Date of marriage	Sons				Daughters			
	Total (N)	Range (yrs)	Median (yrs)	Younger than 20 years (%)	Total (N)	Range (yrs)	Median (yrs)	Younger than 16 years (%)
1450–99	9	15–34	28.0	22	4	13–17	13.5	75
1500–49	25	16–50	25.0	20	25	13–28	18.0	28
1550–99	33	19–43	24.0	6	45	13–44	22.0	11
(Catholic/Protestant)	(16/17)	(20–43/19–34)	(24.0/25.0)	(0/12)	(22/23)	(13–32/19–44)	(18.0/24.0)	(23/0)
1600–49	33	15–46	27.0	3	35	15–34	22.0	3
(Catholic/Protestant)	(20/13)	(15–31/21–46)	(26.0/27.0)	(5/0)	(18/17)	(15–33/16–34)	(22.0/21.0)	(6/0)
1650–99	41	19–46	27.0	5	43	15–35	19.0	5
(Catholic/Protestant)	(26/15)	(19–46/19–36)	(27.0/23.0)	(0/13)	(24/19)	(16–31/15–35)	(19.5/19.0)	(0/11)

Note: The median is the age by which half of the persons in the category have married. It is a more useful measure than the mean in this case, since the mean is affected by a few individuals with ages much higher than the rest of the sample, whereas the median is not affected by a few outliers.

of the sixteenth century, no Protestant daughters married below the age of nine-teen, whereas 18 percent of the Catholic daughters married before they reached sixteen.[29] However, marriages of daughters at very young ages became rare in both confessions in the seventeenth century. Among women who married between 1600 and 1699, only one Catholic and two Protestants were under the age of sixteen.

Only one woman in the Zimmern family married extremely young: Maria, the sixth of the nine surviving daughters of Froben Christoph married in 1570 at the age of fourteen. Seven of the chronicler's other daughters married between the ages of sixteen and twenty-one. It is unclear why Maria (b. 1555) married so much younger than her sisters or why she married before her older sister Leonora (b. 1554), who eventually married in 1573 at the age of eighteen. Sisters did not always marry in birth order, for prospective husbands were often given the choice of one out of several sisters. Froben Christoph's wife Kunigunde von Eberstein, who was sixteen at the time of her marriage, had three unmarried older sisters. It is possible that Leonora suffered from some defect that made her less attractive on the marriage market than Maria, in spite of the latter's extreme youth.[30]

Studies of other European nobilities after 1550 imply that marriages arranged in childhood became rare except among royalty, but few statistics are available on the actual proportion of children marrying at young ages. No data are available on the German high nobility after the mid-sixteenth century. However, among the lower nobility of the Weser region between 1500 and 1700, no daughters married before the age of fifteen and no sons married before the age of twenty.[31] Although no engagements were actually concluded in childhood, marriage negotiations still began at a young age, particularly in the case of daughters. The diary of Landdrost Kaspar von Fürstenberg (1545–1618) notes overtures from a suitor for his eldest daughter in 1581, when the girl was only seven years old; the marriage took place ten years later when she was seventeen. Her younger sister had a suitor at the age of fifteen but did not marry until the age of twenty-three.[32]

Stone describes a decline in marriages at young ages in the British aristoc-racy in the late sixteenth and early seventeenth centuries, with a movement in the

---

[29]The late marriage ages of Protestant daughters in the years between 1550 and 1599 were prob-ably due to the burden of arranging marriages for large numbers of daughters in the first generation after the Reformation rather than to ideological opposition to marriage of girls in their teens. In the seventeenth century, some Protestant daughters married at the ages of fifteen and sixteen.

[30]Leonora became the second wife of a much older husband, the imperial general Lazarus von Schwendi, who regarded a marriage into the Zimmern family as a social promotion. See Jenny, *Graf Froben Christoph von Zimmern*, 199. Schwendi was the illegitimate son of a father from the lower nobility, and thus of lower social status than the husbands of Leonora's sisters. Together with the fact that Leonora married after her younger sister Maria, this suggests that she was not considered as desir-able a match as her sisters.

[31]Hufschmidt, *Adelige Frauen im Weserraum*, 121–22.

[32]Hufschmidt, *Adelige Frauen im Weserraum*, 129–31.

age of peers and their male heirs "out of the middle teens into the early twenties." He states that "by the seventeenth century very young aristocratic marriages were becoming rare," referring to marriages in which both parties were in their early teens. However, a third of peers and their heirs still married in their teens in the first half of the seventeenth century.[33] T. H. Hollingsworth, who gives data on all sons of peers rather than just the heirs, states that "one-tenth of the men who were born about 1560 were married by the age of seventeen."[34]

Stone does not give statistics for the age at marriage of daughters of peers. However, Hollingsworth states that the median age of marriage for women was about twenty years for women born between 1550 and 1624 and rose among those born after 1620, and that one-tenth of all daughters born around 1560 were married by the age of fifteen.[35] This suggests a marked reduction in marriages of daughters at very young ages during the course of the sixteenth century, since Barbara Harris found that 77 percent of the English aristocratic women born between 1450 and 1550 were aged sixteen or under at the date of their first marriage.[36]

Dukes and peers of France, unlike their counterparts in the British aristocracy, continued to marry off most of their children in their teens even in the late seventeenth and eighteenth centuries. Louis Henry and Claude Lévy note that these marriages at young ages in the French high aristocracy were out of step with the trends in other European elites after 1650.[37]

Although southwest German counts and barons preserved an inheritance strategy that was becoming old-fashioned in the sixteenth and seventeenth century, their strategy with respect to age at marriage followed the prevailing trends among European ruling families. They abandoned the practice of marrying children at very young ages earlier than did some other European aristocracies. This trend toward higher age at marriage has been associated with increased individual freedom of choice, and a larger role for the children themselves in the process of marriage negotiations.[38]

NUMBERS OF SONS AND DAUGHTERS MARRYING

In making decisions about family strategy, family heads had to take into consideration not only how many sons should inherit a portion of the estate, but also how many daughters should receive dowries and what provision should be made for unmarried sons and daughters. The number of heirs and of dowries had to be adjusted to available economic resources, and the Reformation limited the options of Protestant fathers in providing for unmarried children.

[33]Stone, *Crisis of the Aristocracy,* 653, 792 app. 33.
[34]Hollingsworth, "Demography of the British Peerage," 16, 18.
[35]Hollingsworth, "Demography of the British Peerage," 18.
[36]Harris, *English Aristocratic Women,* 56–57.
[37]Henry and Lévy, "Ducs et pairs sous l'ancien régime," 813–14.
[38]Stone, *Crisis of the Aristocracy,* 654.

Over the course of these three centuries, 59 percent of all sons and 73 pecent of all daughters of southwest German counts and barons married (see table 3.5). Marriage strategy was extremely restrictive in the fifteenth century, when only 53 percent of all sons and 56 percent of all daughters married. Approximately a third of all children—30 percent of all sons and 37 percent of all daughters—entered the church, accounting for the majority of the unmarried sons and almost all of the unmarried daughters. In the sixteenth century, the proportion of children who married increased dramatically, to 67 percent of all sons and 76 percent of all daughters. In all the groups born after 1500, the proportion of daughters who married exceeded the proportion of sons who married. Although the proportion of sons marrying declined slightly in the seventeenth century (to 59 percent), the proportion of daughters marrying continued to rise (to 81 percent).

Protestants married off a higher proportion of both sons and daughters than did Catholics. The higher proportion of Protestant sons who married cannot be attributed to a greater willingness of Protestant fathers to divide their estates, since it has already been demonstrated that Protestant and Catholic fathers followed very similar inheritance strategies. Demographic accident appears to have played a large role. More Protestant than Catholic sons succeeded to the estates of collateral relatives and thus were able to marry even though they did not receive a share of the paternal estate. Moreover, three of the four Protestant families died out in the male line in the early eighteenth century. The group born in the late seventeenth century contained few sons; even if only one son per generation married, this represented a high proportion of all surviving sons.

The increase in the proportion of children marrying after 1500 cannot be attributed solely to the Protestant Reformation and the loss of the church as a financial support for unmarried sons and daughters. Catholics as well as Protestants married off a higher percentage of their sons and daughters in the sixteenth century than in the fifteenth century. Moreover, the majority of unmarried Catholic sons in all the groups born after 1500 remained laymen, and the majority of unmarried Catholic daughters in all the groups born after 1600 remained laywomen rather than becoming nuns.

NUMBER OF SONS AND DAUGHTERS MARRYING PER GENERATION
The number of sons and daughters who married per generation reflected a father's ideological preference: either to maximize the number of marriage alliances or to consolidate as much property as possible in the hands of the lineage. However, it also reflected pragmatic considerations: the number of children a father actually had to provide for in a given generation.

Family heads had no major decisions to make about family strategy if they had only one surviving son (or no sons and all) and/or only one surviving daughter (or no daughters at all). They almost invariably arranged a marriage for an

Table 3.5: Percent of Sons and Daughters Marrying, Entering Church, and Unmarried

Date of birth	Total (N)	Sons						Daughters					
		Married		Entered Church		Unmarried laity		Married		Entered Church		Unmarried laity	
		(n)	(%)	(n)	(%)	(n)	(%)	(n)	(%)	(n)	(%)	(n)	(%)
Before 1400	46	26	57	15	33	5	11	11	58	7	37	1	5
1400–49	51	24	47	19	37	8	16	23	59	12	31	4	10
1450–99	54	30	56	12	22	12	22	20	51	17	44	2	5
Subtotal to 1499	151	80	53	46	30	25	17	54	56	36	37	7	7
1500–49 (Catholic/Protestant)	49 (41/8)	33 (25/8)	67 (61/100)	6 (6/0)	12 (15/0)	10 (10/0)	24 (24/0)	51 (34/17)	76 (69/94)	11 (11/0)	16 (22/0)	5 (4/1)	7 (8/6)
1550–99 (Catholic/Protestant)	65 (37/28)	45 (26/19)	69 (70/68)	5 (5/0)	8 (15/0)	15 (6/7)	23 (16/29)	54 (30/24)	76 (71/83)	8 (8/0)	11 (19/0)	9 (4/5)	13 (10/17)
1600–49 (Catholic/Protestant)	62 (38/24)	37 (20/17)	60 (53/71)	9 (9/0)	25 (24/0)	16 (9/7)	26 (24/29)	53 (36/17)	84 (86/81)	3 (3/0)	5 (7/0)	7 (3/4)	11 (7/19)
1650–99 (Catholic/Protestant)	57 (45/12)	33 (25/8)	58 (56/67)	9 (9/0)	16 (20/0)	15 (11/4)	26 (24/33)	56 (32/24)	79 (71/92)	6 (6/0)	8 (13/0)	9 (7/1)	13 (16/8)
Subtotal 1500–1699 (Catholic/Protestant)	233 (161/72)	148 (96/52)	64 (60/72)	29 (29/0)	18 (18/0)	56 (36/20)	24 (22/28)	214 (132/82)	79 (74/87)	28 (28/0)	10 (16/0)	30 (18/12)	11 (10/13)
Total 1400–1699	384	228	59	75	20	81	21	268	73	64	17	37	10

only son or an only daughter, even if they had surviving children of the other sex. Exceptions chiefly involved children who survived to the age of fifteen but died before reaching the average marriage age for their sex. However, the majority of fathers who had any children at all surviving to the age of fifteen had at least two surviving children of the same sex. They therefore had to decide how to apportion their economic resources, whether to divide their estates to allow more than one son to marry and whether to provide dowries to allow more than one daughter to marry (see table 3.6).[39]

During periods of economic difficulty, families allowed only one son per generation to marry. Even in more affluent eras, they normally divided the patrimony between only two sons. Only six divisions among three sons and one among four sons occurred between 1400 and 1700. All but two of these seven divisions among three or more sons took place between 1559 and 1609, an era of unusual agricultural prosperity. However, providing dowries for several daughters did not have such severe economic consequences as dividing the patrimony among several sons. It was therefore possible to pursue a strategy of maximizing alliances by marrying off more than one daughter even in hard times and marrying off virtually all daughters when economic circumstances permitted.

The chances of a son's marrying were determined by his succession to an estate. Over 90 percent of all sons who succeeded to all or part of an estate eventually married (91 percent of those who succeeded to their father's estate and 94 percent of those who succeeded to that of a collateral relative). Only 13 percent of the sons who survived their father but did not inherit an estate were ever able to marry. Nonheirs who married, such as Wilhelm Werner von Zimmern, were usually in the service of a prince. They were either able to purchase an estate out of the income from their office or benefited from the favor of a patron who arranged a marriage for them.

Between 1400 and 1699, 62 percent of all the families with two or more surviving sons included two or more sons who eventually married, but only 28 percent of families with three or more sons included three or more sons who eventually married (see tables 3.7 and 3.8). There were marked differences over time in the willingness of families with several sons to allow more than one of them to marry. The proportion of such families which actually contained more than one married son ranged from a low of 36 percent in the early fifteenth century to a high of 82 percent in the late sixteenth century (based on the date of the father's marriage).

---

[39]Of the ever-married men who had any children surviving to age fifteen, 57 percent had two or more surviving sons (21 percent had two, 19 percent had three, and 17 percent had four or more sons). Fifty-two percent of these men had two or more surviving daughters (18 percent had two, 14 percent had three, and 20 percent had four or more daughters).

Table 3.6: Number of Sons and Daughters Surviving to Age 15 per Sibling Group and Number Marrying per Sibling Group

Date of father's marriage	Total sibling groups (N)	Sons			Daughters		
		Total surviving to age 15 (n)	Mean surviving per sibling group (n)	Mean marrying per sibling group (n)	Total surviving to age 15 (n)	Mean surviving per sibling group (n)	Mean marrying per sibling group (n)
1400–49	23	47	2.0	1.1	39	1.4	1.1
1450–99	21	48	2.2	1.3	45	1.7	1.4
Subtotals 1400–99	44	95	2.2	1.2	84	1.9	1.2
1500–49	23	54	2.3	1.5	76	3.3	2.0
(Catholic/Protestant)	(17/6)	(40/14)	(2.4/2.3)	(1.5/1.8)	(55/21)	(3.2/3.5)	(1.9/2.5)
1550–99	29	67	2.3	1.6	77	2.7	2.0
(Catholic/Protestant)	(18/11)	(40/27)	(2.2/2.5)	(1.6/1.6)	(45/32)	(2.5/2.9)	(1.8/2.3)
1600–49	30	55	1.8	1.0	49	1.6	1.4
(Catholic/Protestant)	(19/11)	(35/20)	(1.8/1.8)	(1.1/1.0)	(34/15)	(1.8/1.4)	(1.5/1.2)
1650–99	32	65	2.0	1.2	71	2.2	1.7
(Catholic/Protestant)	(22/10)	(52/13)	(2.3/1.3)	(1.3/0.9)	(49/22)	(2.2/2.2)	(1.5/1.9)
Subtotals 1500–1699	114	241	2.1	1.3	273	2.4	1.8
(Catholic/Protestant)	(76/38)	(167/74)	(2.1/1.9)	(1.3/1.3)	(183/90)	(2.4/2.3)	(1.7/1.8)
Total 1400–1699	158	336	2.1	1.3	357	2.3	1.6

Note: A sibling group consists of all of the surviving issue of an ever-married man by all of his marriages; it contains one or more children. Cases in which an ever-married man had no children surviving to age 15 are excluded from this category.

Note: Survival to age 15 is one of the criteria for inclusion in the sample of southwest German counts and barons, in order to avoid problems caused by the underrecording of children who died young. Such children would not in any case have been candidates for marriage.

Table 3.7: Number of Sons Marrying in Sibling Groups as Percentage of Possible Cases[a]

Date of father's marriage	N sibling groups	Sibling groups with the following numbers of sons marrying (% of all sibling groups)					Marriages as a percentage of all possible cases			
		0 marry	1 marries	2 marry	3 marry	4+ marry	1+ marry as % of all with 1+	2+ marry as % of all with 2+	3+ marry as % of all with 3+	4+ marry as % of all with 4+
1400–49	23	13	65	22	0	0	91	36	0	0
1450–99	21	23	38	29	10	0	94	57	22	0
Subtotal 1400–1499	*44*	*18*	*52*	*25*	*5*	*0*	*92*	*43*	*13*	*0*
1500–49	23	13	30	13	22	23	95	67	50	40
(Catholic/Protestant)	(22/1)	(14/0)	(32/0)	(14/0)	(22/100)	(18/0)	(95/100)	(58/100)	(23/100)	(50/100)
1550–99	29	17	34	28	10	10	96	78	60	43
(Catholic/Protestant)	(18/11)	(11/28)	(44/18)	(28/28)	(11/9)	(6/18)	(100/89)	(73/85)	(33/75)	(25/67)
1600–49	41	22	44	29	2	2	89	64	12	6
(Catholic/Protestant)	(30/11)	(23/18)	(40/55)	(30/27)	(3/0)	(3/0)	(88/90)	(66/50)	(15/0)	(8/0)
1650–99	21	52	24	19	0	5	83	56	25	50
(Catholic/Protestant)	(11/10)	(45/60)	(28/20)	(28/10)	(0/0)	(0/10)	(67/100)	(5/67)	(0/50)	(0/100)
Subtotal by confession 1500–1699 (Catholic/Protestant)	*114 (81/33)*	*25 (22/33)*	*37 (40/30)*	*25 (27/21)*	*6 (6/6)*	*6 (5/9)*	*91 (91/92)*	*69 (67/71)*	*34 (30/45)*	*35 (27/60)*
Total 1400–1699	*158*	*23*	*41*	*25*	*6*	*4*	*92*	*62*	*29*	*25*

Note: "Marriages as a percentage of all possible cases" indicates the number of sibling groups in which 1 or more, 2 or more, 3 or more, or 4 or more sons married as a percentage of all the sibling groups which contained that number of surviving sons. This eliminates variation attributable to demographic accident rather than deliberate strategy

Table 3.8: Number of Daughters Marrying in Sibling Group as Percentage of Possible Cases

Date of father's marriage	N sibling groups	Sibling groups with the following numbers of daughters marrying (% of all sibling groups)					Marriages as a percentage of all possible cases			
		0 marry	1 marries	2 marry	3 marry	4+ marry	1+ marry as % of all with 1+	2+ marry as % of all with 2+	3+ marry as % of all with 3+	4+ marry as % of all with 4+
1400–49	23	30	39	21	9	0	84	63	40	0
1450–99	21	29	33	24	10	5	79	62	38	20
Subtotal 1400–1499	*44*	*30*	*36*	*22*	*9*	*2*	*82*	*63*	*38*	*13*
1500–49	23	22	35	4	9	30	90	67	83	70
(Catholic/Protestant)	(22/1)	(22/0)	(35/0)	(5/0)	(9/0)	(27/100)	(89/100)	(64/100)	(82/100)	(67/100)
1550–99	29	31	34	3	10	21	95	71	82	75
(Catholic/Protestant)	(18/11)	(39/18)	(22/55)	(6/0)	(17/0)	(17/27)	(92/100)	(70/75)	(75/100)	(60/100)
1600–49	41	17	59	12	7	5	97	63	56	50
(Catholic/Protestant)	(30/11)	(10/36)	(60/56)	(17/0)	(10/0)	(3/9)	(96/100)	(69/33)	(50/50)	(33/1.2)
1650–99	21	14	33	24	14	14	100	79	60	100
(Catholic/Protestant)	(11/10)	(18/10)	(27/30)	(27/10)	(9/40)	(18/10)	(100/100)	(75/83)	(60/60)	(100/100)
Subtotal by confession 1500–1699 (Catholic/Protestant)	*114* (81/33)	*21* (21/21)	*43* (41/48)	*11* (12/6)	*10* (11/6)	*16* (15/18)	*96* (94/100)	*69* (69/71)	*69* (66/80)	*72* (63/100)
Total 1400–1699	*158*	*23*	*41*	*14*	*9*	*12*	*92*	*67*	*62*	*58*

Note: "Marriages as a percentage of all possible cases" indicates the number of sibling groups in which 1 or more, 2 or more, 3 or more, or 4 or more daughters married as a percentage of all the sibling groups containing that number of surviving daughters. This eliminates variation attributable to demographic accident rather than deliberate strategy

As might be expected, the chronological pattern for marriages of more than one son follows very closely the pattern of divisions of estates: it rises sharply from the fifteenth to the sixteenth century, then declines in the seventeenth century. Of the sixteen cases in which three or more sons in a sibling group married, only seven were the result of deliberate family strategy, that is, a division of estates among three or more sons. The other cases occurred when a third or later-born son succeeded to the estate of a collateral relative, or when he did not inherit an estate but was able to marry through his own efforts.

Southwest German counts and barons were more likely to allow several daughters in a sibling group to marry than to allow several sons to marry. Throughout the period of 1400 to 1699, they preferred a strategy of marrying off two daughters, even in periods when they were reluctant to divide estates to support two sons. This was a continuation of a medieval marriage pattern: between 1200 and 1500, three-quarters of all the families of counts and barons in the Mainz region with two or more surviving daughters allowed at least two daughters to marry. However, few families in the Middle Ages married off a third daughter and even fewer married off more than three.[40]

The sixteenth century saw a sharp increase in the willingness of southwest German counts and barons to give dowries to three or more daughters. Between 1400 and 1699, 59 percent of all families in this group who had three or more surviving daughters actually allowed at least three of them to marry. There is a dramatic contrast between the fifteenth century, when only 33 percent of such families gave dowries to three or more daughters, and the sixteenth and seventeenth centuries, when 69 percent did so. The proportion rose to a peak of 83 percent of such families in the late sixteenth century and, even in the depression of the late seventeenth century, it remained as high as 50 percent.

This increase was due in part to a new strategy of marrying off all—or almost all—the daughters even from large sibling groups of four or more daughters. Such large groups of daughters were not rare; they made up 20 percent of all sibling groups. Before 1500 no family married off more than three daughters in a single generation. However, there was an abrupt change of policy in the early sixteenth century. Between 1500 and 1699, sixteen families married off four or more daughters, and in twelve of these cases, they married off five or more daughters. Two fathers, including the chronicler Froben Christoph von Zimmern, married off eight daughters apiece.

This trend toward marrying off three or more daughters in a single generation was not merely the result of the Protestant Reformation, which removed the option of putting daughters in a convent. Protestants were indeed more willing than Catholics to allow three or more daughters to marry: 77 percent of the Protestant families with three or more daughters did so, as compared to 66 percent of

[40]Spiess, *Familie und Verwandtschaft,* 368.

the Catholic families. Religion was clearly a key factor in the decisions of two Protestant families, the Schenken of Erbach and the Schenken of Limpurg, to marry off four or more daughters in a single generation. Both were relatively poor families that had recently risen from the lower nobility and had a strong tradition of placing younger children in the church. In the two generations just before their conversion to Protestantism, two fathers in the Limpurg family had each married off only one daughter in a group of four daughters, sending the others into the church. In the late sixteenth century, however, Karl II von Limpurg married off all five of his daughters and Friedrich VI von Limpurg married off five of his nine daughters.

However, the trend toward marrying off large groups of daughters was not solely due to the Reformation. This trend began before the Protestant Reformation, and eight of the sixteen fathers who married off four or more daughters were Catholics.[41] Two Catholic fathers married off four daughters apiece during the economic depression of the late seventeenth century, even though the option of placing daughters in the convent remained open to them. This suggests a deliberate strategy of investing in alliances through daughters in a period when divisions of estates and marriages of younger sons had to be curtailed due to unfavorable economic conditions.

Comparisons to Other Elites

Did the family strategy of southwest German counts and barons represent patterns typical of German nobles, and did German nobles differ from other European elites? Spiess's studies show that the higher the rank of the father, the higher the proportion of children who married. Between 1200 and 1550, 77 percent of the sons and 82 percent of the daughters of imperial princes married, as compared to 55 percent of all sons and 65 percent of all daughters of counts and barons of the Mainz region. The difference was chiefly due to the greater economic resources of the princes, which allowed them to divide their estates more frequently to fulfill the ideal of equality among brothers. They could also afford to provide dowries to more daughters.

Most of the unmarried children of counts and barons in Mainz were placed in the church, accounting for one-third of all sons and one-third of all daughters. In addition, about one-tenth of all sons remained unmarried laymen, whereas the proportion of unmarried laywomen (at least of recorded ones) was negligible.[42]

Among counts and barons of the Mainz region, the proportion of sons and daughters who married declined in the late Middle Ages. Among those born

---

[41]Marriages of large groups of daughters also became more common in the English peerage in the early sixteenth century. The examples cited by Harris all occurred before the Henrician Reformation, indicating that religious ideology was not the cause: *English Aristocratic Women,* 49.

[42]Spiess, "Social Rank in the German Higher Nobility"; and idem, *Familie und Verwandtschaft,* 279, 367, tables 19 and 33.

between 1350 and 1500, only about one-half of all sons and all daughters married, a proportion similar to sons and daughters of southwest German counts and barons born before 1499. It is not surprising that the family strategies were similar; both groups consist of the nonprincely nobility in adjacent regions. However, it is not clear whether these restrictive marriage strategies were typical of German nobles in other regions in this period, since no data on the proportion of sons and daughters who married are available for other regions.

Such data are only available for the period after 1650. Pedlow's study of Hessian knights finds that among those born between 1650 and 1699, 63 percent of the men and 74 percent of the women who survived to the age of twenty eventually married.[43] This is similar to the proportions among southwest German counts and barons born in the same years, where 64 percent of the men and 79 percent of the women who survived to the age of fifteen eventually married.

Table 3.9: Mean Number of Sons and Daughters Marrying per Sibling Group in Southwest Germany Compared to Other German Nobilities

Date of father's marriage	Sons (n)			Daughters (n)		
	SW Germany	Austria[a]	Rhineland[b]	SW Germany	Austria[a]	Rhineland[b]
1400–99	1.2	1.5	—	1.2	1.9	—
1500–49	1.5	1.8	—	2.0	2.2	—
(Catholic/Protestant)	(1.5/1.8)	(—/—)	(—/—)	(2.0/NA)	(—/—)	(—/—)
1550–99	1.6	1.5	—	2.0	1.9	—
(Catholic/Protestant)	(1.6/1.6)	(—/—)	(—/—)	(1.9/2.5)	(—/—)	(—/—)
1600–49	1.0	1.6	—	1.5	1.6	—
(Catholic/Protestant)	(1.1/1.0)	(—/—)	(1.5/NA)	(1.5/1.2)	(—/—)	(1.9/NA)
1650–99	1.2	1.1	—	1.7	1.7	—
(Catholic/Protestant)	(1.3/0.9)	(—/—)	(1.2/NA)	(1.5/1.9)	(—/—)	(1.8/NA)
1700–49	1.4	1.1	—	1.6	1.6	—
(Catholic/Protestant)	(1.4/1.2)	(—/—)	(1.2/NA)	(1.5/1.8)	(—/—)	(1.7/NA)

Note: NA = not applicable, no Protestants in this group.
[a]Mitterauer, "Zur Frage des Heiratsverhaltens," table 5, 187.
[b]Duhamelle, "Parenté et orientation sociale," 70.

The only other study of a German nobility that extends over the entire time period covered by this study is that of Michael Mitterauer on Austria, which uses data calculated in the form of the number of sons and daughters marrying per sibling group rather than data in the form of percentages marrying per birth cohort.[44]

[43]Pedlow, *Survival of the Hessian Nobility*, 37.

[44]The chronological trends using these data are not exactly comparable to the percentage marrying in each birth cohort, since the cohorts are defined by the date of the father's marriage rather than by the date of the child's birth. Moreover, when few children in a given generation survive to age fifteen, the percentage marrying may be high even though the mean number marrying per generation is low.

The overall trend in the number of sons and daughters marrying per generation was similar in southwest Germany and in Austria, rising from the fifteenth to the sixteenth century, then declining in the seventeenth century. However, there were also some noticeable differences. In the fifteenth century, the marriage strategy of Austrian nobles was much less restrictive than that of southwest German counts and barons, and the mean number of sons and daughters marrying per generation peaked in Austria in the first half of the sixteenth century rather than in the second half of the century. Both Austrian and southwest German nobles practiced an extremely restrictive marriage policy in the late seventeenth century, allowing barely one son per generation to marry. Although this policy was abandoned by the southwest German counts and barons after 1700, it continued among the nobles of Austria and the imperial knights of the Rhineland.[45]

The most striking similarity among all these regional studies of German nobilities is that a higher proportion of daughters than sons eventually married. This gender gap is especially striking in the second half of the seventeenth century, when marriages of sons were drastically restricted but marriages of daughters continued at a level similar to earlier periods. However, these regional comparisons also suggest the counts and barons of southwest Germany may have practiced an unusually restrictive marriage policy in the fifteenth century and an unusually permissive one around 1700. These uniquely southwest German characteristics are even more marked when the nobles in this study are compared to other European nobilities outside of Germany.

COMPARISONS TO OTHER EUROPEAN ELITES

Peller's study of European ruling families found that 41 percent of all sons born in the sixteenth and seventeenth centuries who survived to the age of fifteen remained bachelors.[46] In the same time period, 36 percent of sons of southwest German counts and barons remained unmarried. Their celibacy rate was thus lower than the average for European ruling families, even though mere counts and barons would normally be expected to marry off fewer of their sons than higher-ranking families such as those included in Peller's study. Unfortunately, Peller does not offer any estimates of the proportion of daughters who remained unmarried. Statistics for European nobilities in specific countries are given in tables 3.10 and 3.11.

When southwest German counts and barons are compared to nobles in other European countries, the most striking phenomenon is the relatively low percentage of all southwest German sons and daughters who married in the fifteenth century and the relatively high percentage who married in the late seventeenth

---

[45]Mitterauer, "Zur Frage des Heiratsverhaltens," 189; Duhamelle, "Parenté et orientation sociale," 65–67.

[46]Peller, "Births and Deaths among Europe's Ruling Families," 89.

and early eighteenth century. Although differences between the confessions make it difficult to compare nobles in different countries after 1550, it is clear the trends among Catholic counts and barons of southwest Germany differed from those of Catholic nobles elsewhere in western Europe.

Among Catholics, the percentage of sons and daughters remaining unmarried is closely linked to the proportion entering the church. The percentage of sons and daughters of southwest German counts and barons who entered the church in the fifteenth century was higher than in any other European elite for which statistics are available. Among daughters of English peers, only 2 percent of those born between 1450 and 1550 became nuns. Among sons and daughters of the high aristocracy in Spain and Portugal, only 10 to 15 percent of the children of fathers born in the fifteenth century entered the church. These figures stand in sharp contrast to the children of southwest German counts and barons born in the same period, where 29 percent of the sons and 37 percent of the daughters entered the church.[47] Clerics made up only a minority of all unmarried sons in Iberian and Italian elites in the fifteenth century, whereas they made up the majority of unmarried sons in southwest Germany in this period.

However, the percentage of sons and daughters entering the church fell among southwest German nobles in the sixteenth century, whereas it rose sharply among elites in other Catholic countries in the same period. Anthony Molho speaks of a "rush to the convent" among Florentine patrician women in the sixteenth century; and Jutta Sperling estimates that in Italy as a whole, "between 1550 and 1650, aristocratic girls were more likely to become nuns than wives."[48] In Portugal, the proportion of daughters of the high aristocracy who entered the church rose from 11 percent of those whose fathers were born around 1400 to 40 percent of those whose fathers were born after 1490, while the corresponding proportion of sons entering the church rose from less than 15 percent of those whose fathers were born around 1400 to about 30 percent of those whose fathers were born in the seventeenth century.[49]

In the seventeenth century, the percentage of both sons and daughters entering the church was lower in southwest Germany than in Italy or Iberia or in the French high aristocracy. Only a minority of the unmarried sons and daughters of

---

[47]Statistics on nuns in the English aristocracy are taken from Harris, *English Aristocratic Women,* 11. On Iberia, the figure of 10 to 15 percent of sons and daughters is given for Castile by Beceiro Pita and Córdoba de la Llave, *Parentesco, poder y mentalidad,* 162. Statistics for Portugal are from Boone, "Parental Investment and Elite Family Structure," 873.

[48]Molho, *Marriage Alliance,* 306; and Sperling, *Convents and the Body Politic,* 18. In Florence, only 4.3 percent of the daughters enrolled in the dowry fund (*Monte delle doti*) between 1425 and 1499 who survived to the date of the fund's maturity entered a convent. The proportion of nuns rose to 19.7 percent of all survivors among daughters enrolled between 1500 and 1529, and to 31.4 percent of all survivors among daughters enrolled after 1530. See Molho, *Marriage Alliance,* 306.

[49]Boone, "Parental Investment and Elite Family Structure," 874; and Gonçalo Monteiro, "Casa, reproduçao social e celibato," 919.

Table 3.10: Percent of Sons and Daughters Remaining Unmarried and/or Entering Church, Britain and Italy

Area / social group	Date	Sons Unmarried (%)	Sons Entered church (%)	Daughters Unmarried (%)	Daughters Entered church (%)
	Date of birth				
Britain / dukes[a]	1330–1479	9.0	—	7.0	—
	1480–1679	7.0	—	6.0	—
Britain / peers[b]	1450–1550	—	—	6.0	2.0
Britain / peers[c]	1550–74	2.5	—	9.0	—
	1575–99	13.9	—	4.2	—
	1600–24	22.9	—	12.8	—
	1625–49	15.0	—	17.9	—
	1650–99	17.9	—	15.1	—
	1700–24	21.9	—	23.8	—
	1725–49	20.1	—	26.3	—
	Date enrolled				
Florence / girls in dowry fund[d]					
	1425–99	—	—	—	4.3
	1500–29	—	—	—	19.7
	1530+	—	—	—	31.4
Total		—	—	—	7.2

Area / social group	Date father born	Unmarried at age 50 (%)	Surviving to age 15 (%)	Unmarried at age 50 (%)	Surviving to age 20 (%)
Florence / patriciate[e]	1500–99	48.0	—	30.0	26.2
	1600–99	60.0	—	55.0	48.1
	1700–99	38.0	—	14.0	9.6
Milan / patriciate[f]	Before 1650	49.0	30.9	75.0	—
	1650–99	56.0	22.0	48.5	—
	1700–49	50.5	12.0	34.5	—
	1750–99	36.5	5.0	13.0	—

Note: "Unmarried" means never-married. "Entering church" is a subset of "unmarried"; however, most sources give data for only one category or the other.

Note: "Unmarried at age 50" is the demographers' definition of "permanent celibacy"; it is the percentage of all those surviving to age 50 who had never married before reaching that age.

[a]Hollingsworth, "British Ducal Families," 364.

[b]Harris, *English Aristocratic Women*, 11, 18.

[c]Hollingsworth, "Demography of the British Peerage," 25.

[d]Molho, *Marriage Alliance*, 306. Percentages are for all girls surviving to date of maturity of the investment in the fund.

[e]Litchfield, "Florentine Patrician Families," 195, 197.

[f]Zanetti, *Demografia del patriziato milanese,* 83–84.

Table 3.11: Percent of Sons and Daughters Remaining Unmarried and/or Entering Church, Iberia and France

Area / social group	Date	Sons		Daughters	
		Unmarried (%)	Entered church (%)	Unmarried (%)	Entered church (%)
Castile / high aristocracy[a]	late 14th–15th century	—	—	—	10.0 to 15.0
Extremadura[b] / titleholders	1454–1516	—	20.0	—	—
Extremadura[b] / knights	1454–1516	—	7.0	—	—
	Date father born				
Portugal / high aristocracy[c]	Generation 1 (1380–1430)	24.5	ca. 10	—	ca. 11
	Generation 2 (ca. 1418–68)	21.1	ca. 10	—	ca. 20
	Generation 3 (ca. 1455–1505)	29.4	ca. 13	—	ca. 33
	Generation 4 (ca. 1492–1542)	39.6	ca. 12	—	ca. 40
	Generation 5 (1530–80)	44.3	ca. 15	—	ca. 42
Portugal / titleholders[d]	Before 1651	48.1	31.0	42.0	35.9
	1651–1700	42.1	30.4	44.6	34.4
	1701–1750	43.5	12.9	41.8	18.4
	1751–1830	23.0	4.3	28.5	4.6
Paris / Parlement of Paris[e]	1345–1454	—	36.0	—	7.0
Lyons / nobility[f]	1340–1500	—	—	—	31.0
France / siblings of dukes and peers[g]	1589–1660	—	30.0	34.0	27.0
	1661–1723	—	27.0	42.0	37.0
Toulouse / 15 noble families[h]	1670–99	50.0	15.6	48.7	27.0
	1700–29	51.4	31.4	61.4	25.0
	1730–59	39.4	15.2	59.9	22.7
	1760–89	32.4	0.0	28.0	0.0
Brittany / petty nobles[i]	17th century	10.7	1.8	—	—
	18th century	16.3	8.2	—	—

Note: "Unmarried" means never-married. "Entering church" is a subset of "unmarried"; however, most sources give data for only one category or the other.

[a]Beceiro Pita and Cordoba de la Llave, *Parentesco, poder y mentalidad,* 162.
[b]Gerbet, *Noblesse dans le royaume de Castile,* 165.
[c]Boone, "Parental Investment and Elite Family Structure," 873.
[d]Gonçalo Monteiro, "Casa, reproduçao social e celibato," 919.
[e]Arnaud, "Le mariage et ses enjeux," 412.
[f]Lorcin, *Vivre et mourir en Lyonnais,* 78.
[g]Labutat, *Ducs et pairs,* 108–9.
[h]Forster, *Nobility of Toulouse,*129, cited in Cooper, "Patterns of Inheritance and Settlement," 289.
[i]Nassiet, *Noblesse et pauvreté,* 265.

southwest German counts and barons entered the church in the seventeenth century, whereas the majority of the unmarried sons and daughters did so in most of the other Catholic aristocracies for which statistics are available.

Few comparisons over time are possible between Protestant counts and barons of southwest Germany and other Protestant elites. In the sixteenth and seventeenth centuries, the proportion of sons remaining unmarried was higher among southwest German counts and barons (28 percent of those born between 1500 and 1699) than among Dutch noblemen and British peers. The proportion of daughters of Protestant southwest German counts and barons remaining unmarried (13 percent of those born between 1500 and 1699) was much lower than the percentage among Dutch noblewomen and similar to the percentage among daughters of British peers.[50] The gender gap between the percentage of sons and the percentage of daughters who remained unmarried was greater among southwest German counts and barons than among British peers.

In the period around 1700, it is possible to compare the marriage strategies of men and women in the German nobility with more numerous studies of Catholic and Protestant elites in other western European countries. In his study of inheritance practices, J. P. Cooper demonstrates that Catholic elites practiced much more restrictive inheritance practices during the late seventeenth and early eighteenth centuries than did Protestant elites. In Florence before 1700, Milan before 1750, Toulouse before 1760, and among the dukes and peers of seventeenth-century France, about half the sons and half the daughters remained unmarried.[51] Nuño Gonçalo Monteiro likewise finds that by the mid-seventeenth century Portuguese titleholders conformed to what he calls the "common aristocratic model" in which only one son and one daughter married per generation, with almost half of all sons and all daughters remaining celibate and about a third of each sex entering the church.[52] This model is remarkably similar to the strategy practiced by southwest German counts and barons in the fifteenth century. Among Protestant elites, in contrast, less than a quarter of all sons and all daughters remained unmarried in the patriciate of Geneva and in the English aristocracy of the late seventeenth and early eighteenth century.[53]

The marriage strategies of German nobles around 1700 appear to set them apart from both Catholic and Protestant elites in other countries. The most striking difference is the high proportion of southwest German noblewomen who married, compared to their coreligionists in other elites. Whereas the percentage of Catholic sons born between 1650 and 1699 who remained unmarried (44 percent) was

[50]Hollingsworth, "Demography of the British Peerage," 20; and Nierop, *Nobility of Holland,* 54.

[51]Cooper, "Patterns of Inheritance and Settlement," 287 (Florence and Milan), 289 (Toulouse, French dukes and peers), 290 (British peers), 304, 304n324 (Geneva).

[52]Gonçalo Monteiro, "Casa, reproduçao social e celibato," 920.

[53]Cooper, "Patterns of Inheritance and Settlement," 290 (British peers), 304 (Geneva); Hollingsworth, "Demography of the British Peerage," 25; and Stone, *Family, Sex and Marriage,* 44, 47.

comparable to that of Catholic noblemen elsewhere, the percentage of Catholic daughters born in the same period who remaned unmarried (29 percent) was much lower than in other Catholic elites. Moreover, unmarried Catholic daughters in southwest Germany were less likely to become nuns than were those in other Catholic regions. Among Protestants, 33 percent of the sons of southwest German counts and barons born in this period remained unmarried, a higher percentage than in Protestant elites in Geneva or Britain. In contrast, only 8 percent of the southwest German Protestant daughters remained unmarried, a much lower percentage than in Geneva or Britain.

These data suggest that around 1700, the southwest German counts and barons practiced a distinctive pattern of inheritance and marriage. First, they continued to practice a system of partible inheritance in an era when it was falling into disuse among nobles in other European elites and even among nobles in some other parts of Germany. Second, they followed a marriage strategy that maximized alliances by marrying off several daughters per generation even when they restricted the number of sons who married. Such a surplus in marriages of women over marriages of men within an elite group is associated with a strategy of marrying sons up and daughters down. This pattern was characteristic of medieval and early modern German nobilities, but it was not uniquely German; it was also found in other western European aristocracies in the period between 1400 and 1700.

CHAPTER 4

Intermarriage
and Rank of Spouses

German nobles, like members of other European elites, followed a family strategy designed to maintain and enhance their social position through marriage alliances. Spiess observes that the duty of the noble family was to "maintain and elevate the lineage [*Stamm und Nam*]," that is, to continue the family in the male line and to enhance its territorial base and its prestige through marriage alliances with other families of at least equal rank. This meant, at a minimum, avoiding unequal marriages to partners of lower status. "The social criteria for the choice of marriage candidates aimed at partners who were as equal as possible in rank or even of higher rank. This maxim is rarely to be found fixed in writing, but it is easy to test through marriage practices."[1] Similarly, Stone says of the sixteenth-century English aristocracy that "the greatest fear in a society so acutely conscious of status and hierarchy was of social derogation in marriage, of alliance with a family of lower estate or degree than one's own."[2]

However, the German nobility may have taken a different view of what constituted social derogation than did other European nobilities. Regional studies of medieval and early modern German nobles suggest that cases in which the marriage partners were unequal in status generally involved the marriage of a woman of higher rank to a man of lower rank. This marriage pattern (known in anthropology as *hypogamy*, in which the woman marries down) is the opposite of the one described for early modern England, where noblemen were willing to marry women of lower rank in order to secure larger dowries.[3] The latter pattern

---

[1]Spiess, *Familie und Verwandtschaft*, 9, 49.

[2]Stone, *Family, Sex and Marriage*, 87.

[3]Statistics on the social origins of the wives of British peers in the period of 1540 to 1660 are given in Stone, *Crisis of the Aristocracy*, 628–32 and app. 30. Harris implies that hypergamy was the

(known as *hypergamy*, in which the woman marries up) is usually represented as the norm in studies of early modern European nobilities. For example, Jonathan Dewald says, "a long succession of alliances joined aristocratic young men with wealthy women from lower ranks, the daughters of officials, bankers and merchants; marriage of impoverished but noble women with wealthier men happened much less often but was not unheard of."[4] Olwen Hufton says that "truly prestigious families did not without very special reasons marry their daughters into families of lesser social standing even if they had condoned or encouraged that of a son to someone of less standing who had money."[5]

Two historians of the medieval German noble family, John Freed and Karl-Heinz Spiess, have argued that its hypogamous marriage strategy is due to the unique characteristics of the German nobility. Freed views the pattern of marrying sons up and daughters down as a consequence of the legal disabilities attached to unequal marriages between members of the freeborn high nobility (counts and barons) and those of the lower nobility made up of unfree ministerials.[6] Both Freed and Spiess note that the strategy would have been encouraged by the dowry system of the medieval German nobility. Dowries were fixed by the rank of the husband, so a family using a hypogamous marriage strategy would receive a larger dowry from a son's wife than it would have to pay out to a daughter's husband. Since dowries remained unchanged (at least in face value) over long periods of time, there was little market orientation that might allow wealthy members of the urban patriciate or the lower nobility to marry their daughters into the high nobility by paying extraordinarily high dowries.[7]

The *Zimmern Chronicle* reflects the strong prejudice of the high nobility not only against marriage with nonnobles but also against intermarriage with the lower nobility. The boundary between the latter two groups had become more permeable in the fifteenth century, once ministerials ceased to be legally unfree. In the early sixteenth century, Truchsess Hans von Waldburg liked to boast that "he and his ancestors had mixed themselves in with the counts and barons like mouse-droppings in the pepper" (*ZC* 3:146). In the same period, Schenk Wilhelm von Limpurg complained that the high nobility was being diluted by intermarriage with families whose claims to be equal to barons were more recent than that of the Limpurgs. Wilhelm taunted his mother-in-law by talking in her presence about lesser nobles marrying into families of counts and barons. "But with each

---

dominant pattern in the English aristocracy between 1480 and 1540: "within the limits set by their own economic, political, and social resources, ... [t]he ultimate goal was to secure sons-in-law with more of these assets than their own." *English Aristocratic Women*, 43–44.

[4]Dewald, *European Nobility*, 169.

[5]Hufton, *Prospect Before Her*, 109.

[6]Freed, *Noble Bondsmen*, 101.

[7]Spiess, *Familie und Verwandtschaft*, 364–66; and Freed, *Noble Bondsmen*, 179.

odious example he would say, 'But my lady, I don't mean *you*'" (*ZC* 3:146). The mother-in-law in question was a countess of Leiningen, whose husband came from the somewhat dubious von der Laiter family.[8] The chronicler implies that Wilhelm von Limpurg's other examples also involved hypogamous marriages of new men from the lower nobility to wives from the higher nobility.

The chronicler's concern with this issue may have been partly due to personal circumstances. Froben Christoph von Zimmern had been brought up by his grandmother Elisabeth von Werdenberg, a countess who had remarried a mere nobleman named Philipp Echter. Froben Christoph was embarrassed by the low social status of Echter's relatives and friends, including his own godfather, the hedge-knight Froben von Hutten.[9] However, the chronicler's attitude also reflects the increasing rigidity of social and legal boundaries between the lower and higher nobility in the sixteenth century. According to Georg Schmidt, the offspring of a marriage between a husband from the high nobility and a wife from the lower nobility were accepted as social equals of the father in the fifteenth century but not in the sixteenth century, when "intermarriage lessened not only the marriage opportunities of the children, but those of the entire family."[10]

RANK OF SPOUSES

The Zimmerns, like other German nobles, hoped to increase the prestige of their lineage through marriage alliances with families of higher rank. The chronicler's accounts of marriage negotiations in the first half of the sixteenth century vividly illustrate both an obsession with maintaining existing status and an aggressive pursuit of wives of higher status, even in a period when the financial fortunes of the family were at their lowest ebb. However, these financial difficulties led the children of the exiled Johann Werner I to make an unusually large number of marriages across social boundaries in the opening decades of the sixteenth century. In the chronicler's view, the marriage of sons to wives of lower status would pose a much more serious threat to the social standing of the lineage than would the marriage of daughters to men of lower status.

The most striking demonstration of this attitude is the description of the match Johann Werner II's patron, Margrave Christoph von Baden, tried to arrange for him with a wealthy widow from the urban patriciate of Strasbourg. The match would have gone far to rescue Johann Werner II from his heavy debts, and almost all of his friends and relatives urged him to accept it on the grounds that the widow's fortune would enable his two brothers to marry according to their rank. Nevertheless, Johann Werner II ultimately rejected the unequal match,

---

[8]On the ambiguous status of the von der Laiter family of Bavaria, who were descendants of an illegitimate branch of the Della Scala of Verona, see Euler, "Wandlung des Konnubiums," 60–61.

[9]Jenny, *Graf Froben Christoph von Zimmern*, 66, 198.

[10]Schmidt, *Wetterauer Grafenverein*, 482.

since it would bar his children from tournament societies. Froben Christoph von Zimmern praises his father for rejecting the unequal marriage, even though he thereby lost the favor of his patron (*ZC* 2:148–50). Although Johann Werner II's decision hurt the Zimmern family financially in the short run, it maintained the prestige of the family in the long run.

Both of Johann Werner's younger brothers eventually made upwardly mobile marriages through their own efforts. With the aid of his patron Duke Ulrich von Württemberg, Gottfried Werner succeeded in marrying Countess Apollonia von Henneberg (granddaughter of Margrave Fredrich V von Brandenburg) despite the opposition of her father. Although the chronicle depicts the marriage as a love match, Gottfried Werner boasted of his coup in marrying a "princess"(*Fürstin*) and argued that the higher status of his wife entitled him, rather than his elder brother, to possession of the main Zimmern estate at Messkirch (*ZC* 2:316). Wilhelm Werner, who was granted the title of count as a reward for his services as an imperial judge, married as his second wife the widowed Amalia von Leuchtenberg. Since the landgraves of Leuchtenberg were considered equal to princes, Wilhelm Werner celebrated his climb up the social ladder with an ostentatious homecoming feast to which he invited "most of the nobility from the circles of the Black Forest and the Neckar" (*ZC* 3:50–51).

Statements in the *Zimmern Chronicle* about the goals of marriage always refer to the marriages of males; the assumption is that men must avoid marriages to social inferiors and should seek to marry up. In the handful of cases in which a nobleman married a nonnoble woman, his own status or his fitness to be head of the family might be called into question. The marriage of Schenk Wilhelm von Limpurg to Anna von der Laiter, whose family's status as high nobility was questionable, is adduced as evidence of his childishness and lack of judgment: "Much was said about this marriage.... Still, wine and great foolishness often bring couples together" (*ZC* 3:140). The alleged clandestine marriage of the profligate Count Christoph Friedrich von Zollern to his mistress Anna Rehlinger, a member of the urban patriciate, was part of the evidence of his unfitness adduced by his kinsmen when they forced him to resign the Zollern estates in 1535 (*ZC* 2:466). Similarly, a count of Isenburg who took as his fourth wife the widow of his forester was deposed as family head by his children from previous marriages.[11]

The marriage of a woman to a man of lower status had fewer long-range implications than that of a man to a woman of lower status. Since the lineage was traced only through the male line of descent, the woman's marriage would not directly affect the status of future members of the lineage. The upwardly mobile marriages seen as desirable for men were also downwardly mobile marriages for the women concerned, and the chronicler seems to accept such downward marriages of

---

[11]Schmidt, *Wetterauer Grafenverein,* 482; the woman was probably Isenburg's current or former concubine.

women as part of normal family strategy. He comments only on cases in which the woman made a personal choice to marry a partner who was greatly inferior in status.

Three such cases of women marrying husbands of lower status occurred among the daughters of Johann Werner I von Zimmern. Margarethe and Barbara entered into secret engagements with and ultimately married men of the lower nobility. They evidently feared that their older brother Johann Werner II would leave them unmarried in order to avoid burdening the newly recovered Zimmern estates with the cost of their dowries.[12] The chronicler expresses sympathy for both women and blames their brother for failing in his duty to arrange matches for his sisters with their social equals (*ZC* 2:160–63). In a more shocking violation of social norms, Katharina von Zimmern, the last abbess of the Frauenmünster in Zurich, married after the convent was closed by city authorities. Her husband Eberhard von Reischach, an ardent follower of Zwingli, belonged to a prominent family of the lower nobility. The chronicler denounces Katharina for her marriage "without her brother's knowledge and consent, to one not suitable or equal to her in ancestry and birth" and notes with satisfaction that her lawsuit for a dowry was denied. Surprisingly, the Catholic chronicler does not criticize on principle the marriage of a former nun (*ZC* 2:156–57). Other Catholic family heads were much more outspoken in their condemnation of such marriages. When Anna Westphalen, the former prioress of Lippstadter Kanonissenstift, married Heinrich von Schorlemer in 1585 without the consent of her family, her older brother Friedrich Westphalen not only refused her a dowry on the grounds that she had been adequately provided for when she entered the cloister, but also declared that he could not support her decision to leave the religious life and give herself over to "pleasures of the flesh."[13]

In the view of both sixteenth-century nobles and modern historians, marriages of either sons or daughters with members of the lower nobility could harm the marriage and career opportunities of their kin and even jeopardize the family's status in the high nobility.[14] However, there is little direct evidence that misalliances actually ruined the marriage opportunities of collateral relatives or more remote descendants. The counts of Waldeck in Wetterau were able to marry into princely families even though they made six marriages to their social inferiors (including one to a woman of burgher status) between 1450 and 1648.[15] The kinsmen of Johann

---

[12]This was not an unreasonable fear; in Normandy collateral male relatives (brothers and uncles) had a reputation for marrying women off cheaply or refusing consent to their marriages in order to save money on their dowries. Brunelle, "Dangerous Liaisons," 80.

[13]Hufschmidt, *Adelige Frauen im Weserraum*, 145.

[14]For example, Schmidt classes the Bickenbach and Rodenstein families as members of the lower nobility because of their poverty and their marriages into the lower nobility, *Wetterauer Grafenverein*, 482.

[15]Schmidt, *Wetterauer Grafenverein*, 482.

Werner II von Zimmern did not believe that his brothers would have difficulty marrying according to their rank if Johann Werner married a widow from the urban patriciate. Rather, they believed that the brothers could make better matches under these conditions than they could if the family's finances were not restored. The fiasco of three Zimmern women marrying their social inferiors in the 1520s did not damage the marriage prospects of their grandnieces, the daughters of Froben Christoph von Zimmern.

RANK OF SPOUSES IN THE SOUTHWEST GERMAN NOBILITY

Thus far the choice of spouses has been examined only in the cases of exceptional marriages that crossed the boundaries between different levels of the nobles. In order to see whether German nobles had a general strategy of marrying sons up and daughters down, it is also necessary to examine the normal marriages that took place within the high nobility. The sample of eleven families in the *Zimmern Chronicle* includes 441 first marriages that took place between 1400 and 1699. The status of the spouse (indicated by the title of the groom or of the bride's father at the date of the marriage) is known in 422 cases (194 marriages of men and 228 marriages of women).[16]

The rank of princes (*Fürsten*) includes dukes (*Herzoge*), margraves (*Markgrafen*), and landgraves (*Landgrafen*), and, in the seventeenth century, the newly created title of prince (*Fürst*). The high nobility (*Hochadel*) is divided into two categories: counts (*Grafen*) and *Schenken*/barons. The latter category includes both barons with the title *freie Herren* and certain ministerial families who were recognized as equal to barons even without being granted new titles. These families continued to bear titles reflecting their original offices at princely courts, such as *Schenk* (cupbearer) or *Truchsess* (steward). The category "other" includes the lower nobility and the burghers.

During the period from 1400 to 1699, significant changes took place in noble orders and titles. Although certain ministerial families had gained recognition as members of the high nobility during the course of the fifteenth century, the rise of the territorial princes at the end of the fifteenth century established new political and social barriers between the high and the lower nobility. Most of the lower nobility became subject to the authority of the princes, whereas the high nobility were subject only to the authority of the emperor. The high nobility sought to distance themselves further from the lower nobility by obtaining new titles from the emperor, either by service or by purchase. By the end of the sixteenth century, the

[16]The spouses whose rank could not be identified (seven wives and three husbands in first marriages) were chiefly members of foreign nobilities. In addition to the 441 first marriages included in this sample, there were eighty-five remarriages (forty-eight for men and thirty-seven for women). Spiess refers to "the confirmed tendency of widows to marry a lower-ranking partner in a second marriage" (*Familie und Verwandtschaft*, 405); however, no such trend was evident in this sample either for widows or for widowers.

title of count (*Graf*) had been granted to most of the surviving families of the old freeborn nobility, as well as to certain families of ministerial origin. In the seventeenth century, the elite counts, who had long considered themselves equal to princes, obtained the title of prince (*Fürst*) and joined the constitutional order of princes. A similar inflation of honors, in which rulers created new noble titles which "could be sold for cash, as a way of balancing budgets, or…given to men who were already powerful, to secure their gratitude and political allegiance," occurred in all major western European kingdoms in the sixteenth and especially in the seventeenth century.[17]

This inflation of honors over the course of the three centuries under discussion must be kept in mind in analyzing the status of marriage partners. In the fifteenth century, it was very rare for members of these eleven families of southwest German counts and barons to marry into princely families. However, by the end of the seventeenth century, three of the families (Fürstenberg, Oettingen, and Zollern) had obtained the rank of prince. For them, marriages into princely families were now marriages to social equals rather than to social superiors.

Marriages to spouses below the high nobility were rare for both sexes (see tables 5.1 and 5.2). Only seven such first marriages occurred in three centuries, even though one family, the Schenken of Erbach, was reputed to have achieved its rise into the high nobility through a strategy of marrying sons to women of higher rank and daughters to men from the lower nobility.[18] At least three of the seven marriages into the lower nobility (those of the three daughters of Johann Werner I von Zimmern) were the result of personal choice rather than of family arrangement. Family heads clearly tried to avoid matches for their daughters that were legally or socially considered misalliances. However, a comparison of the status of daughters' husbands to that of sons' wives shows that women were more likely than men to marry a spouse whose rank within the high nobility was lower than their own.

Over the entire period of 1400 to 1699, men in these eleven southwest German noble families were more likely than women to marry spouses from princely families, whereas women were more likely than men to marry spouses from families in the lowest rank of the high nobility (*Schenk* or baron). The majority of men married into families of counts or princes throughout the period; it was not until the sixteenth century that any women married princes and that the majority of women married counts rather than *Schenken* or barons.

---

[17]Dewald, *European Nobility,* 26–27. Dewald gives statistics on the expanding membership of the high nobilities of England, France, Naples, Spain, and Lower Austria. For a detailed analysis of the inflation of honors in England in the early seventeenth century, see Stone, *Crisis of the Aristocracy,* 59–60, 64–128.

[18]On the marriage strategy of the Erbachs, see Böhme, *Fränkische Reichsgrafenkollegium,* 60–64; and Spiess, *Familie und Verwandtschaft,* 348.

The greatest contrast between the status of daughters' husbands and that of sons' wives occurred in the late fifteenth century, when two-thirds of the daughters but only a quarter of the sons married spouses from the lowest rank of the high nobility. Since this was a period of economic hardship, families may have invested their resources in the one heir who was allowed to marry, while economizing on the marriages of daughters. The rise in dowry levels among the high nobility in this period also provided an incentive to marry off daughters to husbands of lower rank, who would be willing to accept smaller dowries.

During the first half of the sixteenth century, the number of men who married spouses from princely families increased dramatically, whereas no such increase occurred for women. Men in this sample were able to marry up into princely families while they were still only counts. With the exception of one case in the Oettingen family, women did not marry into princely families until their own fathers had obtained the rank of prince.

Greater equality between the status of daughters' husbands and of sons' wives is evident in the late sixteenth and early seventeenth centuries. In the late seventeenth century, family strategy seems to have reversed itself; more women than men married spouses from princely families, and more men than women married spouses from the lowest rank of the high nobility.

The observed changes in the late seventeenth century are difficult to explain. The increase in marriage of women into princely families is partly due to changes in titles. These women were the daughters of counts who had recently obtained the title of prince, and many of the princes they married were members of other families recently elevated to princely rank. However, there is no obvious reason why more men than women should have married spouses of lower rank during the economic depression of the late seventeenth century, reversing the pattern that prevailed during the depression of the fifteenth century. Since few other regional studies of marriage in the German nobility analyze the period from 1650 to 1699, it is not clear whether this apparent reversal of earlier strategy was due to factors unique to this sample or was part of a more general trend. Major changes in marriage patterns were taking place in the French and English nobilities in the late seventeenth and early eighteenth centuries; it is possible that long-term shifts were also under way in the German nobility.[19]

ELDEST VS. YOUNGER CHILDREN

Birth order had some effect on the rank of sons' wives, although even younger sons almost never married below the high nobility. Younger sons who received a smaller portion of the paternal estate or eventually succeeded to the estates of collateral relatives were less likely to marry daughters of princes and more likely to marry daughters of barons than were their elder brothers. However, they were just

[19]Hollingsworth, "Demography of the British Peerage," 9, 18–19.

Table 4.1: Rank of Spouses of Sons, 1400–1699

Date of marriage	Total (N)	Rank of wife's father							
		Prince		Count		Schenk or Baron		Other	
		(n)	(%)	(n)	(%)	(n)	(%)	(n)	(%)
1400–49	32	0	0	20	63	11	34	1	3
1450–99	26	2	8	20	77	4	15	0	0
1500–49	30	7	23	17	57	5	17	1	3
Subtotal 1400–1549	*88*	*9*	*10*	*57*	*65*	*20*	*23*	*2*	*2*
1550–99 (Catholic/Protestant)	46 (17/29)	2 (0/2)	4 (0/7)	32 (12/20)	70 (71/69)	11 (5/6)	24 (29/21)	1 (0/1)	2 (0/3)
1600–49 (Catholic/Protestant)	48 (29/19)	4 (3/1)	8 (10/5)	32 (19/13)	67 (66/68)	12 (7/5)	25 (24/26)	0 (0/0)	0 (0/0)
1650–99 (Catholic/Protestant)	48 (29/19)	9 (3/6)	19 (10/32)	30 (21/9)	63 (72/47)	9 (5/4)	19 (17/21)	0 (0/0)	0 (0/0)
Subtotal 1550–1699 (Catholic/Protestant)	*142 (75/67)*	*15 (6/9)*	*11 (8/13)*	*94 (52/42)*	*66 (69/63)*	*32 (17/15)*	*23 (23/22)*	*1 (0/1)*	*1 (0/1)*
Total 1400–1699	*230*	*24*	*10*	*151*	*66*	*52*	*23*	*3*	*1*

Note: All the sons and daughters of a German nobleman inherited their father's rank; a woman retained her father's surname and rank even after her marriage.

Table 4.2: Rank of Spouses of Daughters, 1400–1699

Date of marriage	Total (N)	Rank of husband							
		Prince		Count		Schenk or Baron		Other	
		(n)	(%)	(n)	(%)	(n)	(%)	(n)	(%)
1400–49	22	0	0	11	50	10	45	1	5
1450–99	23	0	0	8	35	15	65	0	0
1500–49	38	0	0	19	50	16	42	3	8
Subtotal 1400–1549	83	0	0	38	46	41	49	4	5
1550–99	54	1	2	33	61	20	37	0	0
(Catholic/Protestant)	(27/27)	(0/1)	(0/4)	(17/16)	(63/59)	(10/10)	(37/37)	(0/0)	(0/0)
1600–49	65	6	9	38	58	21	32	0	0
(Catholic/Protestant)	(43/22)	(4/2)	(9/9)	(22/16)	(51/73)	(17/4)	(40/18)	(0/0)	(0/0)
1650–99	50	13	26	32	64	5	10	0	0
(Catholic/Protestant)	(29/21)	(8/5)	(28/24)	(20/12)	(69/57)	(1/4)	(3/19)	(0/0)	(0/0)
Subtotal 1550–1699	169	20	12	103	61	46	27	0	0
(Catholic/Protestant)	(99/70)	(12/8)	(12/11)	(59/44)	(60/63)	(28/18)	(28/26)	(0/0)	(0/0)
Total 1400–1699	252	20	8	141	56	87	35	4	2

Note: All the sons and daughters of a German nobleman inherited their father's rank; a woman retained her father's surname and rank even after her marriage.

as likely to marry the daughters of counts as were their older brothers. Younger sons who did not inherit estates usually married late after a career in the military or in court service, and, not surprisingly, married at a lower social level than did heirs. Only one of the twenty nonheirs in this group married into a princely family, and the majority married daughters of barons.

Table 4.3: Marriages of Elder and Younger Children and Rank of Spouse

Men	N	Prince	Count	Schenk/ Baron	Other
		Rank of wife's father (%)			
Eldest heir	113	12	67	19	2
Younger heir	61	8	66	25	2
Nonheir	20	5	35	60	0

Women	N	Prince	Count	Schenk/ Baron	Other
		Rank of husband (%)			
Eldest daughter	97	6	64	27	2
Younger daughter	131	8	56	34	2

Birth order was less significant for daughters than for sons; younger daughters were just as likely as eldest daughters to marry into princely families. The husbands of second-born and even of third-born daughters were similar in rank to those of eldest daughters. However, in large sibling groups of four or more daughters, the later-born daughters were more likely than their elder sisters to marry barons rather than counts.

CATHOLIC AND PROTESTANT MARRIAGE STRATEGIES

Did the Protestant Reformation affect the rank of spouses, since a higher proportion of sons and daughters married in Protestant families? The first generation of Protestant counts and barons in southwest Germany were able to marry off almost all of their children, both sons and daughters. After the first generation, the gap between the percentage of daughters marrying and the percentage of sons marrying was consistently wider among Protestants than among Catholics. The continued high rate of marriage for German Protestant noblewomen in the seventeenth century stands in sharp contrast to the decline in marriage rates for women in other Protestant nobilities in this period.[20] Under these circumstances, one

[20]In the British peerage, unmarried daughters made up only 5 percent of all daughters born in the second half of the sixteenth century, but 15 percent of those born in the first half of the seventeenth century, and 20 percent of those born in the second half of the seventeenth century. A third of

might expect to find more Protestant women than Catholic women being forced to settle for husbands of lower social rank than their own. However, this does not appear to be the case: the trend in the period from 1550 to 1699 was toward greater equality in rank between daughters' husbands and sons' wives, and this held true for both Protestants and Catholics.

COMPARISONS TO OTHER GERMAN NOBLES

Studies of the Franconian high nobility find that counts and barons in that region were highly endogamous. More than 80 percent of their marriages were to other families of the nonprincely high nobility, and marriages outside their own order were more likely to be to higher-ranking than to lower-ranking families.[21] The extremely low number of marriages below the high nobility in the eleven southwest German families is consistent with Schmidt's finding that the lower nobility and bourgeoisie "played practically no role" in the marriage strategy of the counts and barons of Wetterau in the sixteenth century.[22] Although Ernst Böhme finds a higher proportion of marriages of counts and barons into families below the high nobility, most of these marriages took place within one family, the Schwarzenbergs, who had only recently been elevated from the rank of knight to baron. Their continued intermarriage with families of the lower nobility may indicate that they were still not fully accepted as equals by the old high nobility.[23]

Table 4.4: Social Status of Spouses of Counts and Barons in Regional Studies

Region	Date	N	Princes (%)	Counts and Barons (%)	Lower nobility (%)	Burghers (%)
Mainz[a]	1200–1500	630	6.3	87.5	6.2	0
Franconia[b]	1475–1525	58	6.9	70.1	18.9	3.4
Wetterau[c]	1450–1648	499	12.4	83.5	3.6	0.4
Southwest Germany	1400–1699	482	9.1	89.4	0.8	0.6

[a]Spiess, *Familie und Verwandtschaft*, 398.
[b]Böhme, *Fränkische Reichsgrafkollegium*, 12–14.
[c]Schmidt, *Wetterauer Grafenverein*, 481.

---

the daughters of the Dutch *Ridderscap* in the late sixteenth and early seventeenth centuries remained single. Hollingsworth, "Demography of the British Peerage," 20; and Nierop, *Nobility of Holland*, 54.

[21]Spiess, *Familie und Verwandtschaft*, 398; and Schmidt, *Wetterauer Grafenverein*, 481, table 5.

[22]Schmidt, *Wetterauer Grafenverein*, 481–82.

[23]Böhme, *Fränkische Reichsgrafenkollegium*, 12–14. Similarly, Carl suggests that a significant percentage of Swabian counts and barons married into families of the lower nobility. He argues that political cooperation between members of the high nobility and the lower nobility in the Swabian League around 1500 was due to intermarriage between families of the two orders. *Schwäbische Bund*, 139–40. However, his argument rests almost entirely on the marriages of one family, the Truchsessen von Waldburg, who were in the process of rising from the lower to the high nobility.

All studies of the marriage patterns of German nobles in the High Middle Ages and the early modern period conclude that marriages between different levels of the nobility were usually hypogamous.

Freed calls marriages of men from Salzburg ministerial families to women of free noble status "fairly common" in the twelfth century, whereas marriages between noblemen and ministerial women were rare. In the thirteenth century, ministerials were increasingly forced to intermarry with their social inferiors, the knights, and "[o]nce again, it was predominantly ministerial women, like the noblewomen before them, who married downward."[24]

Kurt Andermann's and Peter Müller's studies of the lower nobility of the Palatinate and of Alsace during the late Middle Ages find that the only cases of intermarriage between the lower and the high nobility involved men marrying wives of higher rank. Müller states that in the Fleckenheim family of Alsace, "the wives of sons were generally from more prominent families than the husbands of daughters."[25]

Spiess questions whether counts and barons of the Mainz region actually paid greater attention to rank in choosing wives for sons than husbands for daughters. Although sons were slightly more likely than daughters to marry into princely families and less likely than daughters to marry into families of the lower nobility, he does not regard the difference as significant.[26] He also doubts that counts and barons deliberately sought spouses of lower status for their daughters than for their sons for economic reasons, such as achieving a "positive balance of payments" in dowries given and received. Nevertheless, his evidence shows that in ten of fifteen families, the average value of dowries received from sons' wives was higher than the average value of dowries given to daughters. This indicates that the wives of sons were usually of greater wealth and higher status than the husbands of daughters, even when both partners were members of the high nobility.[27]

In studies extending into the sixteenth and seventeenth centuries, Böhme states that between 1475 and 1525 the counts of Franconia were "more conscious of rank in choosing marriage partners for sons than in giving away daughters." He characterizes downwardly mobile marriages for daughters as "marriages for financial support" (*Versorgungsheiraten*), which were less significant for the family than

[24]Freed, *Noble Bondsmen*, 99–100, 139–40.
[25]Andermann, *Pfälzischen Niederadels*, 217–18; and Müller, *Die Herren von Fleckenstein*, 320.
[26]Between 1200 and 1500, 8.7 percent of sons and 5.8 percent of daughters of counts and barons married into princely families, while 6.9 percent of sons and 7.2 percent of daughters married into families of lower nobility. Spiess, *Familie und Verwandtschaft*, 400. A pattern of marrying daughters down is more clearly evident among imperial princes in the same period: only 23.5 percent of sons of princes as compared to 39.5 percent of daughters of princes married children of counts and barons. Spiess, "Das Konnubium der Reichsfürsten im Spätmittelalter."
[27]Spiess, *Familie und Verwandtschaft*, 364–65. For dowries given and received by individual families, see ibid., 344–60; and graph 32, 365.

the marriages of sons.[28] Schmidt's study of the counts of Wetterau also finds that throughout the period 1450 to 1648, "it was primarily sons who married partners from princely houses."[29]

Freed attributes this hypogamous marriage pattern to the legal disabilities attached to unequal marriages between free nobles and unfree ministerials, and Spiess attributes it to the dowry system of the medieval German nobility. However, neither of these factors can explain the existence of the pattern in different German regions for several centuries. Hypogamy could not have been caused originally by the German dowry system, since it existed in Salzburg even before dowry replaced brideprice. The pattern also could not be due solely to the legal consequences of inequality of birth, since it persisted long after ministerials ceased to be unfree and was found even in marriages within the high nobility, which were not legally unequal. While a pattern of marrying sons up and daughters down was encouraged by the rigidity of the German definition of nobility and penalties for inequality of birth, it was not caused by uniquely German factors.

COMPARISONS TO OTHER EUROPEAN ELITES

A surplus of marriages of women over marriages of men, which is consistently found among late medieval and early modern German nobles, also occurred in other European elites. Molho has suggested that in the Florentine patriciate, this pattern is associated with a hypogamous marriage strategy: "if a larger number of marriageable men than women ended up not marrying, men would be in a better position to marry well."[30] Those men who did marry would be able to raise the status of their lineages by marrying women of rank and wealth greater than their own, since not all women could find spouses of their own rank.

Writers on the French and English aristocracies from the sixteenth to the eighteenth century note that French or English noblemen were more willing than German noblemen to marry the daughters of lawyers and merchants.[31] However, much of the evidence on ranks of spouses among European nobilities comes from the late seventeenth and eighteenth centuries, and may not be applicable to earlier periods. Several of the studies summarized by Cooper show a marked discrepancy between the number of men and the number of women remaining unmarried. In these studies, the ones in which a higher number of daughters than of sons remained unmarried (consistent with a hypergamous marriage strategy) dated from the later seventeenth and eighteenth century, whereas those in which a higher number of sons than daughters remained unmarried (consistent with a hypogamous marriage strategy) dated from the sixteenth and seventeenth

---

[28]Böhme, *Fränkische Reichsgrafenkollegium,* 13.

[29]Schmidt, *Wetterauer Grafenverein,* 484.

[30]Molho, *Marriage Alliance,* 290–91.

[31]Nassiet, "Réseaux de parenté," 119; Le Roy Ladurie and Fitou, "Hypergamie féminine," 139, 141.

centuries.[32] This suggests that a hypogamous marriage strategy was not uniquely German and that it had been more widespread in European elites in earlier periods than it was toward the end of the seventeenth century.

The most definitive evidence of hypogamy in late medieval and early modern European elites is that of Florence in the fifteenth century. David Herlihy and Christiane Klapisch-Zuber state that the *castato* (tax assessment) of 1427 verifies the "assumption that women tended to marry down while men married up." In a large majority of the marriages between members of the wealthiest families, the bride's family was wealthier than the groom's family.[33] Molho finds a similar pattern in his study of marriages in the Florentine ruling class in the fifteenth and early sixteenth century, which analyzes the social status of marriage partners rather than merely their wealth.[34]

However, studies of Italian elites in the sixteenth and seventeenth centuries suggest an increasing trend toward hypergamy. According to Molho, the ruling class of Florence became more endogamous in the sixteenth century, and it therefore became more difficult for lineages below the ruling class to marry either daughters or sons into more distinguished families. The dramatic increase in the sixteenth century in the number of girls from ruling-class families who entered convents suggests that these families increasingly desired to keep surplus daughters unmarried rather than marry them to their social inferiors.[35] Sperling describes a similar pattern in Venice between 1550 and 1650: increased endogamy for patrician women and a tendency to place daughters in convents rather than marry them to husbands of lower status. In Venice, unlike Florence, this pattern was associated with an increase in hypergamous marriages for men of the patrician class: more patrician men married wives of lower status who brought large dowries.[36]

In his pioneering studies of the structure of the French nobility in the middle ages, Duby notes that the mother's lineage was often more prestigious than the father's and concludes that the normal marriage strategy was one in which *new men* confirmed their status by marrying women from established noble families. Duby links this hypogamous pattern to increasingly strict inheritance policies, which forced younger sons to forgo marriage unless they could find "a good heiress." A strategy of "marrying all the daughters, keeping all the sons but the eldest unmarried, resulted in the supply of women greatly exceeding the demand

---

[32]Cases in which a higher percentage of sons than of daughters remained unmarried include the Florentine patriciate between 1500 and 1700 (Cooper, "Patterns of Inheritance and Settlement," 287), British peers' children born between 1575 and 1625 (ibid., 290), and Castilian noble families in the sixteenth century (ibid., 291). Cases in which a higher percentage of daughters than sons remained unmarried include the nobility of Toulouse born between 1700 and 1760, British peers' children born between 1625 and 1825 (ibid., 290) and the Genevan elite born between 1650 and 1749 (ibid., 304).

[33]Herlihy and Klapisch-Zuber, *Tuscans and Their Families*, 227–28.

[34]Molho, *Marriage Alliance*, 291.

[35]Molho, *Marriage Alliance*, 306–7, 326.

[36]Sperling, *Convents and the Body Politic*, 20–21.

on…the marriage market…. This again reinforces the structure of noble societies, where generally the wife comes from a kin group richer and more glorious than that of her husband."[37] This medieval French pattern is similar to that practiced by southwest German nobles from the fifteenth to the late seventeenth centuries.

According to Michel Nassiet, "the hypogamy of daughters is the model to which half the marriages of daughters appear to conform" in the fifteenth century, and hypogamy remained the dominant pattern in the French nobility until at least the middle of the sixteenth century.[38] Nassiet states that the usual strategy of noble families was to marry off at least one daughter (usually the eldest) within her own social group, but to marry some of the younger daughters down in social status. In the seventeenth century, this strategy changed to one of stricter endogamy, in which French noble families married off only one daughter per generation and placed a larger number of daughters in the church.[39] Emmanuel Le Roy Ladurie and Jean-François Fitou demonstrate that by the end of the seventeenth century, hypergamy was the dominant pattern among the highest nobility at the court of Versailles.[40] However, hypogamy persisted among the provincial nobility; studies by James B. Wood and Donna Bohanon show that even in the seventeenth century, recently ennobled men in Bayeux and Aix-en Provence were still able to marry wives from the older nobility.[41]

Scholars studying the noble family in the Iberian peninsula also assume that hypogamous marriage was the norm in the High Middle Ages; they associate this pattern with feudal values and attribute its origins to a brideprice system. James Casey describes the Cid as having "built up his following by marrying off the ladies of his household to his trusty captains, a downward movement of brides fairly typical of early feudal society, where no dowry was given and where the main emphasis was on acquiring followers."[42] Even after the adoption of a dowry system, Spanish and Portuguese nobles married off a very high percentage of both sons and daughters in the late Middle Ages.[43]

---

[37]Duby, "Le mariage dans la société du haut moyen âge," 31; and Duby, "Structure de parenté et noblesse dans la France du Nord," 276.

[38]Nassiet, *Parenté, noblesse et états dynastiques,* 136–56, 322.

[39]Nassiet, "Réseaux de parenté," 115,119; and Nassiet, *Parenté, noblesse et états dynastiques,* 148.

[40]Le Roy Ladurie and Fitou classify 1366 marriages mentioned in the *Memoirs of Saint-Simon* as follows: 54 percent endogamous, 28 percent hypergamous (chiefly daughters of the nobility of the robe marrying men from the nobility of the sword), and only 10 percent of the marriages as hypogamous (most of them involving higher and lower ranks within the nobility of the sword). They state that hypergamy was "without doubt, the most striking of marriage forms other than endogamy." "Hypergamie féminine," 139, 141.

[41]Wood, "Endogamy and Mésalliance," 375–92; and Bohanan, "Matrimonial Strategies," 504–6.

[42]Casey, *History of the Family,* 81. See also Beceiro Pita and Córdoba de la Llave, *Parentesco, poder y mentalidad,* 143–45, citing principally studies of Catalonia.

[43]On the high percentage of children who married in Iberian nobilities, see Beceiro Pita and Córdoba de la Llave, *Parentesco, poder y mentalidad,* 162; Gerbet, *Noblesse dans le royaume de Castille,*

In the sixteenth century, the Iberian nobilities severely restricted marriages, often choosing to place daughters in convents rather than marry them to their social inferiors.[44] Casey associates this trend toward endogamy with dowry inflation which made it increasingly attractive to marry sons to wealthy wives of lower social status.[45] However, this trend may have affected only the highest levels of the nobility. James L. Boone III Boone says of the Portuguese high nobility born between 1380 and 1580 that "at the lower end of the social scale, more women marry than men; at the top, more men than women."[46] This suggests that the highest ranks (the titleholders or grandees) may have practiced a hypergamous marriage strategy while other ranks continued to practice a hypogamous strategy.

Even in the middle of the seventeenth century, Spanish and Portuguese nobles were more reluctant than those of France and England to "manure their fields" by marrying richly dowered daughters of merchants or financiers. The author of a handbook on marriage in 1651 endorsed values consistent with a hypogamous marriage system when he advised noblemen to economize on dowries by recruiting as sons-in-law young men of lower social rank who "stood well at court or were very wealthy or were eminent in arms or letters."[47]

Even the British aristocracy, which is usually viewed as the exemplar of a hypergamous system, underwent major changes in marriage patterns between the late sixteenth and the early eighteenth century. In his classic demographic study of the British peerage, Hollingsworth speaks of a revolution in marriage patterns among those born at the end of the seventeenth century and marrying around 1720. Among peers' children born between 1550 and 1699, daughters were more likely to marry than sons, and daughters were more likely than sons to marry spouses whose fathers were not peers. It was only after the revolution that the pattern shifted: women became less likely to marry than men, and more likely than men to marry within their own social class.[48] Until the eighteenth century, then, hypogamy was actually a more common strategy among British nobles than was hypergamy. This pattern has attracted little attention, however, since noblewomen married down only into the gentry. Unlike sons of peers, daughters of peers did not marry outside the landed elite; their numerous marriages downward did not excite as much comment as did the rare but conspicuous marriages of noblemen to daughters of wealthy merchants.[49] A similar system in which men (but not

166; and Boone, "Parental Investment and Elite Family Structure," 865.

[44]Beceiro Pita and Córdoba de la Llave, *Parentesco, poder y mentalidad,* 148.

[45]Casey, *History of the Family,* 82–83.

[46]Boone, "Parental Investment and Elite Family Structure," 867.

[47]Casey, *History of the Family,* 84. The handbook by Francisco Manuel de Mello is quoted in Casey, *Early Modern Spain,* 147.

[48]Hollingsworth, "Demography of the British Peerage," 9, 18–19.

[49]On marriages of daughters, see Stone, *Crisis of the Aristocracy,* 627. Between 1540 and 1660,

women) of the high aristocracy could marry down into the nobility of the robe or even into the bourgeoisie prevailed among the court aristocracy in France in the late seventeenth century.[50]

Thus the marriage strategy of the German nobility, unusual though it was for European elites in 1700, was typical among European elites of the Middle Ages and the sixteenth century. Hypogamy appears to have been the preferred strategy for Italian, French, and Iberian elites until at least the sixteenth or early seventeenth century. Even in the English peerage, daughters were more likely than sons to marry down until the eighteenth century.

There is therefore no need to seek uniquely German causes for the origin of this hypogamous marriage strategy; however, the unique German definition of nobility by quarters, which placed high barriers against intermarriage between different social groups, probably helped to preserve this pattern even after hypergamy became more common in other European elites. Even at the end of the seventeenth century, German nobles continued to perceive the marriage of a nobleman to a woman of lower status as compromising the status of the children of the marriage. This was true even when such marriages were not legally unequal. Mme. Palatine, the German sister-in-law of Louis XIV, denounced the marriages of high-ranking courtiers at Versailles to noblewomen of lower rank much more harshly than did the French memoirist, the Duc de Saint-Simon. Unlike Saint-Simon, who "pays attention only to the paternal line, and considers the children born of these unions as full members of the paternal group," Mme. Palatine "demonstrates a typically Germanic noble prejudice.... Madame pays attention to both sides of the genealogical tree, paternal and maternal. In the case of an ill-matched marriage, Saint-Simon rages, but forgets it after the second generation, whereas Mme. Palatine condemns it definitively."[51]

This view that maternal status affected the status of the children of the marriage helped to maintain a rigid dowry structure that discouraged hypergamy even when other elites were adopting this strategy under the pressure of dowry inflation. Studies of elite marriages in Italy, France, England, and Spain have found that dramatic increases in dowry levels during the late sixteenth and early seventeenth century were associated with an increase in the proportion of marriages of elite men to wives of lower social status.[52] No such dramatic dowry inflation has been demonstrated in the German nobility in this period, and there was

---

about 9 percent of the marriages of British peers were to wives from outside the landed classes (daughters of lawyers, merchants, and royal officials). Ibid., 628–32 and app. 30, 789.

[50]Le Roy Ladurie and Fitou, "Hypergamie féminine," 146; and Labutat, *Ducs et pairs,* 189.

[51]Le Roy Ladurie and Fitou, "Hypergamie féminine," 145.

[52]Studies associating hypergamy with higher dowry levels in Rouen, England, and Barcelona are cited in Molho, *Marriage Alliance,* 325. See also, on Venice, Sperling, *Convents and the Body Politic,* 20–21; and, on Spain, Casey, *History of the Family,* 82–83.

no increase in marriages of counts and barons to wives beneath the high nobility. In their hypogamous marriage strategy as well as in their partible inheritance strategy, German nobles were conservative. They preserved strategies that had once been dominant among medieval European elites but were becoming obsolete in other aristocracies in the early modern era.

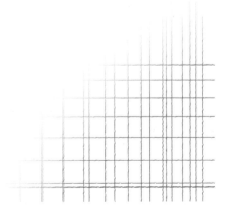

Part II Marriage

CHAPTER 5

Choice of Marriage Partners

In the aristocratic or lay model of marriage, marriage was an alliance between two families, based on pragmatic considerations. In the ecclesiastical model, on the other hand, marriage was a union of two individuals, formed by their mutual consent and based on affection. The persistence of the lay model even into the eighteenth and nineteenth centuries is well documented among European elites. Stone's theory of the stages of development of the English family between 1500 and 1800, which has had great influence on discussions of the European noble family, holds that little change in this model occurred before 1650: "Marriage among property-owning classes ... was a collective decision of family and kin, not an individual one. ... Property and power were the predominant issues which governed negotiations in a society so acutely conscious of status and hierarchy," and it was not until the mid-seventeenth century that "most parents [in the aristocracy] ... at last admitted the need not merely for acquiescence but also for 'affection.'"[1]

However, scholars have increasingly questioned the conventional wisdon that the European family before the mid-seventeenth century was an authoritarian institution in which marriages were arranged for purely pragmatic economic or political purposes. It is now clear that at all levels below the aristocracy, parents did not play such a dominant role in the choice of marriage partners, and that personal preference was a significant factor.[2] Children in German urban elites actively participated in their own marriage negotiations in the late fifteenth century. By the early sixteenth century, they demanded that the potential for affection

---

[1]Stone, *Family, Sex and Marriage,* 87; Stone, *Crisis of the Aristocracy,* 597. However, younger sons in the English aristocracy and gentry, who were not expected to inherit the estate, did enjoy more freedom of choice than did heirs. Stone, *Crisis of the Aristocracy,* 599; and Heal and Holmes, *Gentry in England and Wales,* 60.

[2]For a summary of this argument, see Watt, *Making of Modern Marriage,* 5–10.

be considered in addition to other criteria for marriage, and they exercised the power to veto parental choices when this potential was absent.[3]

European landed elites were slower than urban ones to accord children these powers. The higher the rank of the family, the stronger the degree of parental control. In the sixteenth century, arrangement of marriages by the lineage or the parents "does not seem invariably, or even generally, to have been the case" among the Dutch gentry, but it remained the norm in the high aristocracy throughout western Europe.[4] Nevertheless, some exceptional cases in the French and Castilian aristocracies in the fifteenth and early sixteenth centuries show children playing a role in choosing their spouses or resisting plans made by their parents, possibly due to the influence of the literature of courtly love.[5] A few marriage contracts of French nobles in the late fifteenth century mention personal affection between the potential spouses.[6]

By the mid-sixteenth century, children of French and English nobles had the opportunity to meet their potential spouses before the marriage contract was concluded, although this practice was apparently not widespread in the Castilian aristocracy.[7] In the late sixteenth and seventeenth centuries such "brief and formal encounters" formed the basis of acceptance or refusal of a potential spouse among the English aristocracy; however, "the pair were till often more or less strangers to each other, for it was quite usual for them to have been permitted no more than a few hours in each other's company before the marriage."[8] Recent scholarship has taken a more optimistic view than Stone did of marriage in the English aristocracy; even before 1550, there was some room for personal affection and free choice of partners, and daughters as well as sons had the power to veto partners they disliked.[9] Many sixteenth-century English peers in their testaments cautioned

---

[3]Ozment, *When Fathers Ruled,* 72–80; Ozment, *Magdalena and Balthasar,* 27–43; and Beer, *Eltern und Kinder,* 86–96.

[4]Marshall, *Dutch Gentry,* 4. On the practices in European high aristocracies, see Beceiro Pita and Córdoba de la Llave, *Parentesco, poder et mentalidad,* 128–35; Constant, *La noblesse française,* 117, 121; Grimmer, *La femme et le bâtard,* 110–11; Caron, *La noblesse dans le duché de Bourgogne,* 212; and Nassiet, *Parenté, noblesse et états dynastiques,* 150.

[5]Beceiro Pita and Córdoba de la Llave, *Parentesco, poder et mentalidad,* 361; and Constant, *La noblesse française,* 126.

[6]Nassiet, *Parenté, noblesse et états dynastiques,* 150; and Caron, *Noblesse dans le duché de Bourgogne,* 212.

[7]Nassiet, *Parenté, noblesse et états dynastiques,* 156; Caron, *Noblesse en le duché de Bourgogne,* 212; Grimmer, *Le femme et la bâtard,* 127; and Stone, *Crisis of the Aristocracy,* 649–50. However, Beceiro Pita and Córdoba de la Llave (*Parentesco, poder et mentalidad,* 361) state that a literary account of a hero "meeting his future wife before betrothal with the approval of both their families does not correspond to the marriage contracts of the [Castilian] oligarchy but could happen among servants or at the royal court."

[8]Stone, *Crisis of the Aristocracy,* 649–50.

[9]Rosenthal, "Aristocratic Marriage and the English Peerage," 192; and Harris, *English Aristocratic Women,* 55–56.

executors against forcing their daughters into marriages to which the women objected.[10]

PARENTAL CONTROL AND PERSONAL PREFERENCE

In the absence of letters such as are available for patrician families, knowledge of marriage among southwest German nobles in the late Middle Ages must be derived largely from legal documents. Statements about the motives for marriage in these documents are largely formulaic and give little insight into personal relationships. Discussions of fourteenth- and fifteenth-century marriages in the *Zimmern Chronicle* usually state only that the parents "married" or "arranged the marriage of" their children: in 1372, "Anna [daughter of Werner von Zimmern] was married by her father to Baron Ulrich von Schwarzenberg"(*ZC* 1:184) and around 1400, Johann III "married his daughter Anna" to Count Eberhard von Werdenberg (*ZC* 1:205). Of the marriages of Johann IV in 1418 and Johann Werner I in 1474, the chronicle states in each case that "the marriage was arranged by his father" (*ZC* 1:234, 423), while the marriages of Verena (fl. 1439–55) and Anna (fl. 1439, d. 1492) were "arranged by their brother Werner"(*ZC* 1:318). In none of these cases is there any hint that the son or daughter was personally involved in the process of choosing the spouse, nor is there any hint that their desires conflicted with those of the family head.[11]

The same impression of complete parental control is given in the fifteenth-century documents analyzed by Spiess, but there are also some indications of opposition. According to canon law, the consent of the bride and groom was necessary for a valid marriage and a marriage contracted under duress was invalid. Nevertheless, "parents were determined not to let the child wreck carefully laid family plans."[12] Although parents usually relied on persuasion, secular law gave them the right to punish undutiful children who married without familial consent. Late medieval German law codes contained provisions denying inheritance rights to undutiful children or imposing heavy fines on them. According to the fourteenth-century *Schwabenspiegel*, a daughter who married without the consent of the head of her family was to be deprived of her inheritance if she was under twenty-five years old. The *Carolina* or imperial criminal law code of 1532 provided that the daughter was to be "kept enclosed" (under house arrest) and all her property confiscated.[13] Some princely families actually kept undutiful daughters under

---

[10]Harris, *English Aristocratic Women*, 58–89.

[11]The only exception in the fifteenth century is Werner VIII (fl. 1440–d. 1483), for which the chronicle does not rely on legal documents. His marriage to Anna von Kirchberg is depicted as the result of romantic love. However, this may be a literary device of the chronicler's.

[12]Spiess, *Familie und Verwandtschaft*, 28–29.

[13]Ellrichshausen, *Die uneheliche Mutterschaft*, 24n57. For other statutes and local customaries providing for disinheritance or banishment in cases of marriages of minors without parental consent, see Harrington, *Reordering Marriage and Society*, 173–74.

house arrest in the fifteenth century: Margravine Agnes von Baden was imprisoned for thirty-seven years for opposing her brothers' plans for her remarriage,
and the brothers of Margravine Barbara von Württemberg imprisoned her for
promising marriage to a man of lower rank.[14]

The *Zimmern Chronicle* suggests that the counts and barons of southwest
Germany did not resort to such extreme measures in the fifteenth and early sixteenth centuries. Although family heads did use their power of house arrest to
punish female kin for sex outside of marriage, the chronicle does not mention any
such punishments for promising marriage to inappropriate suitors or for resisting
marriages arranged by their family. Surprisingly, it describes several instances in
which daughters married without familial consent but nevertheless secured their
dowries. This reluctance to invoke financial penalties suggests that the degree of
parental control was decreasing in the early sixteenth century among southwest
German counts and barons.[15]

Sons were able to exercise a greater degree of independence than daughters
since they usually did not marry until their midtwenties. If they were minors, they
had greater independence if their fathers were dead: "Guardians were less successful than parents or siblings in enforcing obedience, at least from males."[16] The
majority of southwest German counts and barons were able to negotiate their own
marriages, since their fathers were already dead. In the eleven families of southwest German counts and barons, 70 percent of the ever-married men born
between 1400 and 1699 did not marry until after their father's death; this percent
is similar to that found by Mitterauer for Austrian nobles.[17] In other European
nobilities, French noblemen were also likely to marry after their father's death,
since their average age at first marriage was high (29.5 years in the sixteenth century).[18] In contrast, English aristocrats in the sixteenth and early seventeenth centuries tried to marry off their heirs in their own lifetime in order to avoid
wardship. An eldest son could choose his own wife if he was over twenty-one
years of age and still single at his father's death, but Stone implies that this was

[14]Spiess, *Familie und Verwandtschaft,* 29.

[15]Parents below the level of princes seem to have been reluctant to invoke strong sanctions.
Spiess describes a case in 1499 in which Countess Agnes von Eppstein-Münzenberg was given only a
token dowry when she made a secret marriage in order to avoid a marriage arranged by her father.
Nevertheless, Agnes was later able to negotiate a larger settlement described as her inheritance rather
than her dowry. *Familie und Verwandtschaft,* 209. Among commoners, financial punishments for
undutiful children became less common in the sixteenth century as "more and more [German]
municipal and territorial codes restricted the parents' right to disinherit children in unapproved marriages." Harrington, *Reordering Marriage and Society,* 198.

[16]Spiess, *Familie und Verwandtschaft,* 30–31.

[17]In the period from the fifteenth to the nineteenth century, three-quarters of all the noblemen
in Mitterauer's study married after the death of their fathers. "Zur Frage des Heiratsverhaltens," 185.

[18]Nassiet, *Parenté, noblesse et états dynastiques,* 43, and Nassiet, *Noblesse et pauvreté,* 272–73.

exceptional. Younger sons, who were not heirs, were more likely to be able to negotiate their own marriages.[19]

Daughters always remained under the authority of the male family head (father, brother, or guardian), so their options were more limited. Harris states that in the English aristocracy, "the ubiquity of marriages arranged by parents for economic and political reasons does not mean that they were indifferent to their daughters' happiness or always unresponsive to their wishes."[20] The same may be true of German noble parents, but there is little direct evidence of the daughters' views in the era of the *Zimmern Chronicle*. In the late sixteenth and seventeenth centuries, letters and diaries allow more insight into their feelings. Thirty years after the chronicle was written, Landdrost Kaspar von Fürstenberg noted the reaction of his daughter Goda (1574–1614) to the marriage to Bernd von Heiden that had already been arranged for her by her family: "When he announced to her 'my wishes and those of her friends [that is, kin],' he found only 'maidenly shame and sadness on her part,' but no strongly marked antipathy; therefore the marriage took place."[21] Goda's lack of enthusiasm for the match was not sufficient reason to call it off; however, her father implies that he would not have forced her into the match if she had expressed a strong aversion to her potential husband.

Daughters of German counts and barons generally accepted their parents' choice of spouse for the same reasons that daughters did so in other European aristocracies. First, they had been brought up to regard marriage as the most desirable vocation for women, and to accept parental authority. They had to accept their parents' choice of marriage partner in order to be allowed to marry at all. Second, daughters needed a large dowry to maintain their status, and the amount of the dowry was dependent on the goodwill of the parents. A marriage for love might not be attractive if it involved sacrificing one's social status and standard of living. Third, daughters married at a young age and had few opportunities to meet young men on their own unless they were sent to court or to a great noble household. Finally—and this consideration applied to sons as well as daughters—"parents and children shared the same view of the purpose of noble marriage and the criteria for choosing partners."[22]

Although women generally accepted their family's candidate in their first marriage, they had greater opportunity to express their personal preference when they were widowed and therefore financially independent. Some widows allowed

---

[19]Stone, *Crisis of the Aristocracy*, 599, 609.

[20]Harris, *English Aristocratic Women*, 55.

[21]Hufschmidt, *Adelige Frauen im Weserraum*, 140.

[22]Spiess, *Familie und Verwandtschaft*, 35. See also, Harris, *English Aristocratic Women*, 56; and Beceiro Pita and Córdoba de la Llave, *Parentesco, poder y mentalidad*, 134. In addition to the opportunities available at court or in a great household, some German noblewomen managed to meet suitors on their own during their education in a cloister far from parental supervision. Hufschmidt, *Adelige Frauen im Weserraum*, 144–45.

themselves to be persuaded by the family council to make another marriage that furthered the interests of their natal or marital families. Countess Magdalena von Oettingen married a cousin of her first husband, Count Ulrich VII von Montfort, to ensure that Ulrich's estates remained in the Montfort family.[23] In his will of 1480, Count Philipp von Eppstein-Königstein "took into account the possibility that his widow would be ordered by her relatives to remarry, and that she would have to obey this demand."[24] However, other widows now felt free to resist familial pressure: in 1525, Countess Katharina von Stolberg (the widow of a count of Wertheim) rejected her father's proposal that she marry Count Ludwig von Löwenstein. Her father then offered Löwenstein her younger sister instead, saying "I have another daughter, sixteen years old, that I have control over." The unmarried daughter could be compelled to accept her father's choice, whereas the widow could not.[25]

It was common in the late Middle Ages for southwest German counts and barons to arrange marriages for children who were still under the canonical age of marriage (twelve years for females and fourteen years for males). Several such marriage contracts for minor children were negotiated in the Swabian house of Montfort in the late fifteenth century. The heiress Magdalena von Oettingen was betrothed to Ulrich VII von Montfort-Tettnang in 1485, when she was ten years old; her daughter Ursula "was betrothed in the very year of her birth [1497] to Georg III von Waldburg" (later called Peasant George, who would have been nine or ten years old at the time). In 1476, when Count Hugo XVII von Montfort-Bregenz was fourteen years old, he was betrothed to a daughter of Count Hugo XIII of Montfort-Tettnang, who was still under age.[26]

As these examples indicate, such marriages of minors were often arranged for dynastic reasons (for example, to reunite two lines of the family) or to secure the wealth of an heiress. Regarding Helene von Zollern and Truchsess Johann von Waldburg, who were betrothed in 1468 but not married until sixteen years later, Ulshöfer remarks, "it is evident from this that even men could be forced into marriage."[27] However, promises of future marriage by minors could be undone without serious legal consequences,[28] and two of the contracts mentioned above never resulted in a marriage. If the groom's father died before both parties reached the canonical age of marriage, it was easy for the newly independent young man to break the contract with his child bride. Karl Heinz Burmeister

[23] Burmeister, *Grafen von Montfort,* 284.

[24] Spiess, *Familie und Verwandtschaft,* 183, 183n190.

[25] Spiess, *Familie und Verwandtschaft,* 30, 30n38. The widowed older sister would have been the more desirable match, since she would bring not only her dowry but her widow's pension from her first marriage.

[26] Burmeister, *Grafen von Montfort,* 279, 281, 290.

[27] Ulshöfer, *Hausrecht der Grafen von Zollern,* 51.

[28] Spiess, *Familie und Verwandtschaft,* 114.

remarks that "possibly after the death of his father in 1482, Count Hugo [XVII von Montfort] no longer felt himself bound by this contract."[29] It is noteworthy that when Count Christoph von Werdenberg wanted to make a dynastic alliance in 1509 to end the feud between the Werdenberg and Zimmern families, he did not offer Johann Werner II a match with his daughter Anna, who was still under age. Instead, he offered him one of his two adolescent nieces, Katharina and Anna von Erbach, the daughters of his sister Elisabeth von Werdenberg. Possibly Christoph felt that a marriage with a bride who was already of canonical age (which would be binding immediately) was a better guarantee of alliance than one with a child bride, which might be broken before Anna came of age.

The only case mentioned in the *Zimmern Chronicle* of a marriage contact for a minor also never came to fruition. During his exile in Switzerland, Johann Werner I von Zimmern tried to arrange a marriage for his youngest son, Wilhelm Werner, to the only daughter and heiress of Count Gaudenz von Mätsch, another of the banished councilors of Sigismund of Tyrol. He "arranged a match between this girl and Wilhelm Werner, when the latter was of age, so he would inherit both from [Jörg von] Werdenberg[-Sargans] and from Mätsch, but this was not kept. Johann Werner died shortly thereafter and no one pursued the matter" (*ZC* 3:2). In this case, it appears that the bride may have already reached the canonical age of twelve, although the groom was less than ten years old.

The chronicler does not mention any matches in his own experience as being arranged in childhood, although it is possible that some of the matches proposed for his cousin Anna "in her youth" and one of the matches proposed for Froben Christoph himself were put forward when the prospective brides were still under the canonical age of marriage (*ZC* 2:452, 3:508). A trend away from child marriages is consistent with other evidence suggesting that in the early sixteenth century, sentiment among German counts and barons was turning towards giving the parties a greater opportunity to express their personal preferences—if not in actually initiating the match, then at least in vetoing one to which they objected.

Allowing the bride and groom to meet before the marriage contract was signed became a common practice among the urban elite in Germany by the late fifteenth century, and a few cases are documented among southwest German nobles in the same period. The 1479 marriage contract of Philipp von Virneburg-Neuenahr and Walburga von Solms states that "the two should meet each other in order to see whether they please each other" before the marriage project would proceed any further; and a similar formula occurs in a contract of 1499.[30]

The first reference in the *Zimmern Chronicle* to the practice of meeting the potential spouse refers to the marriage negotiations of Johann Werner II in 1509. When he was seeking a match with the daughter of his old friend Count Ludwig

[29]Burmeister, *Grafen von Montfort,* 281.
[30]Beer, *Eltern und Kinder,* 99; and Spiess, *Familie und Verwandtschaft,* 34.

von Löwenstein, negotiations reached the point at which "Count Ludwig invited him to visit him to see the girl and handle matters in person" before the contract was drawn up (*ZC* 2:193). However, the visit never took place because Johann Werner II accepted the offer of a Werdenberg match instead. Christoph von Werdenberg and his brothers invited him to Sigmaringen to choose between their two nieces, who had been fostered out to Christoph's household: "They left the choice between the two girls up to him; he preferred the older one, Katharina" (*ZC* 2:194).

By midcentury, the bride also had the opportunity to express her personal preference, as is evident in Froben Christoph von Zimmern's description of his visit to meet his prospective bride in 1544: "Shortly before the meeting to sign the marriage contract at Hechingen, the young Count Froben Christoph and [his intermediary] Count Jos [Niklaus] von Zollern rode to Eberstein to see the Fräulein von Eberstein and *also to let himself be seen*" (*ZC* 3:513, emphasis added). The last phrase suggests a more definite veto power on the part of the bride than in the case of Johann Werner II's negotiations a generation earlier.

The chronicler clearly believes that children should have a veto power in the choice of marriage partners, although it is not clear whether daughters actually enjoyed this right in the early decades of the sixteenth century. He criticizes as tyrants those parents or guardians who force children into marriages against their will, and indicates that this view was shared by the older generation of nobles. He also believes that parents should not oppose love matches to partners of suitable status. By the middle of the sixteenth century, such views were widespread among nonnobles in Germany, for both Catholic and Protestant states passed laws forbidding parents to force children into marriage or to oppose marriages without valid grounds.[31]

Froben Christoph himself vetoed a proposed marriage to a girl with whom he was already acquainted. Although his uncle Gottfried Werner von Zimmern strongly favored the match on political grounds, he allowed the matter to drop when Froben Christoph made it clear that he disliked the girl, "for the old lord did not want to force his nephew into any marriage" (*ZC* 3:507).

The chronicler criticizes guardians or patrons who force girls into marriage. As one of several examples of Jos Niklaus von Zollern's abuse of his power of guardianship over his illegitimate cousin Anna, he states that "although [Anna] had already promised marriage to a young Esslinger, Count Jos Niklaus forced her to marry his clerk, Philipp Lindenfels, much against her will" (*ZC* 2:467). The chronicler also criticizes the behavior of the Duchess of Nürtingen toward her niece, Elsa von Brandenburg: "A young Saxon prince at the court of Ulrich [von

---

[31] Electoral ordinances in the Palatinate in 1562, the decree *Tametsi* of the Council of Trent in 1563, and the marriage ordinance of the Prince-Bishopric of Speyer in 1582 all declared that parents were not to force children into marriage. The electoral ordinance in the Palatinate also reiterated existing imperial laws forbidding parents from hindering a marriage "without just and legitimate grounds." Harrington, *Reordering Marriage and Society,* 200.

Württemberg] had special love and affection for [Elsa]. He would have liked to marry her, and Duke Ulrich favored the match." Nevertheless, the duchess forced Elsa to marry her weak-willed cousin, Margrave Ernst von Baden. The marriage was an unhappy one: "The old Duchess of Nürtingen could not make everything crooked straight again" (*ZC* 2:437–38). The chronicler implies that this incident made her more willing to countenance a later love match between another niece, Apollonia von Henneberg, and Gottfried Werner von Zimmern.

Apollonia's father, Count Hermann von Henneberg, comes in for the most severe criticism for his "grim and stern" behavior toward his daughters. According to the chronicle, he tried to use force to prevent Apollonia's marriage to Gottfried Werner and never forgave her for her disobedience. He then took out his anger on another daughter who was a canoness: "fearing that she might also marry whoever she wanted," he forced her to enter a closed convent where she had to take binding vows of celibacy.[32] "How could good fortune accompany such tyrannical acts?" demands the chronicler, who sees the extinction of the Henneberg family in the male line as divine punishment for Count Hermann's behavior. "Although the higher authorities in this world look the other way in such cases, experience shows that punishment follows eventually" (*ZC* 2: 448–50).

Daughters who married without familial consent did not actually experience the severe punishments permitted by law, and the chronicler's attitude toward them is surprisingly sympathetic. Of the three sisters of Johann Werner II who entered into promises of marriage to men of lower rank without their brother's consent, only the ex-abbess Katharina von Zimmern is criticized for her behavior; she was also the only one denied a dowry. The other two sisters, Margarethe and Barbara, are depicted in the chronicle as victims of male behavior: their brother failed to arrange suitable marriages for them, and they were tricked by their suitors into secret engagements.

Although the two oldest daughters of Johann Werner I von Zimmern had been placed in convents during their father's exile, Margarethe and Barbara were allowed to remain laywomen in the hopes that they would eventually be able to marry. In 1503, shortly before recovering the Zimmern estates, Johann Werner II secured an appointment for Margarethe as a lady-in-waiting to the wife of his patron Margrave Christoph von Baden. Margarethe thus had hopes of finding a match at court; however, Barbara was kept at home in Messkirch to oversee her brother's household (*ZC* 2:161, 163). Margarethe was now twenty-two and Barbara about twenty or twenty-one years old, so they were already past the average age of marriage for southwest German noblewomen. Moreover, they had little prospect of dowries sufficient to marry according to their rank, since the Zimmern estates were heavily in debt. Although the chronicler claims that a count

---

[32]Unlike a professed nun, a canoness (*Stiftsdame*) did not take final vows and was capable of contracting a valid marriage.

and a baron each offered to marry one of the sisters without a dowry, this seems more likely to be a face-saving device than a statement of reality. It allows him to blame Johann Werner II for his sisters' subsequent misalliances by claiming that he did not take advantage of opportunities to secure matches for them with husbands of the high nobility (*ZC* 2:160–61).[33]

According to the chronicler, at the court of Baden Margarethe met the knight Wolf von Affenstein, who "through arts" brought her to promise marriage to him. Her mother then took her away from court to her own residence at Oberndorf, where Affenstein married Margarethe.[34] The chronicler strongly implies that it was Margarethe's mother, Countess Margarethe von Oettingen, who enabled her daughter to marry despite the opposition of her son, the nominal head of the family.[35] The strong-willed countess had faced down far more formidable opponents during her long struggle to maintain her children's claim to the Zimmern inheritance, and it is not surprising that Johann Werner II was forced to acquiesce in the fait accompli. However, he was so enraged by the marriage that he refused to grant Margarethe a dowry, and he rejected her pleas for reconciliation even when she was on her deathbed in 1513 (*ZC* 2:161–62).

In the meantime, Barbara was managing the household of her bachelor brother. A frequent visitor to the house was Johann Werner's good friend Hans Wilhelm von Weitingen, who, according to the chronicle, was "sly" and got Barbara to promise marriage to him. When Johann Werner found this out, he sent Barbara away to one of his other estates for a year, but Hans Wilhelm continued to "lay suit to Johann Werner and his friends asking for friendship [that is, alliance in marriage]." In 1506 friends and relatives arbitrated an agreement. Johann Werner promised Barbara to Hans Wilhelm, with a dowry of 2000 gulden, and the marriage took place shortly thereafter (*ZC* 2:163).

Although the chronicler does not describe the women's feelings toward their suitors, one may assume that the marriages were based at least in part on personal inclination. After all, Margarethe and Barbara had both known their suitors for a long time. However, pragmatic considerations probably played a part as well. By this time, both women undoubtedly feared that their brother would leave them

---

[33]This argument that the family head was to blame for failing to arrange a suitable marriage for the woman was a standard claim in lawsuits in which a woman who married without familiar consent (or a husband, acting in her name) sued for her dowry or inheritance. Hufschmidt, *Adelige Frauen im Weserraum,* 145–47.

[34]The chronicle discusses Margarethe's marriage before Barbara's, implying that it took place earlier. However, Barbara married in 1506 and Margarethe in 1512. Schwennicke, *Europäische Stammtafeln NF,* 12:84.

[35]Harris notes that in the English aristocracy, "mothers may have been more sympathetic to daughters who married without consent than fathers, brothers, and other male kin.... Their lack of voice in their own first marriages seems to have made them more sensitive to the feelings of daughters who faced the prospect of unattractive matches or were being forced to give up men they loved." *English Aristocratic Women,* 58.

old maids in order not to burden the Zimmern estates with their dowries. In both of these cases, the chronicler presents the women as victims of intriguers seeking to raise their own social status by marrying women from the high nobility. Here he may be applying the traditional legal view that females were weak by nature and thus bore less responsibility for their actions than did men. He may also be reluctant to admit that women could act on their own behalf; it was less humiliating for the Zimmern family to admit that its head had been outwitted by another man than by a woman.

One of the most surprising aspects of these marriages is that Margarethe eventually received a dowry of 2000 gulden, even though her brother initially refused to pay her any dowry since she had married without his consent. This amount was equal to the dowry of her sister Barbara, who did receive his consent before the actual marriage ceremony. Apollonia von Henneberg also eventually received a dowry of 4000 gulden, even though her father was bitterly opposed to her marriage to Gottfried Werner von Zimmern and initially refused to pay her any dowry (ZC 2:448, 450). In neither case was the dowry granted due to a personal reconciliation. Rather, it was negotiated by kinsmen who evidently felt that it was better to grant a dowry and obtain a renunciation than to run the risk that the daughter or sister might later lodge a claim for a share of the inheritance. Both Margarethe von Zimmern and Apollonia von Henneberg received dowries smaller than those normally granted by their families to daughters who married husbands of their own rank. However, in each case the dowry was equal to the amount normally received by the husband's family. There was thus no real financial punishment for daughters who married without familial consent. Studies of daughters in other German nobilities from the late fifteenth through the seventeenth centuries have also found that daughters who married without familial consent were not usually deprived of their inheritance, although they sometimes received a smaller dowry than usual.[36] It would be interesting to know whether undutiful daughters were equally fortunate in countries in which inheritance laws were less favorable to female inheritance.

CRITERIA FOR CHOICE OF MARRIAGE PARTNER
Such marriages initiated by the parties themselves were highly exceptional among southwest German counts and barons in the fifteenth and early sixteenth centuries. For German nobles, as for European elites in general, "marriage was not a personal matter between the two parties but a connection between the two family groups they represented,"[37] and the criteria for choice of a marriage partner centered on the characteristics of the family rather than those of the individual. In his

---

[36]Speiss, *Familie und Verwandtschaft,* 209; and Hufschmidt, *Adelige Frauen im Weserraum,* 146–47.

[37]Spiess, *Familie und Verwandtschaft,* 73.

survey of 130 marriage contracts for counts and barons in the Mainz region from the thirteenth to the fifteenth centuries, Spiess concludes that the ideal marriage partner "came from a family that was socially respectable, influential, and as rich as possible." No individual characteristics mattered except that the prospective partner "met the biological requirements for the continuation of the lineage."[38]

These criteria are similar to those that prevailed in other aristocracies in the fifteenth and early sixteenth centuries, although the German nobles may have given a higher priority to status (as opposed to wealth) than some other elites. In the high aristocracy of Castile, the goal was "to obtain a member of the richest and most powerful family possible, who brought not only a good dowry or possessions, but also the backing of a lineage with the greatest possible social prestige and political influence"; this definition includes no personal characteristics at all.[39] French noble parents in the sixteenth and seventeenth centuries similarly mentioned wealth and the social and political connections of the family of the spouse as the most important criteria; as for the bride herself, "above all, one wished her to be capable of bearing children."[40] In England between 1450 and 1550, the chief characteristics that aristocratic parents desired in a son-in-law were wealth, social status, and political connections; in the rare cases where the individual's personal qualities were even mentioned, "character was an addition to, not a substitute for, wealth."[41]

In Germany, an increased emphasis on individual characteristics was evident in the marriage contracts and letters of townsmen much earlier than in those of nobles—it is seen in the late fifteenth century, among German artisans and lesser merchants, and in the early sixteenth century among patricians. In the first half of the fifteenth century, the letters of Nuremberg patricians mentioned only the wealth, status, and reputation of the family of the potential spouse. However, as time went on, the individual characteristics of the potential spouse (especially physical attractiveness) and affection for or inclination toward the potential spouse were increasingly mentioned—in addition to the standard family characteristics, not as a replacement for them.[42]

"Marriage to an honorable family" was the most important criterion for nobles in the *Zimmern Chronicle*. The main goal of marriage negotiations was "friendship and honor," that is, alliance with a family of at least equal rank and descent. Some nobles even professed (at least rhetorically) to be willing to take a bride without a dowry in order to marry into an old and prestigious family (*ZC* 2:160). Avoidance of unequal marriages below the high nobility was the minimum

---

[38]Spiess, *Familie und Verwandtschaft*, 81.

[39]Beceiro Pita and Córdoba de la Llave, *Parentesco, poder y mentalidad*, 147.

[40]Constant, *Noblesse française aux XVI–XVIIe siècles*, 117–23; and Nassiet, *Parenté, noblesse et états dynastiques*, 30.

[41]Harris, *English Aristocratic Women*, 44, 55.

[42]Beer, *Eltern und Kinder*, 90, 95–96.

requirement; the goal was to marry a partner of the same rank or preferably higher. When the two partners did not hold identical ranks within the high nobility, the usual pattern was for men to marry women of higher rank than their own.

Many marriage alliances were political or dynastic in nature, intended to reconcile feuding families, to reinforce a political alliance by forging a kin tie, or to reunite collateral branches of a family. Ecclesiastical authors regarded bringing peace between feuding families as an especially praiseworthy motive for marriage.[43] In dynastic marriages (which included virtually all of the marriages negotiated for underage children), it did not matter which individuals actually married each other. In early sixteenth-century negotiations, potential husbands were still offered "one of the daughters" in a certain family. Sometimes the groom made his selection in person, as in the case of Johann Werner II von Zimmern. Although fathers sometimes promised to marry their daughter to whichever son was selected as heir, it does not appear that daughters were ever allowed an opportunity to select their husband personally from among several sons.[44]

The interchangeability of family members is especially evident in marriages between the Werdenberg and the Zimmern families in the sixteenth-century; in the absence of a son or daughter of the right age, more distant family members could be substituted. Eager to end the long-standing feud between their two families, Christoph von Werdenberg offered Johann Werner II von Zimmern one of his two nieces, rather than his underage daughter. Christoph later wanted to reinforce his friendship with Gottfried Werner von Zimmern by marrying his son Joachim to Gottfried Werner's daughter Anna. This plan for a marriage alliance was thwarted by the early death of Joachim, but it was later carried out by substituting Jos Niklaus II von Zollern (the nephew of Christoph's second wife) as the bridegroom (ZC 2:454).

Marriages could also reinforce personal friendships or reinforce political alliances. Before accepting the dynastic marriage to end the Werdenberg-Zimmern feud, Johann Werner II had been deep in negotiations with Count Ludwig von Löwenstein. "Johann Werner particularly wished friendship [that is, a marriage alliance] with Count Ludwig, since he had known him since his youth at court at Heidelberg. He had given Johann Werner much advice and support in his poverty" (ZC 2:192). The impoverished baron undoubtedly hoped that the marriage would guarantee the continuation of Löwenstein's aid and protection.

---

[43]Spiess, *Familie und Verwandtschaft*, 36. Such reconciliation marriages were vital elements of family strategy in all European elites. In the Castilian high aristocracy they often involved a double marriage, providing a backup to maintain the truce if one member of a couple died. Rosenthal, "Aristocratic Marriage and the English Peerage," 186; and Beceiro Pita and Córdoba de la Llave, *Parentesco, poder y mentalidad*, 146–47.

[44]For example, in a contract of 1495, Eitelfriedrich II von Zollern promised to marry his daughter Wandelberte to a son of Count Kraft von Hohenlohe, whom his father would select later. Ulshöfer, *Hausrecht der Grafen von Zollern*, 52.

Just as a marriage could reinforce friendship or end tensions between families, the rejection of a match might also exacerbate such tensions. When Froben
Christoph von Zimmern was offered a match with Anna von Zollern, the sister of
the powerful Count Karl I von Zollern, his uncle Gottfried Werner "would gladly
have had him make the marriage; he felt that it would lead to a long-lasting relationship of neighborliness, and he was afraid that if the marriage was rejected, it
would lead to ill will and enmity" (ZC 3:506).

Political and dynastic considerations often made it desirable to undertake
repeated marriages within a small circle of families. Although the church forbade
marriages within the fourth degree of kinship (a common ancestor within four
generations), nobles could easily obtain dispensations for the third and fourth
degrees. Marriages within the second degree (first cousins) were virtually
unknown among southwest German counts and barons.[45]

Marriages requiring dispensations were largely confined to the families of
highest rank and greatest political power. The marriage of Magdalena, daughter of
Count Ludwig von Oettingen, to Count Ulrich VII von Montfort-Tettnang in
1485 required a papal dispensation for the second and third degrees of affinity. A
marriage between such unusually close relatives demonstrated the great political
significance of the alliance of the Oettingen and Montfort families.[46] Only one
marriage in the Zimmern family required a dispensation—that of Anna, the
daughter of Johann III, to Count Eberhard von Werdenberg in 1402. This was
probably a political marriage designed to ward off territorial conflicts between the
two families. The chronicler's naïve surprise at the high cost of obtaining the dispensation for the relationship of Eberhard and Anna in the fourth degree suggests
that dispensations were not common in his circle of acquaintance (ZC 1:205).

Endogamous marriages between collateral lines of the same family were
important as a means of reuniting divided territories. They were particularly significant when they involved an heiress, so that the estates of a line lacking male
heirs would pass to the other line.[47] In the Waldburg family, the males of the Sonnenberg line (extinct in the male line in 1511) married their daughters into the

---

[45]Spiess states that the forbidden degrees of kinship did not seriously limit the choice of marriage partners, since it was easy to get a dispensation for the third and fourth degree. He found no
cases of dispensations for the second degree (first cousins). *Familie und Verwandtschaft,* 47. At the
highest levels of the English and Castilian aristocracies, a high proportion of marriages were endogamous and dispensations were routinely required. However, there was no difficulty in obtaining them,
especially for the third and fourth degrees. Rosenthal, "Aristocratic Marriage and the English Peerage,"
184–87; and Beceiro Pita and Córdoba de la Llave, *Parentesco, poder y mentalidad,* 148–60.

[46]Burmeister states that this marriage "make[s] it clear that herre a portion of the Swabian nobility was drawing itself closer together. Families that had long been related by marriage had the declared
goal of protecting themselves against the threat of mediatization by the Empire and the princes" (that
is, of losing their importance and being subjected to the power of the territorial princes). *Grafen von
Montfort,* 279.

[47]Spiess, *Familie und Verwandtschaft,* 61.

Trauchberg and Zeil lines in 1507 and 1509. In the Zollern family, the last count of the Haigerloch line married his daughter into the Sigmaringen line in 1608.[48] In both the Waldburg and the Zollern families, house treaties already provided that the estates of a branch extinct in the male line should revert to the other branches; however, the endogamous marriages ensured that these provisions would actually be carried out.

Even when dynastic or political considerations are not paramount, the *Zimmern Chronicle* consistently stresses the importance of marrying for rank rather than for riches. This emphasis on status rather than wealth was true of the German nobility in general and also of the urban patriciate, although mere merchants might put the greatest emphasis on wealth.[49]

The most detailed discussion in the chronicle of the proper criteria for marriage occurs in the account of Margrave Christoph von Baden's attempt to help his client Johann Werner II von Zimmern out of his financial difficulties by arranging a marriage to the wealthy widow Sophia Böcklin. Not only was Sophia the heiress to a patrician family of Strasbourg, but she would also bring into the marriage her widow's pension from her first marriage to Count Conrad von Tübingen.

As the price for her consent to marry a man of lower rank and less wealth than her first husband, Sophia made what the chronicler considers exorbitant demands. She did not want to marry a mere baron, so Johann Werner must obtain the title of an old earldom (not merely acquire a newly minted title) and give up the name of Zimmern. Nevertheless, most of his friends and relatives advised him to accept Sophia's conditions

> since the family was so impoverished by persecution by the Werdenbergs and the money would do so much to restore the family. Sophia was a good enough match for a count in her first marriage, and even though the match was an unequal one for Johann Werner, it would allow his brothers to marry according to their rank and continue the family line so that their descendants could participate in tournaments. (*ZC* 2:148–49)

However, according to the chronicle, Christoph von Baden's son, Archbishop Jakob von Trier, persuaded Johann Werner II to reject the match. The long speech the chronicle puts into the mouth of the archbishop presumably reflects the views of the chronicler himself, as well as the conventional wisdom of moralists:

> He should remember his ancestry. His ancestors had made honorable marriages looking only for friendship and honor, and therefore married into the most prominent families and did not bargain for money or goods. Moreover, marriages for money were rarely happy or durable.... He would have no children by this old woman. She would despise him because of her wealth. In short, he would never have a happy day with her. (*ZC* 2:149–50)

[48]Schwennicke, *Europäische Stammtafeln NF,* 5:148, 154; and Isenburg, *Europäische Stammtafeln,* 1:153, 155.

[49]Beer, *Eltern und Kinder,* 95.

This speech mixes considerations of personal happiness with those of lineage loyalty: maintaining the traditions of one's ancestors and begetting children to carry on the family name. However, the primary considerations are those of maintaining the proper social order. Marriages for money will be unhappy because they upset the proper social hierarchy and the proper power relationship within the family. Wives should be subject to their husbands, but here the wife from a lower social order will despise her higher-ranking husband, and will exercise greater power within the family because of her wealth. [50]

The chronicler's set of values led him to criticize the pursuit of heiresses and wealthy widows that was a major preoccupation of nobles in real life. Although such pursuit is attributed to nobles in other families, it is rarely acknowledged among members of the Zimmern family. The marriages of Werner VIII to Anna von Kirchberg and of Gottfried Werner to Apollonia von Henneberg, which will be examined in detail later, are depicted as motivated by romantic love, not by pursuit of wealth and status.

An heiress was the greatest prize on the marriage market. Since Gottfried Werner's only lay daughter, Anna, would have been his heiress under customary German law, she was courted by members of high-ranking families who did not usually intermarry with the Zimmerns. One of these was Count Konrad von Tübingen zu Liechteneck, "whom her father would gladly have accepted." However, Konrad's intermediary stipulated "that he would only marry her on condition that Gottfried Werner make her his heir in his will…. Gottfried Werner was greatly displeased at this, that his goods and his inheritance were valued even more than his friendship and even more than his daughter," and he rejected the suit (*ZC* 2:453). Gottfried Werner had already made a pact between brothers stating that in the absence of male heirs, his estate was to go to his brother Johann Werner and the latter's descendants.

Landgrave Jörg von Leuchtenberg also made overtures on behalf of his son, but he too wanted a guarantee that Anna would inherit Messkirch after Gottfried Werner's death. Gottfried Werner again refused, and the chronicler adds, "It would have been a great improvement for him [Leuchtenberg], much as his ancestors had improved their fortunes through a marriage to a Countess von Rieneck, who had no agnates and inherited the estate of Grünsfeld from her childless brother" (*ZC* 2:453–54). Although the chronicler does not mention the parallel, the Zimmerns had also improved their fortunes through the marriage in 1319 of Werner VII to Anna von Waldburg, the heiress of Messkirch.

In one case, the chronicler does acknowledge the financial attractiveness of an heiress. He criticizes his father for not pursuing an opportunity in 1531/32 to

---

[50]Letters by urban patricians also express scorn for those who married merely for money and warn that a man who married a rich wife might be under her thumb. Beer, *Eltern und Kinder*, 91, 92, 95.

arrange a marriage between the chronicler's older brother Johann Christoph and Schweickhart von Gundelfingen's adopted daughter, who later married Ulrich von Helfenstein: "through his negligence he missed the opportunity to obtain a capital sum of over a hundred thousand gulden, for the family became extinct within a few years and the Gundelfingen estates all passed to the Helfensteins" (ZC 2:368–69).[51]

Marriage to a widow might be even more advantageous than marriage to an heiress, for a widow brought her widow's pension into her second marriage and the groom had cash in hand immediately.[52] Marriage to the widow of a prince or a high-ranking count could bring wealth far beyond what most counts or barons could hope to obtain by marriage to a never-married woman. When Countess Veronika von Sonnenberg married Count Hugo XVII von Montfort in 1488, she brought with her over 11,000 gulden: 6000 from her dowry from her father and 5000 from the matching payment and morning gift from her first marriage to Count Ludwig von Oettingen.[53]

In one case, the chronicler does acknowledge that a member of the Zimmern family married a widow solely for her money, but he is careful to depict the ill consequences of such a marriage. Wilhelm Werner is usually portrayed in the chronicle as a positive role model—especially in contrast to his spendthrift brothers[54]—but here he appears greedy and overhasty in concluding his second marriage.

A mutual friend had proposed a match between the widower Wilhelm Werner and Margarethe, the daughter of the late Count Leonard von Haag and his wife, Landgravine Amalia von Leuchtenberg. However, when Wilhelm Werner and his intermediary went to see the prospective bride and to conclude the marriage, the widowed mother "paid attention to Wilhelm Werner and gave him so many good words that he believed there was a great deal of money at hand. Although he had ridden down that morning to commit himself to the girl, he was convinced by the mother to take her instead." The contract was concluded immediately and the wedding was held a few days later at Haag, even though Wilhelm Werner had not brought any suitable clothing with him (ZC 3:41–42).

Wilhelm Werner then behaved like a nouveau riche, putting on a lavish homecoming feast: "It was a grand homecoming that was celebrated for eight days

[51]Schweikhart's adopted daughter was Marie de Bonnard, dame des Gomignies (d. 1565), the granddaughter of his mother's sister. On 4 May 1536, Marie married Count Georg II [not Ulrich] von Helfenstein (1518–73). After Marie's death, Georg von Helfenstein married (on 28 February 1567) Apollonia von Zimmern, the second daughter of the chronicler Froben Christoph, and ultimately one of the two coheiresses of the Zimmern estates. At the time of Apollonia's marriage, however, her brother Wilhelm was still alive, and there was no reason to expect that she would become an heiress. Isenburg, Europäische Stammtafeln 5:125; and Schwennicke, Europäische Stammtafeln NF, 12:59.

[52]Spiess, Familie und Verwandtschaft, 60–61.

[53]Spiess, Familie und Verwandtschaft, 159–60; and Burmeister, Grafen von Montfort, 291.

[54]Wolf, Von der Chronik zum Weltbuch, 343.

with great expense.... This all helped to squander the money and may have been the beginning of the problems that occurred shortly afterward and led them into a dark age (*tenebrose saeculo*) and misfortune" (*ZC* 3:51). In the chronicler's view, the unhappy marriage was a consequence of Wilhelm Werner's disregard of the proper criteria for marriage. It turned out that Amalia was less wealthy than she had led her new husband to believe; a family friend is quoted as saying that "they had both deceived each other: she had cheated him out of a good thing and promised him in its place a great deal of money she didn't have, so he was never well-disposed to her after that" (ZC 3:42).

The account in the chronicle actually softens the evidence for Wilhelm Werner's greed and social climbing, for it represents the marriage as an impetuous decision and the bride as "of a suitable age to bear children" to her second husband (*ZC* 3:58). In reality, almost a year and a half elapsed between the signing of the marriage contract on 17 March 1524 and the wedding ceremony on 30 November 1525. Moreover, Amalia was fifty-five years old (sixteen years older than her new husband) when the marriage contract was signed. It is not clear whether Wilhelm Werner deliberately misrepresented the facts about his second marriage in the stories he told his nephew or whether the chronicler decided that the true story was too unflattering to his favorite uncle.[55]

Although status and wealth receive far more attention than any other issue in marriage negotiations in the *Zimmern Chronicle,* some characteristics of the individual as well as those of the family were considered among the criteria for marriage. In the fifteenth century, the only relevant aspect of the individual was biological: the bride's ability to bear children. Physical appearance mattered only insofar as it bore on this point.[56] The *Zimmern Chronicle* shows that by the sixteenth century, nobles were considering some of the same additional criteria as urban elites: character and moral reputation, economic ability, and potential for affection. However, it appears that physical beauty and the potential for affection played a lesser role among nobles in the early sixteenth century than they did among patricians. These characteristics did assume greater importance in the correspondence of German nobles in the late sixteenth and seventeenth centuries.[57]

---

[55]Schwennicke, *Europäische Stammtafeln NF,* 12:84. Amalia did not marry for the first time until 1504, when she was already thirty-five years old, although she had a younger sister who married in 1491. This suggests that she had some serious handicaps on the marriage market. Isenburg, *Europäische Stammtafeln,* 4:107. Wilhelm Werner's first wife, Countess Katharina von Lupfen (1486–1521), was also thirty-five years old at the time of their marriage, which lasted only sixteen weeks before she died in a fall from a horse. Schwennicke, *Europäische Stammtafeln NF,* 12:84.

[56]Spiess, *Familie und Verwandtschaft,* 37, 39.

[57]According to Hufschmidt (*Adelige Frauen im Weserraum,* 133), "A certain intelligence, good moral reputation [*Tugendhaftigkeit*] and an attractive appearance counted as the most important qualities a future bride should exhibit" among the lower nobility of the Weser region in the late sixteenth and seventeenth century. In this era, a new consideration also became crucial: the religious allegiance of the spouse.

Since the *Zimmern Chronicle* describes marriage negotiations only from the point of view of the groom, it never explicitly discusses the personal characteristics sought in a potential husband. However, it implies that they included good health and the ability to manage an estate. The letters of German nobles in the late sixteenth and seventeenth centuries show that the criteria for a potential husband, as well as for a potential wife, included not only the family characteristics of noble birth, wealth, and social and political connections, but also the individual characteristics of good health, economic ability, suitable age, and good appearance. A potential groom in 1593 was described as "upstanding, honorable, and intelligent" (aufrichtig, ehrlich, *verständig*). He had achieved recognition for his services to the prince, came from an old and respected family, and possessed a residence that could support a decent household.[58]

Since the chief goal of marriage—especially a noble marriage—was to produce heirs to continue the line, the ability of the bride to bear children was crucially important. "A woman had the best chance on the marriage market if she was young, healthy, and not physically deformed (lame or hunchbacked)"; says Spiess; beauty was an additional advantage only because an ugly wife would not arouse her husband's sexual interest and would therefore be less likely to bear children.[59]

The bride's age was significant, since a young wife had a longer potential period of childbearing. The daughters of southwest German counts and barons generally married before the age of twenty in the fifteenth and sixteenth centuries. One of the chief objections to marrying a widow was that she would be too old to bear children; Johann Werner II was warned that "he would have no children by this old woman," Sophia Böcklin (*ZC* 2:150). However, in an era when many women were widowed at early ages, it would not necessarily be the case that a widow would be too old to have children.

The importance of health is evident in the account of the negotiations for the marriage of Froben Christoph to a daughter of Wilhelm von Eberstein. The oldest daughter Amalia "had been suggested…at first as a possible match, but the girl several years before had become ill…and developed a disease of the lungs. So the young man was advised not to take her, since it was not likely that she would have many children or even live very long." These fears proved well founded, since Amalia died a year and a half after Froben Christoph's marriage to her sister Kunigunde (*ZC* 3:516).[60] While the health of the potential groom is rarely mentioned in accounts of marriage negotiations, the chronicle shows that it was also a consideration. Froben Christoph feared that a severe case of smallpox he suffered in

---

[58]Hufschmidt, *Adelige Frauen im Weserraum,* 136. The description comes from a letter in which the brothers of Sophia von Saldern promoted a match for her daughter with a widower aged between thirty and forty. They added that his daughter from a previous marriage would not pose a problem.

[59]Spiess, *Familie und Verwandtschaft,* 37, 39.

[60]Health was also a consideration among patricians. Beer, *Eltern und Kinder,* 93.

his student days would lead to rumors that he had syphilis and thereby ruin his chances for marriage (*ZC* 3:329–30). However, biological factors played less of a role in the case of men than in the case of women.[61]

When the chronicler mentions the personal qualities of potential spouses at all, he emphasizes general social and moral background. Personal qualities are mentioned far more often for females than males. A girl should have good manners and be well-bred and God-fearing: Gottfried Werner's wife Apollonia was brought up "in all modesty and good behavior" (*in aller zucht und gueten geberden*) and Gottfried Werner and Apollonia raised their daughter Anna "in all modesty and fear of God" (*in aller zucht und gotzforcht*) (*ZC* 2:443, 452). Intelligence is also valued, for Amalia von Eberstein is described as "a well-bred and intelligent young lady" (*ZC* 3:516). A reputation for chastity is essential for women; a potential bride could even be ruled out of consideration because of the bad moral reputation of her family, even if no scandal was alleged against her personally (*ZC* 3:507). [62]

The economic skills of individuals were considered in addition to the wealth of their families. The daughter of Count Franz Mörsperg was recommended as a potential match for Froben Christoph because she was "a good household manager" (*ZC* 3:507). Gottfried Werner was reputedly offered many good matches not only because of his prospects for advancement at the court of Ulrich von Württemberg, but also because of his skill in managing his small estate: "He had provided it with capable officials and tried to improve the estate as much as possible" (*ZC* 2:443). It is somewhat surprising that nobles mentioned household and estate management skills, since patricians—unlike mere merchants—did not do so in their correspondence.[63]

From the mid-fifteenth century onward, affection became an important factor in the choice of a spouse among urban elites. Correspondence in marriage negotiations among Nuremberg patricians referred more and more often to the bride's beauty or to love between the potential spouses, and by the early sixteenth century almost all correspondence mentioned the appearance of the bride or expressed feelings. However, the ideal was "a moderate love, that does not overshadow all other criteria." Marriages based solely on personal inclination that ignored the traditional considerations of wealth and status would still lead to conflict with the family.[64]

---

[61]Spiess, *Familie und Verwandtschaft,* 40. In the case of males, of course, the presence of bastard children might provide evidence of their ability to beget heirs.

[62]On the emphasis on the "socially recognized moral character" of the girl and her family, see Beer, *Eltern und Kinder,* 82, 85.

[63]Beer, *Eltern und Kinder,* 90. Members of the lower nobility in the late sixteenth and seventeenth century also mentioned household management skills. Hufschmidt, *Adelige Frauen um Weserraum,* 133.

[64]Beer, *Eltern und Kinder,* 87, 90, 96.

The evidence of the *Zimmern Chronicle* suggests that nobles were less likely than urban elites to take personal appearance into account as a criterion for marriage. References to good looks (of men as well as women) occur frequently in descriptive passages based on literary models, but not in discussions of actual marriage negotiations. The use of literary models from courtly romance is most evident in the passages describing the courtship of Werner VIII von Zimmern and Anna von Kirchberg (the widow of Johann von Fürstenberg), and of Gottfried Werner and Apollonia von Henneberg. According to the account in the chronicle, Werner fell in love with Anna in a classic *coup de foudre* (love at first sight) at her sister's wedding: "The ladies were all adorned with splendid clothing and jewelry, and among them the Countess von Fürstenberg was praised above both her sisters and all the other women, so that no one could compare to her in beauty and good upbringing" (*ZC* 1:323). In a similar vein, Apollonia von Henneberg is depicted as falling in love with Gottfried Werner, who "had a splendid, handsome, straight body" (*ain herrlich, schöne, gerade person*). Gottfried Werner in turn became enamored of Apollonia, who was "extraordinarily beautiful" and had been "brought up in all good manners" (*ZC* 2:443).

In a passage also based more on imagination than reality, Margarethe and Barbara von Zimmern, the two younger daughters of Johann Werner I von Zimmern, are described as being "unusually beautiful" and therefore able to attract suitors despite their family's impoverished state (*ZC* 2:160). However, all of these passages refer to the distant past. The only suggestion that beauty might play a part in marriages in real life comes in an anecdote about the chronicler's eldest daughter Anna (1545–1602). As a child, Anna was so lovely that Count Karl von Zollern used to joke that he would marry her for her beauty when she grew up, saying, "A man would make a fool of himself over her beauty." The chronicler adds, "I believe it was a prophecy on his part, for she later prevented his eldest and favorite daughter from making a fine marriage" (*ZC* 3:540).[65]

In the descriptions of his own marriage negotiations, Froben Christoph received information about the upbringing, moral character, and management skills of potential brides. However, the chronicler says nothing about the women's appearance. If he did not inquire about physical appearance at all, Froben Christoph was distinctly old fashioned by the standards of contemporary urban elites. He apparently did not feel that his own badly pockmarked face would be an obstacle to marriage, provided it was clear that the scars were the result of smallpox rather than syphilis. Beautiful women and handsome men were de rigeur in chivalric romance, but not necessarily in real life.

It is difficult to tell whether matches were based on personal inclination unless they resulted in conflicts with other kin who felt that the parties were

---

[65] Anna married Count Joachim von Fürstenberg, who (the chronicle implies) chose her over Karl's daughter Marie because of her beauty.

neglecting the appropriate criteria of rank and status. If affection supplemented the appropriate criteria, it was unlikely to elicit comment. As Harris says of the English aristocracy, "Many parents were willing to provide dowries and negotiate jointures for daughters who fell in love with men of appropriate status and wealth.... What neither parents nor guardians would accept or support was love matches that disparaged their daughters."[66]

Widows and widowers often considered themselves free to express their personal preferences, once they had fulfilled their obligation by following the advice of kin in their first marriage. According to the chronicler, the twice-widowed Jeanne de Bailleul described her betrothal to Philipp von Eberstein as based on her personal inclination: "I hear that she told her friends...that she had followed their advice twice before and married according to their advice; and she reminded them how that had turned out each time. Therefore, she had decided the third time to marry according to her own pleasure, as long as it was to an honorable family" (*ZC* 4:367–68).

The chronicler describes several matches in the Zimmern family as initiated by the parties themselves and presumably based at least in part on personal affection. His attitude toward these matches largely depends on whether he sees them as advantageous or disadvantageous to Zimmern family interests. Margarethe and Barbara von Zimmern, who married husbands from the lower nobility, are depicted as the victims of sly intriguers who tricked them into secret engagements. The chronicler does not describe the women's feelings toward their suitors. However, when a male member of the Zimmern lineage married a woman of higher rank, the chronicler presents it as romantic love rather than as deception by a scheming social climber.

The story of Werner VIII von Zimmern's marriage in 1444 to Countess Anna von Kirchberg, widow of Count Johann von Fürstenberg, is portrayed as an episode from chivalric romance.[67] At the wedding of his friend Count Ulrich von Mätsch to Anna's sister Agnes, says Wolf, "Werner and Anna stand out as the best looking and appear destined for each other according to the rules of courtly love" even though Anna is already married to Johann von Fürstenberg.[68] Her husband challenges Werner to a duel, in which he is killed "by accident and by Werner's strength." Ulrich von Mätsch and his wife then facilitate a marriage between Werner and the widowed Anna by inviting both of them to visit them a few months later (*ZC* 1:323–24).

---

[66]Harris, *English Aristocratic Women*, 55–56.

[67]As Wolf notes, this is part of the chronicle's general depiction of Werner's career at the court of Württemberg in terms of courtly literature; Werner is the "last knight" of the Zimmern family. *Von der Chronik zum Weltbuch*, 249.

[68]Wolf, *Von der Chronik zum Weltbuch*, 249. Wolf erroneously describes the incident as taking place at Anna's marriage to Johann von Fürstenberg.

The entire story of the duel may be fictitious, although it is true that Anna was the widow of Johann von Fürstenberg and that she married Werner von Zimmern less than a year after the death of her first husband.[69] The romantic story in the chronicle may be designed to avoid any suspicion that Werner was just an ambitious social climber seeking to increase his wealth and status by marrying the rich widow of a member of a leading Swabian family of counts.

The chronicle uses similar literary devices to embellish the story of Gottfried Werner von Zimmern's courtship of Apollonia von Henneberg, the granddaughter of Margrave Friedrich V von Brandenburg and a member of the most powerful family of counts in Franconia. Around 1510, Gottfried Werner met Apollonia at the court of his patron, the young Duke Ulrich von Württemberg. Apollonia was a member of the household of her aunt, Margravine Elisabeth von Brandenburg (called the Duchess of Nürtingen or the old duchess in the chronicle). Since the old duchess was the widow of Duke Ulrich's uncle, she and her ladies were frequent visitors at the court of Württemberg.

Only at a court could a young nobleman "associate with young women of high birth sufficiently frequently and freely for mutual attachment to develop."[70] In scenes straight out of courtly romance, the chronicler describes Apollonia as falling in love with Gottfried Werner, who had "distinguished himself in war and other matters, was handsome and upright, and was cherished and honored by Duke Ulrich and many others." He had previously rejected several offers of marriage to daughters of the leading families in Swabia (Montfort, Werdenberg, and Waldburg) and "many believed he intended to remain single all his life" (ZC 2:443). Now, says Wolf, "[Gottfried Werner] acts as a knight of courtly love (*Minneritter*) who is attracted by the extraordinary beauty and exemplary upbringing of Apollonia" and tries to win her love by his performance in tournaments.[71]

According to the chronicle, "Duke Ulrich did his best to further the match and gain the goodwill of Apollonia's father" by working through the old duchess. He set up opportunities for Gottfried Werner to meet Apollonia by taking him along on visits to Nürtingen and by inviting the duchess and her ladies to hunting parties. Gottfried Werner ingratiated himself with the old duchess by "entertain[ing] her so

---

[69]Johann von Fürstenberg married Anna von Kirchberg in 1436. He died on 30 March 1443, and she married Werner VIII von Zimmern on 21 March 1444. If Werner did in fact kill Johann von Fürstenberg in a duel, the incident could not have taken place at the wedding of Fürstenberg's sister-in-law Agnes von Kirchberg to Werner's friend Ulrich von Mätsch in 1443. Anna von Kirchberg had no sister named Agnes, and the Agnes von Kirchberg who married an Ulrich von Mätsch died in 1407. Isenburg, *Europäische Stammtafeln* 4:127; 5:122; and Schwennicke, *Europäische Stammtafeln NF,* 12:83.

[70]Stone, *Crisis of the Aristocracy,* 609. On the importance of princely courts as a milieu in which noblewomen could meet suitors away from parental supervision and enter marriages based on personal inclination, see also Hufschmidt, *Adelige Frauen im Weserraum,* 144.

[71]Wolf, *Von der Chronik zum Weltbuch,* 334.

much with his stories and good conversation that she preferred him to all others and liked to have him near her" (*ZC* 2:443–44).

Thus far, there is a certain basis of reality to the story, in that Duke Ulrich von Württemberg was promoting an advantageous match for one of his courtiers by using his connections with Apollonia's relatives. However, the story then moves into the realm of literary fantasy as Gottfried and Apollonia promise marriage to each other: "As in courtly models, the secret engagement…takes place during a dramatic thunderstorm at night."[72] When Gottfried Werner asked for the old duchess's approval, she was displeased with her niece for acting without the consent of her kin, but agreed to intercede with her brother-in-law, Apollonia's father.

According to the chronicle, Count Hermann von Henneberg sent two old noblemen with a wagon, telling Apollonia that "her father wanted her to come home at once so that he could outfit her with clothes and other necessities" for the wedding. Apollonia suspected a trap and refused to go home. Fearing that the Henneberg messengers might carry Apollonia off by force, Gottfried Werner had the streets of Nürtingen guarded by soldiers supplied by Ulrich von Württemberg and forced the messengers to leave without her. The troops stayed in the town until it was clear that the Henneberg messengers were not coming back and the duchess promised that she would not let them harass the girl in the future. Gottfried Werner then took leave of Duke Ulrich, collected Apollonia from her aunt's castle, and married her in "a small but gracious and joyous wedding at Messkirch" (*ZC* 2:444–46).[73] According to the chronicle, Count Hermann von Henneberg never forgave his daughter for her marriage to a man of lower social and economic status. He refused to grant Apollonia a dowry, but ten years later arbiters reached an agreement giving Apollonia a dowry of 4000 gulden (*ZC* 2:448, 450).

Wolf argues that the love story of Gottfried Werner and Apollonia is used to provide the justification for a marriage decision that turned out in the long run to be a poor one from the dynastic point of view: the dowry was lower than expected.[74] Moreover, Apollonia produced no male heirs, and she died shortly before her last remaining brother, so that the Henneberg inheritance never came to the Zimmerns. Although Wolf does not mention it, the love story also helps to divert attention from the fact that Gottfried Werner exploited this marriage to a higher-ranking wife for his immediate social and economic advantage. It is unlikely that an impoverished baron (and a younger son, at that) would actually

---

[72]Wolf, *Von der Chronik zum Weltbuch,* 334.

[73]Wolf argues that the entire story of the Henneberg messengers is borrowed from courtly romance, since the messengers could scarcely have made a quick getaway with Apollonia in a cumbersome wagon. Moreover, Count Hermann would have been unlikely to risk such an insult to Duke Ulrich von Württemberg. Wolf, *Von der Chronik zum Weltbuch,* 335–36.

[74]Wolf, *Von der Chronik zum Weltbuch,* 336. Gottfried Werner and Apollonia had evidently hoped for more, for in her renunciation Apollonia reserved the right to inherit from her childless brothers (*ZC* 2:448).

have been sought out as a son-in-law by leading families of Swabian counts, as the account in the chronicle claims.[75] Gottfried Werner used the favor of Duke Ulrich to secure a much more prestigious match than he could ever have achieved on his own. Shortly after his marriage, he talked his brother Johann Werner II into exchanging estates with him, on the grounds that he could not maintain a princess (*Fürstin*) on his small estate of Zimmern vor Wald (*ZC* 2:316).

Despite the chronicler's use of the literary model of courtly love to describe two courtships in past generations, his account of his own marriage negotiations shows that in the mid-sixteenth century, romantic love still played little role in the normal process of choosing a spouse. However, children did have a larger role in choosing their spouses than they had in the late Middle Ages; parents were less likely to arrange marriages in childhood, and children now had the right to veto. The potential for affection was acknowledged as a relevant consideration even in the aristocracy, and the partners met before the marriage contract was signed in order to determine whether such potential existed. Family heads did not exercise their legal right to disinherit undutiful female kin who married without familial consent, even when such marriages resulted in permanent estrangement between the woman and her father or brother.

However, the chronicle does not assume a dichotomy between patriarchal power and lineage interests on the one hand and affection and personal autonomy on the other. Rather, it supports the argument made by Mathias Beer about the German urban elite, by Sherrin Marshall about the Dutch gentry, and by Nassiet about the French nobility: interest and emotion were not necessarily opposed to each other, and family interests and personal preferences formed what Marshall calls an intricate "mesh of interests and motivations" in the selection of marriage partners.[76]

First, children internalized the norms of their society, and concern over the potential for affection supplemented rather than replaced traditional criteria.

---

[75]The chronicle claims that Gottfried Werner was offered matches with "[Eva] the daughter of Ulrich von Montfort; she later married Baron Christoph von Schwarzenburg" and "the only daughter of Count Andreas von Sonnenberg; she later married Truchsess Wilhelm von Waldburg;" furthermore, "he could easily have obtained Count Christoph von Werdenberg's daughter [Anna], who later married Count Friedrich von Fürstenberg" (*ZC* 2:443). The Montforts were one of the few major families of Swabian counts who never intermarried with the Zimmerns, so it is unlikely that they would have sought a marriage alliance at this low point in the latter's fortunes. Andreas von Sonnenberg had no daughters; Sybille, who married Truchsess Wilhelm von Waldburg, was one of the five daughters of his brother Johann. Since Sybille's marriage in 1507 was part of a series of endogamous marriages designed to ensure that the estates of the Sonnenberg line passed to the Zeil line, it is unlikely that she would have been offered to Gottfried Werner. The Werdenberg match is more plausible, since Christoph von Werdenberg was at this time actively seeking a marriage alliance with the Zimmerns to end their feud. However, in 1509 he offered Johann Werner II a choice between his two nieces; it seems unlikely that he would have offered the more prestigious alliance with his daughter to the younger son Gottfried Werner.

[76]Marshall, *Dutch Gentry,* 10.

Even when they negotiated their own marriages, they chose their spouses largely on grounds approved by their elders: status, wealth, and moral reputation. Children did not object to a match on the grounds that they were not acquainted with their potential spouses; they objected only when they *were* acquainted with them and actively disliked them. As Stone says of the English aristocracy, "it was on the basis of a lack of positive antipathy revealed by a little polite conversation that many, perhaps most, noble marriages were concluded."[77] Secondly, as even Stone concedes, "in practice, as anthropologists everywhere have discovered, the arranged marriage works far less badly than those educated in a romantic culture would suppose, partly because the expectations of happiness from it are not set unreasonably high, and partly because it is a fact that sentiment can fairly easily adapt to social command."[78] Even if nobles came to consider the potential for affection a prerequisite for marriage, Nassiet says, "many women love[d] those assigned to them by social destiny." In letters written by members of the La Trémoille family, children who met their prospective partners only on the eve of signing the marriage contract declared that they had "fallen in love" on the basis of this brief acquaintance. Thus, "love did not necessarily conflict with a marriage of reason."[79]

[77]Stone, *Crisis of the Aristocracy,* 651.

[78]Stone, *Family, Sex and Marriage,* 104.

[79]Nassiet, *Parenté, noblesse et états dyastiques,* 151–52, 156. In a letter dated 1484, the writer fell in love in only three hours; in a letter dated 1521, it took three days.

CHAPTER 6

Marriage Negotiations

The lengthy description of Froben Christoph von Zimmern's courtship in the *Zimmern Chronicle* is far more detailed than those in the autobiographies of other nobles, who generally devote only a few lines to the topic of their marriage.[1] In the absence of collections of personal letters of German nobles comparable to those of urban patricians, it is the most complete account available of the process of courtship and marriage in the sixteenth-century German nobility. Three entire chapters of the chronicle are devoted to "the preliminaries, planned and failed marriage negotiations, prophecies, the wedding itself, the descent of the Eberstein family, the homecoming at Messkirch, and the birth of the eldest daughter."[2] In addition, the chronicle contains accounts of courtships of other family members and acquaintances that shed additional light on the process.

Marriages among nobles were usually between parties not personally acquainted with each other. Some exceptions occurred in the cases of young men and women who were brought up in the same noble household or at the same court, as in the cases of Margarethe von Zimmern and Wolf von Affenstein and of Gottfried Werner von Zimmern and Apollonia von Henneberg. Tournaments and weddings provided opportunities for fathers to show off eligible daughters and for young men to scout out prospective brides, as in the story of Werner VIII von Zimmern and Anna von Kirchberg.[3] However, nobles had fewer opportunities to see potential spouses in person than did patricians, who often lived in the same city and could see the prospective partner at church or at a fair.[4] Marriage projects often began with conversations between the two fathers (if they were personally acquainted) or between other friends or relatives of one party with friends

---

[1]An exception is the early seventeenth-century autobiography of Heinrich von Schweinichen (1552–1616), excerpts of which are given in Dülmen, "Heirat und Eheleben," 159–61.

[2]Wolf, *Von der Chronik zum Weltbuch*, 383.

[3]Spiess, *Familie und Verwandtschaft*, 37.

[4]Beer, *Eltern und Kinder*, 90.

or relatives of the other. The *Zimmern Chronicle* implies that most men and women were involved in several marriage projects before one of these resulted in an actual marriage, and this impression is borne out by surviving letters and diaries. Spiess says that, in the fifteenth and early sixteenth centuries, "many unfulfilled projects are alluded to in letters, but the reasons for failure are rarely given."[5] In the last quarter of the sixteenth century, Landdrost Kaspar von Fürstenberg recorded in his diary the number of candidates for the hands of each of his children. The first and second daughters had six suitors apiece, the third and fourth daughters had five suitors apiece, and nine candidates were considered as potential brides for his only son.[6]

Even adults negotiating their own marriages were expected to take the advice of their friends (that is, their kin) in choosing a marriage partner. Marriage contracts usually include the statement that the parties are acting "with the advice of friends on both sides."[7] Intermediaries—usually relatives of one or both parties—played a crucial role throughout the process of marriage negotiations. Even fathers who were personal friends relied on intermediaries to carry out the business aspects of the negotiations for a marriage between their children, as in the case of Johann Werner II von Zimmern and Ludwig von Löwenstein (*ZC* 2:192). In many cases, the intermediary appears as the driving force behind the marriage from the beginning, setting out to kindle the interest of one or both parties in the match. For example, Count Christoph von Tengen promoted a match between his friend Wilhelm Werner von Zimmern and the daughter of the late Count Leonard of Haag; "He was closely related to the counts of Haag, so he made particular efforts to bring about this match" (*ZC* 3:41). If the project was successful, the intermediary usually helped to draw up the marriage contract and acted as one of the witnesses.[8]

Intermediaries might have their own political motives for promoting a match. This was especially true of princes or other patrons who were in a position to arrange marriages for their clients, but even relatives might have their own political or personal agendas. Froben Christoph von Zimmern complains that in the negotiations to end the Werdenberg-Zimmern feud through a dynastic marriage, the intermediary Schenk Christoph von Limpurg "undertook the matter as a relative of both sides [*gemainer freund*] but was more pro-Werdenberg than pro-Zimmern" (*ZC* 2:193). Froben Christoph depicts his own marriage negotiations as a tug-of-war between the rival Fürstenberg and Zollern families (*ZC* 3:507–9). Spiess notes that in the negotiations in the *Zimmern Chronicle,* intermediaries were usually relatives in the female line and relatives by marriage rather than

---

[5]Spiess, *Familie und Verwandtschaft,* 83.
[6]Hufschmidt, *Adelige Frauen im Weserraum,* 131–32.
[7]Spiess, *Familie und Verwandtschaft,* 83.
[8]Spiess, *Familie und Verwandtschaft,* 82–84.

agnates such as brothers or paternal uncles. He suggests that agnates were not trusted since they might try to increase their own inheritance by arranging a disadvantageous match for their kin.[9]

Ruling princes—whether secular or ecclesiastical—could reward their officials and courtiers for their services by arranging marriages to heiresses or rich widows. Such marriages provided the clients with a source of income at no expense to the princes themselves; they also helped the patrons reinforce their clients' dependence on them, build up their own political power, and prevent marriages that might upset the political balance of power.[10] This strategy is most obvious in the case of emperors and their generals. In 1505 Felix von Werdenberg was "given a wife" by Emperor Maximilian I, who made use of the provision in feudal law that the heiress of a vassal could not be married without the consent of the overlord. In this case, the heiress was Elisabeth, daughter of the late Count Claudius de Foy et Neuchâtel, who had large landholdings in Luxembourg.[11]

According to an anecdote in the chronicle, Maximilian also rewarded his general, Andreas von Sonnenberg, with a marriage to a rich widow in the Netherlands. Unfortunately, she had already contracted a secret marriage to her steward, so the marriage to Sonnenberg was bigamous and was later annulled (*ZC* 2:298–99).[12] Charles V probably also promoted the marriage of his general, Philipp von Eberstein (the chronicler's brother-in-law), to the rich widow Jeanne de Bailleul. Jeanne not only had a large inheritance from her father, but had inherited substantial sums from her two previous husbands (*ZC* 4:367).

While serving at the courts of Baden and of Württemberg, Johann Werner II and Gottfried Werner von Zimmern both benefited from the efforts of patrons to secure advantageous marriages for them. Margrave Christoph von Baden took Johann Werner with him on visits to Strasbourg, where he invited the widow Sophia Böcklin to banquets and dances to promote a match between them (*ZC* 2:147–48). Although Duke Ulrich von Württemberg may not have initiated the match between Gottfried Werner and Apollonia von Henneberg, he "did his best to further the match and gain the goodwill of Apollonia's father." He took Gottfried Werner on trips to visit the Duchess of Nürtingen, in whose household Apollonia was being brought up, and invited the duchess and her ladies to hunting parties. If

---

[9]Spiess, *Familie und Verwandtschaft*, 89, 95–96.

[10]For an analysis of the marriages arranged by the Electors Palatine for their clients (including the Erbach family), see Spiess, *Familie und Verwandtschaft*, 105–10. Spiess suggests that at least at the regional level, "princes were clever enough to suggest marriages consistent with the existing connubium [circle of marriages]" and therefore provoked little opposition to their arrangements. Ibid., 111.

[11]Vanotti, *Grafen von Montfort und von Werdenberg*, 451.

[12]The Waldburg genealogy does not record this alleged first marriage, but it does show that Andreas von Sonnenberg married a widow, Margarethe von Starhemberg, whose first husband was a Hapsburg official in Austria. Since the Waldburgs rarely married outside Swabia, it is likely that this marriage was arranged by the emperor. Schwennicke, *Europäische Stammtafeln NF,* 5:148.

the chronicle is to be believed, he was also willing to use armed force to protect Apollonia against abduction by her father (*ZC* 2:443–46).

It might seem—especially from the anecdote about Andreas von Sonnenberg's apocryphal first wife—that the women in these cases had no option but to obey the command of the emperor or the prince. Wards probably did have little choice, but widows evidently had the power to veto a match. Margrave Christoph von Baden did not issue orders to Sophia Böcklin; he had to try to persuade her to accept Johann Werner II von Zimmern. When Johann Werner called off the match, Margrave Christoph angrily demanded that he should pay back "several thousand gulden that [Christoph] had spent on entertainments promoting the match" (*ZC* 2:150).

The marriage contract was signed by the bride's male representative; that is, her father, brother, or guardian. The groom signed the contract himself if he had reached the age of majority (usually eighteen or twenty-one years, depending on the family).[13] If the groom was a minor, the contract was signed by his father or guardian.

The majority of noblemen were able to negotiate their own marriages, since their fathers were already dead. However, fathers might arrange marriages even for sons under the canonical age of fourteen, who would not be expected to inherit for many years. Some fathers arranged a son's marriage in expectation of their own death; Werner VIII von Zimmern is said to have arranged the marriage of his son Johann Werner I to Margarethe von Oettingen in 1474, "since he was old and feeble, and his only son, on whom the continuation of the lineage depended, was still unmarried" (*ZC* 1:423). The chronicle says Johann Werner "had reached a suitable age," but he was probably less than twenty years old at the time of his marriage.[14]

Mitterauer suggests that the tendency for sons not to marry until after the father's death was a deliberate attempt to avoid the frictions caused by coresidence.[15] While the quarrels between Johann Werner I and his father for the remaining nine years of the latter's life would certainly provide evidence to support this argument, the tendency to marry after the father's death was probably due primarily to demographic factors. Southwest German counts and barons normally married in their late twenties. Since in this era the life expectancy for noblemen who survived to the age of twenty was only twenty to thirty more years, a

[13]Ulshöfer, *Hausrecht der Grafen von Zollern,* 64. The Zollerns were unusual in setting the twenty-fifth birthday as the age of majority for their male members.

[14]Isenburg gives Johann Werner's birthdate as 1444, which would make him thirty years old at the time of his marriage; however, Schwennicke gives his birthdate as around 1455, which would make him only eighteen or nineteen years old. Isenburg, *Europäische Stammtafeln* 5:123; and Schwennicke, *Europäische Stammtafeln NF,* 12:83.

[15]Mitterauer, "Zur Frage des Heiratsverhaltens," 185.

father who married in his late twenties was likely to die before his eldest son reached the same age.[16]

An adult son who married during his father's lifetime might still negotiate his own marriage, as in the case of Froben Christoph himself. A son who was financially independent might arrange his own marriage without even consulting his father, though he would still observe the formality of requesting his consent. Philipp von Eberstein, a thirty-five-year-old officer in the army of Charles V, merely wrote to his father after the negotiations for his marriage to Jeanne de Bailleul were already completed. He asked his father's consent in the same letter in which he invited him to the marriage (ZC 4:368).

A marriage project usually began by circulating the news among the kinship network that the family was looking for a partner for a son or daughter, and by consulting trusted kin for their recommendations for potential partners.[17] Urban patrician families often received overtures from an intermediary claiming to hear rumors of a search, and the language of the *Zimmern Chronicle* suggests similar behavior among nobles.[18] Ordinarily, the groom's side made the first move. However, the chronicler always avoids suggesting that the Zimmerns themselves took the first steps in initiating direct contact with the other party; it was more prestigious to be sought after than to make the first overtures.

Froben Christoph had considerable freedom to negotiate his own marriage, even though it took place during the lifetime of his father and his uncle Gottfried Werner, the de facto head of the family. He was estranged from his father, Johann Werner II, who took no part in the negotiations. His uncle Gottfried Werner, with whom he resided and whom he served as secretary, participated in the negotiations and gave his consent to the marriage.

In 1543, when the twenty-five-year-old Froben Christoph had been in his uncle's service for about a year, "the old lord made up his mind to marry the young man into an honorable family" (ZC 3:506). Relatives by blood and by marriage volunteered or were asked for suggestions from among their own circle of relatives and friends.

The first overtures came through letters from the Zollern family, to whom the Zimmerns were already related by marriage; Gottfried Werner's daughter Anna was the wife of Jos Niklaus von Zollern. Johanna von Zollern, the widow of

---

[16]Nassiet emphasizes that these demographic factors meant that French noblemen usually married after the death of their fathers. *Parenté, noblesse et états dynastiques,* 43. For data on the life expectancy of noblemen in Britain, France, and Holland from the fourteenth to the seventeenth century, see ibid., 180–86. Nassiet's calculations of remaining life expectancy at age twenty, based on princely houses, are 25.0 more years for those born between 1426 and 1499, 20.5 more years for those born between 1500 and 1549, and 28.4 more years for those born between 1550 and 1599.

[17]Among the English gentry, "one of the most important functions of the wider kin network was to propose and vet suitable candidates for marriage." Heal and Holmes, *Gentry in England and Wales,* 60.

[18]Beer, *Eltern und Kinder,* 99.

Truchsess Jakob von Waldburg, suggested that Froben Christoph should marry her sister Anna. However, Froben was already acquainted with Anna and had no desire to marry her. "Many letters were written back and forth about the matter, and the Truchsessin took a great interest in it. But the young man did not want to commit himself too far in writing, and took great care to write without giving any promises" (ZC 3:506).

Johanna and her sister then followed up on the letters by visiting Messkirch several times to win the favor of Gottfried Werner and his wife. Gottfried Werner "would gladly have had [Froben Christoph] make the marriage; he felt that it would lead to long-lasting neighborliness and he was afraid that if the match was rejected, it would lead to ill will and enmity." However, "it did not appeal to the young man ... so the matter was politely allowed to drop, for the old lord did not want to force his nephew into any marriage" (ZC 3:506–7).

It is not clear why Froben Christoph did not want to marry Anna von Zollern. His sarcastic remarks about the failure of earlier marriage projects for Anna show that he thought the Zollerns viewed him as a last resort for a woman who was no prize on the marriage market: "Since they needed a fool, they looked for one in Messkirch" (ZC 3:506).[19]

Several aspects of this episode are worth noting. First of all, the groom made the decision himself. The initial overtures were addressed to him, although his uncle "was aware of all these suits," and the bridegroom exercised an effective veto. Gottfried Werner defined his role as that of giving advice and consent; he was willing to use persuasion, but not coercion. Second, personal characteristics were evidently a decisive factor. Froben Christoph never mentions affection as a prerequisite for marriage, but he here refused to accept a politically advantageous match in which the potential for affection was lacking. Lastly, women played a large role; Anna's sister acted as her intermediary, and the two women courted the support of Gottfried Werner's wife Apollonia von Henneberg. Even though her consent was not formally required, they obviously believed that Apollonia would play an important role in making the decision.[20]

After rejecting the match with Anna von Zollern, Froben Christoph turned to his mother's sister, Anna von Erbach, the wife of Count Jörg von Lupfen.

---

[19]Anna "had previously been supposed to marry Count Ladislaus von Haag, Baron Hans Christoph von Falkenstein, Christoph von Landenberg, and others.... The Zollern girl remained single and several years later reentered the convent of Buchau on the Federsee, where she is to this day" (ZC 3:506). The Zollern genealogy confirms that Anna died unmarried at some time after 1544, but it does not record that she entered the church. Isenburg, Europäische Stammtafeln, 1:153.

[20]In a contemporary marriage negotiation in the Nuremberg patriciate, the father of Sibylla Baumgartner made his consent to the suit of Hans Ölhaufen "conditional on the consent of his wife and daughter." Beer, Eltern und Kinder, 109. Women also played key roles in the marriage negotiations of lesser nobles in the late sixteenth and seventeenth centuries, though they were less active in negotiations for sons than in those for daughters. Hufschmidt, Frauen im Weserraum, 131–39.

> Among other pieces of advice (for women give strange advice and one must use one's judgment and not follow all of it), she thought he should marry a Fräulein von Mörsperg, one of Count Franz's daughters, for she was well brought up and good at managing a household; it would be a good marriage. Moreover, since all the Zimmern affairs were going awry and it was like an old dilapidated house that might fall down any minute, she advised him to tell Count Friedrich von Fürstenberg about his need and lack of money, and to tell him how matters stood. (*ZC* 3:507)

Froben Christoph evidently felt defensive about asking advice from women; he rejected his aunt's suggestion by showing off his knowledge of old scandals in the girl's family. "As for the marriage, it melted away, for there was much talk about the household of the Mörspergs" (*ZC* 3:507). The aunt's comments clearly suggest that she thought wealth should be the major consideration in the match and that she was willing to overlook the gossip. Her comments also show the importance of invoking ties to influential kinsmen by marriage such as Friedrich von Fürstenberg, who belonged to one of the highest-ranking families of counts in Swabia.

Although the family ties were indirect—Friedrich von Fürstenberg was the husband of a cousin of Froben Christoph's mother and aunt—Fürstenberg was also a good friend of Froben Christoph and had a political interest in helping him.[21] Fürstenberg had been a rival of Karl von Zollern for the Werdenberg inheritance and he would not want to see the Zimmerns drawn more closely into the Zollern sphere of influence by a marriage alliance. Fürstenberg promoted a match for Froben Christoph with Elisabeth, the eldest daughter of Count Hugo XVI von Montfort-Tettnang-Rothenfels. "Count Friedrich von Fürstenberg had many talks with the young man in favor of this match, for he and Count Hugo had been friends for many years.... [I]t would have been an honorable marriage from the standpoint of family, descent, and convenience" and also, although the chronicler does not mention it, from the standpoint of wealth (*ZC* 3:508). However, it is unclear whether the Montforts themselves were interested in the match. Since the Montforts were a more prestigious and powerful family than the Zimmerns, it is hard to believe that Froben Christoph would have pursued a match with the poorer and less prestigious Eberstein family if he had felt there was any chance of success with the Montfort match.[22]

---

[21]Friedrich von Fürstenberg was married to Anna, the daughter of Christoph von Werdenberg; Anna was a first cousin of Katharina and Anna von Erbach, Froben Christoph's mother and aunt. The personal friendship between Fürstenberg and Froben Christoph would be cemented with a marriage alliance in the next generation, when Fürstenberg's son Joachim married Froben Christoph's eldest daughter Anna in 1562. Isenburg, *Europäische Stammtafeln,* 4:127.

[22]Elisabeth von Montfort was the oldest of Hugo's daughters; she was presumably born before 1535, since her younger sister Katharina was born before 1536. However, she may well have been under the canonical age of twelve at the time of the negotiations. Hugo was clearly in no hurry to make a

The chronicler, however, implies that the Zimmerns were distracted from the Montfort match by the intensive campaign of Jos Niklaus von Zollern on behalf of the daughter of *his* old friend, Count Wilhelm von Eberstein. "In this confusion, Jos Niklaus von Zollern dealt in such a manner with the old lord, with the young man, and with the women, that a Fräulein von Eberstein came into the picture" (*ZC* 3:508). The implication is that the Zollerns, despite their failure with their first candidate, were determined to reinforce their ties to the Zimmerns and to break up any match that would have drawn the Zimmerns closer to the Fürstenbergs. Again the intermediary is depicted as paying special attention to influencing the women of the family.

If the Zimmerns were seeking to shore up their "dilapidated old house" through a rich marriage for Froben Christoph, it is surprising that they would choose the Eberstein family. Although they were an old family of counts, the Ebersteins were now impoverished and of little political significance; they had even made some marriages into the lower nobility. The chronicle candidly admits that they had "lost one feather after another" from their once-rich territorial possessions (*ZC* 3:530–31).[23]

Since the Ebersteins themselves had so little to offer, it was necessary for the chronicler to justify the match. As Wolf notes, "Froben could have used the model of a love match as in the case of Gottfried Werner and Apollonia von Henneberg, but he uses the religious paradigm instead, and names providence as the basis of marriage. God and not love is the best argument against the demands of kin" who wanted a marriage for wealth.[24] The justification might be called superstitious rather than religious; the chronicler claims that he had followed traditional rituals on St. Andrew's eve in the hopes that "one would see in one's sleep the person he or she would marry. The young count tried this a year before the marriage contract and the Fräulein von Eberstein, whom he later married, appeared to him in a dream, although he had never seen her before" (*ZC* 3:509).

The real reasons for the decision to pursue the Eberstein match are not clear. The Eberstein family already had a friendly relationship with the Zimmern family; in 1541, they had asked Wilhelm Werner to research their genealogy.[25] However, the chronicle never mentions Wilhelm Werner in connection with the match. The Eberstein match may have been favored by Gottfried Werner as a means of preserving good relations with the Zollern family without forcing Froben Christoph

---

match for her, or indeed for any of his daughters, for none of them married until 1551. Although Elisabeth was the eldest, she did not marry until 1556. Schwennicke, *Europäische Stammtafeln NF,* 12:55.

[23]Wolf notes that the chronicle's comments on the descent of the Ebersteins are much more perfunctory than those on other families into which the Zimmerns had married. Any attempt to depict a glorious past for them would only accentuate their present decline and imply that an alliance with them was a step downward for the Zimmerns. *Von der Chronik zum Weltbuch,* 385.

[24]Wolf, *Von der Chronik zum Weltbuch,* 385.

[25]Jenny, *Graf Froben Christoph von Zimmern,* 175.

to accept a candidate he disliked. The chronicler stresses the dominant role played by Jos Niklaus von Zollern in negotiating the match. Froben Christoph later came to see Jos Niklaus as an enemy of the Zimmern family because of his insistence on the claim of his wife Anna to the Zimmern inheritance. In retrospect, the chronicler views the earlier efforts of Jos Niklaus to promote the Eberstein match as a Machiavellian intrigue that forced the Zimmerns into a match that was not really in their best interests. He cites a tasteless joke made by Jos Niklaus at the signing of the marriage contract and his failure to attend the wedding ceremony as evidence that he was not fulfilling his proper role as an intermediary.

The proposed match was for "one of the daughters" of Wilhelm von Eberstein, not for a specific individual. The first candidate suggested was the eldest daughter Amalia, but Froben Christoph was advised not to accept her because of her poor health. The fourth daughter Kunigunde was then suggested, but the prospective groom did not actually meet her until the business aspects of the marriage negotiations had been completed. Shortly before the contract was to be signed at Hechingen (on 6 February 1544), "the young Count Froben Christoph and Count Jos Niklaus von Zollern rode to Eberstein to see the Fräulein von Eberstein and also to let himself be seen." The only emotion the chronicler records at this visit was embarrassment at having to wear his uncle's old-fashioned clothes: "he had a cloak that was his best outfit, trimmed with a great deal of velvet. This had belonged to the old lord, but it was too big and too long for the young man, and also out of fashion" (ZC 3:513). He says nothing about the appearance or personality of Kunigunde herself.

After the signing of the marriage contract, Jos Niklaus hinted none too subtly that Froben Christoph would have preferred to marry Amalia: "Count Jos Niklaus made a joke and said to the old lord, 'My young kinsman would be well advised to sneak after both sisters.' Everyone standing by laughed loudly, but not everyone was pleased" (ZC 3:508). In describing Amalia's death and burial two years later, the chronicler states that "she was laid in the grave in a black dress; her hair hung down her back, and she wore a green wreath" (ZC 3:516–17).[26] The emphasis on the unbound hair and the wreath—the attributes of a bride—suggests that Amalia might indeed have been the bride Froben Christoph wished he had taken.

The account in the *Zimmern Chronicle* of Froben Christoph's marriage negotiations shows even a groom who negotiated his own marriage could put the interests of the lineage ahead of his personal preference. Although Froben Christoph

---

[26]Amalia was born in 1524 and therefore would have been nineteen years old at the time negotiations began in 1543; she died in 1546. Kunigunde, born in 1528, would have been fifteen years old. Wilhelm also had two other daughters older than Kunigunde: Elisabeth (b. 1525, died unmarried in 1555) and Felicitas (b. 1527, became abbess of Herford). The fact that neither of these girls was mentioned as a candidate, and that neither of them ever married, suggests that they suffered from drawbacks even more serious than Amalia's. Isenburg, *Europäische Stammtafeln*, 4:133.

apparently preferred Amalia von Eberstein, he heeded his kinsmen's advice to choose a bride more likely to bear children to perpetuate the lineage. In several ways Froben Christoph's marriage negotiations were old-fashioned by the standards of the urban patrician men of his day. The groom did not suggest any potential brides out of his own circle of personal acquaintance; the personal appearance of the bride and the potential for affection between the spouses were not overtly discussed in conversations about potential brides; and the prospective spouses never met in person until the property negotiations were already completed.

Since the chronicle presents the negotiations from the groom's point of view, it is difficult to analyze the role of the prospective bride. Anna von Zollern certainly played an active—even aggressive—role in her proposed match; she called on Froben Christoph's uncle and aunt in the company of her intermediary. However, in this case the call could be disguised as a family visit; it is unlikely that prospective brides visited families to whom they were unrelated.

In all the other proposed matches, the marriage was discussed between the groom (and his intermediary) and the bride's kinsmen, with no mention of active participation by the bride herself.[27] This would not be unusual, for women were often not apprised of a proposed match until the business aspects of the negotiations were concluded. In 1547, Hans Ungnad von Weissenwolff forbade his wife to discuss with their daughter Judith the negotiations under way for her marriage to Juan de Hoyos, in case the project fell through. Only after the marriage contract had been negotiated did he speak to Judith about the marriage. He then "called on her as a dutiful daughter, assured her of her groom's wealth and nobility, and stated that, with the use of their common sense, they would get along with each other very well. In the same breath, he regretted that 'the other daughters were [not] also so well married. I think they will have to sit a long time,'" implying none too subtly that if Judith did not accept this match, she could not expect a better one any time soon.[28] Wilhelm von Eberstein's daughters evidently had no say in which one of them would be offered the match with Froben Christoph, nor do we know what they thought of the potential groom. One suspects that Kunigunde von Eberstein may not have been overly impressed by her awkward suitor with his pockmarked face and hand-me-down clothes. However, her family was not wealthy and she had three unmarried elder sisters, so she may have been relieved

---

[27]In contrast, the patrician Margarethe Beheim "insisted on a husband that *she* liked as the only basis for a happy marriage; she was not interested in being 'married off'" (emphasis in original). Margarethe was involved in discussions of potential spouses from the beginning, rejected her guardians' demands that she choose one of two proposed candidates, and eventually chose her own husband. Beer, *Eltern und Kinder,* 104–7. Some noblewomen in the sixteenth and seventeenth centuries successfully set conditions for acceptable candidates or rejected candidates chosen for them by their families. See Hufschmidt, *Adelige Frauen im Weserraum,* 132–40; and Bastl, *Tugend, Liebe, Ehre,* 156.

[28]Bastl, *Tugend, Liebe, Ehre,* 161.

to be assured of a marriage at all. Despite the new emphasis on the potential for affection as a requirement in marriage, the decision of both parties in this match was probably based largely on pragmatic grounds.

ʃ❧ ʃ❧ ʃ❧

From the legal point of view, the most important step in contracting a marriage was the betrothal (*Verlobung* or *Ehegelöbnis*), which took place after the marriage contract was signed. Several months later—or even years later, if the bride was young—the marriage itself was celebrated through the *Trauung* (exchange of vows) and the *Kirchgang* (blessing in the church). The final stage of the marriage was the bedding of the bridal couple to consummate the marriage (*Beilager*).[29] Among the southwest German nobility, the wedding festivities usually took place at the bride's residence, although it would be held at the groom's residence if the bride lived a great distance away. If the wedding was held at the bride's residence, she usually remained there for several months before being welcomed to her husband's residence with a homecoming feast.[30]

Both the wedding festivities and the homecoming feast allowed the families of the bride and the groom to display their wealth and status. The lavishness of such festivities among princely families became legendary, as in the Landeshut Wedding of 1475 in which Duke Georg the Rich of Bavaria married the daughter of King Casimir of Poland. The splendor of such weddings was often measured by the number of horses (that is, guests of honor and their attendants), which would range between two and four thousand at a princely wedding; princes traveled with two to three hundred horses apiece.[31] However, weddings among the counts and barons were on a much more modest scale. At the marriage of Countess Elisabeth von Isenburg-Büdingen to Count Sigmund von Gleichen in 1482, there were only 173 horses, with eight close relatives of the bride and groom bringing about twenty apiece.[32] The weddings in the *Zimmern Chronicle* are further evidence of the small scale of many weddings among the nobility.

Only one wedding mentioned in the *Zimmern Chronicle* was a court festivity celebrated on a grand scale with tournaments: the wedding of Count Philipp von Eberstein to the widow Jeanne de Bailleul. It took place at St. Thomas in the

---

[29]On the sequence of ceremonies, see Spiess, *Familie und Verwandtschaft*, 113–19, 127.

[30]In ten examples of wedding festivities in Spiess's sample of counts and barons of the Mainz region, five were held at the bride's residence and four at the groom's; one double wedding was held at a neutral site; Spiess, *Familie und Verwandtschaft*, 121–24, 127.

[31]Spiess, *Familie und Verwandtschaft*, 119–20, 123. Zeilinger devotes an entire book to a detailed analysis of the most lavish princely wedding in Swabia in this era, that of Count Eberhard V von Württemberg and Barbara Gonzaga of Mantua in 1474. *Urarcher Hochzeit 1474*.

[32]Spiess, *Familie und Verwandtschaft*, 122–23.

Netherlands and was sponsored by Philipp's patron, Emperor Charles V.[33] The chronicle devotes two entire chapters to a description of the journey of the Eberstein family to the Netherlands and the festivities associated with the wedding.

> The wedding began the next day. A Mass was held in the hall, but only a minority of the lords attended; those who belonged to the new faith or Augsburg Confession left the room. After the Mass, the bride and groom were married to each other; this occurred on 7 April 1556.... It is impossible to describe the pomp and splendor of this wedding, with such expensive foods and the best wines, with such banquets with music and everything else that is fitting and customary; no expense was spared on anything. There were several tournaments on horse and on foot, and several jousts, all held with splendor. Then there was running at the ring.... The wedding lasted several days. (ZC 4:392–96)

Attendance at such a wedding was a once-in-a-lifetime experience for nobles who did not reside at court. The weddings in the Zimmern family itself were on a much more modest scale. Some were quite small because they took place under unusual circumstances. The marriage of Gottfried Werner to Apollonia von Henneberg in 1511 was opposed by the bride's father, so the wedding was held at the groom's residence with only a few of his friends and relatives in attendance. The bridegroom Gottfried Werner, accompanied by his brother Johann Werner II, brought a wagon to pick up Apollonia at the residence of her aunt and patroness, the Duchess of Nürtingen. His close friend Dietrich von Späth escorted them back to Messkirch, where they were met by Gottfried Werner's mother Margarethe von Oettingen and his sister Katharina, the abbess of the Frauenmünster in Zürich. "A small but gracious and joyous wedding" followed (ZC 2:446–47).

The marriage of Gottfried Werner's daughter Anna to Jos Niklaus von Zollern in 1531 was also small, for plague broke out in Messkirch the day of the wedding and Gottfried Werner ordered the house quarantined. The guests of honor included only Johann Werner II and his wife (the bride's aunt and uncle), Count Christoph von Werdenberg and his wife (the groom's aunt), and the groom's cousin, Count Christoph Friedrich von Zollern. The wedding would have had to be a small one in any case, due to the family's financial circumstances. The silver plate used for the wedding was borrowed from Wilhelm Werner von Zimmern, who did not attend the ceremony. When it came time for the gifts, Gottfried Werner "gave" his daughter a gilded cup, but it actually belonged to Wilhelm Werner and had to be sent back to him along with the rest of the plate (ZC 2:454–45).

The marriage in 1524 of Wilhelm Werner to his second wife, the widowed Countesss Amalia von Leuchtenberg, was also a small one. According to the chronicle, the ceremony took place hastily, only a few days after Wilhelm Werner

---

[33]Another example of a lavish wedding sponsored by a prince for his retainer is that of Hans von Schweinichen, described in Dülmen, "Heirat und Eheleben," 159–60.

had arrived at her residence with his intermediary, with the intention of signing a marriage contract with Amalia's daughter.[34] "No one had prepared for the wedding, and neither Christoph nor Wilhelm Werner had brought clothing or other necessities," since ordinarily the ceremony would not take place until several months after the contract was signed. The chronicler foreshadows the unhappy outcome of this marriage by recounting ridiculous events said to have occurred at the wedding. On the first night of the festivities, Wilhelm Werner was exhausted after "dancing all day and also in the evening after dinner." When he went to bed, his servants laid his pants on a hot stove to dry, but they were so careless that the fly burned away. Since he had no other set of clothes to wear, "the church and other matters had to wait until a new fly was sewn in, which everyone took for a bad omen" (ZC 3:42).

The wedding of Froben Christoph to Kunigunde von Eberstein is thus the only normal one described in detail in the *Zimmern Chronicle*. This "small but joyous wedding" took place at Eberstein on "Monday after Misericordia Sunday" 1544 (28 April 1544), with the festivities lasting from Sunday night until Thursday (ZC 3:514, 517). Froben Christoph's description of the wedding concentrates on the feasting and drinking, and surprisingly enough, does not mention the bride at all. Likewise, he does not describe any of the formal stages of the marriage; not the exchanging of vows, the blessing in the church, or the consummation. However, from his remarks about other weddings, it can be assumed the date and time for the bedding of the couple were set for an astrologically auspicious hour in order to assure the fertility of the marriage. The chronicler charges that Christoph von Werdenberg's wife, Johanna von Börsell, planned the wedding of her nephew Jos Niklaus von Zollern to Anna von Zimmern so that "the consummation took place at an inauspicious hour, which experience shows augured badly for the fruitfulness of the marriage." He claims that Johanna did this to ensure that the inheritance would fall not to the offspring of Jos Niklaus but to her own children by Eitelfriedrich von Zollern. In contrast, at the wedding of Truchsess Wilhelm von Waldburg to Johanna von Fürstenberg in 1545, "his father counted off the minutes so that the young people would come together under a lucky and fruitful sign" (ZC 2:456).[35]

The chronicler's most vivid memory of his own wedding was the embarrassment caused him by his father and uncles. In his view, they failed to properly outfit him according to his status, and they made a public spectacle of themselves by

---

[34]The chronicle's account must be taken with a grain of salt, since the contract for the marriage of Wilhelm Werner and Amalia von Leuchtenberg was signed on 17 March 1524 and the wedding ceremony did not take place until 30 November 1525; Schwennicke, *Europäische Stammtafeln NF,* 12:84.

[35]Grimmer describes a similar concern for auspicious hours of espousal and consummation among the French nobility in the sixteenth century. Some nobles carried out the actual marriage ceremony at night in the presence of only a few guests out of fear that enemies might induce impotence by "tying a knot" at the moment of marriage. *La femme et le bâtard,* 128.

revealing the disharmony within the Zimmern family. It was customary for wedding guests to outfit all their attendants in new clothes of a matching color. In this case the bridegroom's father, Johann Werner, and his uncle, Gottfried Werner,

> could not agree on their clothing; neither was willing to dress to please the other. Gottfried Werner dressed his household all in red, while Johann Werner dressed his in green.... He had also convinced his brother Wilhelm Werner, and the two old lords and their servants were dressed in green. Many people wondered at the contrast and were surprised that the brothers had not been able to agree on the smallest thing. (*ZC* 3:514)

Froben Christoph's father and uncles also embarrassed him by their miserliness on an occasion when generous spending was essential to display status. "The bridegroom was outfitted very frugally for the wedding.... His uncles had given him twenty-four gulden, and that was all his ready cash. In addition, he had secretly borrowed another fifty gulden. He was not endowed with any superfluity of clothing, nor arrayed to dazzle the eye" (*ZC* 3:514–15). He does not say whether the bride, who came from a poorer family, was dressed any more lavishly.

The guests at the wedding included, from the Zimmern side, Froben Christoph's father and his uncle Wilhelm Werner. Neither was accompanied by his wife, since both men were informally separated. Gottfried Werner was ill, but his wife Apollonia and daughter Anna attended. Anna's husband Jos Niklaus von Zollern "was supposed to come to the wedding as the negotiator of the marriage, but he had to appear at the Reichstag in Speyer...or perhaps he personally did not want to come" (*ZC* 3:514). The chronicler does not explain this dark hint.

Those appearing from the Eberstein side, in addition to the bride's parents, included her uncle Count Johann Jakob (or Hans Jakob) von Eberstein and his wife, her uncle Count Philipp von Hanau zu Lichtenberg, her four brothers, and her sister Amalia (*ZC* 3:516). It is surprising that her other three sisters are not mentioned, since the two who were not nuns would presumably still have been living at home.

Additional relatives on both sides arrived after the ceremony was over: the bridegroom's older brother, Johann Christoph, a canon of Strasbourg, and his younger brother, Gottfried Christoph. The latter amazed the entire company by his capacity for drink, and startled his family by his request to become a canon like his brother. As soon as these two men had left, another canon of Strasbourg arrived, the bride's uncle Bernard von Eberstein. He had not attended the wedding itself because he did not want to encounter Johann Christoph, who had taken up with his former mistress (*ZC* 3:518, 527).

Although Froben Christoph does not describe the formal ceremonies, he has a good deal to say about the drinking and dancing.

> They say one should be drunk at weddings and homecomings, and that is what happened. After the wedding was over, Count Hans Jakob [Johann

Jakob] von Eberstein invited all the guests to his residence.... Many were merry, and in accordance with German custom, no one came away sober. That included the bridegroom; that night when they came back to Eberstein, he fell down like a block while dancing, and many were frightened that it might have a more serious cause. But the next morning after some sleep he felt better....it was only the wine. (*ZC* 3:519–20)

❧ ❧ ❧

If the wedding took place at the bride's residence, the homecoming feast took place a few months later. The procession of the bride to her new home allowed her to show off her best clothing and jewelry, while the groom went out to meet her with an entourage that displayed his own status.

Wilhelm Werner had used an ostentatious homecoming feast after his marriage to Amalia von Leuchtenberg to display his increase in status by marrying a "countess from a family equal to princes" (*gefürstete Gräfin*) and what he thought was his new wealth from a rich wife. "Most of the nobility of the Black Forest and Neckar circles were invited. It was a grand homecoming that was celebrated for eight days at great expense. The citizens of Rottweil came five hundred strong with carriages and banners to meet the bride. They were all maintained at the couple's expense, and this helped to squander [their] money" (*ZC* 3:50–51).

The homecoming for Froben Christoph's wife Kunigunde was much more modest. It took place in October 1541, less than six months after the wedding. "This was because the countess became pregnant immediately, and if the homecoming was delayed any longer, it might not be possible to hold it at all. Moreover, it was inconvenient for [Froben Christoph] to have to travel so frequently through the rough and dangerous Black Forest" to visit Kunigunde at Eberstein (*ZC* 3:532).

The Eberstein party consisted of the bride, her parents, and two of her older sisters, Amalia and Elisabeth. The Zimmerns were represented by Froben Christoph's father and his two uncles. Once again Froben Christoph was embarrassed by his relatives' behavior. His uncle Gottfried Werner became so engrossed in drafting a business letter that "the guests—including Johann Werner and Wilhelm Werner—might as well have ridden away.... A messenger came to say that the guests from out of town were already there, but since the time for receiving guests was so short, they merely met each other at Rohrdorf," whereas etiquette called for the hosts to ride out to meet their guests farther away (*ZC* 3:532). In the end, all turned out well on this occasion. As the chronicle states,

> the homecoming was a small one with little pomp; moreover, the guests could not be accommodated in a new castle that was still under construction. Nevertheless, Gottfried Werner as family head had provisioned it with the best German and foreign wines, also all kinds of game and fish from Lake Constance and other sources, so that the guests were well treated according to the

old German manner—which is really the best—and lived exceedingly well.
(*ZC* 3:533)

✿ ✿ ✿

Unlike most Swabian counts and barons, Froben Christoph was not able to set up
an independent household with his new bride. Since the chronicler was in the service of his uncle Gottfried Werner, he did not possess his own residence. The couple lived at Messkirch under the authority of Gottfried Werner, who was still the
head of the household until his death in 1554. By the time Froben Christoph succeeded to his estate, the couple had been married for ten years and Kunigunde
had given birth to six of their eleven children. The chronicler chafed under the
authority of his eccentric uncle. He acknowledges that

> he enjoyed a great advantage, in that his uncle, Gottfried Werner, maintained
> him with his wife and children; as the proverb says, "no one is ever badly off
> when he can lay his knife down on the table and the tavern-keeper has
> already been paid." However, a whole chapter could be written about what
> vexations he had to endure and what he had to listen to. (*ZC* 3:468)

He compares his position to that of "a stableboy who has to yield his seat to
others and give everybody fair words" (*ZC* 3:468). Moreover, his dependence on
his uncle kept him from enjoying the respect he felt was due to him as head of his
own nuclear family.

Such coresidence with the parents of the groom (or more rarely with those
of the bride) was the norm among the English aristocracy, where men married
at a younger age than did German counts and barons.[36] It was also common in
the German patriciate, although here the couple usually resided with the bride's
parents.[37] According to Spiess, coresidence (always with the groom's father) was
not uncommon among counts and barons of the Mainz region.[38] In Swabia, the
testament of Count Eitelfriedrich II von Zollern in 1512, which left the entire
estate to his eldest son, provided the options of coresidence or independent
households for the other sons. Younger brothers who wished to marry were to
be maintained by the family head at the ancestral seat or else provided with a
seat of their own and an annuity. The latter provision suggests that some sons

---

[36]Harris, *English Aristocratic Women,* 62–63. Harris depicts coresidence as an arrangement that
benefited the young wife by allowing her to learn through apprenticeship how to manage the household and by providing her with practical assistance and emotional support during childbirth. However, she notes that the wife often found it hard to assert herself against a forceful mother-in-law even
after the couple had their own household.

[37]Beer, *Eltern und Kinder,* 113.

[38]Spiess, *Familie und Verwandtschaft,* 173. Some marriage contracts assume coresidence, making provision for the inheritance of household goods in the event that the son predeceases his father.

preferred greater independence and wished to avoid the frictions inherent in long-term coresidence.[39]

Froben Christoph expresses his frustration with coresidence and subordination to the older generation not only in direct statements about his uncle Gottfried Werner but also indirectly in discussions of other examples of coresidence in the Zimmern family.[40] As another example of disastrous friction between generations, he cites the experience of Johann Werner I and his father Werner VIII von Zimmern. Johann Werner and his wife Margarethe von Oettingen actually coresided with his father for only two years after their marriage, for in 1476 Werner turned Messkirch over to his son and retired to a house in the town. "Although each had a separate household from the other, they were not able to get along with each other because their characters were so different." Werner constantly criticized Johann Werner for neglecting the management of the estate. One night at dinner "matters became so tense that Johann Werner drew a long dagger...against his father, and almost stabbed him. But the good God prevented this terrible crime of parricide in the Zimmern family," for his pregnant wife Margarethe von Oettingen and two nobles grabbed his arm in time to stop him (ZC 1:441).[41]

Another example of friction due to coresidence occurred in the case of Jos Niklaus von Zollern and his father-in-law Gottfried Werner. Jos Niklaus, who was only seventeen years old at the time of his marriage to Anna von Zimmern, did not have a residence of his own. "Since his father Count Joachim gave him little help, he asked his father-in-law Gottfried Werner to maintain him with his wife, children, and household at his cost for three years after the marriage. This gave rise to much friction" (ZC 2:458–59). Only after inheriting the estate of his cousin, Christoph Friedrich von Zollern, was he able to establish his own household at Hechingen.[42]

> In the meantime, he behaved strangely toward everyone. He had the stables broken open in his father-in-law's absence and did other things that scarcely pleased his father-in-law. Although he was at that time in great poverty, he was so arrogant that he openly allowed people to hear him say, "he would rather be anyplace else, than where people disliked him." (ZC 2:468)

[39]Ulshöfer, Hausrecht der Grafen von Zollern, 39.

[40]Wolf describes some of the chapters of Schwänke (farcical tales) in the Zimmern Chronicle as Froben Christoph's justification of his own behavior in subordinating himself to the power of his uncle. "After the break with his father, Froben was dependent on his uncle and also wanted to inherit from him. He could bear his humiliation by his uncle only through reason and self-control, a psychological as well as strategic master-achievement." Von der Chronik zum Weltbuch, 389.

[41]Wolf casts doubt on the authenticity of this story, describing it as "a spectacular explanation, based on literary models" for Johann Werner's decision to undertake a pilgrimage to the Holy Land in 1483. Von der Chronik zum Weltbuch, 263.

[42]The length of stay given in the chronicle is inconsistent with the actual date of death of Christoph Friedrich von Zollern in 1536, five years after the marriage of Jos Niklaus. Isenburg, Europäische Stammtafeln, 1:153.

However, Gottfried Werner acted "like a wise and reasonable man" and ignored Jos Niklaus's petulant behavior as much as possible. The chronicler concludes that

> this shows that living together on a day-to-day basis, especially when quarrelsome people are involved, brings about much misunderstanding and ill will that might otherwise be avoided. Therefore, everyone who gives his daughters dowries is taking the risk that he may be ruined, so he must not maintain his sons-in-law in his house. (*ZC* 2:468)

As far as can be ascertained, Froben did not have to face this problem with the two daughters who married in his lifetime. In his descriptions of courtship and marriage, the chronicler always concludes with the birth of the couple's first child.[43] It was not the marriage ceremonies but the birth of a child that marked the most important change in the social role of the couple, making them heads of an established nuclear family.

---

[43]For example, the description of the marriage of Johann Werner II and Katharina von Zimmern concludes with the birth of their first son, Christoph Werner (*ZC* 2:195); that of Gottfried Werner von Zimmern and Apollonia Henneberg with the birth of their first daughter, "Anna" (*ZC* 2:447); and that of Froben Christoph and Kunigunde von Eberstein with the birth of their first daughter, Anna (*ZC* 3:538).

CHAPTER 7

Marital Happiness and Marital Breakdown

In the sixteenth century, lay writers addressing a middle-class audience increasingly espoused an ideal of companionate marriage and affection between spouses. A popular marriage manual published in 1578 by the Strasbourg poet Johann Fischart depicts marriage as a "legally unequal, yet mutually respectful and functionally sharing, domestic partnership between husband and wife."[1] Although often identified with Protestant or Puritan authors, this view of marriage as based on affection (*dilectio*) was derived from the ecclesiastical model of marriage set forth in the High Middle Ages.[2] Medieval German marriage sermons had long emphasized that the goal of marriage was "loyalty, peace and harmony," which could be achieved only through the efforts of both spouses. For example, a sermon of 1449 describes emotional harmony (*concordia animorum*) as a major goal of marriage and gives a list of commandments on how to achieve love in marriage.[3] The counts and barons of southwest Germany in the era of the *Zimmern Chronicle* did not fully share this ideal of companionate marriage, but they were beginning to redefine what they considered a good and a bad marriage as being based on marital happiness rather than economic considerations. In this new atmosphere, families were also struggling with how to deal with marital unhappiness and marital breakdown at a time when divorce was not widely available.

[1]Ozment, *Ancestors,* 37.

[2]On love in the ecclesiastical model of marriage, see Duby, *Medieval Marriage,* 21, 36, 59.

[3]On the ideal of companionate marriage and affection in medieval German marriage sermons, see Schnell, "Geschlechtergeschichte und Textwissenschaft," 165–72, esp. 171.

Historians of the early modern family have long described the emotional relationship between noble husbands and wives in pessimistic terms. According to Stone, among the sixteenth-century English aristocracy,

> marriage was usually arranged rather than consensual, the outcome of an economic deal or a political alliance between two families. The transaction was sealed by the wedding and by the physical union of two individuals, while the emotional ties were left to develop at a later date. If they did not take place, and if the husband could find sexual outlets through casual liaisons, the emotional outlet through marriage was largely nonexistent for either husband or wife.[4]

Even when nobles accepted the goal of concord in marriage espoused by ecclesiastical writers, they did not necessarily accept the premise that marriage must be based on affection. "What was called conjugal partnership in the Europe of the late Middle Ages and the early modern period … is not love but *concordia* or *caritas conjugalis*—mutual understanding or rather: avoidance of discord."[5] Isabel Beceiro Pita and Isabel Córdoba de la Llave describe marriages of convenience in the Castilian high nobility as "part of a habitual mentality, accepted without major tensions" and state that the goal of concord in marriage did not require close emotional ties.[6] Of course, aristocratic spouses might view their marriages as satisfactory precisely because their expectations of happiness in marriage were set pragmatically low.[7] Despite his pessimistic view of noble marriages, even Stone concedes that

> the majority of marriages survived without open and serious breakdown, and in many cases there developed genuine affection and trust.… The number of aristocratic wills in which husbands refer to their wives in friendly terms, leave them bequests, and saddle them with responsibilities makes it clear beyond doubt that very many unions at any rate provided satisfactory working partnerships.[8]

More recent researchers on the English noble family in the fifteenth and early sixteenth century have taken a more optimistic view, emphasizing this potential for "affectionate, even loving working partnerships" even though aristocratic partners lived apart much of the time.[9] According to Harris,

> fifteenth- and sixteenth-century English aristocratic women and men … certainly did not think of marital love in romantic, erotic terms or consider "falling in love" essential to a good marriage.… What they seemed to mean [by love] … was a combination of affection, fidelity, trust, and kindness, emotions that could develop between a couple after their wedding and that would

---

[4]Stone, *Family, Sex and Marriage,* 102.
[5]Bastl, *Tugend, Liebe, Ehre,* 357.
[6]Beceiro Pita and Córdoba de la Llave, *Parentesco, poder y mentalidad,* 216.
[7]Stone, *Family, Sex and Marriage,* 104.
[8]Stone, *Crisis of the Aristocracy,* 660.
[9]Harris, *English Aristocratic Women,* 75.

facilitate their cooperation as partners in the family enterprise.... Whatever they meant by love, many, though certainly not all, aristocratic couples believed that they experienced it in their marriages and affirmed their affection for each other in their letters.[10]

David Potter describes marriages in the nobility of sixteenth-century France as governed by "the conventions of *amitié* [friendship] and even love between spouses which mitigated the effects of arranged marriage. This sort of convention could also reinforce the conjugal bond."[11] Heinz Reif makes a similar argument apropos of the early modern nobility of Münster; he believes that, although there were few close emotional ties at the beginning of the marriage, in most cases "a kind of married love developed, based on the organized solidarity of the couple to deal with tasks that could only be handled jointly."[12]

It is difficult to evaluate emotional relationships between German noble spouses in the era of the *Zimmern Chronicle,* since few personal documents are available. Some exceptional letters from members of the princely house of Brandenburg show that even the partners in marriages arranged for political purposes could form strong emotional and sexual attachments. Elector Albrecht von Brandenburg and his wife Anna exchanged erotic banter in their correspondence of 1474–75.[13] The Danish princess Dorothea wrote in 1535 to her husband Duke Albrecht of Brandenburg, "I cannot conceal from you how every night, and especially when I have just received your letters, all I dream is that I am lying with my husband, dearest to my heart, and share all joy and pastime with you." The funeral sermon preached for Dorothea in 1547 said, "There was such mutual love between the spouses that one can truly use the old saying, 'Though their bodies are two, their hearts are one.'"[14]

The development of married love is also evident in the letter of the Spanish courtier Juan de Hoyos (1506–61) to his Austrian wife Judith Elisabeth von Ungnad. When Judith's father announced the marriage arrangements to her in 1547, he held out no expectations of romantic bliss, merely saying that "with the use of their common sense, they would get along with each other very well." However, later letters between the couple use greetings such as "my love," "my beloved wife," "my beloved treasure," and "my beloved husband" that were not merely courtesy formulas but expressed real feeling. When separated from his wife by his duties at the Spanish court, Hoyos wrote to her in 1550, "if I could only be with you, all my burdens would be lighter."[15] Unfortunately, no such revealing passages

---

[10]Harris, *English Aristocratic Women,* 73–74. See also Rosenthal, "Aristocratic Marriage and the English Peerage," 188–89, 192.

[11]Potter, "Marriage and Cruelty," 28–29.

[12]Reif, *Westfälischer Adel,* 107.

[13]Nolte, "Verbalerotische Kommunikation," 453–54.

[14]Quoted in Wunder, *He Is the Sun,* 57.

[15]Bastl, *Tugend, Liebe, Ehre,* 161, 356, 365.

occur in the surviving correspondence of southwest German counts and barons. Spiess notes that letters of fifteen Franconian families before 1500 do not shed light on personal relationships. Most surviving documents from the nonprincely nobility are legal records, and expressions such as "beloved wife" in wills may be merely formulaic.[16]

The *Zimmern Chronicle* presents a fairly pessimistic view of marriage among the German high nobility. To some extent this is due to the anecdotal nature of the chronicle—unhappy marriages provide more gossip than happy ones. However, the number of estrangements among the close kin of the chronicler Froben Christoph von Zimmern suggest that happy marriages were the exception rather than the rule in his own personal experience. Although he shares many of the misogynistic stereotypes of his day, he differs from most German lay writers in the sixteenth century in seeing the maintenance of marital harmony as the responsibility of the husband as well as the wife.[17] He places much of the blame for unhappy marriages on husbands, especially those who keep concubines.

Froben Christoph's criteria for a happy marriage are stated explicitly in his comment about Schenk Albrecht von Limpurg (d. 1506) and his wife Elisabeth von Oettingen (d. 1509): "I never heard of any married couple who lived in such unity all their lives, and neither did anything that the other would take amiss nor did they ever have a lasting quarrel" (*ZC* 2:430). The knight Hans von Schweinichen paid a similar tribute to his wife on her death in 1601: "I can well say that we never lay apart any night when we were at home and healthy, nor did we ever go to bed angry with one another; wherefore these twenty years seem a short time. Together we endured cares, troubles, and sorrows."[18] A counterexample of an unhappy marriage in the *Zimmern Chronicle* is that of Margravine Elsa von Brandenburg, whose aunt, the Duchess of Nürtingen, forced her to marry her cousin Margrave Ernst von Baden. Ernst was ridiculed at the court of Württemberg as a coward, so "it is easy to imagine what reputation and love he bore in his wife's eyes—the old duchess could not straighten out what was crooked. The marriage went to pieces. There was little unity or trust between Margrave Ernst and his wife" (*ZC* 2:437–38). Unity, trust, mutual respect, and consideration for each other's feelings are the hallmark of a good marriage; this emphasis on reciprocity is similar to that in sixteenth-century advice literature aimed at a middle-class audience.[19]

---

[16]Spiess, *Familie und Verwandtschaft*, 477–78.

[17]Medieval marriage sermons stressed the need for both spouses to make concessions to maintain marital harmony. Lay writers generally viewed the maintenance of marital harmony as the responsibility of the wife alone, although a few sixteenth-century lay writers charged the husband with some responsibility as well. Schnell, "Geschlechtergeschichte und Textwissenschaft," 165–68; and Walter, *Unkeuschheit und Werk der Liebe*, 290.

[18]Schweinichen's eulogy is quoted in Dülmen, "Heirat und Eheleben," 161.

[19]Maria Müller stresses the growing emphasis on complementarity, or symmetrical relations between spouses in marriage treatises of the sixteenth century, in contrast to the emphasis on subsidiarity, or subordination of the wife in fifteenth-century treatises. "Naturwesen Mann," 58. Walter sees both

How well did the chronicler's own marriage live up to this ideal? Froben Christoph's biographer characterizes his marriage as a happy one, based in part on the fact that the union produced eleven children in twenty years and in part on negative evidence: there is no mention of separations, quarrels, or venereal disease, and no evidence that Froben Christoph kept a mistress or begot illegitimate children. Jenny surmises that "his wife was probably at the helm of affairs in Messkirch."[20] This inference is based chiefly on a passage in which Froben Christoph warns fathers not to criticize an adult son in the presence of the latter's wife, "for the wife will usually take offense and the husband will have less authority and worth in her opinion, but will be greatly despised...then the man is called 'the fellow I have to put up with' and there is nothing but misery in such a marriage" (ZC 3:469). This statement, which occurs in the middle of a long complaint about his treatment by his uncle Gottfried Werner, clearly shows that Froben Christoph felt that his financial dependence on his uncle undermined his own authority with his wife. However, nothing is known about Kunigunde's own behavior.

Froben Christoph's description of his marriage negotiations, written twenty years after the event, strongly implies that he had been maneuvered into the match by an intermediary who later became his bitter enemy. Kunigunde herself is never described in the account of the marriage negotiations and wedding festivities, and the chronicler hints that he would have preferred to marry her sister Amalia (ZC 3:508). As Wolf notes, Froben Christoph never makes any references to romantic love to justify this marriage (a disadvantageous one from an economic point of view), although elsewhere in the chronicle he had used the model of a courtly love match to justify questionable marriages.[21] The chronicler scrupulously avoids any direct statements about his emotional relationship with his wife, but these indirect hints suggest that the marriage was not as happy as Jenny assumes.[22]

Strangely enough, an account of the notoriously unhappy marriage of Maria von Oettingen and Truchsess Georg III von Waldburg is inserted in the middle of the description of Froben Christoph's own wedding. It is unclear whether this juxtaposition is meant to hint at unhappiness in the chronicler's own marriage, but the anecdote is clearly meant to teach a moral lesson about the proper subordination of wives to their husbands.

---

concepts as coexisting in sixteenth-century marriage treatises aimed at a bourgeois audience. *Unkeuschheit und Werk der Liebe,* 289–90.

[20]Jenny, *Graf Froben Christoph von Zimmern,* 193.

[21]Wolf, *Von der Chronik zum Weltbuch,* 385.

[22]The mere fact that Froben Christoph and Kunigunde had eleven children may not be evidence of a happy marriage; after all, the notoriously unhappy marriage between Georg von Waldburg and Maria von Oettingen produced seven children. Stone remarks that the comment "they lived very disagreeably but had many children" (made in 1699 apropos of an English aristocratic couple) "could stand as an epitaph for many sixteenth- and seventeenth-century couples"; *Family, Sex and Marriage,* 103.

In 1514, the widowed Georg married the sixteen-year-old Maria von Oettingen in a match undoubtedly intended to reinforce the political alliance between two of the leading families in the Swabian League. Although the marriage produced seven children in seventeen years, it was marked by discord between the spouses and a long-standing quarrel over the failure of the Oettingen family to pay the full amount of Maria's dowry.[23] According to the chronicler,

> a whole special treatise could be written about how this marriage turned out for [Georg]. They say, she had more than one child by him, but she never wanted to speak a word to him. Once he had been away from home for several months. When he came home unexpectedly late at night and hoped she would welcome him, she deliberately locked him out of her bedroom and would not let him in even if he used force. It is a pity that the pride and strife of such a selfish beast was tolerated. A cudgel and a steady diet of blows could have tanned her hide then and there, though he was too much of an intelligent, magnanimous, and gracious gentleman. (ZC 3:511)

The chronicler attributes Maria's avoidance of her husband to her fear of "the French disease" (ZC 3:511–12). Despite the sympathy Froben Christoph elsewhere demonstrates for the suffering of wives at the hands of adulterous husbands, he here views the risk of infection with syphilis as insufficient grounds for refusing to pay the "marital debt."[24] "People said that he [Georg] could have had nightclothes made without a fly, as old Count Eberhard von Erbach did. His wife lay in bed with him many times, so that he never touched her with his naked body; however, she had several children by him" (ZC 3:512).[25]

The brutal misogyny of the chronicler's comments about Maria is startling to the modern reader, although similar sentiments occur in some of the *Schwänke* in the *Zimmern Chronicle*. Among nonnobles, "some violence was tolerated and even

---

[23]According to an informant who claimed to have heard the story from Maria herself, she was held prisoner in Zeil Castle by Georg's relatives after her husband's death, but escaped by breaking bricks out of the wall of the latrine and letting herself down the wall on a rope she had made out of bed linens. This story does not appear in the *Zimmern Chronicle*, although it is exactly the sort of colorful anecdote Froben Christoph loved. Dornheim reviews the sources for the stories about Maria and notes their possible factual basis in the lawsuits over Maria's dowry in the imperial court at Rottweil and the imperial chamber court in Speyer. A settlement was finally reached in 1560 (five years after Maria's death and twenty-nine years after Georg's death) when the Oettingen family paid Georg's descendants the 4000 gulden for Maria's dowry. Dornheim, *Familie Waldburg-Zeil*, 114.

[24]Some authors of marriage treatises and some secular authorities took the danger of syphilis more seriously. Erasmus advocated granting a divorce (not merely a separation) to the partner of a spouse with an incurable illness, including syphilis. The Protestant marriage courts of Zurich in 1525 and Basel in 1529 accepted venereal disease as grounds for divorce. Christ-von Wedel, "'Praecipua coniugii,'" 134n34. Although this ground was no longer officially recognized in Basel after 1548, the marriage court of Basel granted a divorce in 1586 to a woman who left her husband after she contracted a venereal disease from him. Safley comments, "Such decisions are understandable when one considers the permissible grounds for a divorce. Considering the threat to life and limb, the court held her action to be proper." *Let No Man Put Asunder*, 159.

[25]Eberhard von Erbach's search for a cure for his syphilis is described in ZC 3:272–73.

expected, provided that death or disablement did not result. As part of his authority over his wife and his responsibility to reform her, a husband was allowed to beat his spouse lovingly." Moreover, "total renunciation of the obvious correction of the female partner demonstrated his lack of authority in the household."[26]

It is unclear whether such behavior met with equal social acceptance among the nobility; Jean-Louis Flandrin says, "One may surmise that, among the elites of society, women escaped blows by making the most of their social standing."[27] The Austrian nobleman Bartholomaus von Starhernberg complained in 1675 that "he always had to justify himself before his proud wife" and hardly had any chances to discipline her, "since it is no longer customary among nobles to keep our wives on a tight rein by means of blows like the common man."[28] His use of the words "no longer customary" implies that wife beating had been acceptable among nobles in an earlier era. Beatings did occur in sixteenth-century nobilities, both in Germany and in other countries, and occasionally formed the basis of suit for legal separation.[29]

In the anecdote in the *Zimmern Chronicle,* Maria's willful behavior exemplifies the literary stereotype of the *böse weib* (wicked or ill-tempered wife) who fails to show her husband respect and obedience at all times; she is the antithesis of the ideal *züchtig weib* (modest wife) who patiently suffers in silence even when her husband is in the wrong.[30] In contrast, Georg's self-restraint follows the counsel of sixteenth-century marriage treatises, which hold that a rational and mature man should not lash out in anger.[31]

---

[26]Safley, *Let No Man Put Asunder,* 167; and Walter, *Unkeuschheit und Werk der Liebe,* 302. Maria Müller emphasizes that Joachim Fischart's treatise was unique in rejecting wife beating under any circumstances; other marriage treatises urged rational restraint but allowed force as a last resort. "Schneckengeist im Venusleib," 8.

[27]Flandrin, *Families in Former Times,* 129.

[28]Bastl, *Tugend, Liebe, Ehre,* 366.

[29]For example, Apollonia Meckhen, a noblewoman of Freiburg, complained to the city court of Freiburg in 1603 that her husband, the Bürgermeister Hans Caspar Ingolstatter, beat her severely. The town council ordered the couple to continue living together, but two years later she sued successfully in the ecclesiastical court at Constance for a separation on the grounds of physical abuse. Safley, *Let No Man Put Asunder,* 104–5. Beatings formed the basis for several suits brought by wives in the Castilian high aristocracy for separation on the ground of cruelty. Beceiro Pita and Córdoba de la Llave, *Parentesco, poder y mentalidad,* 217–18. In Verona, witnesses in the separation suit brought by Aurelia, the wife of Count Ercole de Giusti, gave graphic descriptions of how he gave her black eyes and hit her with his sword when she complained about his undue favoritism towards his concubine. Such details were designed to convince the judge that the wife was not disobeying normal husbandly authority and that the husband lacked "the basic mature masculine qualities of reason and self-control." Eisenach, *Husbands, Wives, and Concubines,* 150, 192, 202.

[30]Walter, *Unkeuschheit und Werk der Liebe,* 296.

[31]Even the lay authors of *Schwänke* who do not doubt that the husband has the right and even the duty to use physical force to "correct" an insubordinate wife, warn that he "ought to chastise his wife not too harshly, not as a regular occurrence, and not in an emotional state." Walter, *Unkeuschheit und Werk der Liebe,* 301–2. On the views of ecclesiastical authors on this subject, see Flandrin, *Families in*

Even an unhappy marriage such as that of Maria von Oettingen and Georg von Waldburg did not necessarily result in dissolution or legal separation. The Catholic Church did not recognize divorce, although it did grant annulment (*divortio ad vinculum*) on the grounds of precontract, consanguinity, or affinity (that is, relationships through blood or through marriage), impotence, force and fear, or age (marriage when at least one spouse was below the age of consent). The church also granted legal separation (*divortio a mensa et thoro,* or separation from bed and board) on the grounds of adultery and cruelty, but such a separation did not allow either party to remarry.[32]

Despite the publicity given to the politically motivated divorces of royalty and the highest aristocracy, annulments did not function as a convenient substitute for divorce for the general population, or even for nobility below the level of princes.[33] A legal separation might offer a wife an escape from a bad marriage, but it also had serious drawbacks. The wife would lose custody of her children, who were considered the property of her husband's lineage. Moreover, it was difficult for a wife to support herself financially after a separation.

Among the German nobility, the wife was under the marriage guardianship (*Ehevögtei*) of her husband, who had control over the administration of her dowry and even over her inheritance from her own family. She had little legal recourse if he misused her property.[34] Her natal family's legal obligation to support her ended once they had provided her with a dowry, but she was not entitled to the income from her dowry and matching payment until widowhood. During the marriage, she received only a small income from her morning gift, an amount similar to that granted as pensions to unmarried daughters.[35] Since this would not be sufficient to support her in her own residence, a wife who separated from

---

Former Times, 128–29. The chronicler's praise of Georg von Waldburg for his magnanimity and self-restraint in this episode seems at odds with other accounts of Georg's character. Not only did he acquire lasting notoriety for his ruthlessness in the Peasants' War, but he had a reputation for being quick to take offense on points of honor. Wolf, *Von der Chronik zum Weltbuch,* 48–49.

[32]On the grounds for annulment and separation as they were stated in canon law and as they were actually interpreted by ecclesiastical courts in the late Middle Ages and the sixteenth century, see Brundage, *Law, Sex, and Christian Society,* 509–14; and Helmholz, *Marriage Litigation in Medieval,* 74–77, 90–99. Judges often adopted a broad interpretation of cruelty as a ground for separation and, despite the fact that separations by mutual consent were illegal, sometimes ratified such arrangements by granting a legal separation to couples who refused to resume cohabitation.

[33]Phillips, *Putting Asunder,* 9.

[34]Spiess, *Familie und Verwandtschaft,* 174–77. Charges of misuse of the wife's property were also common among the English aristocracy; men heavily in debt would sell or pawn their wives' jewelry, plate, jointures, or inheritances. Harris, *English Aristocratic Women,* 78–79. In France, "custom gave a husband unchallenged rights over the management of his wife's fortune (though it also protected her rights under separation)." Potter, "Marriage and Cruelty," 26.

[35]At the usual interest rate of 5 percent, the standard morning gift of 1000 gulden would have yielded an annual income of 50 gulden, a figure at the upper range of the annuities paid to nuns or unmarried lay daughters. Spiess, *Familie und Verwandtschaft,* 174, 177, 375–76, 380.

her husband would either have to negotiate an additional financial settlement from her husband or live as a dependent in the household of her father or brother.

The chronicler Froben Christoph disapproves of the divorces of Protestant princes, and writing of an ill-matched couple, quotes "What God has joined together, let not man put asunder" (ZC 3:120). He mentions only one annulment (on the grounds of bigamy) in the chronicle, and does not mention any cases of formal legal separations granted by an ecclesiastical court.[36] Nevertheless, he regards estrangements as normal, if regrettable, occurrences in noble families. The cases mentioned in the Zimmern Chronicle were not taken to ecclesiastical courts for a formal legal separation from bed and board; rather, they were handled privately within the family.

In the case of Count Ladislaus von Haag, the husband had grounds for a legal separation when his wife Emilia Rovello di Pio was forced to enter a convent shortly after their marriage in 1556. However, he did not have grounds in canon law for an annulment that would permit remarriage.[37]

According to the chronicle, Ladislaus "had married as his second wife a Countess of Ferrara, a close relative of the duke. A splendid wedding was held, to which he brought his best silver plate and jewels. But shortly thereafter he quarreled with his mother-in-law," who is said to have attempted to poison him. Ladislaus returned to Germany, but "his wife was not allowed to follow him; she entered a convent.... So he is still saddled with his wife to this day. She is still alive in the convent, and although he is the only one left of his lineage and uncertain about his proper heirs, he cannot marry again during her lifetime" (ZC 3:43–44). Ladislaus spent the last ten years of his life unsuccessfully attempting to dissolve the marriage so that he could remarry and obtain a male heir to perpetuate his line.[38]

The case of Barbara von Hausen represents a common way of dealing with estrangements through private deeds of separation that allowed the wife to claim her widow's pension as a means of support. Barbara had married "a Werdenstein, by whom she had no children. They were later separated [gesöndert] by mediation of their friends. Her husband had to pay her the widow's pension as if he had died, and support her the rest of her life" (ZC 2:543–44).

In some cases, there was no legal agreement between the husband and the wife's kin. In this type of informal separation, the wife usually returned to her own

---

[36]This anecdote refers to the (probably apocryphal) story of the first marriage of Count Andreas von Sonnenberg (ZC 2:298–300).

[37]Canon law stated that "after separation by mutual agreement to allow one party to enter religion, the other might not remarry." Brundage, Law, Sex, and Christian Society, 202. Although the separation in this case was not by mutual agreement, the Protestant Ladislaus von Haag was not likely to receive sympathetic treatment from the Catholic ecclesiastical courts.

[38]For the remainder of his life, Ladislaus lived in concubinage (wilde Ehe) with Margaretha von Trenbach, who bore him a daughter. After his death without legitimate heirs in 1566, the county of Haag was regranted by the Hapsburgs to his archenemy Duke Albrecht of Bavaria. Münch, "Ladislaus."

kin, if they were willing to support her. According to the chronicler, the wife of Baron Franz von Mörsperg tired of his strange household and loose living; she eventually ran off to Switzerland with a clerk (ZC 3:507–8). However, the chronicler earlier refers to Mörsperg's wife as keeping house for her brother, Count Jakob, and states that she had her young daughter with her. It thus appears that when she left her husband's household, she at first returned to her own kin (ZC 3:236).

In other cases, the wife's kin might enforce a separation even if she had not requested it. Barbara von Bubenhofen was married to Hans von Sickingen, a knight at the court of Heidelberg. "They lived in great disharmony—there was much disorder in household management in those days, especially in courts, which usually bring with them *impudici und corruptissimi mores* (the most shameful and corrupt morals)... Because of this disharmony, the Bubenhofen brothers decided to bring their sister back and maintain her at their home." They sent a servant to fetch her from Heidelberg; she arrived "dressed in beggar's clothes." At first the brothers provided Barbara with one of their castles as her residence, but after an alleged affair with her steward, they forced her to reside with them and may have kept her under house arrest (ZC 2:504–5).

The cases of separations in the Zimmern family itself were all of this informal type, which did not produce a property settlement between the husband and his estranged wife. However, they ranged all the way from an amicable agreement to live apart (Wilhelm Werner and Amalia von Leuchtenberg) to the negotiation of a document of formal separation that could be invoked in the case of future disagreements (Gottfried Werner and Apollonia von Henneberg).

The marriage of Wilhelm Werner to Amalia von Leuchtenberg in 1524 had gotten off to a bad start. After courting Amalia's daughter, Wilhelm Werner hastily decided to marry the widowed mother, who led him to believe she had more money than she actually possessed. According to the chronicler, bad omens at the wedding and extravagance at the homecoming feast foreshadowed future unhappiness (ZC 3:42, 50–51).

Amalia was not satisfied with any of Wilhelm Werner's estates as a residence. Immediately after the homecoming, "Wilhelm Werner moved with his wife to [Herren]zimmern castle. However, she had only been there a short time when she decided that she could not endure the place, and asked to live at Oberndorf," where the couple resided until the outbreak of the Peasants' War. During the war, Wilhelm Werner "had his wife brought to Rottweil, where she lived the rest of her life" (ZC 3:53–54, 58). After Wilhelm Werner was appointed to the Imperial Chamber Court in 1529, he resided in Speyer when the court was in session and at Herrenzimmern when it was in recess. However, Amalia did not accompany him. "Because it was better for her health and...because it was rather far to travel, his wife remained in her husband's house in Rottweil, where she had religious services close at hand in the Johanniterhaus. Here she behaved in such a way that she was popular with many and a burden to none" (ZC 3:62).

It appears, then, that the spouses separated informally five years after their marriage. Although Wilhelm Werner owned the house in which Amalia resided, she may have supported herself on her widow's pension from her first marriage. During her final illness in 1538, she made her will and "bequeathed to her husband all her cash, silver plate, and other goods that would otherwise have gone to her son Ladislaus von Haag as her heir if she had died intestate." Her death "happened so quickly...that Wilhelm Werner could not be notified in time to see her still alive" (ZC 3:262). Amalia may have sent for her husband on her deathbed; at the very least, the bequest of her movable goods suggests that their relationship had remained friendly.[39] The chronicle does not record Wilhelm Werner's reaction to Amalia's death. Wilhelm Werner did not mention it in his annals, although he had recorded the death in 1521 of his first wife Katharina von Lupfen, "who lived with me only sixteen weeks."[40]

The marriage of the chronicler's parents, Johann Werner II von Zimmern and Katharina von Erbach, exemplifies Harris's generalization that "fiscal irresponsibility, incompetent management of households and estates, and aristocratic men's estrangement from their wives often went together.... Women in such positions had little hope of relief unless they could enlist men as powerful as their husbands, usually their natal kin, to assist them."[41]

Katharina, who separated from her husband in 1528 due to his maintenance of a concubine, had no such powerful males among her immediate kin. Her father was dead, she had no brothers, and her mother had married a second husband of lower status than her own. The only male relative who could have intervened decisively was her uncle Christoph von Werdenberg, in whose household she had spent her adolescent years. However, Christoph had arranged Katharina's marriage to Johann Werner to reconcile the Werdenberg and Zimmern families, and he was currently engaged in negotiating another match with the Zimmern to reinforce the alliance. Taking his niece's side against her husband might have jeopardized these political calculations; in any event, there is no evidence that Christoph tried to intercede. Without support from her natal male kin, Katharina remained in a precarious financial position after separating from her husband.

Katharina's marriage had been unhappy from the beginning. When she married Johann Werner II in 1510,

> most of the friends on both sides gladly accepted this marriage as a means of promoting peace and unity between the two families.... But [Johann Werner's] mother, the Countess of Oettingen, and his brother Gottfried Werner were greatly displeased with it, because of the insults and injuries they had

---

[39]It is possible that Amalia's main motive in this bequest was to prevent the silver plate from passing to her son Ladislaus von Haag, from whom she had been estranged since his conversion to Protestantism.

[40]Zimmern, "Jahresgeschichten" in *Quellensammlung*, 2:135.

[41]Harris, *English Aristocratic Women*, 77.

received from the Werdenbergs in the past; they did not want to have a
reminder before their eyes every day. (*ZC* 2:194)

The hostility of her in-laws must have made Katharina's life in her new home
uncomfortable in the early days of the marriage; however, "the resentment diminished with time, and Katharina herself was not to blame" for the past actions of
her Werdenberg kin (*ZC* 2:194).

A year after the marriage, Johann Werner was persuaded by his brother Gottfried Werner to exchange the castle of Messkirch for the estate of Zimmern vor
Wald. Gottfried had just married Apollonia von Henneberg and complained that
he could not maintain his high-ranking wife on his original estate. The chronicle
compares this to "a horse in exchange for a pipe," but does not discuss Katharina's
reaction to being demoted in favor of her new sister-in-law. She and her husband
resided temporarily in a "house in the lower court" at Messkirch, then in a series
of rented accommodations before moving to her widow's seat, Seedorf, in 1513
and back to the house in Messkirch in 1517 (*ZC* 2:316). The chronicler depicts
Katharina as playing a key role in averting a fight between Johann Werner and his
brother Gottfried Werner over another inheritance matter. She is also credited
with convincing her husband to move to Seedorf in 1513, presumably to reduce
the friction between the two brothers that had been so intense when they both
lived at Messkirch (*ZC* 2:317–18).

Katharina bore no children for the first four years of the marriage. In 1514,
she gave birth to a son, Christoph Werner, who died at the age of three (*ZC* 2:370).
In 1516, Katharina gave birth to a second son, Johann Christoph. During the
plague epidemic of 1518, Johann Werner sent his pregnant wife and her surviving
son Johann Christoph to stay with her mother in the neighboring region of Franconia. Here she gave birth in 1519 to her third son, the chronicler Froben Christoph, who would be brought up by his grandmother until the age of twelve. When
the plague was over, Johann Werner came to fetch his wife and son home. However, Katharina's mother was angry with him because he had been away for over
six months and scolded him for neglecting his family (*ZC* 2:374, 379). Once they
returned to Swabia, the household resided primarily at Seedorf, where Katharina
gave birth to another son, Gottfried Christoph, in 1524 (*ZC* 2:399). In 1526,
Katharina bore her last child and only daughter, Barbara, who died in infancy (*ZC*
2:406). This is the last point in the chronicle at which it appears that the spouses
were still living in the same household.

In 1524, Johann Werner had purchased the castle of Falkenstein. Here he
established a strange household with his concubine Margarethe Hutler, who eventually bore him four children. This was too much for Katharina, who moved back
to Messkirch around 1528. She presumably left behind her youngest son Gottfried
Christoph, for the latter is said to have been brought up by his father "until he
reached his eighth year" (*ZC* 2:399). When Froben Christoph was summoned

home in 1531 to accompany his brother Johann Christoph to the university, he had a disastrous quarrel with his father at Falkenstein, then requested permission to visit his uncle Gottfried Werner and his mother, "who was residing in the lower court at Messkirch" in the house belonging to Johann Werner (ZC 3:214). Although Froben Christoph had evidently had little or no contact with his mother since infancy, he strongly identified with her grievances against her husband and later fantasized himself as the champion who would avenge her wrongs (ZC 3:308).

> After the year 1528, [Katharina] usually kept her household in the lower
> court at Messkirch; she stayed there until after her husband's death … and
> rarely missed attendance at church. After her husband's death [in 1548] she
> did not want to remain any longer at Messkirch, but preferred … the castle of
> Seedorf; there she wanted to end her days (ZC 4:120).

Katharina von Erbach died at Seedorf a year later. Clearly she did not have a property settlement from Johann Werner granting her the widow's pension during his lifetime, as was often provided in private separation agreements. She did not move to her widow's seat until after his death, even though the chronicler stresses her determination to move to Seedorf as quickly as possible once she had the legal right to do so. It is not clear what source of financial support Katharina relied on during the twenty years she was separated from her husband. She may not even have had the income from her morning gift of 1000 gulden, for Johann Werner had persuaded her to make it over to him in 1524, ostensibly on the grounds that he feared it might otherwise not come to their children after her death (ZC 2:399).

It is also not clear why Katharina chose to live at Messkirch when she presumably had the option of returning to her natal kin. Her mother, Elisabeth von Werdenberg, was still alive in 1528, and was bringing up Katharina's second son, Froben Christoph. Katharina may have preferred maintaining her own household at Messkirch, where she had spent part of her early married life, to living as a dependent in her mother's household. She was evidently on good terms with her brother-in-law Gottfried Werner and his wife Apollonia, and it is possible that Gottfried Werner offered her his protection either out of friendship or in order to spite his brother, Johann Werner. Moreover, one of Katharina's sons was in residence in Gottfried Werner's household during most of the period that she resided at Messkirch. Gottfried Christoph was sent to the household of his uncle for his education between his eighth and his eighteenth year (from 1531 to 1541), and Froben Christoph resided there after entering his uncle's service in 1543.[42]

According to the chronicler's admittedly partisan account, Katharina von Erbach never enjoyed much happiness in her married life. Her husband's open

---

[42]However, Katharina did not attend Froben Christoph's wedding in 1544; this suggests either that the Zimmerns did not consider her one of the family or that she did not wish to meet her estranged husband at the wedding.

maintenance of a concubine provoked her into leaving him, and the couple was never reconciled. The chronicler champions his mother's cause and presents her actions as completely justified. Although he had criticized Katharina's mother for abandoning her children in order to remarry (ZC 2:248–49), he never faults Katharina for leaving her four-year-old son behind to be brought up by the husband she despised.

Froben Christoph's identification with his mother's plight leads him to criticize adulterous husbands in general for the emotional suffering they inflicted on their wives by their extramarital affairs. This attitude is clearly shown in the case discussed most fully in the chronicle, the temporary separation of Gottfried Werner von Zimmern and Apollonia von Henneberg. Unlike Katharina von Erbach, Apollonia had powerful male kin from her natal family whom she succeeded in mobilizing to defend her interests against her unfaithful husband.

The marriage of Gottfried Werner and Apollonia von Henneberg had begun as a love match, at least according to the chronicler. However, Apollonia bore her husband no sons, only two daughters, and "an unfriendly relationship developed between them that lasted many years.… [T]he good woman suffered patiently for a long time and overlooked a great deal"(ZC 3:387), including Gottfried Werner's eight illegitimate children by two different concubines, Anna Fritz of Luberlingen and Anna Landaver of Messkirch (ZC 4:287). Much to the chronicler's disgust, his uncle seemed to favor his illegitimate sons over his legitimate daughters.

The breaking point came in 1539 when Gottfried Werner made no effort to conceal his latest affair with the Faulhans woman, the wife of a mercenary soldier from Messkirch. One day when he was dining with his wife, daughter, and son-in-law, Gottfried Werner asked the page who was serving them, "What's the news?" The boy blurted out, "Nothing, sir, except that the Faulhans woman was sent the same fish" as was being served at the table (ZC 3:383). The diners quickly changed the subject, but Apollonia did not forget the insult. She requested permission to visit her brother Otto, a canon of Strasbourg; once she was back in Franconia, she stayed with her brothers for two years.[43]

"Gottfried Werner's excesses went beyond the norm, so that he alienated not only his wife but also her brothers, the counts of Henneberg" (ZC 3:388). Gottfried Werner feared that his wife's brothers might take violent reprisals and suspected that they might have instigated the actions of a neighboring nobleman who raided his lands: "He did not know who he was safe with or who he could trust; he hardly dared stick his head outside the gate" (ZC 3:386–87).

---

[43]The chronicle does not explain why Apollonia regarded this particular incident as the last straw. However, sending the Faulhans woman the same fish that had been provided to Gottfried Werner's legitimate family implied that the concubine was equal to the legitimate wife. In Verona, such "improperly respectful" treatment of a concubine was seen as an intolerable affront to the honor of the wife and, by extension, that of her natal family. Eisenach, *Husbands, Wives, and Concubines,* 149–50.

"He was justly criticized for his improper behavior," acknowledges his nephew Froben Christoph. Still, the chronicler feels that the lasting "contempt and enmity" professed by Gottfried Werner's friends and relatives was unfair because many other noblemen behaved just as badly without suffering social condemnation. "Many others may lie in the same hospital and perhaps be even sicker, but their reputations don't suffer; it is regarded as a joke" (*ZC* 3:388–89). Froben Christoph took a broader view of what constituted behaving just as badly than did other nobles in his milieu. Moreover, Gottfried Werner's kin may have been anxious to assert their disapproval publicly in order not to be drawn into his quarrel with the Hennebergs; it was dangerous to antagonize one of the most powerful families in Franconia.

After Apollonia had been living in Franconia for a year, her brother Wilhelm and Gottfried Werner's two brothers, Johann Werner and Wilhelm Werner, began to negotiate a formal reconciliation agreement. This provided that Apollonia would return to her husband at Messkirch, that the two of them would henceforth live as man and wife, and that everything that had happened in the past was to be forgiven and forgotten. However, it also provided that any future offenses by Gottfried Werner would trigger a formal separation: "If Count Gottfried Werner gives his wife future cause for offense and does not behave towards her as he should, so that she for this reason no longer can or no longer wishes to remain with her husband or receive her widow's pension," she was to have the right to live with her brothers or with her daughter Anna and to receive an annuity of 500 gulden from Gottfried Werner. In other words, she would have the choice of living either at her widow's seat or with her kin, but Gottfried Werner would be obligated to maintain her in either case.[44] A secret clause in the contract provided that the Faulhans woman was to be sent away (*ZC* 3:393).

The reconciliation of Gottfried Werner and Apollonia was due in large part to the efforts of their daughter Anna, who "worried a great deal about her mother in her absence" and "was heartily grieved that her parents bore such ill will towards each other." Her "letters and many entreaties" finally persuaded her mother to consent to the reconciliation agreement (*ZC* 3:393–94).

Apollonia was escorted back to Swabia by her brother-in-law Johann Werner von Zimmern, and Gottfried Werner met her at Anna's house. "It was almost like a second wedding. . . . Everyone was happy with one another, and no one thought of the old matters at all." However, "the unity was not permanent," and Wolf suggests that from this point on the marriage of Gottfried Werner and Apollonia was *Josephsehe* (without sexual relations) (*ZC* 3:397).[45] Apollonia spent long periods at

---

[44]An annuity of 500 gulden would be slightly higher than the widow's pension normally associated with her dowry of 4000 gulden. Possibly Gottfried Werner had given a higher matching payment or morning gift than usual because of Apollonia's higher rank.

[45]Wolf, *Von der Chronik zum Weltbuch*, 392.

the home of her daughter Anna; Gottfried Werner gave up the Faulhans woman, but probably replaced her with new mistresses (*ZC* 3:393). However, Apollonia never invoked her rights under the reconciliation agreement, and she remained with Gottfried Werner for eight more years until her death in 1549 (*ZC* 4:113).

≈ ≈ ≈

The *Zimmern Chronicle*'s accounts of marriages in the Zimmern family demonstrate the complexity of emotional relationships within noble marriages. It is not clear whether even the chronicler's own marriage had the unity and trust that he considered the basis of a happy marriage, and the marriages of his father and uncles all resulted in temporary or permanent estrangements. Not all unhappiness in noble marriages can be attributed to the fact that they were undertaken for economic and political motives. The rapid breakdown of Wilhelm Werner's marriage to Amalia von Leuchtenberg is described as the natural consequence of greed and deceit, and Katharina von Erbach is depicted as the victim of her own family's political calculations and her husband's financial incompetence and infidelity. However, the marriage of Apollonia von Henneberg and Gottfried Werner von Zimmern had begun—at least according to the chronicle—as a love match straight out of a courtly romance.

How typical were the cases of marital breakdown in the *Zimmern Chronicle* of marriages among southwest German counts and barons, and of marriages in other European aristocracies? The chronicle accurately reflects the preference in the southwest German nobility for mediating both property and marital conflicts within the circle of kin; recourse to either secular or ecclesiastical courts was viewed as a last resort. In the 10,000 marital dispute cases in the diocese of Constance between 1551 and 1600, only thirty-seven plaintiffs were identified as nobles, and no nobles were involved in the 250 separation cases of this period.[46]

Among the counts and barons of the Mainz region, Spiess found only one example of an annulment and one example of a legal separation in the entire period of 1200 to 1550.[47] Consanguinity was occasionally invoked as the grounds for backing out of a proposed alliance that was no longer politically useful. However, southwest German counts and barons did not use it as grounds for dissolution of

[46]Safley, *Let No Man Put Asunder,* 168n3. The thirty-seven noble plaintiffs were identified as *dominus* or *domina.* Separation cases made up only 2 percent of the marital cases before the court at Constance. Although no nobles were involved in separation cases in the second half of the sixteenth century, in 1605 one woman of the lower nobility did bring a successful suit at Constance for a separation based on physical abuse. Ibid., 104–5.

[47]This was the "well-documented case of Count Johann von Hapsburg-Laufenberg and Herzlaude von Rappoltstein, whose marriage [in 1372] could not be consummated due to the husband's impotence." Spiess, *Familie und Verwandtschaft,* 40n77.

marriages that had already been solemnized; rather, a dispensation was obtained when consanguinity was "discovered" after the marriage had taken place.[48]

Although Spiess does not analyze private separation agreements, he shows that they already were in use in the mid-fifteenth century. When Count Philipp von Katzenelnbogen separated from his wife, Countess Anna von Württemberg in 1446, he paid her widow's pension so that she could head her own household at her widow's seat. Only after this private arrangement failed to resolve the conflict did he resort to the ecclesiastical court to obtain a separation from bed and board.[49]

German nobles in other regions of the Holy Roman Empire were also reluctant to bring lawsuits for annulment or separations, although in the late sixteenth and seventeenth centuries, the lower nobility in the Wesser region did resort to the ecclesiastical courts to sue for enforcement of promises of marriage.[50] The Austrian duchess Elisabeth Lukretia von Teschen, who had been married off by her guardian to a man of lower rank, left her husband in 1637 as soon as she inherited an estate from her brother. Declaring that "we loved each other as little as fire loves water," she refused to return to share a residence with her husband, whom she accused of failing to maintain her according to her rank. However, there is no evidence that either spouse sought a formal separation.[51]

In the period after 1550, marital discord often featured conflicts over religion, which had not been an issue in the era of the *Zimmern Chronicle*. This created an additional obstacle to seeking a legal remedy for marital breakdown, since neither spouse was likely to accept the verdict of a court belonging to the opposite confession. The marriage of the Austrian noblewoman Ester von Windischgraetz (1629/30–95) to Bartholomaus von Starhembert (1625–76) had started out with high expectations of happiness. In letters to his fiancée in 1651, Bartholomaus called Ester "my life" and "my sweetheart," and promised to be true to her as long as she lived, declaring, "I would sooner cease to live than cease to love you." However, twenty years later, the relationship had frayed, due to Bartholomaus's spendthrift ways and ill health, and to religious discord. Nobles in the province of Styria were ordered to adopt Catholicism or lose their lands, and after one attempt at resistance led to the confiscation of his land, Bartholomaus converted to Catholicism. However, Ester remained a Protestant and bitterly resented her husband's arrangement of their daughter's marriage in 1671 to a Catholic suitor. In 1673, Ester expressed the hope that "God will hear my prayer and release us from our fetters, since we get along so badly," and two years later Bartholomaus handed his wife

---

[48]Spiess, *Familie und Verwandtschaft*, 46, 48.

[49]Spiess, *Familie und Verwandtschaft*, 180 and 180n180.

[50]For examples of suits for enforcement of promises of marriage, see Hufschmidt, *Adelige Frauen im Weserraum*, 143–46.

[51]Bastl, *Treue, Liebe, Ehre*, 365–67.

over to the custody of one of his Catholic kinsmen. Nevertheless, neither spouse sought a resolution from earthly authorities; their conflict was resolved only with the death of Bartholomaus in 1676.[52] The noblemen and noblewomen of the Hapsburg court who described their unhappy marriages in their correspondence or diaries attributed marital discord primarily to quarrels over money and religion. It is interesting that none of the wives mentioned their husbands' infidelities as a factor in their unhappiness, even in letters to their closest kin or in their personal diaries.[53]

The reluctance of nobles to resort to the court system might adversely affect the interests of noblewomen trapped in bad marriages, for women initiated the majority of actions for divorce or separation in German courts. In the second half of the sixteenth century, they began 69 percent of the cases for judicial separation in the Catholic ecclesiastical court at Constance (which included Upper Swabia) and 56 percent of the suits for divorce before the Protestant town council at nearby Basel in Switzerland. Thomas Max Safley interprets these statistics as evidence that courts offered women significant protection: "Women were encouraged, indeed commanded, to accept the authority of their husbands in all things. Yet when that authority became too arbitrary and tyrannical, women turned to the court as a means of self-defense."[54] German noblewomen, however, did not turn to the courts for self-defense; instead, they relied on the backing of their own natal family. Cordula Nolte states that a German prince's open discussion of his adulterous affairs "would have injured the honor of the princely consort and possibly called her relatives into the matter."[55] Mobilizing her male kin might be a more effective defense than appealing to the courts; the wife's family was normally at least equal in status to her husband's, and the husband might be reluctant to jeopardize a politically valuable relationship with his in-laws.

It is difficult to tell whether marital breakdown was more common or less common among the southwest German counts and barons than in other European aristocracies. Only those rare cases that actually resulted in lawsuits appear in the legal records of any country, and anecdotal evidence chiefly concerns the highest court aristocrats, who were more likely than provincial nobles to dissolve marriages for political reasons.

Nobles in England, like those in Germany, were less likely than commoners to resort to the ecclesiastical courts in cases of marital breakdown. In England in the late Middle Ages, "members of the highest classes ... did not generally figure among litigants in matrimonial causes," and both Joel T. Rosenthal and Stone express surprise at the rarity of annulments in the English peerage in the fifteenth

---

[52]Bastl, *Treue, Liebe, Ehre*, 363–66.
[53]Bastl, *Treue, Liebe, Ehre*, 363–73.
[54]Safley, *Let No Man Put Asunder*, 175.
[55]Nolte, "Verbalerotische Kommunikation," 451.

and early sixteenth centuries.[56] However, members of both the English peerage and the high aristocracy of Castile appear to have been more willing to bring suits for annulments and separations than were the counts and barons of southwest Germany.[57]

In Verona, members of the elite (largely from the lesser nobility) were well represented in cases of marriage dissolution before the ecclesiastical court in the mid-sixteenth century. Elite women actually constituted the majority of all women who initiated suits for separation brought before the diocesan court, mainly because a legal separation was a prerequisite for recovering control of their dowries and elite women had more property at stake.[58]

In cases of informal or formal separation, German noblewomen were in a better financial position than those in other aristocracies who did not receive a morning gift. In the first half of the sixteenth century, English aristocratic women had no income of their own during the marriage. In cases of separation, they either had to rely on support from their natal kin or to convince their estranged husbands to grant them an allowance. Stone suggests that the change in the law of married women's property making it easier for women to obtain a satisfactory financial settlement in the event of a separation was a significant factor in the increased number of separations in the English aristocracy between 1590 and 1620.[59] In Italy, women who left their husbands had no source of financial support unless they won a separation suit in the ecclesiastical court and then persuaded the secular authorities to grant them control of their dotal property as if they were widows.[60]

"Divorces" (that is, annulments) on the basis of consanguinity in both the English and the Castilian aristocracies usually involved the dissolution of betrothals, as they did among southwest German counts and barons. However, some cases involved marriages that had already been solemnized and had produced children. In these cases, consanguinity was probably the excuse for a dissolution desired for political or personal reasons.

Couples normally obtained a dispensation if the consanguinity was "discovered" after the marriage ceremony. Rosenthal states that no cases are known in England in which "aristocratic parties, already satisfactorily married, really had to

---

[56]Helmholz, "Marriage Litigation," 58–59; Rosenthal, "Aristocratic Marriage and the English Peerage," 187; and Stone, *Crisis of the Aristocracy,* 655.

[57]For examples of annulment cases in the English aristocracy in the late Middle Ages, see Rosenthal, "Aristocratic Marriage," 187. For examples in Castile, see Beceiro Pita and Córdoba de la Llave, *Parentesco, poder y mentalidad,* 213–18.

[58]Eisenach, *Husbands, Wives, and Concubines,* 198. Nonelite women with less property at stake were more likely to settle for de facto marriage dissolutions that did not involve the expense of a court suit. Ibid., 186, 197.

[59]Harris, *English Aristocratic Women,* 82–86; and Stone, *Crisis of the Aristocracy,* 661.

[60]Eisenach, *Husbands, Wives, and Concubines,* 198.

dissolve their union because of an ex post facto discovery or realization of an impediment." Even if they married in full knowledge of their kinship, "aristocrats could get what they wanted, particularly since they could and would pay for it."[61] Castilian aristocrats sometimes deliberately failed to obtain dispensations even when they knew of their kinship, thus setting up grounds for an annulment if one should be desired in the future.[62]

In the English peerage in the late fifteenth and early sixteenth century, one wife obtained an annulment for her husband's impotence and another obtained a "divorce at her own suit" (possibly a separation rather than an annulment). At least one husband obtained a separation on the grounds of his wife's adultery. It is not clear whether any English aristocratic women successfully sued for separation on the grounds of cruelty. However, some women in the Castilian high aristocracy did so, citing the same grounds of physical violence used in suits by women from the urban classes.[63]

In Verona, elite women successfully sued for separation in the ecclesiastical court on the grounds of both adultery and cruelty, even though the court set a high standard of proof: "[First], that a husband, *leaving* his wife, keeps other women and commits adultery, [second] that she cannot live with him without *danger to her life*."[64]

In France, where royal courts increasingly asserted jurisdiction in marriage cases, separation on the grounds of adultery was granted only to husbands. However, at least one noblewoman obtained a separation from her violent husband, presumably on the basis of cruelty. Potter notes that in the sixteenth century "the limits of acceptable behavior among the nobility were being demonstrated," for example in the censure of a Picard nobleman "for cheating his wife and ruining her fortune," although such behavior did not constitute legal grounds for separation.[65]

Among nobles in all countries, "many cases of marital conflict...were resolved by the simple physical separation of the spouses who nevertheless remained legally married."[66] As Rosenthal remarks, "there was generally enough latitude within the respectable pastimes and responsibilities of the aristocratic household to allow men and women to stay married and well apart, if they so chose," often in different residences.[67] In addition, de facto separations in which women returned to their natal families or left their husbands in order to live with their lovers are well documented in the English, French, and Castilian aristocracies; however, it does not appear that

[61]Rosenthal, "Aristocratic Marriage," 187.

[62]Beceiro Pita and Córdoba de la Llave, *Parentesco, poder y mentalidad*, 151, 215, 370.

[63]Rosenthal, "Aristocratic Marriage," 187; and Beceiro Pita and Córdoba de la Llave, *Parentesco, poder y mentalidad*, 217–18.

[64]Eisenach, *Husbands, Wives, and Concubines*, 182.

[65]Potter, "Marriage and Cruelty," 26–28.

[66]Beceiro Pita and Córdoba de la Llave, *Parentesco, poder y mentalidad*, 215.

[67]Rosenthal, "Aristocratic Marriage," 191.

private deeds of separation were in general use in any of these countries in the fifteenth and sixteenth centuries.[68]

The only writer who attempts to analyze the total incidence of marital breakdown in all its forms in any European aristocracy is Lawrence Stone. Writing of the English peerage in a slightly later period, he states,

> In view of the tremendous religious, social, legal, and economic pressures directed at holding the family together, it is nonetheless remarkable how many marriages publicly and completely broke up. ... In the ninety years between 1570 and 1659, we find forty-nine known cases of notorious marital quarrels, separations *a mensa et thoro,* or annulments among the peerage, which is about 10 per cent. [*sic*] of all marriages. The worst period seems to have been between 1595 and 1620, when something like one-third of the older peers were estranged from or actually separated from their wives.[69]

The key issue is obviously the number of "notorious marital quarrels," which are likely to be known only through surviving correspondence. Stone acknowledges that marital breakdown in the early Elizabethan period is probably underreported as compared to the better-documented period after 1590. However, his statistics provide a useful context in which to place the evidence of the *Zimmern Chronicle;* it certainly seems plausible that at least a tenth of all noble marriages in Froben Christoph von Zimmern's circle of acquaintance "publicly and completely broke up."

Stone regards the increase in marital breakdown in the course of the sixteenth century as the product of middle-class and Puritan values—rising expectations of affection and companionship in marriage, coupled with increasing public disapproval of the mistresses and illegitimate children who had previously provided a relief, at least for men, in arranged marriages.[70] The *Zimmern Chronicle* shows that all these factors already existed in the first half of the sixteenth century in southwest Germany, among Catholics as well as Protestants. The chronicler regards the potential for affection as a significant criterion in the selection of marriage partners. Not only does he share the ideal of affection and companionship within marriage set forth by contemporary advice literature aimed at a middle-class audience, but he blames unfaithful husbands for the breakdown of their marriages in an era when conventional advice required a noblewoman to turn a blind eye to her husband's extramarital affairs.

---

[68]For cases of separations among the English aristocracy, see Harris, *English Aristocratic Women,* 82–86, 177. For cases of French noblewomen running away with their lovers, see Potter, "Marriage and Cruelty," 27. Private deeds of separation did not come into general use among the English landed classes until after 1640, although individual cases occurred earlier. Stone, *Road to Divorce,* 149.

[69]Stone, *Crisis of the Aristocracy,* 660–61.

[70]Stone, *Crisis of the Aristocracy,* 664.

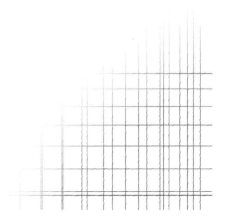

Part III Sexuality

CHAPTER 8

Sexuality
Laws, Attitudes, and the Sexual Honor Code

In 1479, the regulations for a tournament in Würzburg excluded from participation all publicly known adulterers, persons living in concubinage (*Unehe*), and persons born outside of wedlock. It is not clear to what extent the wording of the regulations was dictated by the bishop of Würzburg and to what extent it reflected the views of the knights of Franconia.[1] Nevertheless, the willingness of the knights to include language denouncing adultery and concubinage indicates that by the end of the fifteenth century the church's views on nonmarital sexuality were acknowledged—if not actually obeyed—by a social class whose lay model of marriage accepted premarital and extramarital male sexuality and viewed adultery as an offense that could be committed only by females.

The increasing hostility of ecclesiastical and secular authorities toward sexuality outside of marriage, often viewed as a product of the Protestant and Catholic Reformations, was already evident in canon law and in municipal legislation in the fourteenth and fifteenth centuries. By the early sixteenth century, it was expressed in German imperial and territorial law codes as well. The anecdotes in the *Zimmern Chronicle* make it a uniquely rich source of information on the attitudes of nobles towards sexuality and provide insight into the extent to which the hostile attitudes of the authorities affected German nobles of this period. While

---

[1]Sprandel argues that the regulations were drawn up by the bishop and his advisers and show that "ecclesiastical social policy reached a sphere [that is, the nobility] in which illegitimate persons had previously had free range." "Diskriminierung der unehelichen Kinder," 491. Borchardt interprets the regulations somewhat differently, arguing that the exclusion of bastards primarily reflected the desire of the Franconian knights to restrict the ranks of the nobility rather than the bishop's desire to impose the church's moral standards on the nobility. "Illegitime," 270. Some of the other regulations for the Würzburg tournament definitely showed a concern for social exclusivity rather than morality: one regulation excluded all those who had married outside the nobility, unless the bride had brought an especially rich dowry.

some of the views expressed in the chronicle represent the personal idiosyncrasies of the author, the anecdotes he tells indicate the values he expects his audience to share. Before analyzing the actual behavior of German counts and barons as depicted in the chronicle, this chapter will first examine the relevant provisions of canon and German secular law, the values expressed in contemporary *Schwänke,* and the attitude of the chronicler Froben Christoph von Zimmern.

LAW: ADULTERY, CONCUBINAGE, AND ILLEGITIMATE CHILDREN

In the words of Ludwig Schmugge, "Noble laymen simply did not hold to the sexual norms of the church, which viewed all sexual intercourse outside of marriage as sinful."[2] From the early Middle Ages onward, the Catholic Church condemned both the polygamy of Germanic nobles and the concubinage permitted by Roman law.[3] In the eleventh and twelfth centuries, the church gained legal control over the marriage of the laity, establishing a model of marriage as a monogamous and exclusive institution. Canonists in this period defined adultery as an offense against the institution of marriage, which could be committed by both married men and married women.[4] This ecclesiastical view of adultery conflicted with the concept in Germanic law that adultery was an offense against the husband's authority over his wife. In this view, based on the lay model of marriage, extramarital sex was considered adultery only if the female partner was married and the marital status of the male partner was irrelevant. Germanic law incorporated a sexual honor code that permitted the woman's husband or father to kill adulterers caught in the act. This right to kill (*Tötungsrecht*) maintained a strong hold over the popular imagination, although canonists strongly disapproved of private vengeance and argued that "punishment of adultery was the business of public authority, not a private right to be exercised by aggrieved husbands."[5]

While noble husbands might claim the right to kill wives who conducted extramarital affairs, they took for granted their own right not only to conduct casual affairs but to maintain long-term relationships with concubines. Although the church condemned concubinage by married men, concubinage by unmarried laymen was not forbidden in the High Middle Ages, and some canonists regarded it as equivalent to a de facto marriage.[6]

In the fourteenth and fifteenth centuries, however, canon law increasingly regarded concubinage as illegal and equated it with fornication and prostitution.[7]

---

[2]Schmugge, *Kirche, Kinder, Karrieren,* 227.

[3]Brundage, *Law, Sex, and Christian Society,* 130.

[4]Brundage, *Law, Sex, and Christian Society,* 248, 305–7.

[5]Brundage, *Law, Sex, and Christian Society,* 248. For a useful discussion of the concept of adultery in popular culture in the early modern period, contrasting it with developments in law, see Roth, *Ehebruchsschwänke in Liedform,* 193–217. On the legal definition of adultery, see *HRG,* s.v. "Ehebruch."

[6]Brundage, *Law, Sex, and Christian Society,* 297–300.

[7]Brundage, *Law, Sex, and Christian Society,* 481, 516.

From the thirteenth century onward, regional synods issued threats of excommunication against laymen who kept concubines. While synods in Spain and Italy chiefly prohibited adulterous concubinage, some of those in northern Europe prohibited concubinage even by unmarried men. In the fifteenth and sixteenth centuries, the campaign against lay concubinage moved to the highest levels of church authority. The Fifth Lateran Council in 1514 forbade concubinage both by single and by married laymen, and the prohibition was reiterated in the decree *Tametsi* of the Council of Trent in 1563.[8]

Secular authorities in the High Middle Ages generally took no action against concubinage. In some parts of Europe, especially in Italy and the Iberian peninsula, various forms of concubinage by unmarried persons were legally recognized.[9] Secular authorities in most European countries (including Germany) followed the Germanic concept of adultery as an offense by a married woman against her husband's rights; an extramarital liaison by a married man was not a punishable offense.[10]

In the fourteenth and fifteenth centuries, the church's campaign to abolish lay concubinage led many towns and cities, particularly in northern Italy and southern Germany, to impose financial penalties on men who cohabited openly with women to whom they were not married. The strictest regulations were those passed by cities in southern Germany and Switzerland—the region described in the *Zimmern Chronicle*.[11] Although these regulations forbade concubinage by both single and married persons, prosecution centered on open concubinage by married men.

The driving force behind municipal legislation against extramarital sexual relationships came from the guilds, which were more concerned with threats to the social order than with morality. Augsburg guildsmen in the pre-Reformation era regarded adultery by males as a serious offense only if it was public, particularly if

---

[8]Brundage, *Law, Sex, and Christian Society,* 514–15; and Becker, "Nichteheliche Lebensgemeinschaft," 24–25.

[9]On secular laws in Spain relating to concubinage, see Aznar Gil, "Illegitimen auf der Iberischen Halbinsel," 175–77. On *barrangaría,* a legally recognized form of concubinage based on contract, see also Winterer, *Bastarde in Spanien,* 75–77. The municipal law codes of some Italian cities, especially in the fourteenth century, expressly permitted concubinage by single men. Becker, "Nichteheliche Lebensgemeinschaft," 26.

[10]On the law of adultery in Spain, see Winterer, *Bastarde in Spanien,* 77. On Italy, see Ellrichshausen, *Uneheliche Mütterschaft,* 56. On Germany, see *HRG,* s.v. "Ehebruch." In France, neither Roman law (in the provinces of written law) nor any of the customary law codes allowed a woman to bring a suit charging her husband with adultery. Potter, "Marriage and Cruelty," 27–28.

[11]Italian secular governments began to declare concubinage illegal "as early as 1387 in Cremona but generally in the fifteenth century." Eisenach, *Husbands, Wives, and Concubines,* 137. One of the earliest examples of such municipal legislation in Germany is from Strasbourg, where a 1337 law prohibited open nonmarital coresidence and imposed significant financial penalties on the partners if they did not marry or separate. Other such laws were passed in Ulm (1387), Würzburg (1418), Bern (1459), Frankfurt am Main (1468), Basel (1448, 1498) and Constance (1505). Brundage, *Law, Sex, and Christian Society,* 444, 514–15; and Becker, "Nichteheliche Lebensgemeinschaft," 25.

the couple lived together in open concubinage. A secret liaison between a master and a servant in his household, on the other hand, was viewed as a nonpunishable matter since it posed no offense to the social hierarchy.[12]

By the late sixteenth century, however, municipal authorities in both Protestant and Catholic cities increasingly prosecuted married men for adultery, including master-servant relationships. This represented a significant shift from traditional attitudes in the handling of marital offenses. At the same time, municipal authorities took a stricter view of sexual relations between unmarried persons, leading to prosecutions of lay concubinage by unmarried couples as unchastity (*Unzucht*).[13]

German imperial and territorial law codes of the sixteenth century, as well as municipal regulations, reflected the view that adultery could be committed by both husbands and wives. The code *Bamburgensis* (1507), drawn up in the reign of Maximilian I, followed Italian civil law by defining adultery by the husband as a punishable offense only when it developed into an open and lasting relationship (that is, concubinage). The most influential imperial law code of the sixteenth century, the *Carolina* of Charles V (1532, sec. 120), went further by incorporating the canon law principle that adultery by the husband was legally equivalent to that of the wife. The Imperial Police Regulation (*Reichspolizeiordnung*) of Charles V (1530) followed the Fifth Lateran Council in outlawing all forms of lay concubinage. The *Carolina* set the model for other imperial and territorial police regulations of the sixteenth century; however, it did not specify penalties, which were left up to "customary and imperial law."[14] Although the *Carolina* incorporated the canon law concept of male adultery into secular law, it also reaffirmed traditional rights of family regulation and private vengeance, including the right to kill; "If anyone finds a work of unchastity taking place with his wife or daughter, or another evil crime, and on that account kills the evildoer, he is excused from the punishment or imprisonment specified by law" (sec. 142).[15]

Imperial law codes and police regulations set the model for legislation by territorial princes in the sixteenth century, which also forbade lay concubinage. By the second half of the century, territorial police regulations unanimously prohibited concubinage as unchastity, and therefore subject to heavy punishments because of its offense against Christian moral teachings.[16] This legislation had little direct

[12]Roper, *Holy Household,* 195–99.

[13]Harrington, *Reordering Marriage and Society,* 227–28; and Ellrichshausen, *Uneheliche Mütterschaft,* 50–51.

[14]*HRG,* s.v. "Ehebruch." Living together outside of marriage was a punishable offense in the *Reichspolizeiordnung* of 1330 (sec. 33); the demand for punishment of concubinage was repeated in ordinances of 1548 (sec. 25) and 1577 (sec. 26). However, there is no evidence that concubinage by unmarried persons was actually prosecuted in imperial courts. See Becker, "Nichteheliche Lebensgemeinschaft," 29; and *HRG,* s.v. "Konkubinat."

[15]Quoted in Roth, *Ehebruchsschwänke in Liedform,* 198.

[16]Becker, "Nichteheliche Lebensgemeinschaft," 29–30.

effect on German nobles, even though some law codes expressly stated that they applied both to nobles and to nonnobles. Territorial princes and other nobles who were *reichsunmittelbar* (subject only to the legal authority of the emperor) regulated the sexual behavior of their own family members; in southwest Germany this category included the counts and barons (such as the Zimmerns) and even the imperial knights. Nobles who were *landsässig* (subject to the authority of the territorial princes) were theoretically subject to territorial police regulations. However, they too were able to maintain independence in family matters. The right of nobles to be tried only by their peers meant that, in practice, morals legislation was applied only to townsmen and peasants.[17]

The legal position of children born of nonmarital relationships deteriorated severely in the twelfth century after the church succeeded in imposing its model of marriage as a monogamous union. Canon law now declared illegitimate birth a defect that rendered the bastard "infamous" and ineligible to receive holy orders. Under the influence of canon law, secular rulers in most countries, including Germany, forbade illegitimate children to inherit from their fathers as of right (that is, in cases under customary law where there was no will bequeathing property to them) and imposed severe restrictions on their legal rights. In Germany in the High Middle Ages, illegitimate children were *rechtlos* (unfree at law) and *ehrlos* (dishonorable). They could not hold fiefs, hold public office or positions of honor, become members of guilds, or receive honorable burial.[18]

Bastards' legal status was gradually ameliorated by developments that allowed the removal of the defect of illegitimacy and by alternatives to the customary law of inheritance. Almost as soon as it declared illegitimate children ineligible to take holy orders, the church began issuing dispensations allowing them to do so. Canonists of the twelfth and thirteenth centuries established the right of illegitimate children to receive child support (at least in certain cases) and revived from Roman law the concept of legitimation, either by the subsequent marriage of the parents or by rescript (order) of the prince. Both of these practices were gradually incorporated into secular law in continental European countries, including the German states.[19] Although one of the chief motives for the legitimation of

---

[17]Ellrichshausen, *Uneheliche Mütterschaft*, 88–89.

[18]Brundage, *Law, Sex, and Christian Society*, 543–44; and *HRG*, s.vv. "Bankert," "Uneheliche." Similar restrictions applied in Spain and Italy. Winterer, *Bastarde in Italien*, 58, 109–10; Winterer, *Bastarde in Spanien*, 91–92; and Aznar Gil, "Illegitimen auf der Iberischen Halbinsel," 177–79. In England, bastards were legally free but forbidden to hold public office or to join guilds. Given-Wilson and Curteis, *Royal Bastards of England*, 49–50; and Sheehan, "Illegitimacy in Late Medieval England," 119–20.

[19]On the development of legitimation in canon law and French law, see Génestal, *Légitimation des enfants naturels*, 91–226. On continental Europe in general and Germany in particular, see Schmugge, *Kirche, Kinder, Karrieren*, 70–79. On Italy, see Winterer, *Bastarde in Italien*, 52–53, 95–96; and Kuehn, *Illegitimacy in Renaissance Florence*, 167–205. On Spain, see Winterer, *Bastarde in Spanien*, 79–84, 109; and Aznar Gil, "Illegitimen auf der Iberischen Halbinsel," 177–79. English common law

bastards was to secure male heirs, secular law in most regions did not admit a legitimated son to the succession ahead of a daughter born in wedlock. [20]

The practice of making written testaments allowed fathers to make bequests by will to their illegitimate children, who were not otherwise allowed to inherit. In German law, real estate could not be bequeathed to illegitimate children without the consent of the nearest heirs, though small bequests of movable goods did not require such consent.[21]

Concepts of child support, legitimation, and written testaments began to affect German law only after the reception of Roman law in the fourteenth and fifteenth centuries. Rights granted in German law were more restricted than in some other European countries, especially Spain and Italy. German law followed the distinction made in canon law between different categories of illegitimate children: that is, between *naturales* (natural children) born of an unmarried man and an unmarried woman, and *spurii* (children born of forbidden relationships such as adultery, incest, or clerical concubinage). In Germany, only natural children had an automatic claim against the father for child support, and only they could be legitimated by the subsequent marriage of their parents.[22]

Children legitimated by the subsequent marriage of their parents were known as mantle children from the custom of placing them under their parents' cloak during the marriage ceremony. Canon law regarded them as fully equal to children born after the marriage. Except in England, which did not recognize legitimation in any form, secular courts accorded mantle children greater inheritance

---

refused to recognize legitimation. The principle "once a bastard, always a bastard," stated in the Statute of Merton in 1236, remained in effect until 1920. Sheehan, "Illegitimacy in Late Medieval England," 116–18; and Given-Wilson and Curteis, *Royal Bastards of England,* 44–48.

[20]Cooper implies that recognition of bastards was a solution to the problem of female heirs in an increasingly patrilineal society. "Patterns of Inheritance and Settlement," 302. This may have been the case in some regions; in France (particularly in the provinces of Roman law), a father could choose a legitimated son as his heir in preference to a legitimate daughter or even a legitimate son. Grimmer, *La femme et le bâtard,* 181. However, in most countries legitimated sons were not allowed to succeed ahead of daughters born in wedlock. In Burgundy, "as between a legitimate daughter and an illegitimate son, the daughter normally received the succession." Caron, *Noblesse dans le duché de Bourgogne,* 234. In Castile, bastard sons (preferably but not necessarily legitimated) were in the third rank of succession to *mayorazgos* (entailed estates) after all legitimate male and female descendants and collaterals. Beceiro Pita and Córdoba de la Llave, *Parentesco, poder y mentalidad,* 248. In Florence, fifteenth-century jurists ruled that "legitimation of males should not result in the statutory exclusion of legitimate females." Kuehn, *Law, Family, and Women,* 190. See also Bestor, "Bastardy and Legitimacy," 563.

[21]*HRG,* s.v. "Bankert"; and Dieck, *Legitimation durch nachfolgende Ehe,* 5–6.

[22]In Germany and France, only natural children were entitled to child support. Ellrichshausen, *Uneheliche Mütterschaft,* 114–15; and Demars-Sion, *Femmes séduites et abandonées,* 9. In Spain, only natural children were entitled by law to child support, but the father or his kin could grant support to other illegitimate children as a matter of equity. Winterer, *Bastarde in Spanien,* 108. In Italy, all illegitimate children were entitled to child support, even those born of forbidden relationships. Winterer, *Bastarde in Italien,* 52.

rights than children legitimated by other means.[23] In German law, mantle children were the only legitimated children who had the right to inherit real estate. According to the law of the Holy Roman Empire, they did not have the right to succeed to fiefs. However, some sixteenth-century German jurists argued that mantle children could succeed to fiefs, and it is clear that in practice they were often allowed to do so.[24]

Legitimation by rescript of the prince was the only form of legitimation available for children born of adulterous liaisons (*spurii*).[25] In Italy and the Iberian peninsula, such legitimation conveyed full rights of inheritance and succession, and fathers in Italy, Spain, and Portugal made extensive use of legitimation of bastards to secure male heirs.[26] In the Holy Roman Empire, by contrast, legitimation by rescript of the prince removed civil disabilities but conveyed only limited inheritance rights. Since it usually did not allow the recipient to inherit real estate, it was less significant for German nobles than for those in southern Europe.[27]

The rights of German noble bastards were increasingly restricted in the late sixteenth and seventeenth centuries by laws passed both by the emperors and by territorial princes. This reflected not only the influence of the Protestant and Catholic Reformations but also the concern of nobles with protecting their privileged status. After the middle of the sixteenth century, jurists increasingly denied the right of mantle children to inherit fiefs, and edicts of territorial princes justified restrictions on the inheritance rights of illegitimate children by the need to "maintain the purity of blood of each order, ... so that noble lineages will not

---

[23]On legitimation by subsequent marriage in canon law and in French law, see Génestal, *Légitimation des enfants naturels,* 101, 176–79. On the rights of mantle children, see Given-Wilson and Curteis, *Royal Bastards of England,* 44; Winterer, *Bastarde in Italien,* 95; Winterer, *Bastarde in Spanien,* 84; and *HRG,* s.v. "Mantelkind."

[24]On the exclusion from fiefs, see Winterer, *Bastarde in Italien,* 102; and Winterer, *Bastarde in Spanien,* 84. The rule in German law was the statement in the *Libri Feudorum* that "natural children, even if they are later legitimated, are not to be admitted to succession in fiefs either alone or with others." *HRG,* s.v. "Mantelkind." The arguments of sixteenth-century jurists on this issue are summarized in Dieck, *Legitimation durch nachfolgende Ehe,* 115–17.

[25]On legitimation by rescript of the prince, with examples from France, Burgundy, the Iberian Peninsula, and Italy, see Schmugge, *Kinder, Kirche, Karrieren,* 74–75. In Spain during the High Middle Ages, mere acknowledgment by the father was often tantamount to legitimation, but by the fifteenth century, rulers insisted on formal letters of legitimation. Winterer, *Bastarde in Spanien,* 83; and Gerbet, *Noblesse dans le royaume de Castille,* 163, 199.

[26]Kuehn notes that "legitimation was a legal device used with some regularity in fifteenth-century Florence" to provide male heirs. *Law, Family, and Women,* 176. Cooper says that "the fifteenth-century nobility of Castile, due particularly to the prohibition of marriage for members of the military orders, made considerable use of this expedient." "Patterns of Inheritance and Settlement," 302. In the genealogies of the Portuguese nobility compiled in the seventeenth century, legitimated bastards made up over a fifth of all recorded children of titleholders between 1380 and 1580. Boone, "Parental Investment and Elite Family Structure," 863.

[27]Schmugge, *Kinder, Kirche, Karrieren,* 74–75. The emperor could legitimate noble bastards and allow them to hold imperial fiefs, as in the case of the Este of Ferrara, but such cases were rare. Bestor, "Bastardy and Legitimacy," 565.

become mixed with those that have received a stain from the improper union of their parents."[28]

SEXUALITY IN *SCHWANKLITERATUR*

The crusade against all forms of extramarital sexuality by ecclesiastical and secular authorities in the late fifteenth and sixteenth centuries conflicted with the values of the laity as expressed in the genre of *Schwankliteratur* (merry tales). One of the unique features of the *Zimmern Chronicle* is its inclusion of entire chapters of such tales, and Tilmann Walter notes that even in those portions of the chronicle dealing with the Zimmerns themselves, "the chronicler reports noteworthy events in which there are plot motifs, styles of speech, characters, psychological explanations, and the [role of the] narrator that correspond down to the smallest detail to the stories of the authors of merry tales."[29]

Although merry tales sometimes express moral indignation at the sexual behavior they portray, they frequently trivialize behavior condemned by the church and treat it as harmless. Premarital sex is depicted "primarily as an amusing game, an everyday pleasure, and much less as a deadly sin," and even adultery is treated more as a social offense than a religious one.[30] Although the authors of these tales sometimes suggest that a cuckolded husband might take revenge on his rival by seducing the latter's own wife, they rarely invoke the motif of the husband killing the lover and/or the unfaithful wife, which is a common theme in popular ballads of the period.[31] Not only premarital sex but extramarital sex is treated in the tales as essentially comic; it may cause social conflict, but it does not lead to fatal consequences.

The authors of these tales were chiefly educated members of the middle class, and their cast of characters is made up of townsmen and peasants. However, the tales were addressed to an audience that included nobles as well as nonnobles, and similar erotic literature was enjoyed among the court nobility.[32] Although the *Zimmern Chronicle* is unique in incorporating such sexual anecdotes into a house chronicle that purports to narrate genuine historical events, Froben Christoph

---

[28]Dieck documents the increasingly hostile attitude toward inheritance of fiefs by mantle children in the legislation of territorial princes; the earliest case unfavorable to mantle children occurred in 1543. Dieck, *Legitimation durch nachfolgende Ehe*, 69–113. The quote is from the Bohemian Landesordnung of Emperor Ferdinand III (1640). Ibid., 95.

[29]On this genre, see Walter, *Unkeuschheit und Werk der Liebe*, 151–283, quote at 163.

[30]Walter, *Unkeuschheit und Werk der Liebe*, 154, 159, quote at 154. References to God's commandments or the teachings of the church are more common in the context of adultery than in that of premarital intercourse. Ibid., 224.

[31]Walter, *Unkeuschheit und Werk der Liebe*, 224; and Roth, *Ehebruchsschwänke in Liedform*, 210–11.

[32]On the courtly erotic literature of the late Middle Ages as a source of *Schwänke*, see Walter, *Unkeuschheit und Werk der Liebe*, 157. Walter (212) refers to the "interchangeability of ethical-erotic norms and assumptions of 'courtly' and 'bourgeois' literature, more specifically, texts aimed both at nobles and nonnobles."

could assume that his noble readers would be familiar with such tales in other contexts.

In one of the anecdotes in the *Zimmern Chronicle,* members of the court of Charles V—and even the emperor himself—indulge in bawdy speculation about how the grossly fat Count Christoph von Tengen managed to copulate with his young second wife (*ZC* 3:154–55). Clearly the author believed such public joking about sexual matters would be acceptable among the highest nobility at what was, for its day, a relatively straitlaced court. Noblemen often discussed their extramarital affairs in their letters to each other, which also included ribald jokes about the "work" of procreation within marriage.[33] Moreover, "coarse comedy was not reserved for the world of men, but women could also draw lascivious pleasure from it and even make use of erotic speech."[34] In his correspondence with his wife in 1474–75, Elector Albrecht von Brandenburg asked her to send him good jokes (*gut schwenk*) in her letters. He included open sexual references in his own letters, which were not meant for his wife's eyes alone but were read aloud to the ladies of her chamber. Nolte interprets these letters as imitations of "literary genres such as tales, jokes, carnival plays and fabliaux that also aim to provoke obscene laughter."[35]

The values of the merry tales can therefore be assumed to be familiar, and to some extent acceptable, to the audience addressed in the *Zimmern Chronicle.* Nobles as well as burghers enjoyed playing literary games with obscene metaphors. They also accepted the tales' anticlericalism and the view that neither premarital nor extramarital sex was a serious offense, at least where men were concerned. However, the chronicler himself was somewhat stricter in his own views on sexual matters, especially on the issue of adultery. His views were shaped not only by his milieu but also by his personal experiences.

The Attitude of the Chronicler

Froben Christoph von Zimmen expresses a wide range of attitudes toward nonmarital sexuality, some idiosyncratic and some highly conventional. On the one hand, he takes a detached and scientific view of certain sexual deviants: a male transvestite and a lesbian servant girl are described as freaks whose behavior evokes curiosity rather than horror or moral outrage (*ZC* 2:372, 473). On the other hand, he fervently endorses the popular stereotypes that bastards are evil by nature and that women are untrustworthy and sexually voracious (*ZC* 2:311, 504). The chronicler's views on premarital sexuality are conventional for nobles of his era; he accepts concubinage by unmarried men. However, his views on extramarital

---

[33]Nolte, "Verbalerotische Kommunikation," 458. The joke about the "work" of procreation is quoted from a 1531 letter of Count Wilhelm von Henneberg, one of the brothers of Apollonia, the wife of Gottfried Werner von Zimmern.

[34]Nolte, "Verbalerotische Kommunikation," 459.

[35]Nolte, "Verbalerotische Kommunikation," 452, 459.

sexuality are unconventional. To an extent that is surprising for a layman, he internalizes the canon law concept of adultery as an offense against the institution of marriage, and that both men and women can be culpable. He comments with disapproval on even casual sexual encounters. Schweickhart von Gundelfingen, while on a journey, "behaved so that one might have doubted that he was married." The chronicler compares him to another husband who "while he was engaged in the act with a woman up against a wall," suddenly remembered his wife and "cried out loudly, 'O Martha, Martha (for that was his wife's name), how shamefully I have forgotten you!'"(ZC 2:366).

Some of Froben Christoph von Zimmern's comments on sexuality may reflect his own personality. According to his biographer Beat Jenny, Froben Christoph was only an observer, not a participant, in the boisterous life of hunting, drinking, gambling, and wenching that characterized much of noble society in southern Germany and that he portrayed vividly in the *Zimmern Chronicle*. "The most striking traits of his character are shyness, exaggerated nervousness, a certain reserve, and the inability to make decisions quickly and carry them out quickly.... All of this obviously made him ill suited to be a skirt chaser." During his grand tour of university study and visits to foreign courts, Froben Christoph's lack of sexual adventures contrasted sharply with the experiences of his brother and his friends. He then settled down to a quiet life as a country gentleman. He was evidently faithful to his wife Kunigunde von Eberstein, who bore him ten daughters and one son; the chronicle does not mention any mistresses, illegitimate children, or venereal disease.[36]

It seems that Froben Christoph's avoidance of extramarital sex was not the result of a devout religious outlook. He practiced a largely political Catholicism, and despite the anticlerical jibes in the chronicle, he took little interest in doctrinal questions or in movements for personal spirituality.[37] His outlook seems to be determined less by conventional religious teachings on sexual morality than by his personal experiences, particularly the separation of his parents due to his father's maintenance of a concubine.

Froben Christoph identified strongly with his mother's cause and his fantasy of himself as the champion avenging the insult to her led to his permanent estrangement from his father. When Froben was a university student, he told his friends a story he had read about King Charles VII of France, his mistress Agnes Sorel, and his son, the future Louis XI. The queen was hurt when her husband ignored her in favor of the mistress and unburdened herself to her fourteen-year-old son, "who took his mother's shame so much to heart that he resolved to avenge her." He met the mistress on the way to church the next day, dragged her off her horse and slapped her face, and would have ridden over her if his attendants had

---

[36]Jenny, *Graf Froben Christoph von Zimmern*, 193–94.
[37]Jenny, *Graf Froben Christoph von Zimmern*, 195.

not stopped him. He then had to flee to Burgundy to avoid his father's wrath. "The young man told this story with emotion, as young people do," remarks the chronicler. "This was all brought to the old lord, perhaps with additions. This caused the greatest resentment and mistrust which the old lord felt more and more deeply all his life and never got over" (ZC 3:307–8).[38]

In addition, Froben Christoph's views on sexuality were shaped by his experiences when he accompanied his older brother Johann Christoph to study at universities and visit courts in the Netherlands and France. Although destined for the church as a canon of Strasbourg, Johann Christoph was far more worldly than his younger brother and far more at ease in a milieu in which "no one was considered a gentleman unless he had the great pox [syphilis]" (ZC 3:333). Froben Christoph's comments on his brother's sexual adventures are cautionary. Johann Christoph was lucky not to catch the French disease, as his companions often did, and

> he met with treachery from a maid at an inn…which left him all the rest of his life less able to have children.… I mention this so that every good fellow will take care. Such arts are all too frequently used by women.… I know more than one important person who encountered such practices by a woman; they never afterward begot a child of their body. This creates a good pleasant fellow fit to be a monk. (ZC 3:231)[39]

Froben Christoph himself was ridiculed in his student days for his lack of sexual experience. Conrad Peutinger, a fellow student at Louvain, spread a rumor implying that he was impotent ("as if he were of a cold nature [naturae frigidae]") (ZC 3:249).[40] After the chronicler suffered a severe case of smallpox that left him badly scarred, another friend, Antonius von Schauenburg, joked that Froben Christoph was the last person he would have expected to catch the great pox. However, the smallpox had attacked him instead, so there was still a chance that he could go home as a gentleman (ZC 3:333).

Recognizing that a life at court was not right for him, Froben Christoph spent all of his adult life administering his country estate. Throughout the chronicle he denounces courts as centers of sexual immorality: "They usually have the most shameless and corrupt morals [impudici und corruptissimi mores], which bring with them all kinds of trouble, as I saw for myself in many places years ago" (ZC 2:504).

---

[38]The chronicle calls the mistress "the fair Ameta" (for Agneta, the Latin form of Agnes). Stories about the mistresses of Charles VII, especially Agnes Sorel, were recounted at length in the French and Burgundian chronicles of the period. One chronicler says that Agnes Sorel "lived in greater estate than the queen of France, and the said queen was worth little or nothing in the eyes of the said king Charles, although she was a very good and humble woman, and many people said she was a saintly woman." Quoted in Bousmar, "Alliances liées à la procréation," 41.

[39]The reference here is evidently to magical practices rather than to sterility due to venereal disease. Froben Christoph refers to such practices in an anecdote about a cast-off mistress who turned to them to make her lover sterile in his marriage (ZC 4:362–63).

[40]The reference seems to be to impotence, not merely to Froben Christoph's personality, since it is followed by a series of anecdotes about impotence in other men.

The most lurid example in the *Zimmern Chronicle* of such shameless and corrupt morals is the "filthy satyr" Landgrave Wilhelm von Hesse, whose sexual license posed a threat to the honor of the chronicler's own mother. During a feud against the Erbach family, Wilhelm had tried to seize the young Katherina von Erbach and her sister Anna as hostages. "Everyone, both of high and low station, said openly that if he had gotten them in his power, he would have brought them up to shame and debauchery" (*ZC* 2:255).

Wilhelm is said to have "invented a new form of marital relations" in consummating his marriage; "he laid her on the ground in broad daylight and treated her most shamelessly, to her great pain." He was also in the habit of taking one of the ladies-in-waiting into the woods while the courtiers were strolling after dinner, so that his wife had to see the pair reemerge with "red ears and disheveled hair" (*ZC* 2:255–56). The chronicler reports with satisfaction that Wilhelm finally died "a frightful and shocking death" of syphilis, "consumed by wildfire" (*ZC* 2:258).

Froben Christoph's sexual restraint was not typical of his relatives and acquaintances, and his views on extramarital sexuality cannot be assumed to be broadly representative of his contemporaries. From the point of view of the modern reader, it is particularly interesting that his criticisms of extramarital sexuality and of bastardy are based on psychological and pragmatic arguments rather than on Christian morality. Extramarital affairs are condemned on the grounds that they inflict emotional suffering on the wife: "Their wives had to see it, live with it, and keep quiet, even if it stabbed them to the heart" (*ZC* 3:389). Although Froben Christoph accepts the conventional view that bastards are evil by nature, much of his criticism of bastardy is based on the argument that lavish provision for illegitimate children results in emotional and financial harm to the legitimate children and in financial damage to the patrimony of the lineage. As Wolf notes, Froben Christoph's allusions to his father's concubinage serve to explain

> the causal connection ... between miserliness toward the son, neglect of dynastic obligations, and extravagant spending. From this perspective one can also discern ... the function of the discourse on sexuality in the chronicle. Froben's interest in the effects of sexuality is evidently based on a personal experience in which he saw the mixture of lust and dynastic interest as an extreme threat. His indirect reproach is not of a moral nature; it aims at that juncture between family interest and sexual desire, which makes a private act into a public one.[41]

FEMALE SEXUALITY AND THE HONOR CODE

Although Froben Christoph von Zimmern's criticisms of adulterous husbands demonstrate an empathy with the legitimate wife that is unusual for his social class and his era, the chronicler also endorses the traditional sexual honor code

---

[41]Wolf, *Von der Chronik zum Weltbuch*, 376.

derived from German customary law. Many statements in the *Zimmern Chronicle* reflect the misogynistic stereotypes of the period, which depict women as untrustworthy and sexually voracious.[42] Since women are naturally inclined towards unchastity, says the chronicler, constant vigilance is the only way to ensure their proper behavior: "Some people say that one shouldn't keep close watch over women, or that it doesn't do any good. This might have been true in the good old days of piety, but things are very different in our times, and the opposite is proved in daily experience. But a clever, intelligent man can have and keep a pious wife" (*ZC* 2:504). The chronicler views a wife's adultery as an attack on her husband's honor and believes that the husband has the right to take private vengeance, including killing offenders caught in the act.[43] Family heads also have an obligation to control the sexual behavior of their unmarried female members, since their behavior reflects on the honor of their natal family.

In the numerous sexual anecdotes inserted into the *Zimmern Chronicle,* the most popular theme by far is adultery. Adultery by nonnoble women is treated in the chronicle as the subject matter of comedy, in a manner similar to the treatment of the theme in ballads and collections of *Schwänke*.[44] In these stories the woman is usually the wife of a burgher, her lover often a clergyman. The husband catches them in the act and usually beats the lover or exposes him to public humiliation, while the wife's friends and relatives often intervene to bring about a reconciliation between the spouses (*ZC* 2:523–24, 546–47). The husband thus takes his revenge on the lover, not the wife, and there are no lasting consequences for the marriage. Here the chronicler clearly follows the tradition of the *Schwankliteratur,* in which even adultery is viewed as a harmless amusement.

Adultery by a noblewoman, on the other hand, is portrayed in the chronicle as a tragedy, requiring the husband to exercise his right of private vengeance. In retelling a legend about a nobleman who seduced his friend's wife and was killed in the ensuing feud, the chronicler supplies his own view of an appropriate fate for the adulterous wife: "It is to be hoped that the whore, the shameful, impudent beast" met the same fate as her lover "so that they reaped their just reward" (*ZC* 2:500–1).

This view that adultery by a noblewoman is a particularly grave offense is reflected in some early modern German law codes. In the Bavarian Territorial Police Regulation of 1616, it forms an exception to the usual rule of lighter penalties for persons of higher social status. Noble *men* were accorded the mildest of all the penalties for adultery prescribed for any social class; "the noble *woman*, in contrast, was very harshly punished"[45]—at least in theory, since it is unlikely that

---

[42]On this stereotype of women, see Brundage, *Law, Sex, and Christian Society,* 548.

[43]On the survival in the sixteenth century of traditional concepts of the husband's right of private vengeance for adultery, see Harrington, *Reordering Marriage and Society,* 226–27.

[44]On the treatment of adultery in *Schwänke* and carnival plays, see Walter, *Unkeuschheit und Werk der Liebe,* 221–30.

[45]Roth, *Ehebruchsschwänke in Liedform,* 195.

the laws on the books were actually enforced against nobles of either sex. It is also unclear whether any German noblewomen in this era were actually put to death for adultery by aggrieved husbands or fathers. Clearly the chronicler had not heard of any such cases in real life, since his examples are purely literary.

The legal condemnation of noble adulteresses was evidently more severe in the French nobility, at least in some cases decided by the Parlement of Paris. In 1522, Marie de Quatrelivres ran away for two months with her lover and his brother; she was "sentenced by the Parlement to deprivation of community property and her dower, head shaving and immurement in a convent for life," although Francis I secured her release.[46] However, English noblewomen were not prosecuted under such circumstances; Harris even states that aristocratic English women who left their husbands to live with their lovers were not socially ostracized, though they might suffer the loss of financial support.[47]

In contrast to the numerous stories in the *Zimmern Chronicle* about extramarital affairs by the chronicler's male relatives and friends, there is only one case of alleged adultery by the wife in a family with which he was personally acquainted. When Froben Christoph and his brother were students in Cologne, boarding with their kinsman Count Thomas von Rieneck,

> they were several times invited by [their fellow student] Rheingraf Jakob to come visit him two miles from Cologne. There his sister kept house for him; she was married to Baron Franz von Mörsperg. She had her young daughter with her; nevertheless, it was a strange household about which much could be written. But acting on the advice of Count Thomas and their tutors, the boys politely turned down the invitation and stayed home. (*ZC* 3:236)

Not until much later in the chronicle does Froben Christoph explain the reasons for avoiding the "strange household." When his aunt recommended one of the daughters of Franz von Mörsperg as a potential bride, Froben Christoph rejected her suggestion out of hand because of the rumors about the sexual laxity of the Mörsperg household.

> The father was married to a Rheingräfin.... Once she, the two noble ladies-in-waiting, the housekeeper, and two maids were all pregnant at the same time, some by the lord, some by the clerk, and some by the manservant. How Count Wolf von Solms, a canon of Strasbourg, served as a tutor in this intimate circle,...I will omit at present.... Later she [the wife] took a clerk and fled with her possessions to Switzerland. (*ZC* 3:507–8)

The chronicler admits that much of this sensational story may have been mere rumor. Nevertheless, the damage to the reputation of the Mörsperg family ruled out any possibility of a marriage alliance with them, even though no scandal was alleged against the daughters themselves. This ostracism of a family whose

---

[46]Potter, "Marriage and Cruelty," 28.
[47]Harris, *English Aristocratic Women*, 84–85.

female members were reputed unchaste represents the most severe censure for adultery imposed by nobles in the *Zimmern Chronicle* against members of their own social class.

The chronicler says nothing about Franz von Mörsperg's handling of his wife's behavior, although in popular culture complaisant husbands were themselves considered culpable.[48] He calls the burgher Leonard Hutler, whose wife Margarethe later became the concubine of Johann Werner II von Zimmern, a "wanton, dishonorable man" because he tolerated an earlier affair of his wife's. Hutler is said to have been banished from Messkirch along with his wife after she was convicted of adultery (*ZC* 2:590–91). The chronicler does criticize the general lax management of the Mörsperg household and the sexual behavior of Franz von Mörsperg. Since the countess is described as keeping house for her brother Jakob, it is possible that she and her husband were separated, at least informally. The fact that the wife belonged to a higher-ranking family—she was a countess of the Rhine while he was a mere baron—may have had something to do with her husband's reluctance to take stronger action.

According to Wolf, a series of anecdotes about adultery told in connection with the Bubenhofen family of Falkenstein (*ZC* 2:492–93) shows that "Froben is here struggling with whether the continuation of a house and the maintenance of outward appearances takes precedence over upholding moral norms."[49] In addition, an anecdote about a case of bigamy—which in law was treated as a form of adultery[50]—explicitly raises the question of whether a husband should jeopardize an advantageous marriage alliance in order to punish his wife's sexual behavior.

According to a probably apocryphal story in the chronicle, Count Andreas von Sonnenberg, a general in the service of Maximilan I, was rewarded by the emperor with a splendid marriage to a rich widow. However, the woman had already contracted a clandestine marriage with her steward. When she was pressured by the emperor and her relatives to marry Sonnenberg, she did not dare reveal the secret marriage but went through with the church ceremony. Nevertheless, she continued meeting the steward secretly, and when Sonnenberg found out the truth, "he was unwilling to be made a fool of and brought the matter before the emperor. On the emperor's command and with the consent of her friends she was divorced from the count [the bigamous marriage was annulled] and kept in prison all her life." The steward is said to have "disappeared under the ice," presumably murdered at Sonnenberg's orders (*ZC* 2:298–99).[51]

---

[48]However, in one of his chapters of *Schwänke*, the chronicler inserts a series of three anecdotes about lenient husbands who discover the lovers in flagrante but do not punish them (*ZC* 3:381). This theme is rare in popular literature, and Wolf suggests that Froben Christoph endorsed such pragmatic behavior in at least some cases. *Von der Chronik zum Weltbuch*, 389.

[49]Wolf, *Von der Chronik zum Weltbuch*, 337.

[50]*HRG*, s.v. "Bigamie (Doppelehe)."

[51]The entire story is probably apocryphal, since the Waldburg genealogy does not record any

This is the only case in which an outside authority is said to have intervened in the case of a noblewoman charged with sexual misconduct; clearly the circumstances were exceptional, since the emperor himself was said to be involved. However, even in this case, the imprisonment would probably have been house arrest under the supervision of her family, the usual form of punishment meted out by family heads.

The chronicler adds, "I heard from one of the old-timers that Sonnenberg was widely criticized for giving information against his first wife to the emperor and her relatives and causing her to be punished. But I think he acted honorably" (*ZC* 2:299). Evidently members of the older generation felt it would be unfair to make the wife suffer for the bigamous marriage when she had been forced into it against her will. The chronicler, however, takes the more legalistic attitude that she was guilty of adultery and deserved punishment. He contrasts the behavior of Sonnenberg with that of the husband of a recent case in which the second husband pretended not to know the truth and acted "basely [by] letting himself be a fifth wheel." He comments, "he must have believed that many people would agree with the saying of the Roman Emperor Antonius: 'If I put away my wife, I must also give back her dowry'" (*ZC* 2:299–300).[52] Froben Christoph's criticism of the husband's behavior in this case contrasts with the "realistic, rational approach to life" that Wolf attributes to him in other stories about lenient husbands.[53]

Stories in the *Zimmern Chronicle* that depict family heads as punishing the deviant sexual conduct of female family members are more likely to involve fathers or brothers asserting control over unmarried daughters or sisters than they are to involve husbands asserting control over wives. If it became publicly known that a noblewoman had engaged in sexual relations before marriage or during her widowhood, it would be impossible to arrange a marriage for her. Moreover, her conduct could damage the reputation of the family and jeopardize the chances for other children to make advantageous alliances. Most of the stories in the chronicle in which family heads took action against unmarried female kin were of the type in which public officials might have intervened if the women had not been nobles; that is, they involved out-of-wedlock pregnancies, open cohabitation, or widespread and persistent rumors of a sexual relationship. The penalty imposed in these stories was usually a form of house arrest.

Cases of premarital pregnancy were very rare among noblewomen in the *Zimmern Chronicle*. One such case involved seduction after promise of marriage:

---

such marriage and annulment for Andreas von Sonnenberg. Schwennicke, *Europäische Stammtafeln NF,* 5:148.

[52]The dowry would have to be returned if a bigamous marriage was annulled, since no valid marriage existed. However, a husband who obtained a legal separation on the grounds of his wife's adultery did not have to return her dowry. Brundage, *Law, Sex, and Christian Society,* 388.

[53]Wolf, *Von der Chronik zum Weltbuch,* 389.

Count Ladislaus von Haag had a child by "one of his mother's ladies-in-waiting, an unusually beautiful lady from Bavaria…he is said to have promised her marriage, as the young lady swore, but he cast doubt on the matter" (*ZC* 3:44). Premarital sex would ruin a woman's reputation even if no pregnancy resulted and even if the woman was the victim of sexual attack. This is shown in an anecdote about "la Horion," a lady-in-waiting to the wife of Count Hans von Montfort. The chronicle says that the count's agent Johann Naves "paid court to her so violently that she cried out.… How Naves got along with the countess after perpetrating such an outrage among her ladies, I never found out. It was all hushed up. No one was hurt except 'la Horion.' She was sent home in disgrace, probably with a Uriah-letter, for her brothers imprisoned her shortly thereafter" (*ZC* 3:296).[54]

Stories in the *Zimmern Chronicle* in which young noblewomen were seduced before marriage or contracted secret engagements to young men deemed unsuitable by their families almost always occurred at court, or while the girl was fostered out to the household of a relative or patron. Girls who remained at home before marriage were kept under much stricter supervision by the family head. It was more difficult for family heads to control daughters or sisters who were widowed or separated from their husbands, for these women were sexually experienced and usually possessed their own residences.

The chronicle's stories about these independent women undoubtedly draw on the literary motif of the insatiable sexual appetite of widows.[55] In one such story, after Barbara von Bubenhofen separated from her husband, she was established by her brothers in one of the castles owned by the family. "But the woman was young, and she was used to living at court among people, not among wild beasts, and she began to get bored." Within a year there were rumors about an affair between Barbara and the steward of the castle, Wolf Eisenbart, "who was a tall upright man with a handsome figure." The affair "was so much talked about and rumors spread so widely that Lord Hans Caspar von Bubenhofen took his sister to his own household, where she afterwards lived the rest of her life in peace," presumably under a form of house arrest. According to the story, Barbara's brother Wolf von Bubenhofen had her lover imprisoned in the castle at Schalzburg, and it was rumored that Eisenbart had been secretly thrown over the walls and killed. However, the chronicle gives a different account of his death: fearing that he would be tortured, Eisenbart bribed the jailor to let him escape from the castle but died trying to climb down the steep cliff (*ZC* 2:505–6).

---

[54]The term "Uriah-letter" (a message sealing a person's doom, unwittingly delivered by the victim) refers to the biblical story of David and Bathsheba (I Sam. 2:1–24). King David fell in love with Bathsheba, the wife of Uriah, one of his generals. David had Uriah carry a sealed message to the Israelite military commander ordering him to place Uriah in the fiercest part of the battle so he would be killed.

[55]For a discussion of this theme, see Wolf, *Von der Chronik zum Weltbuch,* 264–69.

The story of Barbara von Bubenhofen—or at least the lurid tale about the fate of her lover—is probably fictitious. However, the most spectacular case of a noblewoman's extramarital sexual behavior recounted in the *Zimmern Chronicle* involved a woman well known to the chronicler. Johanna von Zollern (fl. 1539–50), the widow of Truchsess Jakob von Waldburg, had acted as intermediary in the attempt to negotiate a marriage between her sister Anna and Froben Christoph in 1543. At about the same date, Johanna moved into her dower house in Mengen, inviting her illegitimate half-sister "Black Anna" Zollerer to reside there as her companion (*ZC* 3:481–82).

According to the chronicle, a constant visitor to the house was Jakob Zimmerle, a member of an illegitimate branch of the Zimmern family. He ostensibly came to court Black Anna, but his visit also aroused the suspicions of Johanna's former parents-in-law. Through the efforts of Johanna and of Jakob's kinsman Johann Werner II von Zimmern, Karl von Zollern was finally persuaded to allow his bastard half-sister to marry Jakob Zimmerle. The couple took up residence in Oberndorf, where the Zimmern family were overlords. Here Johanna joined them in a ménage à trois; "the two sisters lived in such harmony with one another that they didn't even quarrel over sharing their rooster Zimmerle" (*ZC* 3:482). Johanna and Jakob were seen taking walks and rides together under suspicious circumstances. The scandal soon reached the ears of Karl von Zollern, who asked Johann Werner von Zimmern to banish the trio from Oberndorf.

Karl von Zollern sent armed men to break into their house early in the morning one day in December 1546.[56] The soldiers tried to carry off Jakob Zimmerle, who undoubtedly feared that Zollern would have him killed. "But he was too clever for them and called on the law of the empire. The burghers of Oberndorf came running and insisted on arresting him according to law" (*ZC* 3:483), thereby thwarting Zollern's private vengeance. The burghers kept Zimmerle in irons in the town hall at Zollern's expense and refused to let him out of their jurisdiction. Zollern was unable to bring any criminal charges against Jakob Zimmerle and finally had to let him go six weeks later.[57] The chronicle states that Zimmerle continued to live in Oberndorf until his death a few years later, suggesting that the town authorities and Jakob's legitimate Zimmern kin protected him against any further reprisals from Karl von Zollern.

Johanna was not so fortunate. "She was kept in custody in Zollern castle for several years. There a special chamber was built for her and she was kept under strict guard. She always had to have one lady-in-waiting with her; she willingly

[56]According to the chronicle, Karl von Zollern sent a veritable army of "fifty or sixty Zollern men on horseback as well as some foot soldiers" (*ZC* 3: 483).

[57]Zollern lacked standing to bring a case under imperial law, since the *Carolina* and imperial police regulations gave the power of accusation primarily to the injured spouse. Public officials could intervene in cases of public adultery (that is, desertion and open cohabitation with another party). *HRG*, s.v. "Ehebruch."

stayed with her in prison." Johanna was finally released from her imprisonment when lightning destroyed the tower containing her room. She died a few years later, "people say, from epilepsy and sheer displeasure" (*ZC* 3:484).

The conditions of Johanna's house arrest may have been less drastic than those portrayed in the chronicle; nevertheless her punishment was more severe than what would have been imposed on a woman of respectable social background by most secular courts in Germany. Women of burgher status were normally fined and/or subjected to public penances for sexual offenses; sometimes brief imprisonments of a week or so were added. In general, women received milder punishments than men for sexual offenses, since judges shared the prejudice that women were weak willed and not fully responsible for their actions.[58] Moreover, Johanna could not have been convicted of adultery under imperial law, which required proof of actual intercourse, although many municipalities would probably have considered the "common fame" of her relationship with Jakob Zimmerle as sufficient grounds to punish her under local law codes.[59]

If the case had been considered one of incest, the penalties might have been much more severe. In France, a noblewoman was actually executed in 1603 for incest with her brother.[60] German territorial and municipal legislation did not distinguish in incest cases between relatives by blood and relatives by marriage, and Harrington cites a case in which a woman was executed for incest with her brother-in-law.[61] However, Safley generalizes that "in the Holy Roman Empire… these forbidden relationships were not severely punished"; and civil authorities in Freiburg and Basel imposed the same penalties for incest as for adultery.[62] Although the chronicler regards the case of Johanna von Zollern and Jakob Zimmerle as scandalous, he never implies that it was incestuous. This suggests that Black Anna, as an illegitimate half-sister, was not considered a real member of the Zollern lineage.

The *Zimmern Chronicle* thus shows that German nobles continued to regard female sexual behavior as a matter to be regulated by the family. Family heads in Germany continued to exercise the power to punish deviant female kin by house arrest in a period when, in France, such matters were passing out of private hands and coming under the jurisdiction of royal courts. German nobles also continued to approve of private vengeance as an appropriate method of enforcing the sexual

[58]Safley, *Let No Man Put Asunder,* 170.

[59]The *Carolina* and imperial police regulations required proof of actual intercourse (*immissio semenis*). Roth, *Ehebruchsschwänke,* 195. Unless Johanna had been pregnant, it would have been almost impossible to produce such proof. On the lower burden of proof in municipal legislation, see Harrington, *Reordering Marriage and Society,* 237; and Safley, *Let No Man Put Asunder,* 99–100.

[60]In a case decided by the Parlement of Paris in 1603, Marguerite de Ravalet was executed for adultery and incest with her brother Julien. Potter, "Marriage and Cruelty," 28.

[61]Harrington, *Reordering Marriage and Society,* 157.

[62]Safley, *Let No Man Put Asunder,* 114–15, 156. The punishment was usually a fine, although repeat offenders were banished from the town.

honor code, at least against the lowborn lovers of noblewomen. The stories of the estate officials allegedly put to death for their affairs with Barbara von Bubenhofen and with the wife of Andreas von Sonnenberg may belong to the realm of legend, but Karl von Zollern's harassment of Jakob Zimmerle took place in real life.

Noble families did not necessarily carry out the precepts of the sexual honor code in every instance of deviant female sexual behavior. Despite the persistence of the right to kill in law as well as in popular culture, nobles in the *Zimmern Chronicle* did not kill their wives—or even repudiate them—for adultery. In this respect, German nobles were similar to other European elites. Despite the frequency with which the motif of the husband's private vengeance appeared in literature, only a handful of such killings of adulterous wives are actually documented in the fifteenth and sixteenth centuries in Spain and France.[63] Unmarried women were more likely to face retribution from their fathers or brothers for violations of the sexual honor code than wives were from their husbands.[64] These family heads had the power to place the women under house arrest with no possibility of appeal to public authorities. Husbands were probably reluctant to jeopardize their relationship with their wives' kin, while family heads might be more willing to punish women whose actions could harm the family's reputation and thereby its chances of arranging prestigious alliances for its members.

---

[63]Beceiro Pita and Córdoba de la Llave cite one case in 1436 in which a Castilian nobleman ordered his wife killed on the grounds of her adultery; however, they stress the uniqueness of this incident and the presence of political as well as sexual motives. *Parentesco, poder y mentalidad,* 218. In France, Grimmer cites two cases in the late sixteenth century in which noblemen killed wives whom they suspected of infidelity. *La Femme et le bâtard,* 134.

[64]Similarly, there is more evidence of vengeance by fathers or brothers than by husbands in the Italian nobility. Ettlinger emphasizes that noblewomen were not punished by their husbands or fathers for adultery with princes; however, she cites two cases in which bastard daughters of princes were executed by their fathers for affairs with men of lower rank. "Visibilis et Invisibilis," 785. The seventeen-year-old Francesco Maria della Rovere killed his sister's lover. Martines, *Power and Imagination,* 228.

CHAPTER 9

Concubines

Throughout the Middle Ages and the early modern period, European noblemen "practiced legal monogamy and social polygamy."[1] They not only conducted casual affairs but were accustomed to keeping a mistress or concubine of lower social status as a secondary wife.[2] Keeping a concubine was one aspect of the noble style of life, demonstrating the aristocratic attributes of wealth, leisure, and dominance over the rest of society. In the early sixteenth century, nobles in England, Castile, and France saw no conflict between the open maintenance of a mistress (usually of nonnoble origins) on the one hand and a respected social position and a stable marriage on the other. Such extramarital affairs by noble husbands were regarded as compatible with the goal of *concordia* or absence of discord in marriage, and even with the ideal of love between spouses.[3] Similarly, both men and women in sixteenth-century German princely families considered concubinage a normal occurrence.[4] However, social conventions prescribed that the husband's attentions to his mistress must not damage the honor of the wife and legitimate family.[5] As already demonstrated in the case of Gottfried Werner, southwest German counts and barons viewed flagrant violations of such conventions with disapproval and felt that they justified a wife leaving her husband and invoking retaliation by her natal kin.

---

[1]Bartolomé Clavero, *Mayorazgo Propriedad Feudal in Castilla (1369–1836)* (Madrid: Siglo Veintiuno Editores, 1974), 98, quoted in Cooper, "Patterns of Inheritance and Settlement," 238.

[2]Gottlieb, *Family in the Western World,* 102; Eisenach, *Husbands, Wives, and Concubines,* 144–46. Writers on the English aristocracy tend to use the term "mistress" for a long-term nonmarital sexual partner of any social class, whereas writers on continental elites sometimes distinguish between the "mistress" of a prince (who might be a noblewoman) and the "concubine" who was of lower social status than her noble patron. This study will use the two terms interchangeably.

[3]On attitudes in European aristocracies, see Stone, *Crisis of the Aristocracy,* 662; Beceiro Pita and Córdoba de la Llave, *Parentesco, poder y mentalidad,* 220, 360; and Potter, "Marriage and Cruelty," 28–29.

[4]Ellrichshausen, *Uneheliche Mütterschaft,* 89.

[5]Eisenach, *Husbands, Wives, and Concubines,* 150.

The strong resistance of nobles to the attempts of ecclesiastical (and later, also secular) authorities to outlaw concubinage was due to the important social functions of the practice. First, concubines were a symbol of wealth, status, and power. "While ordinary men might visit prostitutes, have lovers, or carry on long-term relationships with women from their own milieu to whom they were not married, they did not keep concubines," because of the great expense involved in maintaining the woman in her own household while also supporting a legitimate family.[6]

Second, concubinage served an important emotional function for noblemen, providing married men with relationships based on personal choice in a society in which marriages were primarily based on rank and wealth rather than on the personal qualities of the spouse.[7] Concubines also served as temporary companions to noblemen who did not marry until their late twenties or thirties, and as permanent de facto wives to the large number of noblemen who never married.

Lastly, concubinage served economic functions that complemented the restrictive family strategies associated with lineal consolidation. Younger sons who did not inherit estates could not support a legitimate wife of their own social class, but concubinage enabled them to enjoy stable unions without endangering the family patrimony. Moreover, many widowers took concubines instead of remarrying after the deaths of their wives, so that they would not encumber the estate with additional legitimate heirs.[8] Concubines could also serve as a form of insurance, producing sons who could be legitimated if necessary to provide a male heir to continue the lineage.[9]

The *Zimmern Chronicle* makes it clear that, despite his personal sexual restraint, Froben Christoph von Zimmern shared his social class's assumption that noblemen did not have to abide by the rules that restricted sexual relations to marriage. He expresses surprise that the town council of Strasbourg "many years ago expelled all concubines [*beisitz*] and passed a law that such lewd behavior was not permitted. This was strictly enforced and no one was spared, not even if he was a nobleman or one of the most powerful burghers; this applied not only to

---

[6]Eisenach, *Husbands, Wives, and Concubines*, 146.

[7]However, Beceiro Pita and Córdoba de la Llave question the view that these relationships should be seen as "close to the present-day concept of love." They argue that such liaisons involved sexual attraction and affection, but also social and mental habits that made it customary to maintain mistresses in this society. *Parentesco, poder y mentalidad*, 220.

[8]Spiess, *Familie und Verwandtschaft*, 381; and Eisenach, *Husbands, Wives, and Concubines*, 143. Eisenach (143–44) states that scholars, looking at the institution from the point of view of the men who maintained concubines, "have generally argued that elite concubinage helped maintain the aristocratic marriage system by unofficially giving it greater flexibility," whereas she emphasizes its potential to threaten the marriage system by undercutting the status of elite wives.

[9]The role of the mistress as the mother of potential heirs is a major theme in Ettlinger, "Visibilis et invisibilis," 771–72. For the adoption of illegitimate sons as heirs, see Cooper, "Patterns of Inheritance and Settlement," 302; Boone, "Parental Investment and Elite Family Structure," 863; Given-Wilson and Curteis, *Royal Bastards of England*, 49–53; Grimmer, *La femme et le bâtard*, 181–82; Kuehn, *Illegitimacy in Florence*, 173–74; and Winterer, *Bastarde in Spanien*, 92–112.

married men but also to those who remained single, whether clerical or lay" (*ZC* 4:174–75).

Here the chronicler distinguishes between different forms of concubinage. He disapproves of the keeping of concubines by married men or priests, but—despite the rulings of the Fifth Lateran Council and the imperial law codes of the sixteenth century—he sees no reason to penalize cohabitation by unmarried persons. He draws distinctions not only according to marital status, but also according to social rank; he is shocked that the Strasbourg authorities actually enforced this law even against nobles and urban patricians.

Although he inserts many popular tales about lascivious clergy into the *Zimmern Chronicle*, Froben Christoph is tolerant of concubinage by cathedral canons, including his own kinsmen. Perhaps this is because canons were, in Spiess's words "nobles first and clergy second."[10] He strongly disapproves of the affair between Dorothea Grüniger and his brother Johann Christoph, a canon of Strasbourg; however, his criticism does not focus on the impropriety of a canon's keeping a concubine, but on the fact that the affair led to a lifelong quarrel between Johann Christoph and Dorothea's former lover, another canon in the same cathedral chapter (*ZC* 3:527–28). Their kinsman Count Thomas von Rieneck, a canon of Cologne, had earlier given up his plan to resign his benefices in favor of Johann Christoph because he disapproved of the latter's womanizing. Nevertheless, the chronicler remarks without any apparent irony that Rieneck himself "had a great many bastards, for whom he made appropriate provision long before his death" (*ZC* 2:235).

The *Zimmern Chronicle* expresses no disapproval of noble bachelors for cohabiting with concubines before their marriage. One story retold from a literary source shows the approved model for such a relationship. "Heinrich von Tierstein had a concubine in his youth whom he loved very much. He was persuaded by his friends to marry a Fräulein von Welschen-Neuenberg. He dismissed his lover [*liebhaber*] but gave her an honorable dowry." The jealous concubine asked her mother to help her cast a spell to make her lover impotent in his marriage so that he would take her back. However, she eventually became remorseful and helped him undo the spell (*ZC* 4:362–63). In this story the relationship is based on romantic love, and the man behaves correctly by making appropriate financial provision for his mistress when their relationship is terminated by his marriage to a woman of his own social rank.

The chronicler also does not stigmatize either the lifelong bachelors who maintained concubines or the women who served as their de facto wives. He describes his great-grandfather's brother Gottfried III von Zimmern as a particularly pious man even though "he never married but was blessed with many children" and was still carrying on love affairs when he was over seventy years old (*ZC* 1:416). Stories in the *Zimmern Chronicle* about bachelors who cohabit with

---

[10]Spiess, *Familie und Verwandtschaft,* 468.

concubines do not criticize the men for their sexual behavior but for their drunkenness, swearing, or bad household management. The dissolute Hans von Weitingen "never married in his youth and manhood but kept house with concubines, so you can imagine how the household was run" (*ZC* 3:170); a concubine could not exercise the authority over the household that was accorded a legitimate wife. The concubine herself is sometimes portrayed more positively than her lover: Christoph von Leitingen is called a "child of Bacchus" in contrast to "the good woman, his concubine," who tried to persuade him to go to Mass on Christmas Eve (*ZC* 4:254–55).

Because of his own personality and his experience of his parents' separation, Froben Christoph von Zimmern was undoubtedly more vocal than most noblemen in his censure of married men who kept concubines. However, anecdotes in the chronicle show that in his milieu, extramarital relationships were tolerated, but married men were expected to be discreet.

The concubine of a married nobleman was usually maintained in her own household, either in the town outside the castle or in another location at some distance from his own residence.[11] Some nobles made a serious attempt to keep the affair secret, at least at the beginning. An anecdote about Sixt von Hausen and his "maid or concubine," who was nicknamed Five of Diamonds, specifies that the incident occurred "when she first came to him and the affair was still supposed to be a secret." Sixt maintained her in a townhouse in Messkirch. He was greatly embarrassed one day when he saw two peasants shouting and gesturing in the street below, for he was afraid that they had seen the concubine at the window with him (*ZC* 2:604–5).

According to the chronicle, the notorious murder of Andreas von Sonnenberg in 1511 took place while he was on his way to visit a concubine (*metzlin*) whom he maintained in a house a mile or two away from the castle. His enemy Felix von Werdenberg, who knew that Sonnenberg would be traveling with only a few servants, lay in ambush and stabbed him to death (*ZC* 2:289).[12]

Noblewomen could and did separate from husbands who flaunted their mistresses openly and violated the convention that "dictated that a concubine be treated obviously less well than a wife."[13] Both the chronicler's mother, Katharina von Erbach, and his aunt Apollonia von Henneberg left their husbands for such

---

[11]The same arrangement was customary in Spain. Beceiro Pita and Córdoba de la Llave, *Parentesco, poder y mentalidad,* 223. Ettlinger notes that the favorites of Italian princes often resided not in the palace but in a house in the town outside it, or even in another town. "Visibilis et invisibilis," 777.

[12]According to the *Truchsessenchronik* commissioned by the Waldburg family, Sonnenberg was ambushed while he was hunting in the forest. However, the author of the *Truchsessenchronik* also criticizes Sonnenberg as a womanizer, so the story in the *Zimmern Chronicle* that he was on his way to visit his mistress may have some basis in contemporary gossip. Wolf, *Von der Chronik zum Weltbuch,* 80–82.

[13]Eisenach, *Husbands, Wives, and Concubines,* 148.

behavior, and in each case some of the husband's own relatives and friends took the side of the injured wife. The case of Gottfried Werner von Zimmern is particularly interesting for what it reveals of attitudes toward extramarital relationships in the social milieu of the chronicler.

Apollonia von Henneberg "suffered patiently for a long time and put up with a great deal" from her husband Gottfried Werner, including eight illegitimate children by two different concubines (*ZC* 3:387). Much to the chronicler's disgust, Gottfried Werner showed more favor to his illegitimate sons than to his legitimate daughters (*ZC* 4:286). After an incident in 1539 involving yet another concubine, Apollonia left her husband and returned to her natal family in Franconia. She refused to be reconciled to Gottfried Werner until he signed an agreement entitling her to a separation and a pension in the case of a future offense (*ZC* 3:392–93).

Froben Christoph's sympathies in this case were divided. On the one hand, he felt that his aunt had suffered greatly; on the other hand, he felt sorry for his uncle, who "suffered great scorn and enmity from his friends and relations." Froben Christoph felt that such "gossip and enmity" was unfair because many other noblemen behaved just as badly without being censured by their peers (*ZC* 3:386–87).

The chronicler proceeds to relate a series of anecdotes about relatives and acquaintances whose behavior, in his view, was as bad as Gottfried Werner's. He is particularly scornful of Friedrich von Fürstenberg, who joked about the sexual activities of his wife's father Christoph von Werdenberg and called him "the most whoring father-in-law in the land" (*ZC* 3:389). Froben Christoph was himself highly critical of Christoph von Werdenberg's behavior and particularly of his affair with his illegitimate cousin Leonora Werdenberger (*ZC* 3:129); however, he felt that Fürstenberg was being hypocritical.

He tells an anecdote about an affair Fürstenberg carried on with one of his wife's servants during his wife's illness, and another about an incident at an inn in which Fürstenberg was surprised by other members of his traveling party while he was in bed with a prostitute. Fürstenberg drove the woman out of the room, pretending to be scolding her as a delinquent servant, "so he kept his honor and was believed." "This man," concludes the chronicler, "whom I otherwise knew as a well-respected count, had several children by a concubine [*eine possession*] without his wife's knowledge and got away with it. I am not saying that this is right…, but in the case of one man, it's considered a minor matter, for another, it's condemned as a capital offense" (*ZC* 3:392).

Here it becomes clear how the views of the chronicler Froben Christoph von Zimmern differed from those of other nobles in his milieu. The chronicler sees secret adultery as just as culpable as open concubinage and considers a nobleman's honor compromised even by a brief encounter with a prostitute. However, most other nobles saw male adultery as an offense only if it created a public scandal. The behavior of Christoph von Werdenberg and of Gottfried Werner von Zimmern, which created open discord in their families, was too egregious to be overlooked. However, a nobleman who was discreet in his extramarital affairs and begot children without his wife's knowledge suffered no real social stigma.

All of the incidents examined thus far have looked at concubinage only from the point of view of the men involved, but what about the women? What was their social background? Why did they become concubines, and what happened to them after the relationship with their noble lovers ended? The *Zimmern Chronicle* gives details that help to flesh out the brief mentions such women receive in documentary sources such as wills.

Several of the concubines mentioned in the *Zimmern Chronicle* were servants: Sixt von Hausen kept "a maid [*magd*] or concubine nicknamed Five of Diamonds"(*ZC* 2:605); Christoph von Werdenberg had a child by Endle Garele, his housekeeper (*beschliesserin*), and Friedrich von Fürstenberg also carried on a secret affair with his wife's housekeeper (*ZC* 3:129, 392).

Other concubines came from artisan or middle-class backgrounds: the concubine who cast a spell on her former lover asked advice from her mother, a chair-maker (*sesselmacherin*) (*ZC* 4:362). "The Faulhans woman," one of Gottfried Werner's concubines, was the wife of a mercenary soldier from Messkirch (*ZC* 3:382); and Margarethe Hutler, the concubine of Johann Werner II, was the wife of a burgher of Messkirch (*ZC* 4:86). Leonora Werdenberger, the mistress of Christoph von Werdenberg and his brother Felix, was the bastard daughter of their uncle Hugo von Werdenberg and was married to a furrier (*ZC* 2:310–11). The highest-ranking woman whose background is mentioned in the chronicle is Anna Rehlinger, a member of a patrician family of Augsburg; she became the mistress and perhaps the clandestine wife of Christoph Friedrich von Zollern (*ZC* 2:463).

Why did these women become concubines? In the case of servant women, one may assume that they had little choice, since they were economically dependent on their masters. A concubine may also have hoped that the relationship would ultimately lead to marriage to her lover, an outcome canonists considered a realistic possibility.[14] At the very least, she would enjoy a higher standard of living while the liaison lasted, and the gifts or bequests she received from her lover when it ended would provide a dowry enabling her to settle down as the respectable wife of a man of her own social class.[15]

In the case of married women, the *Zimmern Chronicle* cynically implies that they sought either to fulfill their own sexual desires or to obtain greater wealth and power than they could achieve in their own social class. In some cases, their

---

[14]Brundage, *Law, Sex, and Christian Society,* 446; and Beceiro Pita and Córdoba de la Llave, *Parentesco, poder y mentalidad,* 223.

[15]Eisenach suggests that this prospect of a dowry and a legitimate marriage at the end of the relationship "may indeed have been the main attraction of concubinage for many women." *Husbands, Wives, and Concubines,* 153.

marriages had broken down and they may have been seeking a source of economic support. Personal affection undoubtedly played a role, particularly in relationships that lasted for many years, but unfortunately the chronicle gives little insight into the emotional aspects of these unions.

Several noblemen in the *Zimmern Chronicle* talked about marrying their concubines in order to legitimate their bastard sons as heirs. The bachelor Hans von Weitingen is said to have saved his lineage from extinction by marrying his concubine on his deathbed and thereby legitimating their son (*ZC* 3:171).[16] Two married men with only daughters from their marriages seriously considered the possibility of marrying their concubines after the death of their wives in order to legitimate their bastard sons as heirs. Gottfried Werner von Zimmern hoped to marry Anna Fritz after his wife's death in order to legitimate their son, but she married before his wife died (*ZC* 4:288). The widower Christoph von Werdenberg wanted to marry his housekeeper Endle Garele after she bore him a son. "The old lord took such joy in this that people were sure he would have married her in order to maintain his lineage" if it had not been for the opposition of his brother and his son-in-law, who stood to inherit his estates if he died without male heirs.[17] Nothing actually came of the matter, for both the concubine and the child died shortly thereafter (*ZC* 3:129).

As a point of law, these fathers were probably mistaken in believing that a legitimated son could inherit ahead of a legitimate daughter. Moreover, the requirement of equality of birth in German law meant that even the legitimate children of a marriage between a nobleman and a nonnoble woman were not entitled to inherit their father's noble rank or his estate.[18]

The chronicler describes one nobleman who evidently did marry his concubine in such a morganatic marriage. Count Antonio von Isenburg, who married a nonnoble woman as his second wife, did not live with her in his castle but maintained her in a house in the town. He rode down from the castle on a donkey to visit her and their sons, "who were not considered nobles but only good fellows [*gute gesellen*]. This was done with the consent of their father" (*ZC* 4:288). The living arrangements strongly imply that Isenburg's second wife was his former concubine, who would have been installed in this house before their marriage.[19]

---

[16]Such deathbed marriages in order to legitimate children as heirs also occurred in other elites; Kuehn notes that the practice was "of lively interest to jurists" in Florence. *Illegitimacy in Renaissance Florence*, 170.

[17]Christoph von Werdenberg's fiefs would have passed to his brother Felix and his allodial estates to his daughter Anna, the wife of Friedrich von Fürstenberg. Since Fürstenberg was counting on the Werdenberg inheritance to pay his debts (*ZC* 3:137), he would certainly have mounted a legal challenge if Christoph had tried to make his illegitimate son his heir in place of his legitimate daughter.

[18]On the question of whether legitimated sons could inherit ahead of legitimate daughters, see chapter 8 above, 178n20. On the limited inheritance rights of children of unequal marriages, see *HRG*, s.vv. "Ebenbürtigkeit," "Missheirat."

[19]Another count of Isenburg took as his fourth wife the widow of his forester (almost certainly

Few concubines could realistically expect to marry their lovers, but they did benefit from the relationship. It is clear from the *Zimmern Chronicle* that a German count or baron normally provided the woman with a house at least for the duration of their liaison, and that he was expected to give her a dowry that would enable her to marry after it ended. In the case of a long-term relationship, he would provide for her maintenance after his death. Their illegitimate children would receive support during his lifetime and bequests in his will.

The *Zimmern Chronicle* suggests that little social stigma was attached in most cases to the former concubine of a nobleman; the dowry or legacy he provided made her a valuable catch on the marriage market in spite of her past. In the story of Heinrich von Tierstein, the concubine who was jealous enough to cast a spell to make her noble lover come back to her was also practical enough to make more realistic provisions for the future: "since she had ready cash, she took a clerk [in marriage] and moved to Metz" (*ZC* 4:362). Anna Fritz was equally pragmatic. Although Gottfried Werner von Zimmern hoped that Anna would remain unmarried so that he could marry her after his wife's death and legitimate their son as his heir, "God did not ordain it so: she finally married a forester" (*ZC* 4:288). Even Margarethe Hutler, who had a notorious sexual history long before she spent more than twenty years as the concubine of Johann Werner II von Zimmern, was able to remarry using the money he bequeathed her as a dowry (*ZC* 4:92–93).

Most of the concubines in the *Zimmern Chronicle* merely receive a passing mention in anecdotes about their lovers and are described by the neutral terms *concubina* or *beisitz*.[20] However, the chronicler launches vitriolic tirades against a few women—Dorothea Grüniger, Leonora Werdenberger, Anna Rehlinger, and

---

his present or former concubine). This mésalliance resulted in his deposition as head of the family by the children of his previous marriages. Schmidt, *Wetterauer Grafenverein,* 482.

[20]The chronicle avoids the standard German word for concubine, *Kebse,* as well as the compound forms *Kebsweib* and *Kebsfrau,* which largely superseded *Kebse* in the fifteenth and sixteenth centuries. Luther used *Kebsweib* in his translation of the Bible to refer to Abraham's concubine Hagar (Gen. 16:3); however, the term was considered vulgar and polite authors used the Latin *concubina* or *concubine* as a euphemism. In addition to *concubina,* the *Zimmern Chronicle* frequently uses *Beisitz,* a legal term with the root meaning "possession"; in one instance the chronicle actually uses *eine possession* (from the Latin) to mean a concubine. Other terms are used only once or twice in the chronicle. In only one case does the term refer to an emotional relationship: Heinrich von Tierstein dismissed his *Liebhaberin* (lover) when he had to marry a woman of his own rank. The romantic term is probably borrowed from the literary source of the story. The chronicle uses the term *Metzlein* to refer to the mistress whom Andreas von Sonnenberg was on his way to visit at the time of his murder. *Metzlein* is a diminutive of *Metze* (or *Mätz*), a nickname for Mathilda, which was used to mean "girl" in general. Although not always used in a pejorative sense, *Metze* also acquired the connotation of a woman of loose morals and was used to designate a camp follower or a priest's concubine. The term *Palmesel,* used to describe Leonora Werdenberger, may be a metaphor unique to Froben Christoph rather than a term in general use. A *Palmesel* was a wooden statue of Christ riding a donkey, used in processions on Palm Sunday. Although Grimm's dictionary states that the word was often used in a broader sense, its

Margarethe Hutler—who made a career out of a series of irregular sexual relationships and who exerted power over their lovers. In telling their stories, the chronicler invokes all the misogynistic stereotypes of the era: they are the "unruly women" or "women on top" who disrupt the social order, seeking power and status to which they are not entitled.[21] Particularly in the cases of Leonora Werdenberger and Anna Rehlinger, whose stories draw heavily on rumor and are embellished with many motifs from popular literature, these women are depicted as cruel adventuresses. Insatiable in their sexual appetites, cold and calculating in their manipulation of their lovers, they drag down to ruin and death the men unfortunate enough to be obsessed with them.

Dorothea Grüniger's career included stints as the mistress of three canons of Strasbourg, among them the chronicler's brother, Johann Christoph von Zimmern. According to the chronicle, she brought her first lover, Rheingraf Jakob, "into great debt and misery," so that he was almost forced to resign from the cathedral chapter because of his debts. He sent her away but was unable to resist her, "for she was very beautiful in her youth, and such people are good at blandishments." When she came to him in an old gray peasant dress and fell weeping at his feet, her false tears convinced him to take her back (ZC 3:527).

Although Dorothea had several children by Count Jakob, she also "wandered around" and eventually settled down with Count Bernhard von Eberstein, the chronicler's brother-in-law, who kept her for several years. After leaving him, she became the mistress of Johann Christoph von Zimmern. This led to such enmity between the two men that it disrupted the entire cathedral chapter. "Therefore Count Bernhard took a lasting dislike to him, and the two men did ridiculous and foolish things to each other all their lives." Bernhard von Eberstein did not attend the wedding of his sister Kunigunde to Froben Christoph von Zimmern; he arrived only after the other guests had departed, since he did not want to encounter Johann Christoph. The chronicler remarks in exasperation, "I don't know which of the two counts acted more foolishly; the old one [Bernhard] for letting himself be discarded by such an old, used-up, unfaithful, sly cow (for which he should have thanked God), or the young one [Johann Christoph] for burdening himself with such a stinking, filthy beast" (ZC 3:528).

According to the chronicle, the career of Leonora Werdenberger led to more serious consequences than mere quarrels between canons. Leonora, the illegitimate daughter of Count Hugo von Werdenberg, was brought up in Sigmaringen in or near her father's castle. As a bastard, she was naturally evil, at least in the opinion of

---

two citations from the *Zimmern Chronicle* are the only ones with the meaning "concubine." *Palmesel* was also used as an insult equivalent to "blockhead." Grimm and Grimm, *Deutsches Wörterbuch*. s.vv. "Beisitz," "Kebse," "Kebsweib," "Metze," "Metzlein," "Palmesel."

[21]On this stereotype, see Davis, "Women on Top," 124–51.

the chronicler. Since the categories of women who were sexually available to noblemen included "bastard daughters of their relatives,"[22] it is possible that even in her
youth she might already have had a sexual relationship with one or more of her
legitimate cousins. After her father's death, Leonora was married to a furrier, but
she soon became bored with her uncouth middle-class husband. "As soon as the
Werdenberg gold warmed her neck, it was all over; ...the furrier's trade stank, and
so did her husband." She left him and thereafter "always resided at Sigmaringen;
there the two counts of Werdenberg, Christoph and Felix, built her a house. In
short, she became all-powerful, and anyone who had any business to transact with
the counts or any case for them to handle had to win the favor of this Leonora" (*ZC*
2:310–11). The chronicler is outraged not only by her political influence but by the
emotional suffering caused to the counts' wives by this open scandal: "their wives
had to see it, live with it, and keep silent about it, even if it stabbed them to the
heart, and it is said that it cost both the counts their lives" (*ZC* 3:389).

The most scandalous aspect of this affair is that, according to the chronicle,
Leonora was mistress to the two brothers simultaneously: "The Werdenberg
brothers had a remarkable alternation with a concubine [*palmesel*], and each
brother yielded to the other. She was a great courtesan" (*ZC* 3:389).[23] Presumably
Leonora's primary lover was Christoph, since he was the brother who resided permanently in Sigmaringen. However, it was Felix who, according to the chronicle,
fell madly in love with Leonora and thereby met his downfall. While en route to
Italy with his troops to attend the coronation of Charles V in Bologna, he heard
rumors about Leonora's affairs with other men. Felix suddenly left his regiment
without asking the emperor's permission and returned to Sigmaringen, thereby
losing the emperor's favor and (according to the chronicle) leading the emperor to
order his secret execution (*ZC* 2:308). "It is a pity," says the chronicler, "that this
good count became entangled with this shameful, ravening beast.... All his misfortunes were due to her, for it was on her account that he lost the favor of
Emperor Charles, who had previously held him in especially high regard because
of his loyal service to the Empire and to the House of Burgundy" (*ZC* 2:311).

The kernel of fact underlying the story of Leonora Werdenberger is that she
was reputed to be the mistress of Christoph von Werdenberg. The chronicler elsewhere says of Christoph, "It is said, with good reason, that he enjoyed himself too
much with women and, they say, Leonora Werdenberger was not the least of the
causes of this" (*ZC* 3:129). However, it is difficult to see how Leonora could have
carried on a prolonged affair with Felix, who rarely visited Sigmaringen.[24]

---

[22]Brundage, *Law, Sex, and Christian Society*, 204.

[23]Such a relationship might have attracted less attention in France, where Grimmer says that a
nobleman "was not jealous of his concubine.... It was customary to share her with his friends or relatives." In a case parallel to that of the Werdenberg brothers, Gilles de Gouberville shared his mistress
Hélène Vaultier with his brother Simonnet. Grimmer, *La femme et le bâtard*, 133.

[24]Felix spent much of his time at the imperial court and after his marriage in 1505 resided

Neither is there any historical evidence to support the chronicle's allegations that Felix was secretly executed. Vanotti's chronicle of the Werdenberg family states that Felix died suddenly of a stroke while attending the Diet of Augsburg in 1530, and that his death was widely viewed as a belated divine retribution for his murder of Andreas von Sonnenberg in 1511.[25] It is surprising that the *Zimmern Chronicle* places the blame for Felix's death on Leonora rather than on the notorious Sonnenberg murder, which it elsewhere invokes as the cause of subsequent misfortune for the Werdenbergs and for everyone else even remotely connected to the scandal (*ZC* 2:307, 314).

Anna Rehlinger is described in the chronicle as a femme fatale who was responsible for the death of her lover, Christoph Friedrich von Zollern: "Because he had promised marriage to a Rehlinger woman from Augsburg, and had a daughter Anna by her, he took the matter so much to heart that in desperation he threw himself like Decius into the thick of the battle" (*ZC* 2:463).

So many motifs from literary sources and popular culture are woven into the chronicle's tale of Anna Rehlinger that it is difficult to tell how much factual basis exists for any part of the story of her life before she met Christoph Friedrich. According to the chronicle, Anna was the oldest and most beautiful of three daughters of an Augsburg patrician, a doctor of civil law. She became pregnant by Jakob Adler, a young man of good family; she claimed that he had promised her marriage, but he denied it under oath. Anna's family tried to keep the pregnancy a secret and "the birth was hushed up so that no one would know where it [the child] came from or what happened to it. Jakob Adler did not live long after this but died...of a strange and surprising illness" (*ZC* 2:463–64). Many people in Augsburg regarded Adler's death as punishment for perjury; nevertheless, Anna's reputation was ruined. Unable to make a respectable marriage, she led a reclusive existence in her mother's house.

Gossip more than made up for the lack of public knowledge about Anna; she was rumored to have kept for her private pleasure an apprentice boy who was "exceptionally well made below the belt, just right for her appetite," and to have "plied her trade [as a courtesan] with several important men" (*ZC* 2:465–66). The reclusive beauty became a Garbo-like legend; the young women of Augsburg questioned her tailor and shoemaker to find out what she really looked like and

chiefly on his wife's estates in Luxembourg: "he spent little time in Sigmaringen or on other Werdenberg estates but left them to his brothers" (*ZC* 2:287). If Leonora was actually the mistress of two Werdenberg brothers at the same time, a more plausible candidate than Felix would be his older brother Johann, for both Johann and Christoph resided at Sigmaringen between 1500 and 1510. Vanotti, *Grafen von Montfort und von Werdenberg,* 452. However, the chronicle places this story shortly before Felix's death in 1530; Johann died in 1522.

[25]Vanotti, *Grafen von Montfort und von Werdenberg,* 463. The *Zimmern Chronicle* acknowledges the official version that Felix died of apoplexy, but characterizes it as a cover-up spread by Felix's relatives (*ZC* 2:308).

what clothes she wore. The legend of "the fair Rehlinger woman" intrigued Christoph Friedrich von Zollern, known as "the ash-gray count" because of the pallor caused by his life of dissipation. He spent large sums of money on "banquets, sleigh rides and the like" to win Anna as his mistress (*ZC* 2:466).

"Whether he took her as his wife is uncertain," says the chronicle. "She always gave out that he took her [in marriage] before her friends, which seems quite likely, for she was clever enough. The other counts of Zollern were not willing to acknowledge it" (*ZC* 2:466). Anna moved to the Zollern castle at Haigerloch and lived there openly with Christoph Friedrich. According to the chronicle, it was this alleged marriage to Anna that finally led Christoph Friedrich's kinsmen, long exasperated by his profligate ways, to take drastic action. In 1535 they forced him to renounce his title to the Zollern estates.[26] Perhaps this was the reason that "in the meantime he had come, too late, to regret the matter; he fell into such a depression that out of desperation he joined the campaign" of Charles V against the French and died in battle in 1536 (*ZC* 2:466–67).

After the death of Christoph Friedrich, his cousin and heir Jos Niklaus von Zollern "reached an agreement with the Rehlinger woman that she would leave Haigerloch and go back to her mother's house in Augsburg." Here, according to the chronicle, "she plied her former trade and nourished herself by the hand she sat on." Her daughter Anna was placed under the guardianship of Jos Niklaus and brought up in a convent. However, Jos Niklaus treated his cousin and ward as a bastard; he forced the younger Anna to renounce all claim to the name and rank of Zollern, and married her against her will to one of his estate officials (*ZC* 2:467–68).

The only facts in this story that seem firmly established are that Christoph Friedrich von Zollern lived openly with Anna Rehlinger, that he was widely believed to have married her, and that the other members of the Zollern family refused to recognize such a misalliance with a nonnoble woman, even one from a patrician family. The standard collection of German noble genealogies actually includes the marriage of Christoph Friedrich and Anna Rehlinger in the Zollern genealogy, although it does not mention their daughter Anna.[27] It is possible that some incident in Anna Rehlinger's past accounted for the fact that she had not married, whereas her two younger sisters are said to have married patricians. However, the concern for family reputation in the German patriciate makes it unlikely that Anna's sisters could have found husbands within their social class if she was reputed to be a courtesan.[28] The lurid details of the story in the chronicle tell more about sexual fantasies in popular culture than they do about the real Anna Rehlinger.

[26]However, the Zollern genealogy records the marriage as taking place in 1530, suggesting that the two events were not as closely related as the chronicle implies. Isenburg, *Europäische Stammtafeln,* 5:153.

[27]Isenburg, *Europäische Stammtafeln,* 5:153.

[28]On concern for the respectability of the family (rather than that of the potential bride herself) as a criterion for marriage in the merchant and patrician classes, see Beer, *Eltern und Kinder,* 82–85.

The story of Margarethe Hutler is more prosaic than the legend of the "fair Rehlinger woman." The chronicler is understandably biased against the woman he blamed for destroying his parents' marriage. He calls her a thief and a whore and exaggerates the allegation that she was arrested for attending a disorderly dance into the charge that she attended orgies at which everyone danced naked (*ZC* 4:92). Margarethe Hutler was the wife of Leonard Hutler, a burgher of Messkirch. According to the chronicle, she had established a reputation for sexual misconduct even before she became the mistress of Johann Werner II. She is alleged to have carried on an affair with the burgher Hans Glates that became so notorious she was convicted of adultery, forced to carry the "stone of shame" as public humiliation, and banished from the town. The municipal authorities were so outraged at Leonard Hutler's willingness to tolerate his wife's behavior that they banished him as well (*ZC* 2:590–91).

Exactly how and when Margarethe Hutler became the concubine of Johann Werner II von Zimmern is not recorded in the chronicle, but the affair led Johann Werner's wife to separate from him about 1528. Margarethe lived with Johann Werner at Falkenstein until his death twenty years later and bore him four children. Froben Christoph's anger at the "strange household" at Falkenstein led to a confrontation between father and son in 1539 and a permanent estrangement between them.

Johann Werner feared, with good reason, that Froben Christoph and his other two legitimate sons might refuse to pay the legacies he intended to leave his concubine and illegitimate children. He therefore took special precautions. A year before his death in 1548, he purchased a house and civic rights in the imperial city of Rottweil for Margarethe Hutler and her children. He also made his legitimate sons sign a pledge to pay the mother and each child 200 gulden apiece, and to confirm them in the possession of the house in Rottweil (*ZC* 4:288).

As heir to the estate, Froben Christoph grudgingly carried out these provisions, though he suspected Margarethe Hutler of stealing the family silver and other valuables and of forging documents with Johann Werner's seal as the old man lay dying. The concubine's side of the story is not told in the chronicle; presumably she claimed that the "stolen" goods were gifts from her lover. Public opinion was evidently on her side, for the chronicle is decidedly defensive in tone:

> Concerning the Hutler woman, she was not packed off as her behavior or guilt deserved, but in consideration of the fact that she waited on and remained with the old lord in his great illness…she was graciously allowed to return to her children in Rottweil.… And so that no one could suspect the three brothers of anything in this case…, they allowed the Hutler woman to keep the chest with all the stolen money, silver beakers, golden rings set with precious stones and the horn spoon that had been a Zimmern family heirloom for many years. (*ZC* 4:87–88)

Moreover, "all the children were provided for and lacked for nothing" (*ZC* 4:93).

The family silver and heirlooms were of great symbolic significance, and their concession to the concubine was probably a more bitter blow to the lineage-conscious chronicler than was the mere payment of the legacies. Margarethe Hutler remarried and outlived her second husband, a burgher of Rottweil. The marriage was said to have been quarrelsome, "especially when little of the money for which he married her was left" (*ZC* 4:92–93).

The *Zimmern Chronicle* shows that keeping concubines was socially acceptable for unmarried noblemen in the fifteenth and early sixteenth centuries, and that most nobles (in contrast to the chronicler) had no objection to married men keeping concubines as long as they did not cause a public scandal. Little stigma attached to the concubines themselves, who were usually servants or other women of low social status. Once the liaison ended, they were able to marry men of their own social class, using as dowries the gifts or bequests they received from their noble lovers. However, the chronicle also suggests that married men in the nonprincely nobility were expected to make at least a pretense of keeping their liaisons secret, and that those who allowed their concubines a visible public role met with social disapproval. Concubines who did not keep a low profile come in for harsh criticism in the chronicle. The chronicler stigmatizes as courtesans those women who made a career out of a series of liaisons, and he heaps invective on women who tried to rise above their station through their influence over their noble lovers. In both cases, he expects that his audience will share his values; of course, the exercise of undue influence by lowborn mistresses raises the issue of maintaining social hierarchy as well as issues of morality.

Comparisons to Other German and European Nobles

To what extent are the patterns of concubinage described in the *Zimmern Chronicle* typical of other nobles in Germany and western Europe? Most of the detailed evidence available about the social background of concubines and financial provision for them deals with the mistresses of kings and princes, and may not always be a reliable guide to the behavior of provincial nobles.

The mistresses of princes differed from the concubines of nonprincely nobles in being drawn primarily from the nobility. According to Paul-Joachim Heinig, German ecclesiastical princes in the late fifteenth and sixteenth centuries usually practiced monogamous relationships with women from the higher nobility—that is, women who might have been acceptable marriage partners if the men had been eligible to contract a legal marriage. Very few came from the lower nobility, though at least a quarter of the concubines were nonnobles, probably burghers.[29] An exception to this pattern was the most famous ecclesiastical prince of the era, Cardinal Albrecht von Brandenburg, archbishop of Mainz. Albrecht had five known mistresses, some of whom he is said to have had depicted in the guise of

[29]Heinig, "'Omnia vincit amor,'" 291.

female saints in works he commissioned from Dürer, Grünewald, Cranach, and other artists. Four of these women were nonnobles, including his best-known mistress, Agnes Pless, the widow of a burgher from Frankfurt.[30] Secular princes had a wider variety of sexual partners; usually noblewomen, though rarely drawn from the ladies-in-waiting of the inner court circle. A significant number of their mistresses, however, came from the bourgeoisie of imperial and territorial cities. These included the most famous mistress of Emperor Charles V: Barbara Blomberg, the daughter of an innkeeper in Regensburg.[31]

Royal and princely courts in all countries provided a milieu in which noblemen might conduct affairs with women of their own status. However, such sexual liaisons between social equals were regarded as far more scandalous than keeping a woman of lower social status as a concubine. Stone states that in England, "although court behavior under Henry VIII appears to have been fairly lax, in the middle and late sixteenth century, peers had taken lower-class mistresses but had jealously guarded the honour of their wives. It was only after about 1590 that there developed general promiscuity among both sexes at Court," which damaged the reputation of the court and of the aristocracy in an era when "general disapprobation of loose conduct was rising."[32]

The concubines of nonprincely nobles in all European countries generally fell into the same two categories represented in the *Zimmern Chronicle*: they were either servants (including the attendants of the noblemen's own wives) or residents of the town or village adjoining the castle.[33] Concubines can usually be identified in documentary sources only when they are mentioned as the mothers of the nobleman's illegitimate children, although a few appear in records of episcopal visitations and court cases.

Studies of wills and other demographic sources suggest that the mothers of the illegitimate children of elite men were usually domestic servants. The illegitimate children reported in the tax returns of Florentine patricians were usually the offspring of maids or slave women, as were the illegitimate girls registered in the Florentine dowry fund. The mothers of illegitimate children recorded by memoirists in the Veneto were also domestic servants, while concubines named in episcopal visitations and in separation suits in the diocese of Verona included not only servants but also peasant women from the region surrounding the noblemen's villas, and even one noblewoman in reduced circumstances.[34] In France, the mothers

---

[30]For illustrations of works of art depicting Albrecht von Brandenburg and his mistresses as saints, see "Kardinal Albrecht von Brandenburg als heiliger Martin." On Agnes Pless, see Tacke, "Agnes Pless und Kardinal Albrecht von Brandenburg," 347–66.

[31]Heinig, "'Omnia vincit amor,'" 291–92. On Barbara Blomberg, see ibid., 284–85.

[32]Stone, *Crisis of the Aristocracy*, 664–65.

[33]Beceiro Pita and Córdoba de la Llave, *Parentesco, poder y mentalidad*, 221; Grimmer, "Bâtards de la noblesse," 38; and Lorcin, *Vivre et mourir en Lyonnais*, 99–100.

[34]In the Florentine *castato* of 1458, which is exceptional in naming the mothers of most of the

of illegitimate children who received legacies from noblemen were predominantly servants, though peasant women made up a significant proportion of the mistresses of the petty nobility.[35] In Germany, Spiess finds a wide social range among mothers of illegitimate children of counts and barons of the Mainz region; in addition to domestic servants, they included women from the middle class, and one who probably belonged to a family of the lower nobility.[36]

The provisions made for the support of the concubine and her children are better documented in the cases of princes than in those of the nonprincely nobility. Some of the ecclesiastical princes mentioned by Heinig openly maintained their concubine "like a princess," but in this case, the mistress was not competing with a legal wife. A few princes actually married their concubines, a practice that became more common in the late sixteenth century. Most of Heinig's examples involve ecclesiastical princes who converted to Protestantism and were thus able to convert long-standing monogamous relationships into formal marriages. However, he also cites cases among secular princes, including the morganatic marriage of Archduke Ferdinand II of Austria (d. 1595) to Philippine Welser of Augsburg in 1557.[37]

A secular prince provided for a long-term mistress by giving her a house to reside in, generous gifts of jewelry and cash, and grants for her support paid out of the prince's income and lands. Her children received financial support and were mentioned in their father's will, although the mother herself was rarely named. Nolte notes that there was "no problem … in marrying off former 'bed-partners' of the prince with an appropriate wedding present"; the husbands were usually members of the prince's entourage or officials on his estates.[38] Emperor Charles V granted Barbara Blomberg an allowance of 200 gulden and married her to an imperial official with a dowry of 5000 gulden, equivalent of that of a countess. [39]

Few details of such provision for mistresses can be documented below the princely level. Noblemen undoubtedly arranged some marriages for their former concubines, although the *Zimmern Chronicle* gives the impression that they were more likely to give the woman a dowry and let her make her own arrangements. A few noblemen did marry their former concubines after the death of their wives, as

---

illegitimate children claimed as tax deductions, the majority of the women are described as slaves and servants. Kuehn, *Illegitimacy in Renaissance Florence,* 143. See also Kirschner and Molho, "Dowry Fund," 429. On other Italian elites, see Grubb, *Provincial Families of the Renaissance,* 38; and Eisenach, *Husbands, Wives, and Concubines,* 142, 152–53.

[35]Grimmer, "Bâtards de la nobless auvergnate," 38; and Lorcin, *Vivre et mourir en Lyonnais,* 99–100. Lorcin notes that the children born to noblemen by peasant women remained in their mother's household and never rose above the status of peasants.

[36]Spiess, *Familie und Verwandtschaft,* 383, 385.

[37]Heinig, "'Omnia vincit amor,'" 293–96, 286–90.

[38]Nolte, "Verbalerotische Kommunikation," 450.

[39]Heinig, "'Omnia vincit amor,'" 293–97.

Gottfried Werner von Zimmern and Christoph von Werdenberg had hoped to do. The most prominent case in southwest Germany in the era of the *Zimmern Chronicle* was that of Count Hugo XVII of Montfort-Bregenz, who married "the virtuous lady Dorothea Falckner" two months before his death in 1536 "in order to give greater force" to the provision in his will designating her and their three legitimated children as his rightful heirs.[40]

It is unclear how common this practice was in other European nobilities. Stone does not mention any cases in which English peers married their lowborn mistresses, although he does mention an early-sixteenth-century case of a gentleman who married a long-term mistress from his own social class.[41] However, among the high aristocracy of Castile, it was "fairly common" for a magnate to "marry a woman with whom he had an extramarital relationship, either after the death of his first wife or after living together as single persons." In one marriage contract, the father of an heiress was forced to promise "not to marry the mother of any of his many bastards or any future mistress."[42]

Although Hugo von Montfort and Johann Werner II von Zimmern left bequests to their concubines, the wills of noblemen in all countries typically named only their illegitimate children, not the children's mothers. Spiess finds only two noblemen making bequests to their concubines in his fifteen families of counts and barons in the Mainz region. In 1500, Count Philipp of Hanau-Münzberg left a legacy to Grete Wisskircher and her children, unromantically describing her in the will as "Grete the whore [*Dirne*]." His brother Ludwig had also left bequests to two mothers of his illegitimate children in two wills drawn up in 1484 and 1485.[43]

In France, according to Claude Grimmer, four-fifths of the mothers of illegitimate children of nobles are never named in wills or other documents.[44] In Spain, concubines are rarely identified in wills as the mothers of the noblemen's illegitimate children, although legacies to concubines may be concealed as bequests to servants for "services rendered" or as contributions to their dowries.[45] In England, Stone states that peers made bequests to illegitimate children in their wills until about 1560, but he makes no mention of legacies to mistresses. However, Harris states that between 1450 and 1550, a few peers made bequests to their mistresses and/or illegitimate children in their wills, and that many others probably made other provision for them.[46]

---

[40]Burmeister, *Grafen von Montfort*, 300.

[41]Stone, *Crisis of the Aristocracy*, 663.

[42]Beceiro Pita and Córdoba de la Llave, *Parentesco, poder y mentalidad*, 223.

[43]Spiess, *Familie und Verwandtschaft*, 224, 387.

[44]Grimmer, *Femme et le bâtard*, 150.

[45]Beceiro Pita and Córdoba de la Llave, *Parentesco, poder y mentalidad*, 220.

[46]Stone, *Crisis of the Aristocracy*, 663. Harris states that between 1450 and 1550, 51 of 763 wills of English aristocratic men (6.7 percent) made bequests to their mistresses and/or illegitimate children in their wills. However, she does not indicate how many of the wills specifically mentioned the mistress. *English Aristocratic Women*, 83.

It is likely that many noblemen made provision for their concubines through gifts in their own lifetime rather than through bequests, which might not be honored by their heirs. Thomas Kuehn suggests that in the Florence patriciate, "the testators had already assuaged their consciences by establishing some settlement on the woman, and therefore did not mention her in the will."[47]

Although concubinage was accepted in all European elites, it was always regulated by customs that "limited the possibility of injury to legitimate families, and particularly to legitimate wives." Among southwest German counts and barons, these customs required that a nobleman make at least a pretense of observing secrecy, and one who failed to do so met with disapproval from his social equals. However, this was not necessarily the case in other elites. In Verona, according to Emlyn Eisenach, "from the point of view of the man, it was important that the relationship be publicly known, [since] a concubine was a luxury item, one might say, of conspicuous consumption, like a coach." Nevertheless, "to protect a legitimate wife's, and by extension her family's position, honor, and financial resources, and probably also to help secure her cooperation, convention dictated that a concubine be treated obviously less well than a wife." Wives were dishonored when their husbands showed too much respect to their concubines, for example by dressing them as well as their wives, allowing them to have servants in attendance, or giving them the companionship (*compagnia*) appropriate to a legitimate wife.[48] Similarly, Castilian noblewomen refused to tolerate their husbands' extramarital affairs when the husband lived "under the sway" of his mistress, allowing her the kind of influence that should be exercised only by the legitimate wife.[49]

To what extent did concubinage affect the reputation of the women involved, and that of their families? In Italy, Eisenach notes, "a woman who publicly entered a sexual relationship outside of marriage took a fairly large risk, particularly considering that concubinage relationships were not permanent, and a woman's honor and reputation was determined largely by her sexual conduct."[50] However, the risk seems to have been less severe in Germany than in some other countries. In the fifteenth and sixteenth centuries, canon lawyers increasingly assimilated concubinage to prostitution, and even the testament of one German count referred to his own concubine as "the whore."[51] Nevertheless, the *Zimmern Chronicle* suggests that little social stigma was attached to the concubine of a nobleman as long as she was willing to accept her secondary role in his life; the

---

[47]Kuehn, *Illegitimacy in Renaissance Florence,* 193–94. Canonists of the late Middle Ages argued that both legacies and gifts inter vivos to concubines were invalid. Brundage, *Law, Sex, and Christian Society,* 515. However, secular law codes did not accept this view. See, for example, Eisenach, *Husbands, Wives, and Concubines,* 151, 151n39.

[48]Eisenach, *Husbands, Wives, and Concubines,* 146–48.

[49]Beceiro Pita and Córdoba de la Llave, *Parentesco, poder y mentalidad,* 360.

[50]Eisenach, *Husbands, Wives, and Concubines,* 151.

[51]Spiess, *Familie und Verwandtschaft,* 387.

chronicle criticizes only those mistresses who exercised undue influence over their lovers.

Writers on the French nobility, like those on German nobles, imply that concubinage carried little moral disgrace for lower-class women: "Isn't it an honor to have the local nobleman make love to you?" asks Grimmer in his study of the noble bastards of the Auvergne. "The lords appear to us surrounded by a halo of such prestige that one could not resist them; moreover, they are assiduous [in their courtship] and promise a better future."[52] Similarly, Marie-Thérèse Lorcin notes that the mother of illegitimate child named in the will of a nobleman is often "a peasant woman from the surrounding region, whom the testator names without shame. Perhaps it is for her not a humiliation but a promotion in the eyes of the villagers?"[53]

In Italy and Spain, however, there is more evidence of moral opprobrium directed against concubines and their families. In Verona, it was important for a nobleman to give his former concubine "a generous dowry and proper marriage ceremony and celebration, perhaps at his own house," in order to "confirm...that she was not dishonored and establish...her as a respectable member of society,"[54] whereas the *Zimmern Chronicle* implies that in Germany a former concubine could easily find willing marriage partners on her own once she had been given a dowry. In Castile, according to Beceiro Pita and Córdoba de la Llave,

> there are many references to the enmity directed against these women...
> because, as always in the period, it was they and not their male lovers, who
> are considered guilty of falling into sin and maintaining a relationship offen-
> sive in the eyes of God and man.... This common sentiment assures us that
> the sinful relationship that these women maintained with magnates would
> not have very agreeable results for their parents and closest family,
> ...however much this relationship brought the mistress's kin some indirect
> benefits, such as a much-desired post or office. [55]

This statement that the women, not the men, were blamed for the "sinful relationship" suggests a difference between popular opinion and the views of ecclesiastical and secular authorities, who usually concentrated on prosecuting the men who kept concubines rather than the women themselves. Only on the eve of the Council of Trent did ecclesiastical authorities in the diocese of Verona "attempt to discourage women from considering concubinage by convincing both the women and the communities around them that the risks to their reputations and their souls were very high indeed."[56]

[52]Grimmer, "Bâtards de la noblesse," 38.
[53]Lorcin, *Vivre et mourir en Lyonnais,* 99–100.
[54]Eisenach, *Husbands, Wives, and Concubines,* 154.
[55]Beceiro Pita and Córdoba de la Llave, *Parentesco, poder y mentalidad,* 222.
[56]Eisenach states that episcopal visitations in Verona in the 1520s and '30s viewed concubinage as a crime of the man, threatening to excommunicate him if he did not dismiss his concubine rather

Even in countries where the moral indignation against concubines ran high, many women considered possible social disgrace an acceptable trade-off for enjoying a higher standard of living during the liaison and probably receiving a dowry at the end of it.[57] Such liaisons also "had the additional attraction of attaching the woman's family to the political and social networks of wealthier and more prominent men than they could have hoped to attract into marriage."[58] Some families actually encouraged their daughters to enter concubinage as a means of providing for their financial security without having to pay their dowries, and as a means of securing favors for other family members.

These considerations could be significant even at the highest social levels. Helen Ettlinger notes that concubinage was sometimes an "acceptable or attractive family strategy" for Italian noble families, since the prince assumed financial responsibility for his mistress and thus eliminated one claim on her natal family's wealth. Remaining family members would receive a larger share of the patrimony; moreover, the increased wealth and prestige acquired through princely favors would result in better marriage opportunities for other family members, and the mistress's sisters might not have to go into convents.[59]

🙎 🙎 🙎

The counts and barons of southwest Germany as depicted in the *Zimmern Chronicle* appear typical of the nonprincely nobility in other European countries both in the social status of their concubines and the methods by which they supported these women. They were certainly not unusual in being more apt to criticize concubines for offenses against the social hierarchy and prescribed gender roles than for moral offenses against the institution of marriage. However, the chronicle shows that while southwest German counts and barons accepted concubinage as the norm even for married noblemen, they also expected it to be practiced discreetly. Some other European elites, in contrast, allowed the relationship to be publicly known and objected only when the concubine was treated with as much respect as the legitimate wife. Attitudes toward the open practice of concubinage might be expected to change in the sixteenth century as a result of the Protestant

---

than ordering the couple to separate. *Husbands, Wives, and Concubines,* 174–75. Municipal legislation in German and Italian towns in the late Middle Ages also tended to single out the man as the guilty party, imposing financial penalties on men who cohabited openly with women to whom they were not married. However, some towns regarded both parties as equally culpable, ordering both to pay financial penalties if they did not marry or separate. These orders may have been aimed primarily at cases of nonelite concubinage, in which both parties were of similar social status. Brundage, *Law, Sex, and Christian Society,* 444, 514–15; and Becker, "Nichteheliche Lebensgemeinschaft," 25.

[57]Eisenach, *Husbands, Wives, and Concubines,* 174.

[58]Brundage, *Law, Sex, and Christian Society,* 446.

[59]Ettlinger, "Visibilis et invisibilis," 781.

and Catholic reformations and their emphasis on stricter enforcement of morality. However, an increasingly hostile attitude toward concubines and bastards had been evident long before the Reformation, and it is difficult to show a direct connection between morals legislation aimed at the lower classes and the behavior of noblemen. Evidence about mistresses of noblemen comes largely from royal and princely courts, where concubinage continued to be practiced and may even have become more public by the end of the sixteenth century. However, behavior at court may not be a reliable guide to the attitudes of provincial nobles. It is impossible to know how many German counts and barons shared Froben Christoph von Zimmern's distaste for courts as centers of corrupt sexual morals, but such a view was widespread among the English gentry at the end of the sixteenth and beginning of the seventeenth centuries.

Although extramarital liaisons had always been permitted for noblemen, adulterous liaisons for noblewomen violated the traditional sexual honor code. The promiscuous behavior of nobles of both sexes at the English court after 1590 shocked the landed classes in the countryside.[60] Noblemen at northern Italian princely courts ignored the sexual honor code in order to advance their own careers, sometimes even forcing unwilling kinswomen into concubinage. For example, "Galeazzo Maria Sforza, Duke of Milan, was actively encouraged by men seeking to garner favor at court to make advances to their daughters and even wives."[61] This strategy was undoubtedly practiced at other European courts as well. Moreover, some kings and princes maintained their mistresses openly and even gave them a political role, a practice that in the fifteenth and sixteenth centuries was particularly associated with Italian and French courts. The *prima favorita* of an Italian prince, usually a noblewoman, "was openly recognized as what could be called the prince's alternative wife." In chronicles, "if named, she was given respect equal to a wife," and was designated by the title "domina" or "madonna."[62]

The model of Italian princely courts was less relevant for German nobles than that of France under Charles VII in the late fifteenth century and under Francis I and Henry II in the first half of the sixteenth century. Froben Christoph von Zimmern describes the conspicuous public role of Agnes Sorel at the court of Charles VII as an intolerable insult to the French queen, and draws a parallel between Agnes and his own father's concubine Margarethe Hutler (*ZC* 3:307–8). He also describes Duke George of Bavaria as similar to Francis I of France because the duke rarely visited his wife. Although he maintained her in splendid style, he visited her only twice in three years, while carrying on an affair with a lady-in-waiting at the imperial court (*ZC* 2:419–20).

---

[60]Stone discusses the gentry's disapproval of the "scandalous living" of the court aristocracy as a factor in the political division between court and country in Britain in the early seventeenth century. *Crisis of the Aristocracy,* 664–68.

[61]Ettlinger, "Visibilis et invisibilis," 771, 776, 781, quote at 776.

[62]Ettlinger, "Visibilis et invisibilis," 772–73.

The chronicler also recounts an anecdote about Emperor Charles V that contrasts his reputation for chastity with the licentiousness of the French court. According to the story, which is based on a Roman legend about Scipio, Charles V refused to sleep with a girl from a noble family whom the dauphin had kidnapped and presented to the emperor in his bedchamber. Instead, he had her sent home and gave her a thousand crowns for her dowry. "This act was a strange experience for the French, who aren't accustomed to such behavior from their lords," says the chronicler (ZC 3:316).[63]

Heinig argues that at the courts of German secular princes, "there was a general acceptance of relationships with concubines, but in the second half of the fifteenth century no permanent *Nebenfrau* [literally, secondary wife; a publicly recognized mistress] can be proved." Such reticence stood in marked contrast to the practice at contemporary French and Italian courts. Secular German princes usually engaged in a series of short-lived liaisons, few of which produced more than one child by the same mother, and the general practice of secrecy means that little is known of the life and circumstances of the women involved. However, Heinig argues, relationships with concubines became semipublic in the sixteenth century. Princes increasingly imitated the kings of France by maintaining their mistresses publicly, thus foreshadowing the politically influential official mistresses of the Enlightenment era.[64]

Nolte agrees that discretion was the norm among German secular princes in the fifteenth century. She asserts that Elector Albrecht von Brandenburg would not have referred openly in his letters to any affairs he might have had with his wife's ladies-in-waiting:

> In the first place, if the contents of the letters became known, the reputations of the ladies-in-waiting and their chances of marriage would be jeopardized.... With regard to publicity, a certain discretion was observed about life at court and in the ladies' chamber. Secondly, and this is decisive, such an open discussion of adultery would have injured the honor of the princely consort and possibly called her relatives into the matter. There would at least have been the possibility of serious marital conflicts to reckon with. [65]

Even Martin Luther evidently viewed secondary wives as a prerogative of princely status and was prepared to turn a blind eye as long as the pretense of secrecy was observed. In 1539, Landgrave Philipp of Hesse contracted a bigamous

---

[63]Charles V did have mistresses and illegitimate children, but unlike Francis I, he evidently did not take mistresses during his marriages. His bastards were the offspring of affairs that took place when he was a bachelor or widower. Heinig, "'Omnia vincit amor,'" 284–85.

[64]Heinig, "'Omnia vincit amor,'" 282–86, 292–94, quote at 285. Before the sixteenth century, the secrecy was so great that the names of the mistresses are rarely known. Although Emperor Maximilian I had at least ten and possibly as many as thirty illegitimate children, only two of their mothers can be identified by name.

[65]Nolte, "Verbalerotische Kommunikation," 451. See also Heinig, "'Omnia vincit amor,'" 281.

marriage to his mistress with the consent of his wife Christine of Saxony and the reluctant acquiescence of Luther.[66] In a letter the following year, Luther wrote that he wished Philipp had not insisted on a separation from his wife and a public remarriage. It would have been better for him to "keep an honest girl in a house and have her on account of his dire need and for the sake of his conscience in a secret marriage (although, of course, the world would have considered it adultery) and visit her from time to time, as great lords have often done."[67]

The increased willingness of German princes in the later sixteenth century to give their mistresses a public role occurred, paradoxically enough, at the same time that they were issuing more regulations restricting the sexual behavior of their subjects. Hans Conrad Ellrichshausen notes that the norms of morality that princes chose to enforce depended not only upon their religious confession but on "whether the dynastic family was oriented toward the customs of the French court, where confining sexual relations to marriage was rejected as bourgeois."[68] Heinig states that the gulf between the norms of sexual behavior among the aristocracy and the norms of other social classes increased in this period: "there was a tendency toward increasing acceptance of illegitimate relationships in the milieu of the secular high nobility, who were set apart from the discipline of the subject society."[69] There is thus no proof that the Catholic and Protestant Reformations caused German nobles to become more hostile to the open practice of concubinage in the later sixteenth century. If anything, the institution became, more than ever, a mark of the special status enjoyed by the nobility. It is possible that behavior at court was atypical of nobles as a whole, and that provincial nobles were more apt to share Froben Christoph von Zimmern's distaste for open concubinage. However, little evidence is available to document such attitudes.

During the same period in England, public opinion among the gentry was definitely turning against open concubinage, and this hostility had some effect even on the highest nobility. Stone notes that, although some noblemen in the early sixteenth century were polygamous in practice if not in theory, "presumably in deference to puritan criticism of the double standard, this casual approach to extramarital relationships disappeared between 1560 and 1660." British peers ceased to name their illegitimate children in their wills after 1560, and "between 1610 and 1660 evidence for the maintenance of regular, semiofficial mistresses becomes rare," a development he believes is related to greater acceptance of affection as a criterion for marriage in the choice of marriage partners in the British aristocracy.[70] However, there is little evidence for such a trend in continental elites, where

[66]Heinig, "'Omnia vincit amor,'" 286.
[67]Letter of Martin Luther to Elector John Frederick of Saxony, 10 January 1540, quoted in Phillips, *Putting Asunder*, 76.
[68]Ellrichshausen, *Uneheliche Mütterschaft*, 89.
[69]Heinig, "'Omnia vincit amor,'" 286.
[70]Stone, *Crisis of the Aristocracy*, 663–64.

nobles continued to name their illegitimate children in their wills. According to Eisenach, the efforts of Catholic reformers in Verona during the era of the Council of Trent had much less effect on popular opinion—let alone on the behavior of the elite—than Stone ascribes to those of Puritans in England:

> The churchmen tried to discourage the practice [of concubinage] and to convince the Veronese that keeping a concubine was not a sign of a man's power, but of his weakness and disgrace. There are only a few signs, however, that this message affected popular opinion, even after several decades of authorities' efforts. A lone voice heard in a case in 1582 stands out in its echoing of the religious rhetoric of the time.... Asked to characterize a man involved in a separation suit, the witness, a layman, condemned the husband simply for keeping concubines: "I hold him to be one of those men you find now, a person who, I think, has little fear of God, [and who] is disgraced by keeping whores."[71]

This lone voice was, not surprisingly, that of a commoner rather than a nobleman. Froben Christoph von Zimmern appears to be exceptional not only among German nobles, but among European nobles of any country in the mid-sixteenth century, in internalizing the ecclesiastical view that male adultery was an offense against the institution of marriage and that even secret concubinage and casual affairs were unacceptable. He is also exceptional in denouncing male adultery on nonreligious grounds—the emotional suffering it caused to wives—even in an era when affection was increasingly accepted as a criterion for aristocratic marriage. However, another of his grounds for denouncing concubinage might be expected to resonate even among nobles less attuned to psychological nuances: the practice led noblemen to neglect their dynastic obligations, and extravagant spending on mistresses and on illegitimate children not only deprived the legitimate children of the attention and affection they deserved but also injured the patrimony and the prestige of the lineage.[72]

---

[71]Eisenach, *Husbands, Wives, and Concubines,* 176–77. In fairness, it should be noted that Stone refers to a much longer period of time, and that more change might have been evident in Catholic elites by the mid-seventeenth century.

[72]In Verona, such an economic argument was put forward by Lady Aurelia in her suit against her husband, Count Ercole de Giusti. One of her witnesses alleged that the count "sent half of the household provisions to the whore (*alla puttana*). Part of the hurt to Aurelia was economic, and part of Ercole's crime was that he did not care properly for his legitimate family." Eisenach, *Husbands, Wives, and Concubines,* 149.

CHAPTER 10

Bastards

If a bastard does good, it's a miracle;
If he does evil, he is acting according to his nature.
— (ZC 2:172)

The chronicler Froben Christoph von Zimmern cites several variations on this old proverb and asserts that the bastard who turns out well is as rare as a white raven or black swan (*ZC* 2:172, 311). His attitude towards bastards reflects the social norms evident in legislation of the mid-sixteenth century, but they also reflect his own personal experiences. The chronicler seems to have become increasingly preoccupied with the issue of illegitimate children in the final section of the *Zimmern Chronicle* as he described the death of his father Johann Werner II and his subsequent legal battle against the claims of his father's concubine, Margarethe Hutler. In the addenda he wrote after completing the main narrative, he inserted several moralizing stories about bastards.

The most striking of these addenda makes explicit the chronicler's fear that bastards would inherit along with (or even instead of) the legitimate children. In this tale about the Lichtenberg family, the father separates from his wife and takes a concubine, who persuades him to legitimate their children and to make them eligible to inherit along with those of his marriage. When the legitimate son protests, he is disinherited. The son then kills the mistress and takes the father prisoner, refusing to release him until he promises to take his wife back and change his will back to its original form (*ZC* 3:308–9). Recounting this tale allows Froben Christoph to fantasize the revenge he was unable to take in real life against the concubine who had replaced his mother and the bastards who had replaced him and his brothers in his father's affections. The tale also emphasizes that fathers who diverted property to their illegitimate children posed a threat to the entire lineage: "the other agnates and relatives were on [the son's] side; they either helped him in his actions or at least tolerated them" (*ZC* 3:309).[1]

---

[1] For an analysis of this story (which is probably an invention of Froben Christoph's), see Wolf,

Despite his emotional denunciation of married men who favored their illegitimate children, Froben Christoph von Zimmern never questions the obligation of all fathers to recognize and provide for their illegitimate children. However, he disapproves of fathers who give their bastards anything more than "food and shelter as required by ecclesiastical law " (ZC 3:443).

Strictly speaking, ecclesiastical law and customary German law granted child support only to natural children (the offspring of an unmarried man and an unmarried woman), and denied it to children born of forbidden relationships (adultery, incest, or clerical concubinage).[2] Nevertheless, the chronicler assumes that even married men and clerics have an obligation to provide for their offspring. He remarks that his kinsman Thomas von Rieneck, a canon of Strasbourg, "had a great many bastards, for most of which he made appropriate provision long before his death" (ZC 3:235).[3]

The chronicler regards it as disgraceful for a nobleman to refuse to support his illegitimate children, even those born of casual liaisons rather than long-term relationships. He recounts an anecdote about a woman who came to the imperial court to accuse a certain young duke of refusing to pay support for her child, which she claimed was the offspring of their brief affair. Many of the courtiers thought that the man she was accusing was Wilhelm Werner von Zimmern, and one of his friends chided him, "Cousin, what kind of household do you keep, with your children being carried around in the streets?" Clearly the mother was counting on social pressure from other courtiers to force the duke to meet her demands (ZC 3:443).

The chronicler's views on the proper treatment of bastards are set forth in great detail in three cases of bastards in the Zimmern family in the late fifteenth and early sixteenth centuries. The bachelor Gottfried III (1425–1508) succeeded in establishing his son Junker (Squire) Heinrich at least temporarily in the nobility. Two generations later, Gottfried Werner (1484–1554) also attempted to have his illegitimate sons accepted as nobles, whereas his brother Johann Werner II (1480–1548) provided only sufficient financial support to establish his illegitimate sons as clerics or burghers.

Junker Heinrich was the son of Gottfried III von Zimmern, who had inherited the small estate of Herrenzimmern while his elder brother held the main family estate at Messkirch. Gottfried, who never married, had several daughters and one other son, but the bright and ambitious Heinrich was clearly his favorite. Even the hostile chronicler acknowledged that Heinrich "grew up to be eloquent, intelligent,

---

Von der Chronik zum Weltbuch, 377–78.

[2]On child support, see Ellrichshausen, *Uneheliche Mütterschaft,* 114–15; Demars-Sion, *Femmes séduites et abandonées,* 9; Winterer, *Bastarde in Spanien,* 108; and Winterer, *Bastarde in Italien,* 52.

[3]Three of Thomas von Rieneck's illegitimate children (Jörg Steynborn, Anna Praun, and Kunigunde Rieneck) are listed in the genealogical table in Ruf, *Grafen von Rieneck,* "Stammtafel."

and very quick, and used his mind well." His father gave him a seat in the ancestral castle at Herrenzimmern and the office of chief bailiff (*Oberamtmann*) of his estate of Zimmern vor Wald. Heinrich became wealthy; according to the chronicle, he did so by embezzling revenues from the estate. Since his father "gave him everything he wanted" and his office provided him with a nobleman's income, he was able to live in noble style. He purchased castles and villages, and in 1500 he secured legitimation and a coat of arms from Emperor Maximilian. Henceforth he styled himself "von Herrenzimmern" after the estate his father made over to him. He married a woman of noble birth, a Hegelback, who bore him several sons and daughters; after her death he married another wife from the lower nobility, a member of the Weitingen family (*ZC* 2:166–68).

According to the chronicle, Heinrich squandered money and soon amassed debts, which he tried to cover by selling off estates and by secretly borrowing money in his father's name. The chronicler even blames Gottfried's death on his shock at learning of his son's embezzlements (*ZC* 2:168–170). With grim satisfaction, the chronicler quotes the proverb, "Ill-gotten gains won't last three generations" (*ZC* 2:225). After his father's death, Junker Heinrich was forced to sell his remaining estates to the legitimate branch of the Zimmern family. "The estates he had acquired at the expense of the Zimmerns were dissipated in his lifetime" and he finally died "in great poverty and hunger" (*ZC* 2:226–28). His son Jakob bore the surname Zimmerle, indicating that he was not regarded as a nobleman. Without economic resources sufficient to maintain a noble style of life, Junker Heinrich's son could not maintain the position in the lower nobility that his father had acquired during his lifetime.[4]

The account given by Froben Christoph ignores the positive contributions Junker Heinrich had made to the Zimmern family. Heinrich was one of the few agnates who had come to their aid when Johann Werner I was outlawed; he not only represented the family in appeals to the emperor but also participated in the military raids that recovered the sequestered Zimmern estates (*ZC* 2:57, 79, 94, 104). Gottfried might well have felt that the bequest of Herrenzimmern to his illegitimate son was a just reward for services rendered. However, the chronicler regards Junker Heinrich as a disloyal bastard who threatened the inheritance of the legitimate heirs and presents his downfall as the appropriate punishment for an overambitious bastard.

In the second case, the chronicler seethes with indignation as he describes the favor Gottfried Werner von Zimmern showed to his illegitimate sons. The chronicler condemns both the psychological damage done to Gottfried Werner's legitimate daughters by their father's emotional attachment to his bastards and the

---

[4]Jakob Zimmerle enlisted the help of his kinsman Johann Werner II von Zimmern in negotiating his marriage (*ZC* 3:481). This suggests that the legitimate and illegitimate branches of the Zimmern family maintained a patron/client relationship.

damage to the wealth and prestige of the Zimmern lineage that would result from allowing bastards to be recognized as nobles.

Gottfried Werner von Zimmern, whose wife Apollonia von Henneberg bore him two daughters but no sons, had a total of eight illegitimate children (two sons and six daughters) by two different concubines. At one time, Gottfried Werner had hoped to marry his concubine Anna Fritz after his wife's death and thus legitimate their natural son Gottfried as his heir. "However, God did not ordain it so: she finally married a forester" (ZC 4:287).

Although Gottfried Werner is portrayed elsewhere in the chronicle as an indulgent father to his legitimate daughters, the chronicler here says that his bastard children "unhinged his mind so that he had an unbelievable love for them but paid little attention to and took little interest in his daughters by the Countess of Henneberg." He boasted about his children, "saying they were illegitimate, yet they were held in great respect in foreign nations, just as if they were legitimate. He said that the law [*juditia*] and human inclination were not in agreement."

According to the chronicler, Gottfried Werner's conviction that illegitimate children were the victims of unfair discrimination led him to have a

> special love and affection for all bastards; whenever he could, he favored and advanced them in preference to other people. It seems to me that at one time the majority of his male and female servants were of illegitimate birth.... Many people said, bastards were so favored at Messkirch that if one were hanging from the sky and had to fall, he should choose no place other than Messkirch. (ZC 4:286–88)

The chronicle does not record the names of Gottfried Werner's six illegitimate daughters and says nothing about them except that all the children were given dowries or portions (*ausgesteuert*). However, it gives a detailed account of Gottfried Werner's attempts to have his two bastard sons treated as nobles. He allowed them "during his lifetime to bear a coat of arms ... with a tournament helm. By his order and permission they were allowed to sign themselves 'von Zimmern' as Junker Heinrich had done, although this was not done with the consent of the agnates. He spent a great deal of money on them for universities" (ZC 4:287). It is not clear what careers Gottfried Werner intended his sons to follow; possibly they were to study law as preparation for entering the service of a prince.

Gottfried Werner's efforts, however, met with little success. His elder son, Gottfried, apparently died during his student days; the chronicle reports with satisfaction that "he died miserably, after squandering everything." The other son, Martin, was still alive at the time the chronicle was written in the 1560s, living "on the annual pension assigned to him out of the estate." Martin apparently never married, but there is no mention of his occupation. The chronicle presents the story as an object lesson in the importance of keeping bastards in their proper place: "posterity should take care not to allow people who by ecclesiastical law are entitled only to food and support to inherit the use of the family name and to sign themselves 'von Zimmern'" (*ZC* 4:287).

Johann Werner II, who had three surviving sons from his marriage to Katharina von Erbach, did not make such generous provision for the four children born of his liaison with Margarethe Hutler. However, he took great pains to ensure that his concubine and illegitimate children would be provided for, and that his legitimate sons would not cheat them out of their inheritance. He purchased civic rights in Rottweil for Margarethe Hutler and her children and required his three legitimate sons to sign a pledge to pay the concubine and her children 200 gulden apiece within a month after his death.[5] Froben Christoph, the heir to the estate, grudgingly carried out these directions and insists in the chronicle that "all the children were provided for and lacked for nothing" (*ZC* 4:87–88, 93).[6] After their father's death in 1548, the four illegitimate children purchased a rescript of legitimation from the emperor. However, they made no attempt to purchase grants of nobility as Junker Heinrich had done half a century earlier.

All of the sons received educations with the expectation that they would support themselves through ecclesiastical careers. The eldest son, Christoph, was the only one who actually entered the church; he became a parish priest in Breisgau instead of a monk as he had originally intended. The second son, Hans Christoph, was supposed to become an organist but instead "married a woman well known to many honest men's sons, and moved with her here and there in great poverty. He became the city clerk at Hornberg and died there." The youngest son, Philipp Christoph, was the one who showed the greatest intellectual promise in his youth. He wanted to become a clergyman, and his uncle Wilhelm Werner von Zimmern wrote letters of recommendation for him to two abbots. "He had the best prospects, but as they say, 'still waters run deep.' He was expected to take holy orders but married the daughter of a burgher of Rottweil. Neither he nor his wife had much money, but they were content with what they had" (*ZC* 4:93). Clearly this modest bourgeois existence was what Froben Christoph von Zimmern regarded as appropriate for the bastards even of the high nobility in the middle of the sixteenth century.

The chronicler does not suggest that religious or moral considerations played any role in the treatment of bastards in the Zimmern family. The most significant factor was the presence or absence of legitimate heirs, as well as a growing sense of

---

[5]Similar suspicions are evident in the story of the fifteenth-century Duke of Bavaria who feared that his legitimate son would thwart his intentions to leave 10,000 gulden to a favorite bastard son; the father deposited the money in three imperial cities outside of Bavaria. Sprandel, "Diskriminierung der unehelichen Kinder," 493.

[6]A capital sum of 200 gulden would have provided each of Johann Werner's illegitimate sons with a pension of about 10 gulden a year in addition to his income from an ecclesiastical benefice or a secular occupation. The bequest of 200 gulden to his daughter Barbara presumably represented her dowry, even though she married during her father's lifetime. It was not unusual for dowries to be paid only upon the father's death.

lineage loyalty that mandated the concentration of property in the legitimate male line of descent. The bachelor Gottfried III established his illegitimate son Junker Heinrich on his estate instead of letting it pass to his nephew and grand-nephew, an act the chronicler denounces as showing lack of concern for the interests of the Zimmern lineage.[7] Two generations later, Gottfried Werner, who had daughters but no sons by his marriage, attempted to have his two illegitimate sons accepted as nobles but did not give them estates of their own. His reluctance to bequeath real property to his bastard sons was undoubtedly related to his larger commitment to keeping the Zimmern estates intact; he had designated his brother rather than his daughter as his heir so that his estates would remain in the Zimmern lineage (ZC 2:580). Johann Werner II, who had three surviving legitimate sons, made no attempt to obtain noble status for his three illegitimate sons and provided them only with small pensions that would not constitute a significant burden on the estate of the legitimate heir.

The chronicler Froben Christoph von Zimmern maintains that bastards should not be considered part of their father's lineage: they should not be allowed to use the family name, and they should not be recognized as nobles. He criticizes his uncle Gottfried Werner for allowing his two illegitimate sons to bear the Zimmern coat of arms and to sign themselves "von Zimmern" without the consent of the agnates (ZC 4:287). He evidently conceives of the right to use the name and arms of the lineage as a property right analogous to real property, which in German law could not be bequeathed to an illegitimate child without the consent of the nearest heirs.[8] The indiscriminate extension of this right to those who were not real members of the lineage would diminish the value of the property of the real members.

To what extent were the views on illegitimate children stated in the *Zimmern Chronicle* typical of German and other European nobles in the late fifteenth and sixteenth centuries? This question may be answered by examining the numbers of illegitimate children and the extent to which they were recognized as nobles and considered to be part of their father's lineage; the provisions noblemen made for illegitimate sons and daughters; and how the treatment of noble bastards changed as ecclesiastical and secular legislation became increasingly hostile toward illegitimate children in the Reformation era.

NUMBERS OF BASTARDS

"Would the estimate be too high, if one regarded one-third of the population in the late Middle Ages as of illegitimate birth?" asks Rolf Sprandel, after looking at

---

[7]Gottfried's action violated the pact he had signed in 1444 when he divided the Zimmern estates with his brother Werner VIII; each had promised that if he had no legitimate male heir, his estate would go to his brother or to the latter's descendants (ZC 1:314–15).

[8]*HRG*, s.v. "Bankert"; and Dieck, *Legitimation durch nachfolgende Ehe*, 5–6.

wills and personal chronicles that suggest "the late Middle Ages teemed with illegitimate children," especially in the upper classes.[9] Likewise, Neithard Bulst says, "It appears that in Germany neither the nobility nor the urban patriciate had a uniformly negative attitude toward illegitimate children. Here, too, family chronicles are full of bastards."[10]

Sprandel's impressionistic estimate that a third of the European population in the late Middle Ages was of illegitimate birth is certainly too high for the general population.[11] After a review of quantitative studies of wills, birth registers, and tax registers, Bulst concludes that the true illegitimacy rate was well under 10 percent; Schmugge estimates that illegitimate children made up 3 to 5 percent of the European population in the late fifteenth century.[12] However, research on wills and other demographic sources indicates that illegitimate children were more numerous in the nobility and the urban elites than in the population as a whole. In her study of wills in Lyons, Lorcin found that bastard children of the testator were mentioned twice as often in wills of nobles as in those of any other social group.[13] The illegitimate children reported in the Florentine tax registers in the fifteenth century were concentrated in the wealthier households, and fathers who opened accounts for their illegitimate daughters in the dowry fund of Florence were more likely to come from high-status lineages than were investors in the fund as a whole.[14]

The larger number of bastards in the elites partly reflects the greater willingness of wealthy fathers to recognize and support their illegitimate children, since they could better afford to do so. However, elite men "may also have procreated more bastards because they had access to vulnerable women" of lower social status.[15] Marie-Thérèse Caron generalizes that "there were few noble families who did not have at least one [bastard] in each generation," and Grimmer claims that in France, "illegitimacy in the fifteenth and sixteenth centuries is essentially a noble phenomenon."[16] The family system of the nobility encouraged extramarital sexual relationships: "The husband who emotionally never accepted the wife chosen for him by his family; the widower who did not wish to remarry after his wife's death and burden the estate with more legitimate heirs; the lay younger son

[9]Sprandel, "Diskriminierung der unehelichen Kinder," 487.

[10]Bulst, "Illegitime Kinder," 37.

[11]Sprandel, "Diskriminierung der unehelichen Kinder," 487.

[12]Bulst, "Illegitime Kinder," 30–31; and Schmugge, *Kirche, Kinder, Karrieren*, 8.

[13]Bastard children of the testator were mentioned in 1 out of every 12.1 wills by nobles, as compared to 1 out of every 23.2 wills by citizens of Lyons, 1 out of 29 wills by clergy, and 1 out of 52.2 wills by testators in the surrounding region. Lorcin, *Vivre et mourir en Lyonnais*, 96.

[14]Herlihy and Klapisch-Zuber, *Tuscans and Their Families*, 245; Kuehn, *Illegitimacy in Renaissance Florence*, 128–30; and Molho, *Marriage Alliance*, 279, 284.

[15]Kuehn, *Illegitimacy in Renaissance Florence*, 130.

[16]Caron, *Noblesse dans le duché de Bourgogne*, 233; and Grimmer, *La femme et le bâtard*, 169.

forbidden by his family to marry; the clerical son compelled to celibacy by the church: all begot illegitimate children."[17]

The *Zimmern Chronicle* and the records of the counts of Montfort suggest that southwest German counts produced at least as many illegitimate children as other European noblemen. Between 1342 and 1515, illegitimate children made up at least 38 percent of the surviving offspring of the House of Bourbon, one of the greatest families of the French nobility.[18] In seventeenth-century Auvergne, the illegitimacy rate among nobles stood at 30 percent, while the rate among commoners was only 1.5 percent.[19] Legitimated bastards made up 13 percent of all the recorded offspring who survived to adulthood in twenty-five lineages of Portuguese high aristocracy between 1380 and 1580, and 21 percent of the recorded offspring of the men of highest rank.[20] Since bastards were rarely legitimated by men who had any surviving children from their marriages,[21] the true proportion of bastards among the offspring of the Portuguese high nobility must have been considerably higher.

In Swabia, Burmeister's study of the counts of Montfort identifies twenty-four illegitimate sons and three illegitimate daughters from the middle of the fourteenth to the middle of the sixteenth century. The Montfort genealogies record seventy-three legitimate children (including forty-seven sons) who survived to adulthood between 1350 and 1550. The known illegitimate children thus made up a quarter to a third of the total offspring, and the known illegitimate sons made up a third of all sons.[22] The genealogy of the barons of Brandis from 1396 to 1510 records nine illegitimate children along with thirteen surviving legitimate ones, so that bastards made up 40 percent of the surviving offspring.[23] The *Zimmern Chronicle* and Zimmern genealogies indicate that between 1440 and 1594, the eleven adult male members of the last five generations of barons or counts of Zimmern included at least six fathers of bastards. These men fathered at least twenty-one illegitimate children (including nine sons), as compared to twenty-four legitimate children

---

[17]Spiess, *Familie und Verwandtschaft,* 381.

[18]Harsgor, "L'essor des bâtards nobles," 354.

[19]Grimmer, *La femme et le bâtard,* 169.

[20]Boone, "Parental Investment and Elite Family Structure," 863.

[21]Gerbet, *Noblesse dans le royaume de Castille,* 199.

[22]Burmeister, *Grafen von Montfort,* 103. The statistics on legitimate children are derived from the genealogies in ibid., 307–12. Since illegitimate children who died young are unlikely to appear in records, the comparison to legitimate children who survived to adulthood is more meaningful than the comparison to all legitimate children ever born. It should be noted that several different systems of assigning Roman numerals to the counts of Montfort with identical names are used by different genealogists. Cf. Isenburg, *Europäische Stammtafeln,* 5:53,55; and Weiss, *Grafen von Montfort,* 138–39. This study follows Burmeister's numbering.

[23]Schwennicke, *Europäische Stammtafeln NF,* 12:121. Several of the other genealogies in this updated edition, including those of the Zimmern and the Montfort families, also record some illegitimate children. However, many of the bastards named in other sources do not appear in Schwennicke's genealogies of the Zimmern and Montfort families.

(including eight sons) who survived to adulthood. Thus almost half their known surviving offspring, and over half of their surviving sons, were illegitimate. Sprandel's impression that one-third of the population was of illegitimate birth may not be far off the mark when it comes to the children of noblemen (see table 10.1).

A GOLDEN AGE OF NOBLE BASTARDS?

Although illegitimate children were as numerous in the German nobility as in other western European aristocracies, their legal and social position may have been inferior to that of their counterparts in other countries. Moreover, the position of noble bastards in all countries declined between the fifteenth and the sixteenth centuries. The fifteenth century has been described as a golden age for noble bastards in western Europe, one in which illegitimate sons of noblemen were recognized as nobles, brought up in their fathers' households, and accorded prominent roles at court, in the army, and in estate administration. In Kuehn's view, this concept originated in Jacob Burckhardt's description of the Italian Renaissance and expanded geographically along with the concept of the Renaissance itself. He states that "its essential factual basis in each case remains an awareness of the presence of bastards in princely, noble, and patrician families and their visible role at times in affairs of state."[24]

According to Schmugge, "Children begotten outside of marriage seem to have been considered a 'luxury of male aristocrats' in France. In noble circles here and elsewhere in Europe, illegitimacy was ... not grounds for social discrimination against parents or children."[25] Mikhael Harsgor speaks of the "ascendancy of noble bastards" at the courts of France and Burgundy in the second half of the fifteenth century.[26] Cooper describes a similar phenomenon in Castile and concludes that "a general if superficial impression is that bastards were more numerous and had a more recognized place in noble societies of fifteenth-century Europe than in those of post-Tridentine Europe."[27]

In all of these countries, illegitimate sons served a vital social function for the nobility by holding offices in church and state, which enhanced the power and influence of their fathers' families, while the marriages of illegitimate sons and daughters helped to extend dynastic alliances and patron-client networks. Moreover, the legitimation of bastards served as a method of creating male heirs in the absence of adoption.[28]

[24]Kuehn, *Illegitimacy in Renaissance Florence*, 8–10.

[25]Schmugge, *Kirche, Kinder, Karrieren*, 25–27. The phrase, "a luxury of male aristocrats," is taken from Lorcin, *Vivre et mourir en Lyonnais*, 95. On the concept of a golden age of bastards, see Harsgor, "L'essor des bâtards nobles," 319–54; Cooper, "Patterns of Inheritance and Settlement," 236n144, 302; Winterer, *Bastarde in Italien*, 112; and Winterer, *Bastarde in Spanien*, 117. Additional sources are cited by Kuehn, *Illegitimacy in Renaissance Florence*, 9–10.

[26]Harsgor, "L'essor des bâtards nobles," 319.

[27]Cooper, "Patterns of Inheritance and Settlement," 238n144, 302n320.

[28]Harsgor, "L'essor des bâtards nobles," 335–46; Cooper, "Patterns of Inheritance and Settlement,"

Table 10.1: Fathers of Bastards in the Zimmern Family

Father	Known illegitimate children		Legitimate children surviving to age 15	
	Sons	Daughters	Sons	Daughters
Werner VIII (1423–83)[a]	Hans Schilling	—	Johann Werner I	—
Gottfried III (1425–1508)	Hans Heinrich	At least four (unnamed)	None (unmarried)	None (unmarried)
Johann Werner I (c. 1455–95)[b]	Hans	—	Veit Werner Johann Werner II Gottfried Werner Wilhelm Werner	Anna Katharina Margarethe Barbara
Johann Werner II (1480–1548)[c]	Christoph Hans Christoph Philipp Christoph	Barbara	Johann Christoph Froben Christoph Gottfried Christoph	—
Gottfried Werner (1484–1554)	Gottfried Martin	Six (unnamed)	—	Anna Barbara
Gottfried Christoph (1524–70)	—	Magdalena	None (unmarried)	None (unmarried)

[a] Werner VIII also had a legitimate son Georg who died young.

[b] Johann Werner I also had a legitimate daughter Verena who died young.

[c] Johann Werner II also had a legitimate son Christoph Werner and a legitimate daughter Barbara, both of whom died young.

These generalizations are based primarily on the bastards of kings and great nobles, and even Harsgor acknowledges that "the ambiguity of the social position of the natural children of nobles increased to the extent that the social importance of their fathers decreased. Among the nobles with only one *seigneurie*, or even less than that,...bastards were much less esteemed" than in the high nobility.[29]

There is no doubt that nobles below the level of kings and princes often gave favored treatment to their bastards, and that affectionate ties often existed between noblemen and their illegitimate offspring or half siblings. Throughout Europe, as Shulamith Shahar notes, "bastard sons sometimes became the particular confidants of their fathers, on whose mercies they depended, and served as their faithful assistants and emissaries."[30] Both Lorcin in her study of wills of the Lyonnais region and Nassiet in his study of the petty nobles of Brittany in the late Middle Ages stress the close emotional ties between nobles and their illegitimate sons or half brothers. Grimmer does the same in his study of the petty nobility of the Auvergnat in the seventeenth century and of the French nobility as a whole in the early modern period.[31]

Nevertheless, bastards were always economically inferior to their legitimate kin; they formed part of the large body of servants, clients, poor relations, and other dependents for whom the head of a noble family took responsibility. In late medieval and early modern Spain, many illegitimate children fell into the ambiguous category of *criado* or "reared one" (a term used for a foster child but also for a servant), or became clients of the household head.[32]

Caron, writing about Burgundy in the same period in which Harsgor describes the "ascendancy of noble bastards" at court, takes a pessimistic view of the prospects for the bastards of provincial nobles.

> The illegitimate child...never had anything other than a secondary position; he could not make his birth forgotten...or attain the same standard of living [as a legitimate child].... Even in the best case, when he lived close to nobles recognized as such, the situation of the noble bastard was inferior if not downright wretched; he was treated in his father's family "like a servant."[33]

Although Nassiet is more optimistic than Caron about the status of noble bastards in France, he states that the best they could hope for was to insert themselves as "auxiliaries, adjuncts, [or] clients" in a network of relationships with collaterals.[34]

302; Caron, *Noblesse dans le duché de Bourgogne*, 234; Kuehn, *Law, Family, and Women*, 190; and Beceiro Pita and Córdoba de la Llave, *Parentesco, poder y mentalidad*, 248.

[29]Harsgor, "L'essor des bâtards nobles," 346.

[30]Shahar, *Fourth Estate*, 116.

[31]Lorcin, *Vivre et mourir en Lyonnais*, 97–99; Nassiet, *Parenté, noblesse et états dynastiques*, 83; Grimmer, "Bâtards de la noblesse auvergnate," 48; and Grimmer, *La femme et le bâtard*, 153.

[32]Casey, *Early Modern Spain*, 209; and Gerbet, *Noblesses espagnoles au moyen âge*, 207.

[33]Caron, *Noblesse dans le duché de Bourgogne*, 224, 230, 233.

[34]Nassiet, *Parenté, noblesse et états dynastiques*, 83.

Even in Italy, Kuehn argues, that "it is difficult to credit the notion that the fifteenth century, especially in Florence, constituted a 'golden age' of bastardy"; rather, he characterizes it as "a golden age for contradiction, ambiguity, and liminality for bastards." He emphasizes that illegitimacy "generally carried a stain of some sort" and that even bastards recognized and brought up in the paternal home "were not as well off as legitimate children. Even if legitimated, their prior status was never entirely forgotten—neither at the hands of jurists, nor legislators, nor their own kin," particularly in matters of inheritance. Agnatic kin were likely to challenge inheritance claims even by legitimated bastards; "litigants... may have acted from no more than a visceral sense that they could, or even should, try to claim property away from a bastard."[35]

The political and legal position of noblemen's illegitimate children deteriorated in all continental European countries by the mid-sixteenth century. This change is most often attributed to the influence of the Protestant and Catholic reformations, as both ecclesiastical and secular authorities took a more hostile attitude toward extramarital sexuality and toward the illegitimate children who were its products. However, Harsgor and Grimmer also attribute the declining status of French noble bastards in part to the increasing centralization of power in the hands of the monarchy, which strove to reduce the nobility's numbers and power.[36]

Cooper notes that the increasing reluctance to recognize bastards as inheriting their fathers' noble status may be seen as part of the process of lineal consolidation, by which great landowners tried to concentrate property in the hands of a single patriline. This "process of restricting the number of families and kin" reduced the inheritance rights not only of illegitimate children but also of legitimate daughters and younger sons.[37] Kuehn sees a similar process at work in Florence in the fifteenth century, where increasing preoccupation with issues of family inheritance meant that the claims of bastards on family resources "had to be removed, postponed, or limited."[38]

Recent scholarship suggests that opportunities for noble bastards were more limited in the Holy Roman Empire than in other western European countries even in the fifteenth century, and that the deterioration in their legal, political, and social position was evident long before the Reformation. In his analysis of illegitimacy in the late Middle Ages, Schmugge says, "The [German] nobles acknowledged their natural children, it is true, but they did not climb nearly as high as in France."[39]

[35]Kuehn, *Illegitimacy in Renaissance Florence,* 14, 252.

[36]Harsgor, "L'essor des bâtards nobles," 352; and Grimmer, *La femme et le bâtard,* 178–79.

[37]Cooper, "Patterns of Inheritance and Settlement," 302.

[38]Kuehn, *Illegitimacy in Renaissance Florence,* 15, 203, 253. He notes that over the course of the fifteenth century, jurists became increasingly hostile to the inheritance claims of legitimated sons, a trend due in part to the "more aristocratic cast" of Florentine society.

[39]Schmugge, *Kirche, Kinder, Karrieren,* 27.

No illegitimate sons succeeded to the thrones of German princely states in an era when they often did so in Italy.[40] A few men of illegitimate birth managed to achieve honor and high office at the imperial court even in the sixteenth century, including the imperial general Lazarus von Schwendi, who married one of the daughters of Froben Christoph von Zimmern.[41] However, in 1454, Emperor Frederick III had objected to elevating Borso d'Este to the rank of duke of Ferrara on the grounds that "because Borso was not born in a proper marriage, it would be unseemly to place him higher than the sons born in wedlock."[42] Such reluctance suggests that the Holy Roman Emperors of the fifteenth century were not accustomed to placing noble bastards in prominent positions at the imperial court.

Opportunities for noble bastards in the ecclesiastical sphere were also more limited than in other European countries. Schmugge notes that "in the empire, canonries in cathedral chapters or bishoprics were almost unobtainable even for bastards from noble families," whereas noble bastards in France and Spain frequently entered cathedral chapters and became bishops and abbots.[43]

Scholars differ on the rationale for the less-favored position of noble bastards in German lands. Citing the regulations for a tournament held by the Prince-Bishop of Würzburg in 1479, Sprandel argues that German nobles were more affected than those in other European countries by the church's norms on extramarital sexuality.[44] However, Karl Borchardt interprets the regulations as showing the knights' determination to maintain the exclusivity of their social order. Tournaments, like cathedral chapters, required proof that both the mother and the father of the applicant were of noble descent; the exclusion of bastards was thus merely a by-product of the exclusion of all sons of nonnoble mothers.[45]

Borchardt's argument suggests that social and legal factors unique to the German nobility must be considered in addition to the factors common to other

---

[40]Legitimated bastards succeeded to the throne in several princely families of northern Italy, including the Sforza of Milan, Malatesta of Rimini, and especially the Este of Ferrara, where five illegitimately born sons in a row came to the throne between 1308 and 1450. Ettlinger, "Visibilis et Invisibilis," 782–83; and Bestor, "Bastardy and Legitimacy," 550. The "many natural sons of the Della Scala rulers" also played a prominent role in the politics of Verona. Eisenach, *Husbands, Wives, and Concubines,* 137.

[41]Lazarus von Schwendi, an illegitimately born member of a Swabian family of the lower nobility, was legitimated by Charles V in 1554 and given the rank of baron. He was appointed an imperial councilor in the Palatinate in 1568 and held many other offices under the Hapsburgs; Schwennicke, *Europäische Stammtafeln NF,* 12:154; and *ADB,* s.v. "Lazarus Freiherr von Schwendi."

[42]Sprandel, "Diskriminierung der unehelichen Kinder," 494.

[43]Schmugge, *Kirche, Kinder, Karrieren,* 27, 221–22. Between 1490 and 1530, ten French bishoprics were held by illegitimately born men. Grimmer, *La femme et le bâtard,* 165. Some illegitimate sons of Hapsburg emperors and German princes did become bishops and eventually cardinals, often through appointments to sees outside the Holy Roman Empire. Heinig, "'Omnia vincit amor,'" 299.

[44]Sprandel, "Diskriminierung der unehelichen Kinder," 491.

[45]Borchardt, "Illegitime in den Diözen Würzburg, Bamberg und Eichstatt," 270. The exclusion of bastards from cathedral chapters after the mid-fifteenth century may be a similar by-product of the exclusion of those who lacked noble ancestry on both sides rather than a regulation specifically aimed against illegitimacy. Veit, *Stiftsmässige deutschen Adel,* 11, 15–16.

European countries. In most other western European aristocracies, the legitimate (and sometimes even the illegitimate) children of a nobleman were nobles regardless of the status of their mother. In the Holy Roman Empire, however, noble status required noble descent on both the paternal and maternal sides. The requirement of *Ebenbürtigkeit* (equality of birth) meant that even the legitimate offspring of a marriage between a nobleman and a nonnoble woman did not inherit the rank and estate of their father. The illegitimate offspring of a nobleman and a nonnoble woman obviously had even less claim to noble status than did legitimate children born of an unequal marriage.

🙊 🙊 🙊

The legal status of noble bastards varied greatly in different western European countries, and actual practice in all countries differed from the letter of the law. While the bastards of kings and great nobles were recognized as nobles, the status of those whose fathers were of less exalted rank was more ambiguous. In most continental aristocracies, bastards of noblemen were legally considered nobles only if they were legitimated, either by the subsequent marriage of their parents or by rescript of the prince, granted either by agents of the pope or by secular authorities.[46] In practice, almost all legitimations were by rescript of the prince.

Legitimation was much more common in the lands of Roman law, such as Italy and the Iberian kingdoms, than in lands of customary law, such as northern France and the Holy Roman Empire. English common law did not recognize legitimation at all. Kuehn notes that "legitimation was a legal device used with some regularity in fifteenth-century Florence" to provide male heirs. However, it was not frequent considering the large number of recognized bastards. Only thirteen out of almost a thousand bastards listed in the *castato* of 1458 were described as legitimated, and fewer than a hundred legitimations by acts of the city councils or by rescripts of counts palatine are recorded between the mid-fourteenth and the early sixteenth centuries.[47]

Fifteenth-century Castilian nobles made considerable use of legitimation by rescript of the prince to increase the number of male heirs. Legitimations for the purposes of succession were particularly common among members of the religious military orders, who were required to remain unmarried. The practice remained widespread among Spanish and Portuguese nobles in the sixteenth and seventeenth centuries. In the single year 1626, sixty-five of the approximately six hundred noble families of Valencia petitioned the Cortes for legitimation of offspring

---

[46]On the development of legitimation in canon law and customary law, see chapter 8 above, 178–79.

[47]Kuehn, *Law, Family, and Women,* 176; and Kuehn, *Illegitimacy in Renaissance Florence,* 169, 174–78.

for the purposes of inheritance. The Portuguese high aristocracy not only legitimated large numbers of bastards in the seventeenth century but recorded them in their genealogies alongside their legitimate children.[48]

In France, illegitimate children of noble fathers were noble (and thereby exempt from direct taxation) even without legitimation until their status was changed by an edict of Henry IV in 1600. After this edict, bastards of noble fathers were noble only if they secured legitimation and letters of ennoblement from the king. However, this procedure remained rare in the early seventeenth century. Louis XIII (1610–43) granted only nineteen legitimations and ennoblements of noble bastards, making up 11 percent of the total of 165 ennoblements granted in his reign. [49]

The French theorist Florentine de Thirrat, writing in 1606, drew a categorical distinction between the usage of the Holy Roman Empire by which bastards of noble fathers remained in principle "incapable of all nobility, natural or civil," and the traditional usage of France by which the illegitimate child kept the name, nobility, and arms of his father.[50] However, the distinction was not as hard and fast as Thirrat implied. Even in the fifteenth century, only those illegitimate sons who lived nobly were socially and legally accepted as nobles in France. This implied the possession of at least a small fief, or of a military or political office providing sufficient revenue to maintain a noble style of life. Moreover, French law differed from region to region, with the provinces of customary law in the north and west more hostile to the recognition of noble bastards than the provinces of written law in the south. Over the course of the sixteenth century, the northern provinces largely ceased to recognize the illegitimate children of noblemen as belonging to the nobility.[51]

In his *Traités des ordres et simples dignités* (1666), Charles Loyseau argued that the edict of Henry IV was too rigorous, that it contradicted the ancient custom of France, and that it should not extend to bastards of *seigneurs*. Loyseau suggested that bastards should be considered to rank "one degree below [the legitimate children], so that bastards of kings are princes, those of princes are noblemen (*seigneurs*), those of noblemen are gentlemen (*gentilshommes*), those of gentlemen are commoners (*roturiers*)."[52] This view is remarkably similar to that held by German nobles in the Middle Ages and in the sixteenth century.

[48]Cooper, "Patterns of Inheritance and Settlement," 302; Casey, *Early Modern Spain,* 214; and Boone, "Parental Investment and Elite Family Structure," 861.

[49]For a detailed analysis of the edict of Henry IV and its effects, see Grimmer, "Bâtards de la noblesse auvergnate," 40–47, and Grimmer, *La femme et le bâtard,* 177–91.

[50]Florentine de Thirrat, *Trois traictez* (1606), quoted in Harsgor, "L'essor des bâtards nobles," 328.

[51]Contamines, *Noblesse au royaume de France,* 61; Lorcin, *Vivre et mourir en Lyonnais,* 99; and Grimmer, *La femme et le bâtard,* 175.

[52]Charles Loyseau, *Traités des ordres et simples dignités* (1666), quoted in Grimmer, "Bâtards de la noblesse auvergnate," 41.

In the Holy Roman Empire, bastards of nobles theoretically did not inherit their father's noble status or the right to bear arms unless they were legitimated.[53] However, few German nobles sought to legitimate their children, probably because of the restrictive inheritance laws. Legitimation by rescript of the prince did not confer the right to inherit land, and legitimation by subsequent marriage of the parents could legitimate only natural children, not those born of adultery. Spiess states that "the status and the provision for illegitimate offspring of counts and barons was determined by the fact that even in the case of eventual legitimation, they were granted no share in the lordship (*Herrschaft*) and had no claim to the paternal inheritance."[54]

The *Zimmern Chronicle* reports several cases—including that of Gottfried Werner von Zimmern—in which noblemen considered marrying their concubines in order to legitimate a natural son as heir (*ZC* 3:129, 4:288). However, only one man is reported to have actually done so: Hans von Weitingen, a bachelor from the lower nobility, who saved his lineage from extinction by marrying his concubine on his deathbed (*ZC* 3:171).

Some other German nobles sought legitimation by rescript of the prince in connection with the grant of noble status and coats of arms to their illegitimate children.[55] Count Hugo XVII von Montfort-Bregenz petitioned Charles V in 1532 to raise his three children by Dorothea Falckner—Christoph, Daniel, and Marina—"to the honor and rights of legitimate and noble status." The emperor granted the petition, giving the three children the name "von Flugberg" and their own coat of arms. Four years later, Hugo married their mother in an attempt to give greater force to the provisions in his will designating her and their children as his legal heirs.[56] Burmeister remarks drily, "it is evident that these proceedings did not win unanimous support in the House of Montfort"; Hugo's indulgence toward his bastards led to a marked decline in his reputation.[57]

However, Hugo XVII was the only father in the Montfort family who legitimated any of his children between 1350 and 1550, and Spiess finds only two cases

[53]*HRG*, s.v. "Uneheliche." This also held true in the Netherlands, which were still part of the Holy Roman Empire. In the sixteenth century, "the bastards of the Holland nobles were not reckoned among the nobility," at least not in law. Nierop, *Nobility of Holland*, 53.

[54]*HRG*, s.v. "Bankert"; Dieck, *Legitimation durch nachfolgende Ehe*, 5–6; and Spiess, *Familie und Verwandtschaft*, 381.

[55]Duke Eberhard the Bearded of Württemberg "had two sons legitimated and raised to the nobility by Emperor Maximilian in 1494." Count Adolf von Nassau was legitimated by Emperor Frederick III in 1442 and allowed to carry his father's arms with a "sign of bastardy." Schmugge, *Kirche, Kinder, Karrieren*, 74–75.

[56]Hugo evidently feared that collateral relatives might challenge his will on the grounds that children legitimated by rescript of the prince did not have the right to inherit land. The marriage would strengthen the children's legal claim, since children legitimated by the subsequent marriage of their parents did have this right under German law. *HRG*, s.v. "Mantelkind."

[57]Burmeister, *Grafen von Montfort*, 300–1. Marina's marriage contract described her "as a legitimate daughter of Count Hugo, i.e., not as Marina von Flugberg, but as Marina von Montfort."

in his fifteen families of counts and barons in the Mainz region between 1300 and 1500.[58] The two legitimations mentioned in the *Zimmern Chronicle* (those of Junker Heinrich and of the four children of Johann Werner II von Zimmern) were both obtained by the children rather than the father. It is noteworthy that Gottfried Werner did not legitimate his bastard sons, despite his indulgent treatment of them and his desire to have them recognized as nobles.

Very few German noble bastards thus qualified for noble status according to the letter of the law. Nevertheless, sources from the late Middle Ages and the sixteenth century show that in practice some German nobles were regarded as belonging—even without legitimation—to the social order one step below that of their fathers. Spiess says that in the Mainz region in the fourteenth and fifteenth centuries "the route to the lower nobility (*Ritteradel*) lay open to the illegitimate children of counts and barons.... This pattern of relationships in which illegitimate children are established one step below their father's order (*Stand*) is encountered as well among the princes, for the latter attempted to place their illegitimate offspring in the order of counts."[59]

Nobles in the *Zimmern Chronicle* in the mid-sixteenth century continued to hold the view that the bastard of a member of the high nobility (count or baron) ranked as a member of the lower nobility (a *Junker* or squire). The chronicler complains that bastards of counts and barons claim noble status: "These people usually think themselves great squires and have a high opinion of themselves." He quotes Truchsess Georg von Waldburg as saying of his bastard son Hans Muffler, "Lord Hans is too much, but Squire Hans is right and fitting"(*ZC* 2:173).

The relationship of illegitimate children to their father's lineage was always problematic. Nevertheless, most illegitimate children of counts and barons in the fifteenth and sixteenth centuries identified themselves with their father's family by using some form of their father's surname; they were also given Christian names traditional in their father's lineage.[60] The three illegitimate sons of Johann Werner II, as well as his four legitimate sons, all had names that included the name Christoph. His illegitimate daughter bore the name Barbara, a traditional name for women of the Zimmern family.

Some illegitimate sons used the family name with the noble particle "von" and bore their father's arms, thus claiming the status of nobles: Gottfried Werner

[58]Spiess mentions the case of Adolf of Nassau and one in which a bastard daughter of Count Eberhard von Katzenelnbogen was legitimated by King Ruprecht in 1408, *Familie und Verwandtschaft*, 381.

[59]Spiess, *Familie und Verwandtschaft*, 389. The view that bastards belonged to the order one step below their father's was also prevalent among Salzburg nobles in the High Middle Ages. "The natural son of a king became a count; a noble's son, a ministerial; a ministerial's son, a knight." Freed, *Noble Bondsmen*, 126–27.

[60]Burmeister, *Grafen von Montfort*, 106. This contrasts with the practice described by Freed (*Noble Bondsmen*, 127) in Salzburg in the High Middle Ages, in which bastards were usually given names uncommon in the lineage in order to distinguish them from their legitimate kin. The difference may be due to the use of surnames in the later period.

von Zimmern allowed his bastard sons to style themselves "von Zimmern" and to bear the family arms. In other cases, sons of counts established themselves as members of the lower nobility under names differing from their father's; these were often taken from a family castle. Sons of the fourteenth-century Count Johann II von Sponheim were known as Simon von Argenschwang, Johann von Kreuznach, and Walrab von Koppelstein; and the three children of Count Hugo XVII von Montfort who were raised to the nobility by Charles V were given the name "von Flugberg."[61]

In most cases, bastards used a form of their father's surname without the noble particle "von," indicating that they were not regarded as nobles. Bastards of the counts of Montfort were usually surnamed "Montfort" (without the "von") or "Montforter," while those of the Zimmern family are usually referred to as "Zimmerer" or "Zimmerle." Some bastards, though obviously acknowledged by their fathers, were known by their mother's name: for example, Hans Schilling, the son of Werner VIII von Zimmern.[62]

There is no clear pattern to the use of surnames. Those who used the noble particle "von" and the family arms did not always maintain a noble style of life, for the four bastards who styled themselves "von Montfort" included two parish priests and two burghers of Speyer.[63] Some bastards appeared both with the particle "von" and without it. Others appeared both under the name of their father and the name of their mother: Hans, the son of Gottfried III von Zimmern, received a dispensation under the name Johannes Hirligack, but appears in parish records under the names "Zimmern" and "Zimmerer." Sometimes the same father had children who were known by their mother's name and others known by his own name: for example, the canon Thomas von Rieneck, whose children were called Jörg Steynborn, Anna Praun, and Kunigunde Rieneck.[64] It is possible that in such cases the children who bore their father's name had mothers of higher status than did the children who bore their mother's name.

Some children who bore their mother's name, however, were definitely regarded as nobles. Truchsess Georg von Waldburg called his son Hans Muffler a squire, and two of the most successful careers of bastards in the Montfort family were those of Heinrich and Wilhelm Gabler, the sons of Count Wilhelm V von Montfort. Burmeister speculates that the cleric Wilhelm Gabler wished to conceal his illegitimate birth and therefore avoided using the name and arms of the Montfort family. However, his brother Heinrich also used the name Gabler, even

---

[61]Spiess, *Familie und Verwandtschaft,* 383–86; and Burmeister, *Grafen von Montfort,* 115, 300.

[62]Bastards of the counts of Montfort also bore the surnames Gabler, Stadler, Ziegler, Bechrer, and Rot. Burmeister, *Grafen von Montfort,* 106.

[63]Burmeister, *Grafen von Montfort,* 114–15. The two burghers had two other brothers who used the surname Montforter.

[64]Wieland, "Römische Dispense 'de defectu natalium,'" 295; and Ruf, *Grafen von Rieneck,* "Stammtafel."

though he was proud of his connection to the Montforts and bore on his seal the Montfort arms with a mark of bastardy.[65]

                        ❧ ❧ ❧

In some European aristocracies, it is said that illegitimate children—especially sons— were regarded as members of the family and were often brought up in their father's household alongside the legitimate children. This was particularly true of Italy, where both princes and members of urban elites "accepted them into their households, started sons in careers, arranged marriages for daughters, and ... provided for them in testaments"; a widow was expected to care for her husband's illegitimate offspring after his death.[66] In his analysis of illegitimacy in Florence, Kuehn assumes that the only two options are to abandon bastards to a foundling home or to bring them up in the father's household. He does not consider the possibility of paying child support to a mother residing outside the father's household.[67] Cases of illegitimate children being brought up in the father's household are also documented among nobles in late medieval and early modern Spain, France, England, and the Netherlands.[68]

Such a practice does not necessarily mean that illegitimate children normally resided in their father's household from birth. The bastard children of a married nobleman usually resided with their mother in a separate household, particularly when the children were young. Their chances of being taken into their father's household depended partly on the status of their mother, and partly on whether they were conceived before or after their father's marriage. Of all the bastards of Italian Renaissance princes, only those born of noble mothers were educated in the palace. Similarly, the bastard sons born to petty nobles of the Lyons region by peasant women always remained in their mothers' villages, whereas some of those whose mothers were of higher status were brought up in their fathers' households. Most of the illegitimate children acknowledged on Florentine tax returns were begotten before their father's marriage, as were most of those accepted into the household of the father's heirs among the Dutch gentry.[69] Some noble bastards

[65]Burmeister, *Grafen von Montfort,* 107–9.

[66]Herlihy and Klapisch-Zuber, *Tuscans and Their Families,* 146; and Grubb, *Provincial Families of the Renaissance,* 39.

[67]Kuehn, *Illegitimacy in Renaissance Florence,* 150–51. However, he is skeptical about claims that children brought up in the father's household were truly accepted as members of the family.

[68]On France, see Lorcin, *Vivre et mourir en Lyonnais,* 99–100; Caron, *Noblesse dans le duché de Bourgogne,* 229–34; Grimmer, "Bâtards de la noblesse auvergnate," 38–39; and Grimmer, *La Femme et le bâtard,* 151–61. On Spain, see Beceiro Pita and Córdoba de la Llave, *Parentesco, poder y mentalidad,* 220–24; and Gerbet, *Noblesse dans le royaume de Castille,* 199. On England, see Harris, *English Aristocratic Women,* 84. On Holland, see Marshall, *Dutch Gentry,* 5–6.

[69]Ettlinger, "Visibilis et Invisibilis," 777–78; Lorcin, *Vivre et mourir en Lyonnais,* 99–100; Kuehn, *Illegitimacy in Renaissance Florence,* 135–37, 166; and Marshall, *Dutch Gentry,* 5.

entered their father's household after being orphaned. Others, usually sons, were sent there for their education in much the same way that legitimate children were fostered out to the household of an uncle or of a greater lord.

There is little evidence that bringing up illegitimate children in their father's household was a common practice in Germany at any social level. In a well-known German case, one of the five children born to the merchant Lucas Rem by a woman in Antwerp was brought up in his household in Augsburg. At a lower social level, a court in Memmingen in 1531 ordered a father to bring up his bastard child in his own household, if he was married and had a household of his own. However, German courts usually ordered a father to pay child support to a mother who brought up the child in her own household.[70] The *Zimmern Chronicle* gives the impression that the bastard children of a German nobleman were unlikely to live with their father unless he was unmarried (or separated from his wife) and maintained a household with his concubine. The four children of Johann Werner II von Zimmern and Margreth Hutler were brought up in the "strange household at Falkenstein" that so enraged the chronicler (*ZC* 3:307). However, the concubine of a married man was usually installed in her own house, often in the town outside the castle, and her children resided there with her.

It was evidently the norm for the legitimate sons or other male relatives of the father to become guardians of his illegitimate children after his death, for the chronicler thinks it necessary to give an explanation for his father's decision not to name his legitimate sons as guardians for their illegitimate half siblings (*ZC* 4:86). Karl von Zollern acted as guardian for his illegitimate half sister Anna Zollerer, and Jos Niklaus von Zollern for Anna, the daughter of his cousin Christoph Friedrich von Zollern. However, guardianship did not necessarily entail taking the illegitimate children into one's own household, especially if their mother was still alive. Spiess's analysis of the provisions for bastards in wills of counts and barons of the Mainz region does not suggest that widows were expected to undertake the upbringing of their husbands' illegitimate children.[71]

In only four cases does the *Zimmern Chronicle* imply that an illegitimate child was brought up in a close relationship with his legitimate kin, and only one of these cases involved a son. Johann Werner I had an illegitimate son named Hans (or Hensle), born before his marriage, whom he brought along with his legitimate family when he was exiled to Switzerland. Hans, who must have been in his mid- to late teens by this time, is described in the chronicle as a "coarse, nasty rascal who engaged in all sorts of rude behavior at the instigation of Johann Werner." His behavior particularly irritated a frequent visitor to the Zimmern household, the wife of Johann Werner's friend Count Jörg von Werdenberg-Sargans. "When the countess tried to reform the rascal's manners, he would address her with the

---

[70]Schmugge, *Kirche, Kinder, Karriere*, 194; and Ellrichshausen, *Uneheliche Mütterschaft*, 114.
[71]Spiess, *Familie und Verwandtschaft*, 381–89.

familiar 'du' and speak to her in the most inappropriate manner. This secretly pleased Johann Werner and infuriated his cousin [his friend's wife]" (*ZC* 1:540). Such rude behavior is surprising if Hans had been brought up in a noble household; on the other hand, the fact that Johann Werner brought Hans with him to Switzerland suggests that the bastard son was considered part of the family. In this anecdote, Hans appears in the role of a fool or jester whose antics allow his father to indulge vicariously in behavior forbidden by proper etiquette.

In three other cases, illegitimate daughters may have been brought up in or near their father's household. Leonora Werdenberger, the daughter of Count Hugo von Werdenberg, was brought up at Sigmaringen, possibly in the household of her father or uncle. After the breakdown of her marriage to a furrier, she is said to have become the mistress of two of her legitimate cousins, Counts Felix and Christoph von Werdenberg (*ZC* 2:311–12).

Anna, the daughter of Count Christoph Friedrich von Zollern (d. 1536) and the Augsburg patrician Anna Rehlinger, may not have been illegitimate, for her mother claimed that a clandestine marriage had taken place. However, her father's family refused to acknowledge the marriage and forced Anna to renounce the use of the Zollern name. Anna's guardian, her father's cousin Jos Niklaus von Zollern, is said to have cheated her out of most of the money she should have inherited from her mother and to have acted unjustly by forcing her to marry one of his clerks, even though she had already formed an attachment to another suitor (*ZC* 2:467).

Black Anna Zollerer, an illegitimate daughter of Count Eitelfriedrich III von Zollern, evidently had a close relationship with her half sister Johanna von Zollern. The widowed Johanna invited Anna to reside with her and tried to persuade her brother Karl (Anna's guardian) to consent to Anna's marriage to Jakob Zimmerle. Karl von Zollern initially opposed the match, perhaps because he begrudged paying Anna's dowry. The marriage finally took place after Johann Werner II von Zimmern intervened on behalf of his kinsman; however, it ended unhappily when Jakob, Anna, and Johanna became involved in a ménage à trois that caused a major public scandal (*ZC* 3:481–83).

In three of these cases, the father never married, or the children were born before the father's marriage (the status of Anna Zollerer is unknown). As in other elites, children begotten when the father was unmarried were more likely to be recognized and brought up in their father's household than were those born of adultery.

It is noteworthy that most of these cases in *Zimmern Chronicle* involved daughters. Evidence for other European aristocracies suggests that sons were more likely than daughters to be brought up in their fathers' households and to have close personal relationships with their legitimate kin. However, the chronicle does not give the impression that these illegitimate daughters were treated generously. Both Leonora Werdenberger and the daughter of Anna Rehlinger seem to have been exploited rather than protected by their legitimate kin, and Anna Zollerer's half brother was reluctant to spend the money for her dowry. The sexual relationships in two of these cases imply that Leonora Werdenberger and Anna Zollerer were not considered real members of their noble family, for a sexual relationship with one's legitimate first cousin or the husband of one's legitimate sister would have been considered incestuous.[72]

PROVISION FOR ILLEGITIMATE CHILDREN

Scholars' perception that noble bastards had a good chance of establishing themselves as nobles is due in large part to the fact that children who did so were more likely to appear in the records than those who sank to a lower social level. It was only the lucky ones among the illegitimate children of counts and barons who succeeded in establishing themselves in the nobility one step below the rank of their fathers. Their social position was dependent on the financial provision their father made for them and the interest he took in furthering their careers. They could become members of the lower nobility only if their fathers provided them with resources sufficient to maintain a noble style of life. For a son, this usually meant a castle and/or the income from estate offices; for a daughter, a dowry sufficient to marry into the lower nobility. Children who did not receive such provision would not be regarded as nobles. In such cases, sons were educated for the church or given cash pensions; daughters were occasionally placed in convents but were usually married off with dowries too small to secure a husband of noble rank. [73]

The provision a noble father made for his illegitimate sons may have depended to some extent on the status of the mother, but the most significant factor was the presence or absence of legitimate children or collateral heirs who would be likely to challenge substantial bequests.[74] Bastard sons assumed greater importance to men who—like Gottfried III and Gottfried Werner von Zimmern—were either unmarried or had no male heirs from their marriages.

From the point of view of noble fathers, establishing their bastard sons either in secular or in ecclesiastical careers secured for them "loyal followers to whom the goals of family policy were more important than anything else."[75] Granting fiefs (castles and offices) to illegitimate sons could be advantageous to both the father and the sons. Using bastard sons as officials, counselors, castellans or servants provided the father with employees who were more trustworthy than nonkinsmen

---

[72]Counts and barons in the Mainz region avoided marriages between first cousins. Spiess, *Familie und Verwandtschaft,* 47. For a case of a woman executed for incest with her brother-in-law, see Harrington, *Reordering Marriage and Society,* 257.

[73]Spiess, *Familie und Verwandtschaft,* 383, 389.

[74]Spiess, *Familie und Verwandtschaft,* 383–85. Count Johann II von Sponheim, when making provision for his illegitimate son Simon von Argenschwang in 1335, had the document signed by all the secular counts of Sponheim in order to prevent any future challenges.

[75]Burmeister, *Grafen von Montfort,* 13.

and could be expected to administer the estates in the interests of the family. The income from these offices and fiefs allowed the sons to live in the style of the lower nobility without placing any additional burden on the family's economic resources. Sometimes these illegitimate sons continued to hold office after their father's death, and a few founded families that ranked as members of the lower nobility.[76]

One of the most successful of the illegitimate sons of the Swabian nobility was Heinrich Gabler (fl. 1424, d. 1452). He was the son of Count Wilhelm V of Montfort-Tettnang, who had been a parish priest before succeeding unexpectedly to the Montfort estates. Although Wilhelm later married a noblewoman and begot legitimate children, he was diligent in furthering the careers of the sons born to him earlier by a concubine. Burmeister sums up the career of Heinrich Gabler as follows: "He served Duke Friedrich of Tyrol as governor at Bludenz and Werdenberg. As counselor of the counts of Tettnang, he climbed to the top of the Montforts' administration. As a Junker and the holder of a castle, which was a fief of the counts of Montfort, he founded at a lower level of nobility the new family of Gabler von Rosenharz."[77] This was the sort of career to which Gottfried III von Zimmern aspired—though on a lesser scale—for his son Junker Heinrich.

Similar stories of bastard sons employed as estate officials are told in the *Zimmern Chronicle*. In a passage that grudgingly concedes that a few bastards do turn out well, the chronicler cites past examples of paragons of loyalty who were willing to put the family's financial interests ahead of their own. For example, Adam von Rosenstein, the bastard son of a count of Eberstein, became an official of the Eberstein family and "stood by his lord faithfully in time of greatest need. The son did not marry, so his movable and other goods would fall to his lord after his death" (ZC 2:173). However, the chronicler does not believe that bastards in modern times can be trusted to be so loyal; he deliberately disregards the services rendered to the Zimmern family during the Werdenberg-Zimmern feud by Werner VIII's illegitimate son Hans Schilling and by Gottfried III's illegitimate son Junker Heinrich.[78] Instead, the chronicler cites Junker Heinrich as an example of a bastard who damaged the interests of his legitimate kin by attempting to establish himself in the nobility.

Even Junker Heinrich failed to maintain his position in the nobility after his father's death. The available evidence suggests that few bastards of German counts and barons actually achieved noble status, much less succeeded in passing it on to their children. In his study of fifteen noble families between 1200 and 1550, Spiess

---

[76]Spiess, *Familie und Verwandtschaft*, 383–85.

[77]Burmeister, *Grafen von Montfort*, 108–11.

[78]Hans Schilling acted as a Zimmern estate official in Bregenz, and his own house in that town was confiscated by the Werdenbergs when the Zimmern estates were sequestered. Along with Junker Heinrich, he appeared before the Reichstag and other assemblies to petition for the restoration of the Zimmern estates (ZC 2:41, 57, 151–52).

mentions only eleven illegitimate sons who were clearly regarded as nobles and only two who established enduring lines in the lower nobility.[79] Burmeister notes that illegitimate children of the Montfort family rarely founded new lineages and in general did not establish "a lasting connection with the family of counts."[80] Of the twenty-seven illegitimate children of the counts of Montfort recorded between 1350 and 1575, only eight could be considered nobles or equal to nobles, and only Heinrich Gabler succeeded in establishing himself and his descendants in the lower nobility.[81]

For illegitimate sons who were not given fiefs and offices, the next best form of provision was an education. This normally served as preparation for an ecclesiastical career, but in the late fifteenth and sixteenth centuries some educated sons pursued secular careers as lawyers or bureaucrats. In order to take holy orders, it was necessary for a bastard son to secure a dispensation from the defect of illegitimate birth. Schmugge's analysis of petitions to the papal curia between 1449 and 1553 shows that nobles made up the largest group of laymen who petitioned for such dispensations. In the diocese of Constance, where the Zimmerns resided, over 13 percent of all petitioners were members of the nobility. They included the counts (later dukes) of Württemberg and many of the Swabian noble families mentioned in the *Zimmern Chronicle*, including the counts of Fürstenberg, Lupfen, Montfort, Werdenberg, and Zollern, and the Zimmerns themselves.[82]

Although many illegitimate sons of noblemen entered the church in the late Middle Ages, very few became bishops. In the course of the fifteenth century, it became more and more difficult for them to obtain prebends and other benefices, as cathedral chapters increasingly demanded proof of the noble birth of both parents.[83]

Two of the illegitimate sons of counts of Montfort did succeed in obtaining cathedral canonries in the early fifteenth century. Wilhelm Gabler (fl. 1419–49),

---

[79]In the fifteen families studied by Spiess, only four noble bastards received castles or offices in the fifteenth century and clearly ranked as nobles. In the fourteenth century, the counts of Sponheim had granted castles and offices to seven of their illegitimate sons, two of whom founded the houses of Koppenstein and Allenbach in the lower nobility. In addition, Spiess mentions three illegitimate daughters in these fifteen families who received dowries large enough to marry into the lower nobility; they presumably were considered noblewomen themselves. *Familie und Verwandtschaft*, 383–86, 389.

[80]Burmeister, *Grafen von Montfort*, 105.

[81]The children who could be considered noble or equal to nobles include two male fief holders, two cathedral canons, the three children of Hugo XVII von Montfort-Bregenz who were ennobled by Charles V, and another daughter of Hugo XVII who held a fief. Two fathers (Count Wilhelm V of Montfort-Tettnang and Count Hugo XVII of Montfort-Bregenz) accounted for six of the eight illegitimate children who ranked as nobles. In addition, one parish priest, who styled himself "von Montfort" and used the family seal, might possibly be considered noble.

[82]Burmeister, *Grafen von Montfort*, 112–13; and Schmugge, *Kirche, Kinder, Karrieren*, 240–41.

[83]Schmugge, *Kirche, Kinder, Karrieren*, 230. Heinig notes that the holders of five bishoprics in northwest Germany in the fifteenth century included several who were illegitimately born, but that all the bishops between 1520 and 1650 were of legitimate birth. "'Omnia vincit amor,'" 288.

the son of Count Wilhelm V, followed a typical career for a successful cleric: he secured "at least fifteen benefices, mostly very rich ones, due to the constant influence of his family," particularly his father's connections with the king and with the bishop of Trent.[84]

Since membership in cathedral chapters was closed to those of illegitimate birth by the late fifteenth century, most noble bastards who followed careers in the church had to settle for positions as parish priests or monks. Many of them owed their appointment to their father or to his family: Hans, the son of Gottfried III von Zimmern, became a chaplain at Messkirch and also held a living in the gift of the Zimmern family at Oberndorf (ZC 1:416). Of the nine bastard sons of the counts of Montfort who entered the church, six "were content to receive their incomes as mere parish priests and carry on their lives without anyone hearing anything special about them.... Adequate financial provision was made for all of these individuals, but careers and achievements for the family were absent."[85]

Like other sons of noblemen who entered the church, noble bastards usually studied law, not theology; many used their education to serve their families as estate officials or legal advisers. The most striking example is that of Johannes Hugo (d. 1505), the son of Count Hugo XIII von Montfort. After studying at Vienna, Bologna, Rome, and Basel, he became the legal adviser to the counts of Montfort, frequently representing the family in cases before the Reichstag.[86] At a humbler level, the three illegitimate sons of Johann Werner II von Zimmern were provided with educations to prepare them for ecclesiastical careers; this training enabled one of them to follow a career as a town clerk when he failed to obtain a position in the church.

Sons who neither held fiefs and offices nor received a university education were usually bequeathed small annuities that would not support even a bachelor in a noble style of life. Spiess describes a typical bequest around the year 1500 as a capital sum of 400 to 500 gulden, which would yield a pension of only 20 to 25 gulden a year. Even the wealthy counts of Nassau bequeathed pensions of only 15 gulden a year to several illegitimate sons in the fifteenth century; one of these became a *heckenreuter* (highway robber).[87]

Some illegitimate sons who received these small pensions probably became retainers to other noblemen in their neighborhood, while others entered military

[84]The other canon, the Greek-born Vincenz von Montfort (fl. 1420–80), made his career in Italy as a scholar and medical doctor without assistance from his German kinsmen. In his old age, he made contact with the counts of Montfort-Tettnang, who granted him the right to use the title Count of Montfort and the Montfort coat of arms. This was the only case in which an illegitimate member of the family was allowed to use this title. Burmeister, *Grafen von Montfort*, 104, 107–8, 113.

[85]Burmeister, *Grafen von Montfort*, 114.

[86]Burmeister, *Grafen von Montfort*, 112–13. For other examples, see Schmugge, *Kirche, Kinder, Karrieren*, 240; and Spiess, *Familie und Verwandtschaft*, 384.

[87]Spiess, *Familie und Verwandtschaft*, 386–87.

service at the courts of more distant princes. Burmeister mentions two illegitimate sons of the counts of Montfort who entered the service of Austria and generalizes that "many illegitimate sons...were shoved off into the military...thus they were provided for, without any great cost to the family."[88] However, most of the illegitimate sons in the Montfort and Zimmern families who remained laymen did not follow military careers. Three out of the six Zimmern bastards whose occupation is known were burghers, as were six sons of the counts of Montfort. One of the illegitimate sons of the counts of Montfort was a baker.[89]

Much less is known about illegitimate daughters of noblemen than about illegitimate sons, since women are less likely to appear in legal documents. Only two illegitimate daughters are specifically identified as noblewomen in the records: Christina von Falkenstein (who used the particle "von" with her father's surname and is styled *mulier nobilis*) and Marina von Flugberg, one of the three children of Count Hugo XVII von Montfort-Bregenz who were raised to the nobility by Charles V. Another of Hugo's daughters, Christina, held a fief and therefore must also have enjoyed noble status.[90]

It has been said that among western European elites, the defect of illegitimate birth was considered sufficient reason to send a girl into a nunnery instead of arranging a marriage for her. According to Kuehn, illegitimate daughters enrolled in the dowry fund of Florence between 1425 and the 1530s "were twice as likely as legitimate girls to end up in convents." Nevertheless, the great majority of illegitimate daughters married; fewer than 10 percent of the illegitimate daughters enrolled in the dowry fund of Florence became nuns.[91]

Heinig states that the illegitimate daughters of German princes were often brought up in convents, "where they had no difficulty advancing to the office of abbess."[92] However, southwest German counts and barons seem to have placed relatively few illegitimate daughters in convents. Although several daughters of the bachelor Gottfried III von Zimmern became nuns (*ZC* 1:416), no other cases of illegitimate daughters entering convents are mentioned in the *Zimmern Chronicle*. Spiess finds only one case among fifteen families of counts and barons in the

[88]Burmeister, *Grafen von Montfort,* 114–15.

[89]The three lay members of the Zimmern family who definitely ranked as burghers were Hans Schilling (son of Werner VIII) and Hans Christoph and Philipp Christoph (sons of Johann Werner II). Hans Schilling served as a Zimmern estate official at Bregenz; Hans Christoph became the town clerk at Hornberg, while Philipp Christoph married the daughter of a burgher of Rottweil (*ZC* 4:93). Six of the twenty-four illegitimate sons of the counts of Montfort were burghers. Burmeister, *Grafen von Montfort,* 115.

[90]Wieland, "Römische Dispense 'de defectu natalium,'" 294; and Burmeister, *Grafen von Montfort,* 115.

[91]See Shahar, *Fourth Estate,* 41; Kirschner and Molho, "Dowry Fund," 424–26; Kuehn, *Illegitimacy in Renaissance Florence,* 164-66; and Molho, *Marriage Alliance,* 277, 306.

[92]Heinig, "'Omnia vincit amor,'" 299.

fourteenth and fifteenth centuries; Burmeister also finds only one case in the Montfort family from the mid-fourteenth to the mid-sixteenth century.[93]

Illegitimate daughters always married below their father's rank. They were unlikely to marry into the high nobility unless their father was a king or prince. Count Georg II von Montfort-Bregenz married an illegitimate daughter of King Sigismund of Poland. Even Count Hugo XVII von Montfort-Bregenz, who had his daughter Marina von Flugberg legitimated and ennobled by Emperor Charles V, did not try to marry her into the high nobility. Negotiations for her marriage to an Augsburg patrician failed because of opposition from the young man's mother. Hugo eventually arranged a marriage for Marina to the jurist Johannes von Hirnkofen of Launingen, who saw this connection to the Montforts as a means of raising his own status. However, when Hirnkofen displayed the Montfort arms on his house at Launingen, other members of the Montfort family were enraged at his presumption. It is said that Marina was abducted on the orders of her father, and that Hirnkofen died under judical torture.[94]

Most illegitimate daughters did not enjoy as many advantages as Marina von Flugberg, who had been legitimated and was designated in her father's will as one of his legal heirs. Illegitimate daughters of southwest German counts and barons received much smaller dowries than their legitimate half sisters and had to marry far below their father's status. Spiess finds that counts and barons in the Mainz region usually gave dowries of 100 to 600 gulden to illegitimate daughters in the fifteenth century, equal to a tenth (or even less than a tenth) of the amount given to legitimate daughters in the same families. A few illegitimate daughters with dowries of 400 to 800 gulden were able to marry members of the lower nobility. However, two women who received about 100 gulden apiece married men-at-arms (*Reitknechte*), and a woman who received only a house and vineyard married a burgher.[95]

The marriages of illegitimate daughters in the *Zimmern Chronicle* are consistent with the examples given by Spiess. The largest dowry mentioned in the chronicle is that of 800 gulden for Anna, the daughter of Christoph Friedrich von Zollern, who was forced by her guardian to marry one of his clerks. Anna's dowry was equivalent to those given by many knights and urban patricians. However, this was an exceptional case, for the dowry was paid out of her inheritance from her mother, the Augsburg patrician Anna Rehlinger (*ZC* 2:467).

---

[93]Spiess, *Familie und Verwandtschaft,* 389; and Burmeister, *Grafen von Montfort,* 114. One additional case can be documented among the families studied by Spiess: Kunigunde Rieneck, an illegitimate daughter of canon Thomas von Rieneck, became abbess of St. Vincent in Cologne. Ruf, *Grafen von Rieneck,* "Stammtafel."

[94]Burmeister, *Grafen von Montfort,* 289, 300–1.

[95]Spiess, *Familie und Verwandtschaft,* 365, 380, 382, 385, 388–89. The size of Marina von Flugberg's dowry is unknown; however, if her father was trying to arrange a marriage for her into the Augsburg patriciate, he was probably offering a dowry of about 1000 gulden. Legitimate daughters of the counts of Montfort received dowries of at least 4000 gulden. Weiss, *Grafen von Montfort,* 11.

More typical is the case of Barbara (or Berbelin), the daughter of Johann Werner II von Zimmern, who received 200 gulden as her portion. She married a man nicknamed Reuterhans (Hans the man-at-arms), who served as her father's bailiff at Seedorf (*ZC* 2:413–14). One of the illegitimate daughters of Gottfried III von Zimmern married Lorenz Münzer, an estate official who represented her father and his kin in their suit to the emperor to restore the confiscated Zimmern lands (*ZC* 1:416, 2:41).

The marriages of illegitimate daughters were thus used to bind retainers more firmly to the interests of the family, just as illegitimate sons were employed to serve the family interests as estate managers. However, the chronicle also records some marriages of illegitimate daughters to men who were not in their father's service: Leonora Werdenberger married a furrier and Anna Zollerer married Jakob Zimmerle, the son of Junker Heinrich.

The evidence of the *Zimmern Chronicle,* together with Burmeister's study of the counts of Montfort and Spiess's research on the counts and barons of the Mainz region, suggests that opportunities for noble bastards in Germany were more limited than those in other European elites, and that they were declining by the mid-fifteenth century, long before the Reformation. The causes seem not to be religious or political factors so much as social factors, especially the German definition of nobility and the increasing lineage consciousness of German nobles.

To be sure, the concept of a golden age of noble bastards applies mainly to princely courts, and one should not overly romanticize the position of the bastards of provincial nobles in other countries in the late fifteenth century. Even so, the legal position of noble bastards in Germany was inferior to that in other continental aristocracies. In contrast to France, the illegitimate children of German noblemen were not presumed to inherit their father's noble status, and in contrast to Italy and Iberia, they were almost never legitimated as heirs. At best, some German noble bastards had the opportunity to achieve the social rank one level below that of their father. However, only a few actually achieved noble status, and those who did so were likely to be the offspring of fathers who had no legitimate sons.

In general, Burmeister characterizes the opportunities open to illegitimate sons of the counts of Montfort as "careers at the middle level," and even these were already becoming scarcer by the mid-fifteenth century. "With the passage of time," he says, "the positions available to illegitimate children steadily declined in quality: instead of cathedral canonries there were now only parish churches, chaplaincies, or a place in a monastery. He who became a bailiff [*Vogt*] in the fifteenth century became in the sixteenth century only a forester or a clerk."[96]

Spiess finds fewer noble bastards receiving grants of castles and offices in the fifteenth century than in the fourteenth. Burmeister attributes the declining

---

[96]Burmeister, *Grafen von Montfort,* 105, 114–16.

opportunities for noble bastards to greater exclusivity and lineage consciousness among the nobility. Cathedral chapters required proof of noble ancestry on both sides. Moreover, as university education became a prerequisite for high office at princely courts, nobles increasingly invested in education for their legitimate sons rather than for their bastards.[97]

Some noble fathers in the early sixteenth century did attempt to make generous provision for their bastards, but such efforts met with social disapproval. In the 1530s, Count Hugo XVII von Montfort enraged the other members of his house by marrying his concubine, legitimating his bastards, and designating them as his heirs in place of his agnates. His sexual behavior made him "a lonely man, who had lost not only his land, but his reputation."[98] Hugo demonstrated the same combination of sexual profligacy with indifference to the interests of the lineage with which Froben Christoph reproaches the fathers of bastards in the *Zimmern Chronicle*. His behavior was a real-life example of the chronicler's worst nightmare: that bastards might take the place of the legitimate heirs from the lineage.

None of the Zimmern fathers of bastards went as far as Count Hugo XVII von Montfort. However, the *Zimmern Chronicle* makes it clear that generous provision for illegitimate sons met with disapproval by the middle of the sixteenth century. The attempt of Junker Heinrich to achieve noble status, which might not have seemed remarkable in the fifteenth century, is presented as a morality tale of greed and ambition. Gottfried Werner's efforts to have his sons accepted as nobles and as members of the Zimmern lineage are depicted as the quixotic fantasy of a man unhinged by his irrational affection for bastards. Although the chronicler's outlook may be idiosyncratic, he clearly expects his audience to sympathize with his view that bastards are evil by nature, that their existence injures the legitimate wife and children psychologically as well as financially, and, above all, that they pose a threat to the patrimony and to the prestige of the lineage. By the mid-sixteenth century, the values of the church and of lineage consciousness both agreed that noble bastards must be kept in their proper place: they were entitled to acknowledgment and to basic financial support, but they should not be allowed to share the name or the noble status of their father's lineage.

[97]Burmeister, *Grafen von Montfort,* 114.
[98]Burmeister, *Grafen von Montfort,* 301.

CHAPTER 11

Family Strategies and Pragmatic Morality

While the views on marriage and sexuality expressed by Froben Christoph von Zimmern were often idiosyncratic, he obviously expected his basic assumptions to be accepted by his audience. Moreover, both demographic evidence and documentary records of the actual practice of his contemporaries make it possible to set the *Zimmern Chronicle* into broader context. In discussions of inheritance patterns and marriage strategy, historians of the early modern noble family have usually generalized from the experience of England and northern France. Primogeniture is seen as the normal (or at least the ideal) inheritance strategy, and hypergamy is assumed to be the typical marriage strategy; although aristocratic men might marry below their own rank, it was unthinkable for aristocratic women to do so.

By these criteria, the inheritance and marriage strategies of the German nobles in the *Zimmern Chronicle* certainly appear anomalous. Southwest German counts and barons continued to practice partible inheritance instead of adopting primogeniture. Although they adjusted the number of heirs per generation to the prevailing economic conditions, they remained nostalgically attached to the ideal of equality among brothers and felt that primogeniture lacked moral legitimacy. They married off a larger number of daughters than sons per generation, seeking to increase the number of alliances through marriages of females even when they limited the number of male heirs. They consistently followed a hypogamous marriage pattern in which sons married up and daughters married down. This practice was reinforced by the German concept of nobility, which defined noble status as dependent on the rank of the mother as well as the father.

These German patterns transcended any effects of religious ideology, for after 1550 they are evident among members of both confessions. Protestant fathers followed inheritance strategies virtually identical to those of Catholic fathers. Since a son's ability to marry was contingent on his inheritance of an estate, the Protestant Reformation had little effect on marriage strategy for sons. However, the need for Protestant fathers to provide for daughters in the absence of convents reinforced the existing preference for marrying off more daughters than sons per generation. By 1700, the marriage patterns of both Protestant and Catholic counts and barons in southwest Germany differed from that of their coreligionists in other European elites. This was particularly noticeable in the high proportion of women who married, a corollary of the hypogamous marriage pattern.

The family strategies of southwest German counts and barons exhibited some unique features that deserve further investigation. Their marriage strategy in the fifteenth century was more restrictive than that of any other European elite on which information is available, and Catholic families made less use of the church in their family strategy in the sixteenth and early seventeenth centuries than they had in the fifteenth century.

In other Catholic nobilities, the trend over time was just the reverse: their percentage of children marrying was much higher in the fifteenth century than it was among Catholic nobles in southwest Germany, but thereafter it declined rapidly, with the church playing an increasingly important role in family strategy. By the mid-seventeenth century, a common aristocratic model was established in other Catholic elites, in which only half of all sons and daughters married and a third of each sex entered the church.[1] This pattern is similar to that of southwest Germany in the fifteenth century.

It is possible that rising dowry levels, which have been associated in other elites with restrictions on the number of daughters who married, were not as great a problem for German nobles because of their unusually rigid dowry system. However, more data on dowry levels in the high nobility in the late sixteenth and seventeenth centuries are needed in order to investigate this issue.

Recent research suggests that some inheritance and marriage patterns associated with Germany were not unique to German nobles but were also common in other European nobilities in the fifteenth and sixteenth centuries. As Cooper notes, strategies of lineal consolidation could be pursued within a nominally partible inheritance system, and primogeniture was not always viewed as the ideal.[2] Hypogamy was the dominant marriage strategy in the French nobility at least until the mid-sixteenth century and in the Iberian nobilities well into the seventeenth century; it probably predominated in the English peerage before 1700. Southwest German counts and barons were thus not unique but merely old-fashioned in their inheritance and marriage strategies, preserving partible inheritance

---

[1] Gonçalo Monteiro, "Casa, reproduçao social e celibato," 920.
[2] Cooper, "Patterns of Inheritance and Settlement," 296, 299–305.

and hypogamous marriage into the seventeenth and eighteenth centuries when other European aristocracies were abandoning these practices.

It is more difficult to tell whether there were any distinctly German characteristics in attitudes toward marriage and sexuality. Like other European aristocracies, southwest German counts and barons continued to adhere to the medieval lay model of marriage, which held that control over marriage and sexuality rested with the kin group rather than with the church, and that marriage was an alliance between families rather than a personal union between individuals. In certain respects, southwest German counts and barons seem to have gone further than other contemporary nobles in maintaining the control of the kin group over marriage and sexuality. Although they did not exercise their legal right to kill female kin who violated the sexual honor code, they did keep daughters and sisters under house arrest for doing so, a practice approved by the chronicler. They also were more reluctant to resort to outside ecclesiastical or secular authorities for annulments or legal separations than were the high aristocracies in France, Castile, or England. In cases of marital breakdown, southwest German noblewomen invoked the aid of the male members of their natal families to negotiate a private settlement rather than appealing to the courts.

Like other European elites, southwest German counts and barons based their choice of marriage partners primarily on the characteristics of the family rather than those of the individual. The majority of men were able to negotiate their own marriages, since they married after their fathers' deaths. Nevertheless, they sought guidance from their kin and emphasized criteria consistent with the lay model of marriage: that is, social status, political power, and wealth. Although health was important since it bore on the ability to produce children, other individual characteristics such as beauty and affection were considered only as supplements to the characteristics of the family, not as replacements for them.

However, at least some aspects of the ecclesiastical rather than the lay model of marriage are reflected in the *Zimmern Chronicle*, not only in the views of the chronicler himself but in those of other southwest German nobles. The chronicler's view of marriage as an exclusive sexual union in which harmony depends on the efforts of both spouses is derived from the medieval church. His description of a good marriage as one based on affection, mutual respect, and trust between the spouses is similar to the ideal set forth in medieval marriage sermons and in sixteenth-century treatises on marriage aimed at a middle-class audience.

By the early sixteenth century, the view that the potential for affection should be a criterion in the choice of marriage partner had spread from the urban elite to the landed nobility. The children of southwest German counts and barons had a veto power in the choice of spouses at least as early as did children in any other European nobility for which evidence is available. The rising mean age at first marriage in the sixteenth and seventeenth centuries, and especially the sharp decline after 1550 in marriages at very young ages, suggest that the children were now more personally involved in choosing their marriage partners.

These ecclesiastical elements in the views of marriage held by the counts and barons of southwest Germany in the sixteenth century contradict Stone's view of the aristocratic family as an authoritarian institution in which marriages were arranged purely for economic or political purposes, and affection between spouses was lacking. However, these findings are consistent with the more recent studies of early modern European nobilities, which emphasize the presence of affection as an ideal and a reality in noble families.

It is in the realm of extramarital sexuality that the *Zimmern Chronicle* presents its most fascinating observations. It is also here that the greatest dissonance is evident between the views of the chronicler Froben Christoph von Zimmern and those that prevailed in his social milieu. Although the canon law concept of male adultery as an offense against the institution of marriage was incorporated into imperial and territorial law codes in the sixteenth century, it is clear that most noblemen considered themselves to be set apart from the discipline of the subject society.[3]

Even the chronicler does not completely accept the ecclesiastical view that sexual activity must be limited to marriage, for he has no objection to unmarried noblemen maintaining concubines and believes that even clergymen and married men have an obligation to support their illegitimate children. However, he opposes even secret and casual liaisons by married men, whereas noblemen in his social milieu generally thought it acceptable for a married man to "keep an honest girl in a house" so long as he did not create a public scandal.[4]

If, as Sprandel argues, German nobles were more sensitive than other European elites to ecclesiastical social policy on extramarital sexuality, this was not the result of the Protestant and Catholic Reformations.[5] Even in the fifteenth century, German nobles, unlike those in Italy, believed a married man needed to make at least a token effort to conceal his relationship with a concubine. German princes, who had observed this convention of discretion in the fifteenth century, were increasingly willing by the late sixteenth century to give their mistresses a quasi-public status. Ironically, this development occurred at the same time that these princes, under the influence of Protestant and Catholic reformers, were issuing more regulations against immorality among their subjects. The open practice of concubinage as a symbol of noble status may actually have become more, rather than less, acceptable among German nobles in the late sixteenth century. Thus Froben Christoph's denunciation of concubinage makes him appear to be a lone voice rather than the spokesman for a new set of attitudes among the nobility.

---

[3] Heinig, "'Omnia vincit amor,'" 286.

[4] Martin Luther, quoted in Phillips, *Putting Asunder,* 76.

[5] Sprandel, "Die Diskriminierung der unehelichen Kinder," 491.

In his hostility to bastards, Froben Christoph von Zimmern appears to be more representative of his milieu. Here he not only draws on popular stereotypes of bastards as evil by nature but stresses the connection between a nobleman's attention to his concubines and illegitimate children and his neglect of his dynastic obligations. Even in the so-called golden age of bastards in the fifteenth century, the legal and social status of German noble bastards was less favorable than in many other European countries, partly as a result of the German definition of nobility as based on the status of the mother as well as that of the father. Generous provision for noble bastards met with increasing criticism in the sixteenth century, not only on moral grounds but on the grounds that it diminished the patrimony of the lineage, which should be concentrated in the hands of its legitimate male members.

The *Zimmern Chronicle*, like other sixteenth-century chronicles of German noble families, seeks not merely to record the deeds of family members but to teach moral lessons to posterity. Like other chroniclers, Froben Christoph von Zimmern warns his readers to avoid the mistakes made in the past, particularly the destructive quarrels between brothers that endanger the well-being of the lineage. However, he also warns against mistakes in matters of marriage; he denounces tyrannical parents and guardians who force children into unwanted marriages, as well as greedy men who seek marriage partners on the basis of wealth rather than status. He is unique among family chroniclers in taking as one of his major themes the destructive effects of sexuality, depicting extramarital liaisons and illegitimate children as threats to the reputation of a nobleman and to the economic interests of the lineage.

The author of the *Zimmern Chronicle* is exceptional, not only among German nobles but among all European nobles of his era, in basing his criticism of unfaithful husbands not on Christian morality but on the pragmatic grounds of the financial damage they do to their lineage. He is virtually unique in condemning their behavior on the grounds of the emotional harm they inflict on their wives and children. Despite his professed nostalgia for the rustic simplicity of the good old days of Swabian noble culture, his heartfelt outburst of sympathy for wronged wives seems to anticipate a much later age of sensibility: "Their wives had to see it, live with it, and keep quiet, even if it stabbed them to the heart" (*ZC* 3:389).

APPENDIX

GENEALOGY OF THE ZIMMERN FAMILY

GENERATION I

Johann Werner (I) (c.1455–1495), Baron von Zimmern; Councilor to Archduke Sigismund of Tyrol, banished 1488
    m. 1474 – Countess Margarethe von Oettingen (d. 1528) daughter of Count Wilhelm

GENERATION II

Children of Johann Werner and Margarethe von Oettingen

1. Anna (1473–1523), 1488 nun in Frauenmünster in Zurich
2. Verena (d. 1487)
3. Katharina (1478–1547/8), 1492 nun, 1496–1524 Abbess of Frauenmünster in Zurich
    m. 1525 – Eberhard von Reischach, citizen of Zurich, killed at Battle of Kappel 1531
4. Veit Werner (1479–1499)
5. Johann Werner (II) (1480–1548), 1538 created Count von Zimmern
    m. 1510 – Schenkin Katharina von Erbach (d. 1549), daughter of Schenk Erasmus
6. Margarethe (1481–1513)
    m. 1512 – Wolf von Affenstein (d. after 1550)
7. Barbara (1482–1515)
    m. 1506 – Hans Wilhelm von Weitingen
8. Gottfried Werner (1484–1554), 1538 created Count von Zimmern
    m. 1511 – Countess Apollonia von Henneberg (1496/7–1548), daughter of Count Hermann
9. Wilhelm Werner (1485–1575), 1538 created Count von Zimmern; Imperial judge at Rottweil and Imperial Councilor 1520–41, judge (later president) of the Imperial Chamber Court 1548–54
    m. (1) 1521 – Countess Katharina von Lupfen (1486–1521), daughter of Count Sigmund, died in a fall from a horse only sixteen weeks after the wedding (no issue)
    m. (2) 1525 – Landgravine Amalia von Leuchtenberg (c.1469–1538), daughter of Landgrave Friedrich; widow of Baron Leonard Fraunberger, Count von Haag (no issue)

Based on Schwennicke, *Europäische Stammtafeln NF* 12, Table 84, "Die Grafen von Zimmern"

GENERATION III

Children of Johann Werner II and Katharina von Erbach

1. Christoph Werner (1514–1517)
2. Johann Christoph (1516–1556/7), 1531 canon of Strasbourg, also canon of Cologne, canon of Speyer, dean of cathedral chapter of Strasbourg 1544–53
3. Froben Christoph (1519–1566)
    m. 1544 – Countess Kunigunde von Eberstein (1528–1575), daughter of Count Wilhelm
4. Gottfried Christoph (1524–1570), 1544 canon of Strasbourg, also canon of Bamberg, canon of Constance
5. Barbara (b. and d. 1526)

Children of Gottfried Werner and Apollonia von Henneberg

1. Anna (1513–1579)
    m. 1531 – Count Jos Niklaus II von Zollern in Hechingen (d. 1558)
2. Barbara (1519–after 1552), blind in childhood, nun at Inzigkofen

GENERATION IV

Children of Froben Christoph and Kunigunde von Eberstein

1. Anna (1545–1602)
    m. 1562 – Count Joachim von Fürstenberg (d. 1598)
2. Apollonia (1547–1604)
    m. 1567 – Count Georg II von Helfenstein, Baron von Gundelfingen (d. 1573)
3. Johanna (1548–1613)
    m. 1566 – Truchsess Jakob von Waldburg zu Zeil (d. 1589)
4. Wilhelm (1549–1594), last of the male line; Privy Councilor and Steward to the Archduke of Austria
    m. (ca. 1570) – Countess Sabina von Thurn und Valsassina (d. 1588/94), daughter of Count Franz, Governor (*Landeshauptmann*) of Moravia (no issue)
5. Kunigunde (1552–1602)
    m. (1) 1570 – Truchsess Johann von Waldburg (d. 1577)
    m. (2) 1580 – Baron Berthold von Königsegg zu Aulendorf (d. 1607)
6. Katharina (b. and d. 1553)
7. Leonora (1554–1606)
    m. (1) – 1573 Lazarus von Schwendi, Baron von Hochlandsberg (d. 1583)
    m. (2) – 1586 Schenk Hans IV von Limpurg zu Schmiedelfeld (d. 1608)
8. Maria (1555–1598)
    m. (1) – 1570 Count Georg von Thurn und Valsassina (d. 1591)
    m. (2) before 10 May 1595 – Baron Kaspar von Lanthieri, Baron zu Schönhaus auf Vippach und Reifenberg (d. 1628)
9. Sibilla (1558–1599)
    m. 1574 – Count Eitel Friedrich I von Hohenzollern-Sigmaringen in Hechingen (d. 1605)
10. Barbara (1559–1595)
11. Ursula (1564–after 10 May 1595)
    m. 1585 – Count Bernhard von Ortenburg-Salamanca (d. 1614)

BIBLIOGRAPHY

Abel, Wilhelm. *Geschichte der deutschen Landwirtschaft vom frühen Mittelalter bis zum 19. Jahrhundert.* Stuttgart: Eugen Ulmer, 1962.

Allgemeine Deutsche Biographie. 56 vols. Leipzig: Duncker & Humbolt, 1875–1912. (Cited as *ADB.)*

Andermann, Kurt. *Studien zur Geschichte des pfälzischen Niederadels im späten Mittelalter: Eine vergleichende Untersuchung an ausgewählten Beispielen.* Speyer: Historischen Vereins der Pfalz, 1982.

Ariès, Philippe. *Centuries of Childhood: A Social History of Family Life.* Translated by Robert Baldick. New York: Vintage Books, 1962. Originally published as *L'enfant et la vie sociale sous l'Ancien Regime* (Paris: Librairie Plon, 1960).

Arnaud, Françoise. "Le Mariage et ses enjeux dans le milieu de robe parisien XIVe–XVe siècles." In *La femme au moyen-âge,* edited by Michel Rouche and Jean Heuclin, 407–29. [Mauberge]: Jean Touzot, 1990.

Aznar Gil, Federico R. "Die Illegitimen auf der Iberischen Halbinsel im Spätmittelalter." In Schmugge, *Illegitimität im Spätmittelalter,* 171–206.

Barack, Karl, ed. *Zimmerische Chronik.* 4 vols. Bibliothek des literarischen Vereins in Stuttgart, 91–94. Tübingen, 1869. (Cited as *ZC.)*

———, ed. *Zimmerische Chronik,* 2nd ed. 4 vols. Freiburg: Mohr, 1881–82.

Bastl, Beatrix. *Tugend, Liebe, Ehre: Die adelige Frau in der frühen Neuzeit.* Vienna: Bohlau, 2000.

Bastress-Dukehart, Erica. *The Zimmern Chronicle: Nobility, Memory and Self-Representation in Sixteenth-Century Germany.* Aldershot: Ashgate, 2002.

Beceiro Pita, Isabel, and Ricardo Córdoba de la Llave. *Parentesco, poder y mentalidad: La nobleza castellana siglos XII–XV.* Madrid: Consejo Superior de Investigaciones Científicas, 1990.

Becker, Hans-Jürgen. "Die nichteheliche Lebensgemeinschaft (Konkubinat) in der Rechtsgeschichte." In *Die nichteheliche Lebensgemeinschaft,* edited by Götz Landwehr, 13–38. Göttingen: Vandenhoeck & Ruprecht, 1978.

Beer, Mathias. *Eltern und Kinder des späten Mittelalters in ihren Briefen: Familienleben in der Stadt des Spätmittelalters und der Frühen Neuzeit mit besonderer Berücksichtigung Nürnbergs.* Nuremberg: Stadtarchiv Nürnberg, 1990.

Bennett, H[enry] S[tanley]. *The Pastons and Their England.* Cambridge: Cambridge University Press, 1922.

Bestor, Jane Fair. "Bastardy and Legitimacy in the Formation of a Regional State in Italy: The Estense Succession." *Comparative Studies in Society and History* 38, no. 3 (July 1996): 549–85.

Beutin, Wolfgang. *Sexualität und Obszönität: Eine literaturpsychologische Studie über epische Dichtung des Mittelalters und der Renaissance.* Würzburg: Königshausen & Neumann, 1990.

Bohanan, Donna. "Matrimonial Strategies among Nobles of Seventeenth-Century Aix-en-Provence." *Journal of Social History* 19 (1986): 503–10.

Böhme, Ernst. *Das fränkische Reichgrafenkollegium im 16. und 17. Jahrhundert: Untersuchung zu den Möglichkeiten und Grenzen der korporativen Politik mindermächtiger Reichsstände.* Stuttgart: Franz Steiner, 1989.

Boone, James L., III. "Parental Investment and Elite Family Structure in Preindustrial States: A Case Study of Late Medieval–Early Modern Portuguese Genealogies." *American Anthropologist* 88, no. 1 (1986): 859–78.

Borchardt, Karl. "Illegitime in den Diözen Würzburg, Bamburg und Eichstatt." In Schmugge, *Illegitimität im Spätmittelalter,* 239–73.

Bousmar, E. "Des alliances liées à la procréation: Les fonctions du mariage dans les Pay-Bas bourguignons." *Mediävistik: Internationale Zeitschift für interdisziplinäre Mitteralterforschung* 7 (1994): 11–69.

Brundage, James A. *Law, Sex, and Christian Society in Medieval Europe.* Chicago: University of Chicago Press, 1987.

Brunelle, Gayle. "Dangerous Liaisons: *Mésalliance* and Early Modern French Noblewomen." *French Historical Studies* 19, no. 1 (Spring 1995): 75–103.

Bulst, Neithard. "Illegitime Kinder: Viele oder wenige? Quantitative Aspekte der Illegitimität im spätmittelälterischen Europa." In Schmugge, *Illegitimität im Spätmittelalter,* 21–39.

Burckhardt, Jacob. *The Civilization of the Renaissance in Italy.* Translated by S. G. C. Middlemore. New York: Harper & Row, 1958. Originally published as *Die Cultur der Renaissance in Italien: Ein Versuch* (Basel, 1860).

Burmeister, Karl Heinz. *Die Grafen von Montfort: Geschichte, Recht, Kultur: Festgabe zur 60. Geburtstag,* edited by Alois Niederstätter. [Constance]: UVK, Universitätsverlag Konstanz, 1996.

Byrne, Muriel St. Clare, ed. *The Lisle Letters.* 6 vols. Chicago: University of Chicago Press, 1981.

Carl, Horst. *Der Schwäbische Bund 1488–1534: Landfrieden und Genossenschaft im Übergang vom Spätmittelalter zur Reformation.* Leinfelden: DRW, 2000.

Caron, Marie-Thérèse. *La noblesse dans le duché de Bourgogne 1315–1477.* [Lille]: Presses Universitaires de Lille, 1987.

Casey, James. *Early Modern Spain: A Social History.* London: Routledge, 1999.

———. *The History of the Family.* [Oxford]: Basil Blackwell, 1989.

Chojnacki, Stanley, "Dowries and Kinsmen in Early Renaissance Venice," *Journal of Interdisciplinary History* 5 (1975): 571–600.

Christ-von Wedel, Christine. "'Praecipua coniugii est animorum coniunctio': Die Stellung der Frau nach der 'Eheanweisung' des Erasmus von Rotterdam." In *Eine Stadt der Frauen: Studien und Quellen zur Geschichte der Baslerinnen im späten Mittelalter und zu Beginn der Neuzeit (13.–17. Jahrhundert),* edited by Heide Wunder, 125–49. Basel and Frankfurt: Helbing & Lichtenhahn, 1995.

Constant, Jean-Marie. *La noblesse française aux XVIe–XVIIe siècles.* Paris: Hachette, 1994.

Contamines, Philippe. *La noblesse au royaume de France de Philippe le Bel à Louis XII.* Paris: Presses Universitaires de France, 1991.

Cooper, J[ohn] P. "Patterns of Inheritance and Settlement by Great Landowners from the Fifteenth to the Eighteenth Centuries." In *Family and Inheritance: Rural Society in Western Europe 1200–1800*, edited by Jack Goody, Joan Thirsk, and E[dward] P. Thompson, 192–327. Cambridge: Cambridge University Press, 1978.

Davis, Natalie Zemon. "Women on Top." In *Society and Culture in Early Modern France.* 124–51. Stanford: Stanford University Press, 1975.

Decker-Hauff, Hansmartin, ed., with the collaboration of Rudolf Seigel. *Die Chronik der Grafen von Zimmern: Handschriften 580 und 581 der Fürstlich Fürstenbergischen Hofbibliothek Donauschingen.* 3 vols. Sigmaringen: Jan Thorbecke, 1964–72.

Demars-Sion, Véronique. *Femmes séduites et abandonées au 18e siècle: L'exemple du Cambrésis.* Paris: L'Espace Juridique, 1991.

Dewald, Jonathan. *The European Nobility, 1400–1800.* Cambridge: Cambridge University Press, 1996.

Dieck, C[arl] F[riedrich]. *Beiträge zur Lehre von der Legitimation durch nachfolgende Ehe.* Halle, 1832.

Dornheim, Andreas. *Adel in der bürgerlich-industrialisierten Gesellschaft: Eine sozialwissenschaftlich-historische Fallstudie über die Familie Waldburg-Zeil.* Frankfurt am Main: Peter Lang, 1993.

Duby, Georges. "Family Structures in the West during the Middle Ages." In *Love and Marriage in the Middle Ages.* 105–12.

———. *Love and Marriage in the Middle Ages.* Translated by Jane Dunnett. Cambridge: Polity Press, 1994.

———. "Le mariage dans la société du haut moyen âge." In *Il Matrimonio nella società altomedievale.* 15–39. Settimane di studio del centro italiano di studi sull'alto medioevo 24. Spoleto: Presso la sede del Centro, 1977.

———. *Medieval Marriage: Two Models from Twelfth-Century France.* Translated by Elborg Forster. Baltimore: Johns Hopkins University Press, 1978.

———. "Philip Augustus's France: Social Change in Aristocratic Circles." In *Love and Marriage in the Middle Ages.* 121–26.

———. "Structures de parenté et noblesse dans la France du Nord aux XIe et XIIe siècles." In Duby, *Hommes et structures du Moyen-Âge; recueil d'articles*, 267–85. Paris: Mouton, 1973.

Duhamelle, Christophe. "Parenté et orientation sociale: La chevalerie immédiate rhénane, XVIIe–XVIIIe siècles." *Annales de démographie historique* (1995): 59–73.

Dülmen, Richard van. "Heirat und Eheleben in der frühen Neuzeit: Autobiographische Zeugnisse." *Archiv für Kulturgeschichte* 72 (1990): 153–71.

———, ed. *Kultur und Alltag in der frühen Neuzeit.* Vol. 1, *Das Haus und seine Menschen 16.–18. Jahrhundert.* Munich: Beck, 1990.

Eisenach, Emlyn. *Husbands, Wives, and Concubines: Marriage, Family and Social Order in Sixteenth-Century Verona.* Sixteenth-Century Essays and Studies 69. Kirksville, MO: Truman State University Press, 2004.

Ellrichshausen, Hans Conrad. *Die uneheliche Mütterschaft im altösterreichischen Polizeirecht des 16. bis 18. Jahrhunderts*, Berlin: Duncker & Humblot, 1988.

Ettlinger, Helen S. "Visibilis et Invisibilis: The Mistress in Italian Renaissance Court Society." *Renaissance Quarterly* 47, no. 4 (1994): 770–92.

Euler, Friedrich W. "Wandlung des Konnubiums im Adel des 15. und 16. Jahrhunderts." In *Deutscher Adel 1430–1555: Büdinger Vorträge*, edited by Hellmuth Rössler, 58–95. Schriften zur Problematik der deutschen Führungsschichten in der Neuzeit 1. Darmstadt: Wissenschaftliche Buchgesellschaft, 1965.

Fichtner, Paula Sutter. *Protestantism and Primogeniture in Early Modern Germany.* New Haven, CT: Yale University Press, 1989.

Flandrin, Jean-Louis. *Families in Former Times: Kinship, Household and Sexuality.* Translated by Richard Southern. Cambridge: Cambridge University Press, 1979. Originally published as *Familles, parenté, maison, sexualité dans l'ancienne société* (Paris: Hachette, 1976).

Franklin, Otto. *Die freien Herren und Grafen von Zimmern: Beiträge zur Rechtsgeschichte nach der Zimmerischen Chronik.* Freiburg im Breisgau und Tübingen: Paul Siebeck, 1884.

Freed, John B. *Noble Bondsmen: Ministerial Marriages in the Archdiocese of Salzburg, 1100–1343.* Ithaca, NY: Cornell University Press, 1996.

Gairdner, J[ames], ed. *The Paston Letters, 1422–1509.* 4 vols. Westminster: A. Constable & Co., 1900–1908.

Génestal, R[obert]. *Histoire de la légitimation des enfants naturels en droit canonique.* Paris: E. Leroux, 1905.

Gerbet, Marie-Claude. *La noblesse dans le royaume de Castille: Étude sur ses structures sociales en Estrémadure (1454–1516).* Paris: Publications de la Sorbonne, 1974.

―――. *Les noblesses espagnoles au moyen âge: XIe–XVe siècle.* Paris: Armand Colin; 1994.

Given-Wilson, Chris, and Alice Curteis. *The Royal Bastards of Medieval England.* London: Routledge & Kegan-Paul, 1984.

Glass, D[avid] V., and D[avid] E[dmund] C. Eversley, eds. *Population in History: Essays in Historical Demography.* London: Arnold Edward Ltd., 1965.

Gonçalo Monteiro, Nuño. "Casa, reproduçao social e celibato: A aristocracia portuguesa nos séculos XVII e XVIII." *Hispania: Revista española de historia* 53(3), no. 185 (1993): 907–36. [House, social reproduction and celibacy: the Portuguese aristocracy in the 17th and 18th centuries.]

Goody, Jack. *The Development of the Family and Marriage in Europe.* Cambridge: Cambridge University Press, 1983.

Gottlieb, Beatrice. *The Family in the Western World from the Black Death to the Industrial Age.* New York: Oxford University Press, 1993.

Grimm, Jacob, and Wilhelm Grimm. *Deutsches Wörterbuch.* 16 vols. Leipzig: S. Hirzel, 1854–1960.

Grimmer, Claude. "Les bâtards de la noblesse auvergnate au XVIIe siècle." *XVIIe Siècle* 117 (1977): 35–48.

―――. *La femme et le bâtard: Amours illégitimes et secrètes dans l'ancienne France.* Paris: Presses de la Renaissance, 1983.

Grubb, James S. *Provincial Families of the Renaissance: Private and Public Life in the Veneto.* Baltimore: Johns Hopkins University Press, 1996.

Hajnal, John. "European Marriage Patterns in Perspective." In Glass and Eversley, *Population in History*, 101–35.

Handwörterbuch zur deutschen Rechtsgeschichte. Edited by Adalbert Erler and Ekke-
   hard Kaufmann. 5 vols. Berlin: E. Schmidt, 1971–98. (Cited as *HRG.*)
Harrington, Joel F. *Reordering Marriage and Society in Reformation Germany.*
   Cambridge: Cambridge University Press, 1995.
Harris, Barbara J. *English Aristocratic Women, 1450–1550: Marriage and Family,
   Property and Careers.* Oxford: Oxford University Press, 2002.
Harsgor, Mikhael. "L'essor des bâtards nobles au XVe siècle." *Revue Historique* 253, no.
   2 (1975): 319–54.
Heal, Felicity, and Clive Holmes. *The Gentry in England and Wales, 1500–1700.*
   Stanford: Stanford University Press, 1994.
Heinig, Paul-Joachim. "'Omnia vincit amor'—Das fürstliche Konkubinat im 15./16.
   Jahrhundert." In *Principes: Dynastien und Höfe im späten Mittelalter,* edited by
   Cordula Nolte, Karl-Heinz Spiess, and Ralf-Gunnar Werlich, 277–314. Stuttgart:
   Jan Thorbecke, 2002.
Helmholz, R[ichard] H. *Marriage Litigation in Medieval England.* Cambridge:
   Cambridge University Press, 1974.
Henry, Louis, *Anciennes familles genevoises, étude démographique: XVIe–XXe.* [Paris]:
   Presses Universitaires de France, 1958.
———, and Claude Lévy. "Ducs et pairs sous l'ancien régime: Caractéristiques
   démographiques d'une caste." *Population* 15 (1960): 807–30.
Herlihy, David. "The Making of the Medieval Family: Symmetry, Structure and
   Sentiment." *Journal of Family History* 8 (1983): 116–30.
———, and Christiane Klapisch-Zuber. *Tuscans and Their Families: A Study of the
   Florentine Castato of 1427.* New Haven, CT: Yale University Press, 1985.
Hermann, Paul, ed. *Zimmerische Chronik. Nach der Ausgabe von Barack.* 4 vols.
   Merseburg and Leipzig: Hendel, 1932.
Hess, Rolf-Dieter. *Familie und Erbrecht im württembergischen Landrecht von 1555,
   unter besonderer Berücksightigung des älteren württembergischen Rechts.* Stuttgart:
   W. Kohlhammer, 1968.
Hofacker, Hans Georg. "Die Schwäbische Herzogswürde: Untersuchungen zur landes-
   fürstlichen und kaiserlichen Politik im deutschen Südwesten im Spätmittelalter
   und in der frühen Neuzeit." *Zeitschrift für württembergische Landesgeschichte* 47
   (1988): 71–148.
Holborn, Hajo. *A History of Modern Germany.* 3 vols. New York: Knopf, 1959–69.
Hollingsworth, T[homas] H[enry]. "A Demographic Study of the British Ducal
   Families." In Glass and Eversley, *Population in History,* 354–78.
———. "The Demography of the British Peerage." *Population Studies* 18 (1964), supplement.
Hufton, Olwen. *The Prospect Before Her: A History of Women in Western Europe. Vol 1,
   1500–1800.* New York: Vintage Books, 1998.
Hufschmidt, Anke. *Adelige Frauen im Weserraum zwischen 1550 und 1700. Status—
   Rollen—Lebenspraxis.* Geschichtliche Arbeiten zur westfälischen Landesfors-
   chung. Wirtschafts- und socialgeschichtliche Gruppe 15. Münster: Aschendorff,
   2001.
Hughes, Diane Owen. "From Brideprice to Dowry in Mediterranean Europe." *Journal
   of Family History* 3 (1978): 262–96.

Imhof, Arthur E., ed. *Historische Demographie als Sozialgeschichte: Giessen und Umgebung vom 17. zum 19. Jahrhundert*. Darmstadt and Marburg: Selbstverlag des Hessischen Historischen Kommission Darmstadt und der Historischen Kommission für Hessen, 1975.

Isenburg, W[ilhelm] K[arl] von. *Europäische Stammtafeln: Stammtafeln zur Geschichte der europäischen Staaten*. 5 vols. Marburg: J. A. Stargardt, 1956–78.

———. "Die geschichtliche Entwicklung von Sippenkunde und Sippenforschung bis zum Ende des dreissigjährigen Krieges." *Historisches Jahrbuch der Görregesellschaft* 60 (1940): 1–13.

Jenny, Beat Rudolf. *Graf Froben Christoph von Zimmern: Geschichtsschreiber, Erzähler, Landesherr; ein Beitrag zur Geschichte des Humanismus in Schwaben*. Lindau: Jan Thorbecke, 1959.

Johnson, Christine. "It All Makes Sense Now." Review of *Von der Chronik zum Weltbuch: Sinn und Anspruch suedwestdeutscher Hauschroniken am Ausgang des Mittelalters*, by Gerhard Wolf. *H-German H-Net Reviews*, Jan. 2005, http://www.h-net.org/reviews/showrev.cgi?path= 182501109956237.

"Kardinal von Brandenburg als heiliger Martin," Zum Internet-Geschichte Baden-Württemberg, http://zum.de/Faecher/G/BW/Landeskunde/rhein/geschichte/spaetma/icoclas/Brandenburg.

Kirschner, Julius, and Anthony Molho. "The Dowry Fund and the Marriage Market in Early Quattrocento Florence." *Journal of Modern History* 50, no. 3 (1978): 403–38.

Klapisch-Zuber, Christiane. *Women, Family and Ritual in Renaissance Italy*. Translated by Lydia Cochrane. Chicago: University of Chicago Press, 1985.

Koebner, Richard. "Die Eheauffassung des ausgehenden deutschen Mittelalters," *Archiv für Kulturgeschichte* 9 (1911): 136–98, 279–318.

Kuehn, Thomas. *Illegitimacy in Renaissance Florence*. Ann Arbor: University of Michigan Press, 2002.

———. *Law, Family, and Women: Toward a Legal Anthropology of Renaissance Italy*. Chicago: University of Chicago Press, 1991.

Labatut, Jean-Pierre. *Les ducs et pairs de France au XVIIe siècle: Étude sociale*. Paris: Presses Universitaires de France, 1972.

———. *Les noblesses européennes de la fin du XVe siècle à la fin du XVIIIe siècle*. Paris: Presses Universitaires de France, 1978.

Laslett, Peter. *The World We Have Lost*. New York: Scribner, 1965.

Le Roy Ladurie, Emmanuel, and Jean-François Fitou. "Hypergamie féminine et population saint-simonienne." *Annales ESC* 46, no. 1 (Jan./Feb. 1991): 133–49.

Lévy, Françoise P. *L'amour nomade: La mère et l'enfant hors mariage XVIe–XXe siècle*. Paris: Seuil, 1981.

Litchfield, R. Burr. "Demographic Characteristics of Florentine Patrician Families, Sixteenth to Nineteenth Centuries." *Journal of Economic History* 29 (1969): 191–205.

Lorcin, Marie-Thérèse. *Vivre et mourir en Lyonnais à la fin du moyen âge*. Paris: Éditions du C.N.R.S., 1981.

Marshall, Sherrin. *The Dutch Gentry, 1500–1650: Family, Faith and Fortune*. New York: Greenwood Press, 1987.

Martines, Lauro. *Power and Imagination: City States in Renaissance Italy*. New York: Knopf, 1979.

Mitterauer, Michael. "Zur Frage des Heiratsverhaltens im österreichischen Adel." In *Beiträge zur neueren Geschichte Österreichs*, edited by Heinrich Fichtenau and Erich Zöllner, 176–94. Vienna: Böhlau, 1974.

———, and Reinhard Sieder. *The European Family: Patriarchy to Partnership from the Middle Ages to the Present*. Translated by Karla Oosterven and Manfred Hörzinger. Chicago: University of Chicago Press, 1982. Originally published as *Vom Patriarchat zur Partnerschaft: Zum Strukturwandel der Familie* (Munich: C.H. Beck, 1977).

Molho, Anthony. *Marriage Alliance in Late Medieval Florence*. Cambridge, MA: Harvard University Press, 1994.

Müller, Karl Otto. "Das Geschlecht der Reichserbschenke zu Limpurg bis zum Aussterben des Mannesstammes (1713)." *Zeitschrift für württembergische Landesgeschichte* 5 (1941): 15–243.

———. "Zur wirtschaftlichen Lage des schwäbischen Adels am Ausgang des Mittelalters." *Zeitschrift für württembergische Landesgeschichte*, n.s. 3, no. 2 (1939): 285–328.

Müller, Maria E. "Naturwesen Mann: Zur Dialektik von Herrschaft und Knechtschaft in Ehelehren der Frühen Neuzeit." In *Wandel der Geschlechterbeziehungen zu Beginn der Neuzeit*, edited by Heide Wunder and Christina Vanja, 43–68. Frankfurt: Suhrkamp, 1991.

———. "Schneckengeist im Venusleib. Zur Zoologie des Ehelebens Johann Fischart." In *Eheglück und Liebesjoch: Bilder von Liebe, Ehe und Familie in der Literatur des 15. und 16. Jahrhunderts*, edited by Maria E. Müller, 155–203. Ergebnisse der Frauenforschung 14. Weinheim: Beltz, 1988.

Müller, Peter. *Die Herren von Fleckenstein im späten Mittelalter: Untersuchungen zur Geschichte eines Adelsgeschlecht im pfälzisch-elsässischen Grenzgebiet*. Stuttgart: Franz Steiner, 1990.

Münch, Rudolph. "Ladislaus." In *Haager Chronik*. http://www.iivs.de/haag/kommune/chronik/graf9.htm

Nadler, Josef. "Die Herren von Zimmern: Eine schwäbische Familie von Dichtern und Geschichtsschreibern." *Der Schwäbische Bund* 3 (1920–21): 296–305.

Nassiet, Michel. *Noblesse et pauvreté: La petite noblesse en Bretagne, XVe–XVIIIe siècle*. [France]: Société d'histoire et d'archéologie de Bretagne, [1993].

———. *Parenté, noblesse et états dynastiques XVe–XVIe siècles*. Paris: Éditions de l'École des Hautes Études en Sciences Sociales, 2000.

———. "Réseaux de parenté et types d'alliance dans la noblesse (XVe–XVIe siècles)." *Annales de démographie historique* 1995: 105–23.

Nierop, H. F. K. van. *The Nobility of Holland: From Knights to Regents, 1500–1600*. Cambridge: Cambridge University Press, 1984.

Nolte, Cordula. "Verbalerotische Kommunikation, *gut schwenck* oder: Worüber lachte man bei Hofe? Einige Thesen zum Briefwechsel des Kurfürstenpaares Albrecht und Anna von Brandenburg-Ansbach 1474/5." In *Das Frauenzimmer: Die Frau bei Hofe in Spätmittelalter und früher Neuzeit,* edited by Jan Hirschbiegel and Werner Paravicini, 449–61. Stuttgart: Jan Thorbecke, 2000.

Ozment, Steven. *Ancestors: The Loving Family in Old Europe*. Cambridge, MA: Harvard University Press, 2001.

————. *Flesh and Spirit: A Study of Private Life in Early Modern Germany.* New York: Penguin, 1989.

————. *Magdalena and Balthasar: An Intimate Portrait of Life in 16th-Century Europe Revealed in the Letters of a Nuremberg Husband and Wife.* New Haven, CT: Yale University Press, 1989.

————. *Three Behaim Boys: Growing Up in Early Modern Germany; A Chronicle of Their Lives.* New Haven, CT: Yale University Press, 1990.

Pedlow, Gregory. *The Survival of the Hessian Nobility 1770–1870.* Princeton: Princeton University Press, 1988.

Peller, Sigismund. "Births and Deaths among Europe's Ruling Families since 1500." In Glass and Eversley, *Population in History,* 87–100.

Phillips, Roderick. *Putting Asunder: A History of Divorce in Western Society.* Cambridge: Cambridge University Press, 1988.

Potter, David. "Marriage and Cruelty among the Protestant Nobility in Sixteenth-Century France: Diane de Barbançon and Jean de Rohan, 1561–67." *European History Quarterly* 20 (1990): 5–38.

Reif, Heinz. *Westfälischer Adel 1770–1860: Vom Herrenstand zur regionalen Elite.* Göttingen: Vandenhoeck & Ruprecht, 1979.

Robisheaux, Thomas. *Rural Society and the Search for Order in Early Modern Germany.* Cambridge: Cambridge University Press, 1989.

Rödel, Walter G. *Mainz und seine Bevölkerung im 17. und 18. Jahrhundert: Demographische Entwicklung, Lebensverhältnisse und soziale Strukturen in einer geistlichen Residenzstadt.* Stuttgart: Franz Steiner, 1985.

Röhm, Helmut. *Die Vererbung des landwirtschaftlichen Grundeigentums in Baden-Württemberg.* Remagen: Bundesanstalt für Landeskunde, 1957.

Roper, Lyndal. *The Holy Household: Women and Morals in Reformation Augsburg.* Oxford: Clarendon Press, 1989.

Rosenthal, Joel T[homas]. "Aristocratic Marriage and the English Peerage 1350–1500: Social Institution and Personal Bond." *Journal of Medieval History* 10, no. 3 (September 1984): 181–94.

————. *Patriarchy and Families of Privilege in Fifteenth-Century England.* Philadelphia: University of Pennsylvania Press, 1991.

Roth, Klaus. *Ehebruchsschwänke in Liedform: Eine Untersuchung zur deutsch- und englischsprächigen Schwankballaden.* Munich: Wilhelm Fink, 1977.

Ruf, Theodor. *Die Grafen von Rieneck: Genealogie und Territorialbildung.* Würzburg: Freunde Mainfränkischer Kunst und Geschichte, 1984.

Safley, Thomas Max. *Let No Man Put Asunder: The Control of Marriage in the German Southwest; A Comparative Study 1550–1600.* Sixteenth Century Essays and Studies 2. Kirksville, MO: Sixteenth-Century Journal Publishers, Northeast Missouri State University, 1984.

Schmidt, Georg. *Der Wetterauer Grafenverein: Organisation und Politik einer Reichskorporation zwischen Reformation und Westfälischen Frieden.* Marburg: Elwert, 1989.

Schmugge, Ludwig. *Kirche, Kinder, Karrieren: Päpstliche Dispense von der unehelichen Geburt im Spätmittelalter.* Zurich: Artemis & Winkler, 1995.

————, ed. *Illegitimität im Spätmittelalter.* Munich: Oldenbourg, 1994.

Schnell, Rüdiger. "Geschlechtergeschichte und Textwissenschaft: Eine Fallstudie zu mittelalterlichen und frühneuzeitigen Ehepredicten." In *Text und Geschlecht: Mann und Frau in Eheschriften der frühen Neuzeit,* edited by Rüdiger Schnell, 145–75. Frankfurt: Suhrkamp, 1997.

Schröder, Richard. *Geschichte des ehelichen Güterrechts in Deutschland.* 2 vols. Stettin, 1868.

Schwennicke, Detlev, ed. *Europäische Stammtafeln: Stammtafeln zur Geschichte der europäischen Staaten, Neue Folge.* Marburg: Stargardt, 1978–.

Seigel, Rudolf. "Zur Geschichtsschreibung beim schwäbischen Adel in der Zeit des Humanismus: Aus den Vorarbeiten zur Textausgabe der Hauschronik der Grafen von Zollern." *Zeitschrift für württembergische Landesgeschichte* 40 (1981): 93–118.

Shahar, Shulamith. *The Fourth Estate: A History of Women in the Middle Ages.* London: Methuen, 1983.

Sheehan, Michael M. "Illegitimacy in Late Medieval England: Laws, Dispensation and Practice." In Schmugge, *Illegitimität im Spätmittelalter,* 115–22.

Shorter, Edward. *The Making of the Modern Family.* New York: Basic Books, 1975.

Siegel, Heinrich. *Das deutsche Erbrecht nach den Rechtsquellen des Mittelalters, in seinem innern Zusammenhange dargestellt.* Heidelberg, 1853.

Sperling, Jutta Gisela. *Convents and the Body Politic in Late Renaissance Venice.* Chicago: University of Chicago Press, 1999.

Spiess, Karl-Heinz. *Familie und Verwandtschaft im deutschen Hochadels des Spätmittelalters: 13. bis Anfang des 16. Jahrhunderts.* Stuttgart: Franz Steiner, 1993.

———. "Das Konnubium der Reichsfürsten im Spätmittelalter." Unpublished paper.

———. "Social Rank in the German Higher Nobility of the Later Middle Ages." Paper presented at the annual meeting of the American Historical Association, 5 January, 1997.

Sprandel, Rolf. "Die Diskriminierung der unehelichen Kinder im Mittelalter." In *Zur Socialgeschichte der Kindheit,* edited by Jochen Martin and August Nitsche. 487–502. Freiburg: Karl Alber, 1986.

Spring, Eileen. *Law, Land and Family: Aristocratic Inheritance in England, 1300 to 1800.* Chapel Hill: University of North Carolina Press, 1993.

Stone, Lawrence. *The Crisis of the Aristocracy, 1558–1641.* Oxford: Clarendon Press, 1965.

———. *The Family, Sex and Marriage in England, 1500–1800.* New York: Harper & Row, 1977.

———. *Road to Divorce: England, 1530–1987.* Oxford: Oxford University Press, 1990.

Tacke, Andreas. "Agnes Pless und Kardinal Albrecht von Brandenburg." *Archiv für Kulturgeschichte* 72 (1990): 347–66.

Thiele, Andreas. Forward to *Die britische Peerage: Ein Auszug,* vol. 4 of *Erzählende genealogische Stammtafeln zur europäischen Geschichte.* Frankfurt: R. G. Fischer, 1996.

Thomas, David. "The Social Origins of Marriage Patterns of the British Peerage in the Eighteenth and Nineteenth Centuries." *Population Studies* 16 (1972): 99–111.

Ulshöfer, Wolfram. *Das Hausrecht der Grafen von Zollern.* Sigmaringen: M. Liebners Hofbuchdruckerei K.G., 1969.

Vanotti, J[ohann] N[epomuk] von. *Geschichte der Grafen von Montfort und von Werdenberg.* Bellevue bei Constanz, 1845.

Veit, Ludwig Andreas. *Die stiftsmässige deutsche Adel im Bilde seiner Ahnenproben.* Freiburg in Breisgau: Wagner, 1935.

Walter, Tilmann. *Unkeuschheit und Werk der Liebe: Diskurse über Sexualität am Beginn der Neuzeit in Deutschland.* Studia linguistica Germanica 48. Berlin: Walter de Gruyter, 1998.

Watt, Jeffrey R. *The Making of Modern Marriage: Matrimonial Control and the Rise of Sentiment in Neuchâtel, 1550–1800.* Ithaca, NY: Cornell University Press, 1992.

Weiss, Roland. *Die Grafen von Montfort im 16. Jahrhundert.* Markdorf: Kreisarchiv Bodenseekreis, 1992.

Wieland, Georg. "Römische Dispense 'de defectu natalium' für Antragsteller aus der Diözese Konstanz (1449–1533). Fallstudie an dispensierten Klerikern aus dem Bistum Konstanz." In Schmugge, *Illegitimität im späten Mittelalter,* 293–300.

Wiesner, Merry E. *Working Women in Renaissance Germany.* New Brunswick, NJ: Rutgers University Press, 1986.

Winterer, Hermann. *Die rechtliche Stellung der Bastarde in Italien von 800 bis 1500.* Münchener Beiträge zur Mediävistik und Renaissance-Forschung 28. Munich: Arbeo Gesellschaft, 1978.

———. *Die rechtliche Stellung der Bastarde in Spanien im Mittelalter.* Münchener Beiträge zur Mediävistik und Renaissance-Forschung 31. Munich: Arbeo-Gesellschaft, 1981.

Wolf, Gerhard. *Von der Chronik zum Weltbuch: Sinn und Anspruch südwestdeutscher Hauschroniken am Ausgang des Mittelalters.* Berlin: Walter de Gruyter, 2002.

Wood, James B. "Endogamy and Mésalliance, the Marriage Patterns of the Nobility of the *Élection* of Bayeux, 1430–1669." *French Historical Studies* 10, no. 3 (Spring 1978): 375–92.

Wunder, Heide. *He Is the Sun, She Is the Moon: Women in Early Modern Germany.* Translated by Thomas Dunlap. Cambridge, MA: Harvard University Press, 1998. Originally published as *"Er ist die Sonn', sie ist der Mond": Frauen in der Frühen Neuzeit* (Munich: Beck, 1992).

Zanetti, Dante. *Demografia del patriziato milanese nei secoli XVII, XVIII, XIX.* Pavia: Università, 1972.

Zeeden, Ernst Walter. *Deutsche Kultur in der frühen Neuzeit.* Frankfurt am Main: Akademische Verlagsgesellschaft Athenaion, 1968.

Zeilinger, Gabriel. *Der Urarcher Hochzeit 1474: Form und Funktion eines höfischen Festes im 15. Jahrhundert.* Frankfurt am Main: Peter Lang, 2003.

Zimmern, Wilhelm Werner von. *Die Eichstätter Bischofschronik des Grafen Wilhelm Werner von Zimmern.* Edited by Wilhelm Kraft. Würzburg: Schoenigh, 1956.

———. "Jahresgeschichten des Grafen Wilhelm Werner von Zimmern von 1193 bis 1557." In *Quellensammlung der badischen Landesgeschichte,* edited by F[ranz] J[oseph] Mone, 2:133–36. Karlsruhe, 1854.

———. *Die Würzburger Bischofschronik des Grafen Wilhelm Werner von Zimmern und die Würzburger Geschichtsschreibung des 16. Jahrhunderts.* Edited by Wilhelm Kraft. Würzburg: Schoenigh, 1952.

Zschunke, Peter. *Konfession und Alltag in Oppenheim.* Wiesbaden: F. Steiner, 1984.

ABOUT THE AUTHOR

Judith Hurwich received her PhD from Princeton University and taught for thirty years in independent secondary schools in the New York City area. After retiring from secondary school teaching, Dr. Hurwich has taught as an adjunct professor and lecturer at several colleges, including Fordham University, the University of Connecticut at Stamford, and Purchase College of the State University of New York. She has written numerous articles for journals. *Noble Strategies* is her first book.

INDEX